RELIGION AS CRITIQUE

Islamic Civilization and Muslim Networks
Carl W. Ernst and Bruce B. Lawrence, editors

Highlighting themes with historical as well as contemporary significance, Islamic Civilization and Muslim Networks features works that explore Islamic societies and Muslim peoples from a fresh perspective, drawing on new interpretive frameworks or theoretical strategies in a variety of disciplines. Special emphasis is given to systems of exchange that have promoted the creation and development of Islamic identities—cultural, religious, or geopolitical. The series spans all periods and regions of Islamic civilization.

A complete list of titles published in this series appears at the end of the book.

RELIGION AS CRITIQUE

Islamic Critical Thinking from Mecca to the Marketplace

Irfan Ahmad

The University of North Carolina Press
Chapel Hill

Manufactured in the United States of America
Designed by Rebecca Evans
Set in Merope by Tseng Information Systems, Inc.

The University of North Carolina Press has been a
member of the Green Press Initiative since 2003.

Cover photograph © istockphoto.com/Tassii

Library of Congress Cataloging-in-Publication Data
Names: Ahmad, Irfan, 1974– author.
Title: Religion as critique : Islamic critical thinking from Mecca to the marketplace / Irfan Ahmad.
Description: Chapel Hill : The University of North Carolina Press, [2017] | Series: Islamic civilization and Muslim networks | Includes bibliographical references and index.
Identifiers: LCCN 2017020949| ISBN 9781469635088 (cloth : alk. paper) | ISBN 9781469635095 (pbk : alk. paper) | ISBN 9781469635101 (ebook)
Subjects: LCSH: Islamic philosophy. | Faith and reason—Islam. | Critical thinking. | Criticism. | Reasoning.
Classification: LCC B745.R4 A36 2017 | DDC 181/.07—dc23
LC record available at https://lccn.loc.gov/2017020949

To *Abbī jī*, Ayesha, Mubashshir

— AND —

To the memory of the Aboriginals and their cultures

(in Australia and elsewhere), victims of the Enlightenment

and Western modernity!

صبحِ ازل یہ مجھ سے کہا جبرئیل نے

جو عقل کا غلام ہو، وہ دِل نہ کر قبول

Urdu couplet of Iqbal. Handwritten calligraphy by Mr. Mahmoud Hatamabadi. Used with permission.

Gabriel on Creation's Early Morn, gave me a lesson

Do not accept that heart which is a slave of reason

—MUHAMMAD IQBAL, *Sulṭān ṭīpū kī vaṣīʿat*

(which figures in *Ẓarb-e-kalīm, The Staff of Moses*)

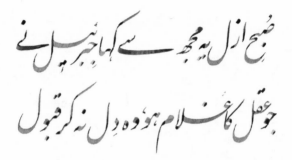

Contents

Preface xi

Acknowledgments xvii

Notes on Transliteration xxiii

PROLOGUE 1

PART I
Formulation

1 ◆ INTRODUCTION 7

The Ubiquitous Absence, or the Received Wisdom 7

The Absent Ubiquity, or the Argument 13

Amartya Sen and *The Argumentative Indian* 19

Design of Intervention 25

2 ◆ CRITIQUE: Western and/or Islamic 30

The Enlightenment as Ethnicity 34

Anthropology and Critique 49

Reconfiguring the Axial Age: Critique before the Enlightenment 54

Islam as Critique 56

3 ◆ THE MODES: Another Genealogy of Critique 63

Critique—*Tanqīd/Naqd*—in Urdu 64

Elements of an Alternative Genealogy 72

Religion and Literature: Believing Ghalib 76

Divine Critique 80

PART II
Illustration

4 ◆ THE MESSAGE: A Critical Enterprise 91

Maududi Dereified 94

Frame and Method: The Permanence of *Ijtihād* and *ʿAql* 99

The Postulates 109

The Aims 116

5 ◆ THE STATE: (In)dispensable, Desirable, Revisable? 120

Rupture and Continuity 123

Forceful Arguments 135

Recovering Universalism 140

Exceptions of the State 151

6 ◆ THE DIFFERENCE: Women and (In)equality 154

Maududi's Janus-Like Neopatriarchate 158

Neopatriarchate in Its Place: Multiple Critiques 163

Context of Transformation 173

Terms for Use 176

7 ◆ THE MUNDANE: Critique as Social-Cultural Practice 179

Critique in Movement 182

Homo Ḳhidmatiqus 190

Critique in Everyday Life: The Power of Proverbs 195

The Greed of the Mullah, the Creed of the Ungodly 196

Epilogue 203

Notes 209

Bibliography 223

Index 257

Figures and Table

FIGURES

Urdu couplet of Iqbal vi

Cover of Manzur Nomani's book, 1980 124

Cover of *Tajallī*, November 1966 125

Special issue "Critique (*tanqīd*) Number" of *Tajallī*, 1965 136

Statues of tigers at Al-Hambra, 2004 207

TABLE

Table 1. Forms of interventions and their status 84

Preface

On 29 August 2012, a day after Tom Holland's debatable documentary *Islam: The Untold Story* (based on his book *In the Shadow of the Sword*) was broadcast on Britain's Channel 4, journalist-writer Ed West published a blog post in the *Telegraph* titled "Can Islam Ever Accept Higher Criticism?" West (2012) summarized the aim of the "atmospheric and intelligent" documentary as an examination of "the early history of the religion [Islam] . . . to explain what evidence we have for the traditional history, as viewed by the faithful." Quoting from Holland, West concluded that this "evidence is almost non-existent." In the rest of his post, West gave one piece of "evidence" after another to endorse Holland's documentary. To mobilize credibility for the film, West clarified that Holland was not "anti-Islam." Toward the end of his post, West referred to Seyyed Hossein Nasr, a well-known scholar of Islam at George Washington University who appears in the documentary, as follows: "He feels culturally under attack from Western-dominated criticism." West concluded with patronizing advice: "If the Islamic world is to go forward . . . it needs to face these uncomfortable questions and embrace the pain of doubt."

West aimed to show that Islam knows no critique and is unlikely to embrace critique in the future, as the title of his post made amply clear. For West, even a professor like Nasr is threatened by Western-dominated criticism. That Muslims have been and are critics was well beyond West's ken. Importantly, in posing the question, "Can Islam Ever Accept Higher Criticism?" it never occurred to West that his own commentary on Holland in the *Telegraph* was far from critical.

In contrast to the conventional wisdom on Islam exemplified by West's blog post in the *Telegraph*—and shared widely by most academics, nonacademic intellectuals, and the general public—*Religion as Critique: Islamic Critical Thinking from Mecca to the Marketplace* demonstrates multifaceted thriving traditions of critique in Islam, laying bare the principles, premises, modes, and forms of critique at work. It discusses believers in Islam as dynamic agents, not mere objects, of critique, for which the standard word in Urdu is *tanqīd* or *naqd*. Based on ethnographic fieldwork in India, it foregrounds critique and tradition as subjects of anthropological inquiry in their own right. Since tradition is reducible neither to nationalized territory nor to its official temporality, the book travels across both. Departing from standard Enlightenment understandings, according to which religions, especially non-Protestant ones, could only be objects of critique, this book in your hands or on your screen theorizes religion as an important agent of critique, viewing Moses, the Buddha, Christ, Muhammad, Abdul Ghaffar Khan, Abul Ala Maududi, and many others as critics par excellence. In the course of this inquiry, *Religion as Critique* offers a different genealogy of critique in Urdu/Islam, transcending as it does ancient Greece and its assumed inheritor, the modern West, as the customary prime loci of critique. Using an anthropology of philosophy approach, it interprets the West's Enlightenment as a sign of its ethnic identity, thereby calling its universalism into question. Engaging with literature on the anthropology of the Enlightenment, it brings the Western Enlightenment tradition of critique into conversation with Islamic tradition to analyze differences as well as similarities between the two. Beyond perfunctory apologia such as, "Muslims also have a notion of critique like the West has," it argues for the specificity of Islam and the need for a genuinely democratic dialogue with different traditions. As it examines the contours and parameters of critique, using sources in English, Hindi, Farsi, and Urdu, it expands the scope of critique, hitherto confined to canonical texts and extraordinary individuals, like salaried philosophers, academics, critics, and intellectuals, to the everyday life intertwined with death of ordinary actors such as street vendor, beggars, and illiterate peasants. In short, *Religion as Critique* brings critique to the academic stage as an ordinary social-cultural practice with an extraordinary salience. Rather than present critique as an isolated, merely mental exercise, the book aspires to lay bare the very life critique belongs to and seeks to enunciate. Thinking past the available descriptions of critique as unmasking, disclosing, debunking, and deconstructing (Fabian 1991), it argues that critique is simultaneously a work of assemblage and disassemblage, with signposts to a world to come. By its very nature, it is neither "neutral" nor "objective" in the sense that these twin words are usually understood or used to claim "impartiality," even "detachment." In many ways, critique indeed presupposes some degrees of attachment as well as detachment.

As will become evident to readers, the notion of critique it employs is also transformative. In 2004, Bruno Latour argued that critique had run out of steam due, among other reasons, to theorization by figures such as Jean Baudrillard, who held that "the Twin Towers destroyed themselves under their own weight . . . undermined by the utter nihilism inherent in capitalism itself."

Taking Baudrillard as representing the ruins of critique, Latour issued a call for the renewal of the critical mind by cultivating a "*stubbornly realist attitude*." In Latour's view, Baudrillard and other French critics lacked a realist attitude. In a mode of "reflexivity," he remarked, "I am ashamed to say that the author was French" (Latour 2004, 228, 231; italics in original). Latour's take is puzzling. He didn't show how Baudrillard's critique was non- or antirealist. Indeed, he didn't engage with Baudrillard's critique beyond the bare mention in the lines quoted above. The critique readers are left with is Latour's expression of shame, which he nationalized rather than rationalized. Parenthetically, it ought to be noted that in contexts including interventions and issues mass-advertised as humanitarian, global, and so on, the national and the rational often work as substitutes, at times even as prostitutes. Returning to and in disagreement with Latour's thesis that critique has run its course, *Religion as Critique* instead maintains that the kind of critique it aims to enunciate has in fact only begun. Vis-à-vis the subject matter of this book and its theoretical horizon, much of critique has been stymied insofar as it has been largely imitative rather than sufficiently reflective, reproductive rather than transformative. For Jacques Rancière (2009), critique realizes itself when it beckons to a world in the offing (see also O'Keeffe 2014).

Religion as Critique aims to contribute, inter alia, to the subfield of anthropology/sociology of philosophy and intellect. If some readers may find it less "ethnographic" (especially in part I), this is because of my realization early on that a meaningful "description" of "data" or "material" must simultaneously describe the very thought and matrix of knowledge behind the description that predescribes (i.e., prescribes) the larger world we inhabit—as migrants; refugees; citizens; permanent residents; "illegals"; Westerners; non-Westerners; cosmopolitans; parochials; Indians; terrorists; feminists, democrats, nationalists; people who identify as religious, secular, patriarchal, tribal, or ethnic; residents of developed or underdeveloped countries; and so on—as well as the specific aspects of inquiry anthropologists and other scholars undertake. A description that doesn't sufficiently describe the condition of its own description to outline another description is itself in need of critical description.

The subject of critique this book tracks is the exposition on Islam by Abul Ala Maududi (1903–79), the founder of Jamaat-e-Islami in colonial India in 1941, and the multifaceted critiques of his exposition by former members (in a few cases current members as well) and sympathizers of Jamaat and its student wing, the Student Islamic Organization (SIO). On some occasions, I also refer to critique by those not formally connected to Jamaat. However, the bulk of discussion on critique is immanent, by those who were or are connected to Jamaat. In the final chapter I move away from Jamaat to focus on critique as everyday social-cultural practice. There I discuss one of the most salient peace movements of the early twentieth century—namely, Ḳhudāī Ḳhidmatgār, launched by Khan Abdul Ghaffar Khan (d.1988) as a movement of critique. This chapter also deals with everyday critique outside the domain of social movements. To this end, I use my own ethnographic materials as well as those of others to discuss the salience of proverbs in everyday life. I take these ethnographic encounters and the Ḳhudāī Ḳhidmatgār movement to understand the issue of critique in general.

Religion as Critique doesn't claim to present *the* genealogy of critique in Islam. Based on a sustained engagement with the traditions, cultures, politics, and histories of Muslims in the Indian subcontinent—frequently but mistakenly deemed marginal in the study of religion in general and Islam in particular—it offers one path to such a genealogy. The book, however, makes a strong claim that its path of genealogy is novel and original for, to my knowledge, it has not been previously charted out, certainly not in anthropology/sociology or religion/Islamic studies with such a theoretical goal and methodological frame. Unlike the available dominant accounts of critique in Western and Westernizing traditions, the book describes and posits God Himself as the source of critique and the prophets He sent over time as critics par excellence. The mission of the prophets God sent was to enact reform (*iṣlāḥ*) through critique. With the conclusion of prophecy, the task of critique and reform fell on *ʿulema* (scholars), deemed heirs to the prophets. It is within this frame (elaborated in chapter 3), defying as it does the dualism and separation—silky to some, thorny to others—between the secular and the religious, that any meaningful enterprise of critique ought to be situated. Such a frame, I suggest, is pertinent to studying social formations of the past as well as those of the contemporary world (dis)order of nation-states led by imperial Western plutocracies. The constellation of reform, critique, *ʿulema*, and the tradition they critically relate to and shape is surely informed by the pervasive, blood-drenched, war-imbued politics of and among the nation-states. However, it is neither reducible to nor to be subsumed within the gory enthusiasm for ethnifying nationalism, the history of which, despite claims by nationalists that it is ancient, sometimes even timeless, is as young as yesterday. Without fully accounting for this constellation alluded to above, we can't adequately understand even the widely agreed common minimum notion of critique (*tanqīd/naqd*) in South Asian Urdu/Islamic tradition—to assess (*jāñchnā/parakh̲nā*) or to distinguish between original and fake, good and bad or not so good.

The genealogy of critique, received wisdom unequivocally maintains, started with Immanuel Kant (e.g., see Shumway 2014). *Religion as Critique,* in contrast, contends that it began much earlier. As a prelude to demonstrate this proposition and enable readers to begin to rethink the whole issue of critique afresh, the prologue presents Shah Valiullah's (d. 1763) work as an exemplification of critique preceding, as well as different from, Kant's.

Acknowledgments

Religion as Critique began as a postdoctoral project in 2006, when I was awarded the Rubicon Grant by the Netherlands Organization for Scientific Research (NWO) for my proposal "Contesting Islamism: Immanent Critique of Jamaat-e-Islami of India, from 1941 to the Present." I completed the postdoctoral research at the former Institute for the Study of Islam in the Modern World (ISIM) at Leiden University in the Netherlands. Building on and expanding prior contacts made during my doctoral research, the postdoctoral project was based on ethnographic fieldwork conducted during 2006–7 in two key locations: Delhi and Aligarh. When relevant, I draw on notes from my doctoral fieldwork. Though I stayed at Karan Palace, a guesthouse close to the university Jamia Millia Islamia in southwest Delhi, I also spent considerable time in Old Delhi, the Walled City. The second site of my fieldwork was the city of Aligarh in the northern state of Uttar Pradesh. The distance between Delhi and Aligarh is about 120 kilometers (75 miles). Occasionally, the fieldwork took me beyond these two sites to places such as Patna, the capital of Bihar. In some ways, the fieldwork continued during my subsequent visits until 2010, and I remained in touch with many interlocutors. I take the people I worked with as interlocutors rather than "informants," who in the dominant old-style anthropology worked more as suppliers of bare "facts" at the local level and less as intellectual interpreters in their own right. As the reader will notice, this book is equally about the books, journals, rejoinders, and writings my interlocutors read, talked about, interpreted, cited, and urged me to consult.

To mark the formal conclusion of the postdoctoral project, I convened an international workshop, "Understanding Immanent Critique: Cultural Politics and Islamic Activism" at Leiden University (28–29 November 2008). The Royal Netherlands Academy of Arts and Sciences, Prince Claus Fund for Culture and Development and Forum (a Dutch organization) awarded financial grants to organize the workshop.

Two articles resulting from this research appeared in *Anthropological Theory* (2011) and *Modern Asian Studies* (2008). Significantly revised, they constitute chapters 2 and 6, respectively, in this book. The article in *Anthropological Theory* was first presented at the 2008 workshop as a concept paper titled "Outline of a Theory of Immanent Critique." I subsequently presented versions of this paper at an anthropology seminar at Monash University (October 2009) and at the sociology department at Jawaharlal Nehru University (JNU) in New Delhi (February 2010). Seminars at the South Asian Studies Center at the University of Chicago and the Committee for the Study of Religion Seminar Series at the City University of New York (both in November 2012) offered me a wonderful opportunity to further reflect on the theoretical part of the project. Titled "Toward an Anthropology of Critique: Secular, Religious, Immanent, Transcendental . . . ," the paper at the University of Chicago received, as it had at Monash University in 2010, largely unsympathetic responses which, if rendered concisely, would read, How can Islam be a source of critique?

I presented earlier and different versions of the article in *Modern Asian Studies* at the Staff Seminar, ISIM, Leiden (2006); the American Anthropological Association Conference, San Jose, California (2006); the South Asia Seminar, Department of Anthropology, University of Sussex (2006); and the Department of Sociology, JNU (2007). I presented parts of chapter 7 in a June 2015 panel discussion at the Institute for Religion, Politics, and Society (IRPS) at the Australian Catholic University (ACU) in Melbourne. The panel, titled "Violence and Peace: Religious and Secular," comprised José Casanova (Georgetown University), Mark Chou (ACU, Melbourne), and myself. My contribution to the panel focused on the ideas and practices of Abdul Ghaffar Khan.

For their critical and constructive comments on the published articles as well as their earlier versions; invitations to seminars and panels where they worked as discussants and offered feedback; their participation in the workshop I convened; and for offering relevant references and personal discussion about the book, I wish to acknowledge my gratitude to Hussein Agrama (University of Chicago), Akhlaq Ahan (JNU), Omair Ahmad (Delhi), Muzaffar Alam (University of Chicago), Ismail Albayrak (ACU), Kamran Asdar Ali (University of Texas at Austin), Robert Audi (University of Notre Dame), Sindre Bangstad (Institute for Church, Religion, and Worldview Research, Oslo), the late Gerd Baumann (University of Amsterdam), Asef Bayat (University of Illinois, Urbana-Champaign), Nabanipa Bhattacharjee (Delhi University), Thomas Blom Hansen (Stanford University), Gary Bouma (Monash University), Kenan Cayır (Bilgi University), Mridula Nath Chakraborty (Monash University), Juan Cole (University of Michigan), Marc de Leeuw (University of New South Wales), Dale Eickelman (Dartmouth College), Patrick French (Delhi/London), Francio Guadeloupe (University of St. Martin), Ghassan Hage (University of Melbourne), Wael Hallaq (Columbia University), Kevin Hart (University of Virginia), Michael Herzfeld (Harvard University), Syed Akhtar Hussain (JNU), Michael Janover (Monash University), Jeanette Jouili (University of Pittsburgh), Shifra Kisch (University of Amsterdam), Michiel Leezenberg (University of Amsterdam), Magnus Marsden (University of Sussex), Waris Mazhari (a Delhi-based *ʿālim*), Julie McBrien (University of Amsterdam), Annelies Moors (University of Amsterdam), Susan Buck Morss (City University of New York), Avijit Pathak (JNU), Caroline Osella (London University), Filippo Osella (University of Sussex), Basharat Peer (Delhi), Frank Peter (Hamad Bin Khalifa University, Doha), Santhosh Raghavan (Indian Institute of Technology, Madras), Samuli Schielke (Centre for Modern Oriental Studies, Berlin), Banu Senay (Macquarie University), Muhammad Shakeel (University of Calcutta), Bhrigupati Singh (Brown University), Benjamin Soares (African Studies Centre, Leiden), Thijl Sunier (Vrije Universiteit Amsterdam), Manindra Thakur (JNU), Manish Thakur (Indian Institute of Management, Calcutta), Martin van Bruinessen (Utrecht University), Peter Van der Veer (Max Planck Institute, Göttingen), Sally Weller (ACU), Salih Yucel (Charles Stuart University, Sydney), Qasim Zaman (Princeton University), and Vazira Zamindar (Brown University).

During my stay at Brown University as a visiting associate professor at the Watson Institute for International Studies in 2014, I had three study sessions with Paul Guyer, a prominent scholar on Kant. To him, an anthropological pursuit on the Enlightenment, Kant, and Islam was less than obvious. For my part, however, I found the sessions beneficial and I thank him. I apologize to those whose names may have escaped my memory; grateful to them obviously I remain.

I am indebted to Rizwan Ahmad (Qatar University, Doha), José Casanova (Georgetown University), and Chris Houston (Macquarie University, Sydney) for reading and commenting on the first draft of the entire manuscript. Kausar Mazhari (Jamia Millia Islamia, Delhi) read chapter 3 and offered many useful suggestions. Tarek Makhlouf, a fresh honors graduate of the University of Melbourne and a visitor to ACU in 2016, read three chapters. So did Sunniya Wajahat, an honors student whose dissertation I supervised. Tarek and Sunniya, among others, let me know the extent to which the manuscript was intelligible to nonanthropologists and readers of their age groups. Special thanks go to Sunniya for a careful scrutiny of references and arranging them in line with University of North Carolina Press style. Raf Rooseleers, administrative officer at IRPS, ACU, where I moved to from Monash University, smilingly helped with the formatting of the manuscript as well as photographs used in the book. I thank Nicholas Morieson, my Ph.D. student at ACU, for proofreading the book.

My thanks equally go to my interlocutors in Delhi, Aligarh, and other places.

They were generous with their time and took part in conversation with much interest. They offered suggestions of multiple kinds, including texts that were unfamiliar to me. They directed me to appropriate bookshops and individuals. Without their participation, this book would not have been possible. I have disidentified them by changing their names.

In 2012, I spent part of my sabbatical at the City University of New York to work with Talal Asad, which was an incredibly rewarding experience. Professor Asad spared time to comment on some chapters of the book draft and offered a variety of rich suggestions. He also arranged for weekend sessions over lunch and tea to discuss thinkers and books relevant to the project. In a style of his own, he would ask, "So, how did you find these writings?" He also introduced me to scholars working in New York and other cities. He was generous enough to offer his office for me to use. On some occasions, it caused unease. Seeing the office door half-open, visitors would knock on the door to find me, not Talal Asad. At times, it led to interesting conversation between visitors and me. What struck me most during my interactions with Professor Asad was his impeccable humility, deep involvement in discussion, pleasant temperament, democratic form of conversation, a willingness to listen, and a caring attitude—all in the midst of what I found to be a rather rushed life in New York. Discussions with Gil Anidjar (Columbia University, whom I first met in Istanbul in 2010) in New York as well as in Sydney have been equally enjoyable.

At the University of North Carolina Press, I wish to express my utmost gratitude to Professors Bruce Lawrence and Carl Ernst. As series editors, they took a keen interest in the manuscript and showed their faith in its author. They enthusiastically supported its theoretical-methodological goal while also paying attention to such matters as translation, transliteration, and more. I thank the anonymous reviewers for their encouraging and constructive comments and suggestions. I thank Executive Editor Elaine Maisner. It is a joy to have an editor like Elaine. From reception of the manuscript through the review process to its production, she guided the project in a timely manner with sound advice and admirable efficiency. I am thankful to Alex Martin for his careful and thoughtful editing. To Dr. Mukta Sai Samant, I am grateful for the first round of meticulous editing of the manuscript. Many of her questions also allowed me to clarify things that I took for granted. To Mahmoud Hatamabadi, a Melbourne-based Iranian calligrapher, I am grateful for his handwriting Iqbal's couplet that forms the book's epigraph. He took no fee for it. Unlike most Indians who call Iqbal simply Iqbal, he, however, called him "Iqbal Lahori," Iqbal from Lahore. This sounded somewhat odd to me, especially because in a couplet Iqbal described himself as a *dervēsh*: neither an Easterner nor a Westerner—his home being neither Delhi or Bukhara nor Samarqand.

I acknowledge my gratitude to my brother, Rizwan Ahmad, a sociolinguist. Over the years, I have benefited from intellectual conversations with him. He offered academic and moral support, at times without being asked.

To my parents, I am grateful for their continued encouragement even if what I was doing was less than comprehensible to them, especially to my mother (*ammī*). This is also the time to ask for forgiveness, especially from *ammī* and YS. They know why. I have always enjoyed intellectual conversation with my father (*abbī jī*), who gave me constant encouragement and had many discussions about the book. In part, it is *abbī jī* 's interest in Farsi and Urdu poetry/philosophy (especially Ghalib, Iqbal, and Jamil Mazhari) and his verbatim recitations of couplets, sayings, and proverbs on occasions most suitable for them that developed my interests as a teenager. Unlike most in my extended family, he was the one who appreciated the life of the mind in its own right. During the course of the project, I was blessed with the arrival of my lovely nephew, Mobashshir Rahman. It is to Mobashshir, Ayesha Rizwan Ahmad (my little niece), and *abbī jī* that I dedicate this book. I found *abbī jī's* interests and thoughts motivating. Mobashshir and Ayesha, when they grow young, would probably find them so, too.

The royalties from this book will be donated to Al-Hira Public School, Shahganj, Patna, India, where my youngest sister (currently a practicing medical doctor) received her early education; my eldest sisters received no formal education. The donation is made to meet the living expenses and tuition fees of orphans enrolled in the school.

Notes on Transliteration

Names of individuals/authors in Arabic, Farsi, Hindi, Sanskrit, and Urdu are untransliterated; they appear as in most social science practices of writings. Unless specified otherwise, all translations into English are mine.

At the first occurrence of non-English words in the text, I provide their approximate English meanings. Italicized words in English in citations from non-English sources indicate they were originally in English in the cited source.

In transliterating words common to Arabic, Farsi, and Urdu, I follow Urdu practices. I write *fiṭ̤rat*, not *fiṭ̤ra* (as in Arabic). Arabic speakers, unlike Urdu speakers, don't pronounce the *t* at the end of a word. Some Urdu speakers now follow the Arabic style.

There are some Sanskrit words, which I have transliterated as per the sources I refer to.

In transliterating Arabic, Hindi, Farsi, and Urdu words, I follow the *Annual of Urdu Studies* (AUS) transliteration guidelines 2007 with the exception that I use the symbol *ch* for the first sound in the word "chaman" rather than Č. I do this because the diacritic above the letter *C* is not well known among most readers with a social science background. I use the symbol *ḳh* for the first sound in the word "ḳhaṭ̤" and g̣h as in "g̣halaṭ̤." *Ḳh*, or *g̣h*, does not exist in Hindi. The Indic sounds "kẖ" and "gẖ," common to Urdu and Hindi (e.g., in "kẖulā," meaning "open," and "gẖ" as in "gẖar," meaning home), are transliterated with a dash below the *h*. Arabic, Farsi, and Urdu words that have become part of English dictionary (for example, hadith, sharia, and so on) have not been transliterated. An exception to this is *ʿulema*; my usage of it differs from its mainstream meaning.

The following are the vowels and consonants I use for transliteration.

VOWELS

Symbol	*Example*	*Meaning*
a	m**a**l	rub
ā	b**ā**l	hair
e	b**e**lā	without
ē	r**ē**l	rail
i	t**i**l	mole
ī	t**ī**n	three
o	b**o**lānā	call
ō	b**ō**l	say
u	b**u**rā	bad
ū	s**ū**q	market
ai	m**ai**l	dirt
au	t**au**l	weigh

CONSONANTS

Letter	*Symbol*	*Example*	*Meaning*
bē	b	**b**āt	talk
pē	p	**p**al	moment
tē	t	**t**an	body
ṭe	ṭ	**ṭ**ōpī	cap
ṡē	ṡ	**ṡ**aqāfat	culture
jīm	j	**j**āʾez	permitted
chē	ch	**ch**aman	garden
ḥē	ḥ	**ḥ**aq	truth
ḳhē	ḳh	**ḳh**āliṣ	pure
dāl	d	**d**īn	religion
ḍāl	ḍ	**ḍ**āk	post
ẕāl	ẕ	**ẕ**ehn	mind
rē	r	**r**izq	provision
ṛē	ṛ	ba**ṛ**ā	big
zē	z	**z**amīn	earth
sīn	s	**s**ar	head
shīn	sh	**sh**arm	shame
ṣvād	ṣ	**ṣ**adāqat	truth
ẓvād	ẓ	**ẓ**amīr	conscience
t̤ōē	t̤	**t̤**āghūt	idol
z̤ōē	z̤	**z̤**ālim	oppressor
ʿain	ʿ	**ʿ**alam	flag
g̣hain	gh	**g̣h**alaṭ	wrong
fē	f	**f**aqīr	beggar
qāf	q	**q**alam	pen
kāf	k	**k**al	tomorrow
gāf	g	**g**āl	cheek
lām	l	**l**ōg	people
mīm	m	**m**aqṣad	goal
nūn	n	**n**iz̤ām	system
vāō	v	**v**aqt	time
hē	h	**h**indī	Hindi
dō chashmī hē	ẖ	b**ẖ**ālū	bear
yē	y	**y**ād	remember
hamzā	ʾ	jā**ʾ**ez	permitted

RELIGION AS CRITIQUE

PROLOGUE

In 1732, at age twenty-nine, the Indian philosopher Shah Valiullah (1703–63) went on a spiritual and educational journey to Hijaz. During his two-year stay there, he studied hadith (*ḥadīṡ*, reports of the words and deed of Prophet Muhammad) and other sciences. In *Fuyudul al-ḥaramain*, an Arabic text rendered into Urdu as *Moshāhidāt v maʿārif*, Valiullah (1947) recorded his experience of "philosophical, political, and collective good" in Hijaz (Sarvar 1947, 3). The journey was a medium enabling Valiullah to undertake "observation of his own interiority [*bāṯin*] and illustration of truths [*ḥaqāʾeq*]."

Fuyudul al-ḥaramain contains forty-seven observations (sing. *moshāhida*) by Valiullah. In consonance with the vocabulary of his time, and especially for the one relating to Sufism (*taṣavvuf*), Valiullah also used "observation" to mean truths (*ḥaqāʾeq*), which his heart underwent and his spiritual eyes (eyes of *qalb v rūḥ*) observed. Dream and light (*nūr*) were integral to that observation, the themes of which included secrets of the universe, love, mysticism, God's creations, a plurality of religions and of schools of thought, a dialectic between multiplicity and unity in the divine plan, and much more. Thus, he dreamed that Hasan and Hussain, grandsons of Prophet Muhammad, handed over a pen from the Prophet to Valiullah. He also saw rays of light emanating from the Kaaba, the mosque in Mecca that is the prime point of the hajj pilgrimage. The source of such *ʿilm* (knowledge) in Valiullah's observation was not exclusively *ʿaql* (reason) but also *qalb* (heart). In the poetry of Maulana Rum (better known in the West as Rumi), the poet-philosopher Muhammad Iqbal (d. 1938) saw many instances of knowledge derived from *vijdān* (intuition) and *bāṯin* (interiority of the self) that are often well beyond the reach of bare *ḥavās* (senses). To Iqbal, the knowledge derived from *bāṯin* and that derived from the senses were not antithetical to each other; rather, they coexisted in a delicately tenuous matrix of interrelationships of complementarity mediated by a "critical eye [*tanqīdī naẕar*]" on the whole (Sarvar 1947, 6–9).

Muhammad Sarvar, a resident of Jamia Nagar, New Delhi, who translated *Fuyudul al-ḥaramain* into Urdu in 1947, invoked Iqbal to convince "some readers" who might think that the issues discussed in the text were "noncredible." By "some readers," Sarvar perhaps meant those educated in and enamored by the "Western" system of knowledge. If so, this apologia—partly veiled, partly manifest—needs unpacking. If absence of a credible source in Valiullah's observation renders it into a fiction, so should the source of "the state of nature" thesis from Thomas Hobbes via Immanuel Kant, to contemporary advocates of realism and neorealism in international relations theory. The state of nature thesis is a pure fiction (Besson 2005, 124–60; Weber 2005 [2001], chap. 2). It is, then, plausible to see dream and the like in Valiullah as conceptually and functionally similar to "the state of nature" in Hobbes—both are unverifiable but galvanized to illuminate a "rational" goal. The unverifiable—one can add even the unsaid, unsayable, and assumed—is no less important to the "scientific" discourses as it is supposed to be central to a "theological" one such as Valiullah's. In fact, without a set of the unsaid, unsayable, assumed, and prior premises, any communication is well-nigh impossible, and certainly not meaningful. Thus viewed, Valiullah's recourse to *qalb* (heart), *nūr* (light), and *bāṯin* (interiority) is neither a renunciation of the *ḥavās* (senses) nor an abandonment of reason in the acquisition of knowledge; it is simply the pursuit of both differently.

I present the very first of the forty-seven observations in the form of a dream by Valiullah as one among many illustrations of critique in the Islamic tradition, well before Kant, with whom "the genealogy of critique starts" (Shumway 2014, 17). In the precinct of the Kaaba and Prophet Muhammad's mosque—Hijaz at large—generally construed as the place of mere submission beyond reason and an uncritical devotion to God, Valiullah enacts argumentation and discussion (*baḥaṡ*). In so doing, he assigns a role to himself—namely to judge, one of the meanings of critique as Reinhart Koselleck (1988 [1959]) outlines it. In Valiullah's text, traces of a Cartesian split or conflict between reason and faith, between heart and mind, between interior and exterior are difficult to fathom; they instead form a connected ensemble. And unlike Kant, who viewed Islam (and other religions) as fanaticism and bestowed rationality solely on Protestant Christianity, for Valiullah Islam was already rational, not in spite of, but due to revelation. His *Ḥujjat Allāh al Bāligha* (*The Conclusive Argument from God*)—the pages of which acknowledge, among others, Ghazali—outlines tenets, rituals, and practices of Islam to explain them in rational terms.[1] Key concepts at the heart of *Ḥujjat Allāh al Bāligha* are *maṣlaḥa* (beneficial purpose and public good), intertwined with the premise that things and events have their *asbāb/sabab/ʿelal* (causes/reasons), the explication and discovery of which is a human task to pursue (Valiullah n.d.; Hermansen 1996, xvi–xix).[2] Below is my summary of Valiullah's (1947) first observation.

◆ ◆ ◆

I dreamed that there was a large community (*jamāʿt*) of godly people (*Allāh vāloñ kī*). On the faces of one group within it, steeped in the remembrance of God, splashed freshness and beauty. These people did not advocate the creed of *vaḥdat al-vajūd* (ontological monism).[3] Upholding ontological monism, members of another group from the same community were busy thinking about the presence and motion of the *vajūd* of God in the universe. In relation to that thinking, since there had been some *taqṣīr* (error) by them vis-à-vis God, who guides the management of the whole universe as well as of human selves, I saw that their hearts were filled with lament and their faces perplexed.

I saw both groups engaged in a debate (*baḥaṡ*). People of the first group said, "Don't you see the light, freshness, and beauty we have benefited from? Do they not prove that, compared to yours, our path is closer to the guidance from God?" In contrast, advocates of *vaḥdat al-vajūd* said, "Is it not that the whole existence [*kul maūjūdāt*] is contained within God? As we have uncovered the secret that is unfamiliar to you, we are better in knowledge than you are."

The discussion between the two groups took the form of a prolonged fight (*nizāʿ*), and they approached me to judge it. This is what I said: "Sciences of truth [*ʿūlūm-e-ḥaqqa*] are of two types: while one type reforms [*iṣlāḥ*] and pursues cultivation/refinement [*tahzīb*] of selves [*nufūs*], the other type does not." Details of this holistic principle are as follows. Human selves are endowed with different capacities and inclinations. When a given self, inclined to a specific type of science of truth in accordance with his capacity, gets fully immersed in it, she or he attains reform and refinement. No doubt the issue of *vaḥdat al-vajūd* pertains to the sciences of truth. As far as the position of those who don't approve of *vaḥdat al-vajūd* is concerned, though they remain unaware of it, they possess the knowledge of the specific type of sciences of truth that they were endowed with. Consequently, their selves were reformed and refined. As for those who supported *vaḥdat al-vajūd*, they reached truth in this regard, but they lacked in the specific type of science of truth they were naturally endowed with. As a result, as they let their reflection roam unconditioned in the valley of thought on the issue of if and how God is present in the whole world, they lost the relational thread of God's greatness—His love and His transcendence. Thus, they neither reached the truth nor achieved reform and refinement of their selves.

"O proponents of *vaḥdat al-vajūd*, upholders of God's *vajūd* being present in the whole world, those among you revealed this secret who indeed were incapable of it." Conversely, the group that had the capacity and inclination for such knowledge remained silent. Some among you—O proponents of *vaḥdat al-vajūd*—are thoroughly unaware of this secret. In this regard, a specific type of reason [*ʿaql*] needed for the attainment of perfection is missing among you. In such a condition, it is natural that there is a lament in your heart and your face wears bewilderment. In reality, the person capable of this secret is he who possesses a specific type and capacity of reason—fresh and blooming.

As I explained, they understood it. I told them that I have the key to these secrets, specially granted by God to me so as to resolve disagreements (*ikhtilāfāt*). All praises are reserved for God who sustains the worlds.

As I finished the discourse, my eyes opened.

PART I
Formulation

1 INTRODUCTION

Insofar as Europe is the source of knowledge, it is also
the center of ignorance [*jehl*]. . . . To her, the criterion for the
health of an event [*vāqeʿā*] is not subject to the strength or
weakness of an argument; rather, the acceptance or denial
of it is based on how it will benefit its own interests
or harm those of its rival/enemy [*ḥarīf*].
—SULAIMAN NADVI (1985 [1914], 132)

On 11 October 2006, the *New York Times* published a curiously long story: "Across Europe, Worries on Islam Spread to Center." It "covered" many aspects, not necessarily congruent. I discuss the criticism and Islam the story dealt with. The first sentence concluded that "more people in the political mainstream are arguing that Islam can't be reconciled with European values." The next sentence was a quote from Patrick Gonman, owner of a "funky wine bar" in Antwerp, Belgium. Speaking about Pope Benedict XVI's speech in Regensburg, Germany, Gonman remarked: "He said Islam is an aggressive religion. And the next day they [Muslims] kill a nun somewhere and make his point. *Rationality is gone*" (Bilefsky and Fisher 2006; italics mine).

◆ The Ubiquitous Absence, or the Received Wisdom

Gonman was described as "hardly an extremist"; rather, he was portrayed as sympathetic to Muslims because he had shut down his restaurant to show his disapproval of a far-right party's anti-Muslim rally held near Antwerp a week earlier. From the far right, the *New York Times* story moved to the center: "centrists across Europe" also share the "worry" that "any criticism of Islam or Muslim immigration provokes threats of violence." Quoting Jack Straw, the British Foreign Secretary, it noted that the veil was a "visible statement of separation and difference." The next paragraph referred again to the pope's speech calling aspects of Islam "evil and inhuman," saying that while Muslims "berated" him, non-Muslims "applauded him for bravely speaking a hard truth." The story then progressed to say how Muslims' lack of rationality toward comments like the pope's showed Europe's "limits of tolerance." It repeated its observation of "the growing fear that any criticism of Islam could provoke violence." To prove this, it cited a few examples. A schoolteacher in France reportedly went underground because he received death threats for calling Prophet Muhammad "a merciless warlord, a looter, a mass murderer of Jews and a polygamist." In Germany, an opera show depicting Prophet Muhammad's severed head was called off for security reasons. German Chancellor Angela Merkel condemned the cancellation. It also referred to protests against the Danish cartoons depicting the Prophet as testimony of Muslims' hostility to freedom of speech. A Belgian woman married to a Tunisian Muslim was quoted as saying that "no amount of explanation about free speech could convince her husband that the publication of cartoons lampooning Muhammad ... was in any way justified" (Bilefsky and Fisher 2006).

The *New York Times* story left no doubt that Islam was a problem. It portrayed the issue in terms of a freedom-loving, enlightened, reason-driven Europe pitted against an uncritical, bigoted, freedom-despising Islam. While Gonman, a secular funky wine bar owner sympathized with Muslims, the Tunisian man had no idea about freedom of speech. While the pope "bravely" spoke "a hard truth," Muslims were perceived as intellectually incapable of any response but to "kill a nun." While Gonman was depicted as an ideal European embodying "Western values," the veiled women only unveiled "separation and differences." Furthermore, Muslims' uncriticality led to violence and protest, thereby setting the "limits of tolerance" in the West. Importantly, the *New York Times* consolidated secular and critical as homologous, on the one hand, and Islam and critique as mutually hostile, on the other. As Gonman said, "Rationality is gone." Writing in *Yale Global Online*, Sadanand Dhume (2008) made the point more flagrantly: "Islamic culture prohibits any criticism of Islamic traditions."

The equation of Islam with the absence of critique has a longer genealogy (see chap. 2) in Western thought, which runs almost concurrently with Europe's colonial expansion. In many ways, the popular image of Islam, from Martin Luther up to the present, bears this out. Luther (d. 1546) likened Muslims to the Antichrist (Quinn 2008, 43). Linking the immobility of Muslim societies with their intellectual traditions, Ernest Renan (1823–92) wrote, "Islam is the disdain of science, ... restricting the human mind, closing it to all delicate ideas, . . . to all rational research" (qtd. in Kurzman 1998, 1). He indeed argued that Islam and knowledge could not go together (Nomani 1955, 168).[1] The same Renan, let's note, exhorted an "eternal war . . . that will not cease until the last son of Ishamel has died of misery or has been relegated to the ends of the deserts by way of terror" (qtd. in Anidjar 2008, 6). Similarly, William Muir observed that the Qur'ān is one of "the most stubborn enemies of Civilization, Liberty . . . which the world has yet known" (qtd. in Lester 1999, 46).

However, the reassertion of Islam's lack of critique in the twentieth century dates to the end of the Cold War in 1989—which Nicole Falkenhayner (2010, 111) calls the "zero year for the envisioning of a new global order"—when the Salman Rushdie affair broke out. I don't want to be misunderstood as saying that religion was absent—as it is usually held—during the Cold War. In fact, the term "Cold War" is linked to Islam. Don Juan Manuel (d. 1348), prince and nephew of Ferdinand II, used the Spanish *guerra fría* (cold war) to describe the relationship between Islam and Christendom as one of neither war nor peace (Trumpbour 2003, 107). Furthermore, the twentieth-century Cold War, as I discuss in chapter 2, was simultaneously religious and secular: Christian democracy versus godless communism. If religion was not absent in the Cold War, an important question is, Did Islam appear as a fault line only after the Cold War? It is relevant to note that the phrase "clash of civilizations," associated with Samuel Huntington, was used as far back as 1964 by Bernard Lewis—also influential in U.S. power circles. In 1964, Lewis wrote: "The crisis in the Middle East . . . arises not from a quarrel between states but from a clash of civilizations" (qtd. in Trumpbour 2003, 93). Already in 1953, Lewis had identified the Cold War with Islam, as the British philosopher Bertrand Russell (1920, 27) had earlier done, likening Bolsheviks to the "successors of Mahomet [*sic*]." "The traditional Islamic division of the world into the House of Islam and the House of War," Lewis wrote, has "obvious parallels in the Communist view of world affairs." He continued, "The call to a *Communist jihad*—a new faith, but against the self-same *Western Christian enemy*—might well strike a responsive note" (qtd. in Trumpbour 2003, 100–101; italics mine). Karl Popper's *The Open Society and Its Enemies* (1969) can be situated within this tradition. "Free debate," use of "reason," and "protection of freedom"—which to Popper (1972) were properties of an "open" society—were available only in the capitalist bloc.

With the 1979 Iranian Revolution and the collapse of communism, the Renan-like imaginary about Islam resurfaced; Ernest Gellner's *Postmodernism, Reason and Religion* is perhaps its most succinct sketch. Gellner saw religious fundamentalism as opposed to "secular wisdom of the age" and "Enlightenment rationalism." However, he felt impelled to say that "in our age fundamentalism is at its strongest in Islam" (Gellner 1992, 4). The Rushdie affair; the publication of *Lajjā* by Taslima Nasreen in the early 1990s; the series of writings and speeches by the Dutch politician Ayaan Hirsi Ali, including the film *Submission* (De Leeuw and van Wichelen 2005; Moors 2005), whose script she wrote; the horrendous murder of Theo van Gough, who directed *Submission*; and writings by tenure-seeking prophets like Irshad Manji have only reinforced this image: Islam is inimical to criticism.

Yet the watershed was the Rushdie affair of 1989, on which much has been written (Asad 1993). One strand of Rushdie's defenders held that at stake was the very freedom of speaking and writing (MacDonogh 1993). Relatedly, some argued that the foundational Christianity of the Enlightenment, with its self-reflexivity, tolerance, and intellectual pluralism, was at a radical variance with Islam's utter lack of these qualities. Falkenhayner (2010, 129n67) quoted the Canadian novelist Margaret Atwood's description of Christianity as a "house with many living quarters" and paraphrased Atwood as arguing that "Christianity is supposed to include criticism as an inherent feature." Muslims' protest, in contrast, showed the sheer absence of such criticism. In a similar vein, Sadik Al-Azm (1991, 13, 20) wrote that the Rushdie affair brought "previously untouchable subjects within the compass of *critical thought, autonomous reason*." Al-Azm concluded his essay on what he called "Rushdie's explosive intervention" with a call that we "desperately need . . . the two great R's of the modern world: Reason and Revolution" (italics mine). That Muslims critical of Rushdie's novel *The Satanic Verses* were far out of the realm of reason, and consequently the modern world, was abundantly evident from Al-Azam's priestly call.

In 2009, on the twentieth anniversary of Ayatollah Ruhollah Khomeini's *fatwa against Rushdie*, New York University's Wagner School of Public Policy and Service collaborated with Irshad Manji, author of *The Trouble with Islam*. As part of its "Moral Courage Project," it organized a conversation with Rushdie. Manji asked him, "Why do you think the controversy on *The Satanic Verses* was and remains so intense?" Rushdie replied: "Free society argues about, disputes, tells and retells and changes its own story." In contrast, in an unfree society "you are not allowed to do that. . . . And I also tell you in what manner the story can be told." He continued, "Because I was trying to do something else, they came after me" (Rushdie 2009).

Any perceptive observer knows well the limits a "free" society too imposes on what to tell and how to tell a story and, therefore, the watertight, Popper-like distinction that Rushdie rehearsed between free and unfree society seems naive. A pertinent example is the trajectory of my own postdoctoral project that this book is based on and which I presented in many venues across the continents. I faced sharp disagreement over, even stiff opposition to, the idea that the Islamic tradition has its own mode of critique. The most eloquent expression of this opposition came in the form of the editorial rejection of the proposal for a special issue—comprising select papers from the workshop on immanent critique (see preface)—that I submitted to *Thesis Eleven*, an interdisciplinary journal that focuses on theories of society, culture, and politics. The editors justified their decision by arguing that "any discussion of immanent critique in Islam must first confront the basic *failure of the Islamic world over the last three centuries to translate immanent critique into a process of reformation.*" They continued: "*No critical* standpoint is articulated in relation to the theme of the proposed issue" (e-mail dated 19 March 2010; italics mine). I found the response curious, showing as it did how free "free society" is. That Islam historically did not have and, therefore, must have a reformation is a story that has resounding sway among many liberals and secularists—both in the West and non-West. This "lack" in Islam and, to use Günter Grass's probing word (qtd. in Rasch 2009, 114), the simultaneous "luck" of the West to have had the Renaissance, Reformation, and Enlightenment cuts across ideological divides in such a way that it becomes central to figures as diverse as William Blunt (d. 1922; see Browers and Kurzman 2004), Grass, Silvio Berlusconi (Ahmad 2002), Jürgen Habermas (1987, 16–17; also see Rasch 2009, 116), Roman Loimeier (2005), and Rushdie (2005). That this narrative is no more than a story, for it is seldom asked how one can precisely demonstrate that one teleologically led to another—that is, Renaissance→ Reformation→ Enlightenment—needs to be stressed. The rejection of my proposal by *Thesis Eleven* illustrated well that a "free" society doesn't necessarily argue about, only selectively disputes, tells, and retells, and rarely changes, its story.

Importantly, in Rushdie's response there was no mention of "listening." Is there an act of telling a story without a notion of a community of listeners? Taslima Nasreen, the Bangladeshi author of the novel *Lajjā*, situates herself in the same league as Rushdie. As do the Indian media, which routinely shower praise on her; her vitriol against Islam is defended in the name of free speech (Dasgupta 2012). However, the same media rarely speak of freedom of speech when activists such as Mirwaiz Omar Farooq, Bilal Lone, and Ali Shah Geelani are punched, hackled, and assaulted, and their seminars are disrupted in Calcutta, Chandigarh, and Delhi (NDTV 2010; *Indian Express* 2010). Disparaging depictions of Islam and Muslims by authors and activists such as Necla Kelek of Germany, Ayaan Hirsi Ali of the Netherlands and United States, Chahdortt Djavann of France, Manji of Canada, and others (often in "realist" genres like autobiographies and personal histories) are thus less about freedom of speech and more about what the audience wants to hear. Such voices offer authentication and evidence as "insiders" (Sieg 2010, 151) to validate what much of the audience is made to and/or likes to hear and which resonates with the mediatized views about Islam.

A number of issues are at stake in thinking about the alleged lack of critique in Islam. In my view, the meaningful question is not about the putative absence of critique in Islam. Rather, it is about the inability of our prevalent frameworks to recognize and study the principles and practices of critique already at work in Islam. The greatest inability of the existing frameworks is found in the Enlightenment legacy, according to which critique is often understood as critique *of* religion other than Christianity, not critique *from within* non-Christian religion. Christianity is exempted from the list of religions because, following Margaret Atwood (cited above), and almost the whole of Enlightenment thinking, Christianity (especially, Protestantism) is already rational, and critique is built into it. Likewise, secularism could emerge only within Christianity (see chap. 2). From this it logically follows that Islam can never be an agent and source of critique; it can only be an object of critique as the Enlightenment postulated it. Mohammed Arkoun's writing is one among several examples. Since "Islam is presented and lived as a definite system of beliefs and non-beliefs which cannot be submitted to any critical inquiry," he stressed "the necessity of starting with a critique of Islamic reason" (Arkoun 2003, 27, 20). In Arkoun's diagnosis, this is due to the "intellectual gap between Muslim orthodoxy and Westernized secular thought," which began in sixteenth-century Europe.

Streaks of current "new atheism" display a distinctly Enlightenment view of Islam, calling for its reformation. This call intensified in the wake of 9/11. Rushdie (2006) called for Islam's reformation and enlightenment (Ahmad 2009b, 166). In a post-9/11 context, "new atheism," says Terry Eagleton (2009), "operates wittingly or not . . . as the sort of intellectual wing of the War on Terror." Eagleton named Rushdie and Christopher Hitchens in this context. This is also the case with the French atheist Michel Onfray. While traveling in Mauritania's desert, Onfray had an intense discussion with his driver, Abduramane, a praying Muslim. Claiming that he "just read" the Qurʾān "pen in hand" and had "memorized several passages," he insisted that Islam preached violence even as Abduramane refuted whatever Onfray (2007 [2005], xii) assigned to Islam—"jihad against unbelievers," "state-of-the art terrorism," and so on—as contrary to what he held was true Islam. Reading Onfray, one is led to believe that Onfray knew more about the correct Islam than did Abduramane.

In the writings of secularists and atheists like Onfray, Islam is not presented as one among many religions; it symbolizes religion in its ultimate essence in a manner that Islam becomes the most religious religion of all. Contemporary discussion of the secular and the religious—presumably encompassing all religions—in significant ways is specific to Islam. Consider the justification of the term "new terrorism" (NT). In *Old & New Terrorism,* Peter Neumann (2009, 29) contends that NT is different from old terrorism (OT) in that while OT was secular-nationalist, NT is "religiously inspired," Islam being its insignia. Neumann devotes chapter 4 of his book ("From Marx to Mohammed? Religion and Terrorism") to his thesis that new terrorism is religious/Islamic. In *Jihad vs. McWorld,* Benjamin Barber used "jihad" as shorthand for "atavistic politics" in general, yet "its evocative power ultimately rests in Islam"—the locus of the "essential jihad" (qtd. in Euben 2002, 6). This move to assign to Islam all that is religious is remarkable. From Christian discourses, which held that "Islam was not a religion" and called Prophet Muhammad an Arab Lucifer and charlatan, Islam has now been rendered as shorthand for all that is religious and hence the signifier of religiously inspired new terrorism. Such is the context that unveils contemporary debate on secularism and religion, Gil Anidjar observes, as "fundamentally related to *anti-Islam*" (qtd. in Shaikh 2004; italics in original).

◆ The Absent Ubiquity, or the Argument

At the center of this book are the well-known figure of Abul Ala Maududi (1903–79) and the lesser-known, diverse critics of Maududi. The founder of Jamaat-e-Islami in colonial India, Maududi is arguably one of the most prominent thinkers of "political Islam," whose influence transcends South Asia (see chap. 4). The book examines the exposition on Islam by Maududi and the multilayered critiques of his exposition by his immanent critics: former members and sympathizers of Jamaat and its students' wing, the Student Islamic Organization (SIO). Through a systematic, contextualized evaluation of critiques of and by Maududi, this book makes a number of interconnected arguments. The foremost among them is my claim that critique—in varying degrees and in different forms and modalities—has been integral to Islamic traditions. The Western/Enlightenment notion of critique is tied to and is an upshot of a distinct, highly local, political-anthropological formation, the generalization of which has limited analytical efficacy in other contexts. Building on and critically engaging with several important recent works, mainly but not only anthropological ones (e.g., Asad et al. 2009; Asad 1993; Bowen 1993; Eickelman 1985; Eickelman and Piscatori 1996; Fischer and Abedi 1990; Kresse 2003, 2007; Marcus and Fischer 1999; Marsden 2005; and Zaman 2012; see chap. 2), my key contention is that the Western notion and practice of critique is not critique per se but simply one among several of its modalities I put to the reader for further discussion. Against the reigning doxa, which views Islam and critique as mutually exclusive domains—Islam *and* critique—I propose we begin to think of Islam *as* critique; indeed, Islam as permanent critique. My position is thus neither one of radical incommensurability between Islamic and Western notions of critique, nor of absolute isomorphism between the two. I am in favor of robust dialogue and comparison between them, recognizing well that each has a different trajectory, each is informed by a specific historical-social formation. By "comparison" (Asad 1986a; De Castro 2004), I mean the work of translation from one tradition or culture into another. However, this translation doesn't presume similarity between or substitutability of the two: translation is not at the service of comparison; comparison is in the service of translation. And a good translation, following Walter Benjamin, is one "that betrays the destination language, not the source language" (De Castro 2004, 3).

My principal contention here is that the Enlightenment—considered *the* reference point for critique and use of reason—was an *ethnic project* as Europe/West constituted its identity in the name of reason and universalism against a series of others (internal and external), Islam being one of them. This is not to say the Enlightenment was nothing else and *only* an ethnic project. It is well known that as an entity the Enlightenment was not constructed before the late nineteenth century (Vincent 2002). Suggesting that there was no single phenomenon called the Enlightenment, historians like J. G. A. Pocock (2008, 1) have recently cautioned against using the definite article before Enlightenment. Pocock also notes the term's deployment in the twenty-first century as "a cause or program—typically a secular liberalism . . . to defend against *its enemies*" (italics mine). That precisely is my point. Like Talal Asad (2003, 16), who draws on Friedrich Nietzsche and Michel Foucault, I work "back from our present to the contingencies that have come together to give us our certainties" about the Enlightenment and its Other.

My argument about the Enlightenment as an ethnic project sharply differs from the existing nonanthropological (e.g., Hampson 1990; Sen 2005, chap. xiii) and anthropological accounts of the Enlightenment, most of which are often like eulogies to the Enlightenment (e.g., Eriksen and Nielsen 2015; Hastrup 2005; Patterson 2009). Some that are critical (e.g., Kapferer 2007), however, posit that critique of the Enlightenment is built into the Enlightenment itself, thereby not sufficiently exploring other modes of critique. Yet other critiques go beyond such a formulation (e.g., see Sahlins 1999; and Vincent 2002), but they don't account for religion, let alone Islam. Paying attention to religion, I argue that the Enlightenment was not a break from Christianity, much less its outright denunciation as is commonly understood, but instead its reconfiguration whereby the West/Christianity/Europe enacted an immunity to protect itself from any critique while subjecting all others—"the Rest," as it were—to critique. To substantiate this argument, I discuss the German Enlightenment as well as the French Enlightenment in eighteenth-century Europe. In relation to the former, I focus on Kant's writings on geography (1801) and his *Anthropology from a Pragmatic Point of View* (1798), which "has rarely been acknowledged—or, perhaps, even read—by anthropologists" (Vincent 2002, 18). As regards the latter, I dwell on the French *Encyclopédie* and the philosophes to show how they constructed reason in opposition to Islam as an enemy of reason. I leave the U.S. Enlightenment out because, among other reasons, in it there was "hardly any anti-religious component" (Casanova 2006, 22).

But what if reason, critique, and reflexivity were not the sole properties of the Enlightenment and they existed much earlier than Enlightenment? Here I turn to literature on the axial age (from 800 to 200 BC), which reads it as an age of criticism. Broadening its frame, I situate Islam in the tradition of Abraham, to read Muhammad's message as a continuation of the message of yore.[2] Like the prophets Moses and Jesus, Muhammad was a critic of the Meccan social order. His was an embodied, comprehensive critique. He was at once an insider and outsider to Meccans. He critiqued the prevalent tenets, practices, and traditions not to dissolve but to reconfigure them. Reform (*iṣlāḥ*), not *inquilāb* (revolution), which became a trope to view the Prophet's life from the early twentieth century on (e.g., see Siddiqi 1999, 414, 488), is the Qurʾānic word to describe Muhammad's mission. That is, Muhammad's was primarily an immanent critique. This idea is central to the commentary on the Qurʾān, *Tarjumānul Qurʾān*, by Abul Kalam Azad (1888–1958), a philosopher and towering Indian leader of anticolonial struggle. In Azad's (2004 [1968], 433–34) interpretation, Allah sent Muhammad not to deny the truth of other religions but to confirm it. Jews opposed Muhammad not because he negated the teaching of Moses; they opposed him because he confirmed the truth of Christianity as well. Likewise, Christians opposed Muhammad because he also endorsed the teaching of Moses. As instructed by Allah, Prophet Muhammad, Azad argued, didn't ask people of other religions to renounce the teaching of their respective religions. Rather, the Qurʾān asked them to get back to and rescue the teaching of their own religions because the true message of all religions is the same. What I call the prophetic critical enterprise didn't disappear with Muhammad's death. It continued.

Engaging with the axial age enables me to examine the hegemonic pedigree of criticism beginning from ancient Greece, via colonizing Britain (Europe), to nineteenth-century India and subsequently. I draft an alternative genealogy of critique emanating from the traditions of Islam. This notion of critique as expressed in the Urdu language transcends the field of literature to include culture, society, politics, and more. I show how for *ʿulema* (scholars; see chap. 3, n. 20) and the "religious" texts they author, a different notion of critique is at work—a notion that does not dismiss Greek, pre-Muhammad, or Western traditions but which at the same time can't be subsumed within them. According to this alternative genealogy, critique doesn't oppose religion; instead, it emanates from God. I trace elements of this genealogy through the Qurʾān, the lives of the prophets, the Sunna, and the early community around Prophet Muhammad. Maududi and his interlocutors poetically worked within that tradition of critique.

My second argument is that in and of itself reason is neither sufficient nor autonomous in arriving at judgements. Reason—unaided, delinked, unhooked, isolated, detached, autonomous, sovereign—doesn't exist; at best it is a mythology that, on close scrutiny, is unable to sustain itself. Left to itself, it is impotent to rationally explain and comprehend the first principles any tradition, worldview, or culture, including the secular one, presupposes. Consider, for instance, "Universalistic Hedonism or Utilitarianism" (Mackenzie 1929, 173). For the purpose of my argument let me state its main tenets (ignoring its diverse strands). Its proponents, such as the British philosophers Jeremy Bentham, John Stuart Mill, and Henry Sidgwick, advocated that maximization of pleasure and happiness was the driver of human action. Once a person accepts this first principle, reason can be harnessed to pursue this goal. However, reason in itself can never satisfactorily explain that the pursuit of pleasure is the only driver of human actions. Nor can it fully account for the tension between two or more competing, conflicting desires and the extent to which reason solitarily and reasonably can address it. Utilitarianism may make sense to its adherents only when one has already embraced the first principle, which, if anything, is far from universal. There are worldviews, alternative, parallel, and rival to utilitarianism, that hold vastly different first principles. For instance, the seventeenth-century Swiss Christian community that migrated to the United States to escape persecution, the Amish, does not valorize pleasure. Vanity, violence (both legal and illegal), adornment (makeup, jewelry, etc.), music, entertainment, use of a camera, premarital sex, excessive dependence on technologies such as electricity and automobiles, to name only a few, are indeed distractions from the divine worldview the Amish follow

(Kraybill 1993a; SBS-1 2012). Is there a solid ground based on which one can say that the Amish worldview is against reason? On the contrary, their worldview, practices, and desire to live their religion "unmolested by the state" (Kraybill 1993b, x) echo reason as long as one doesn't denounce the first principle of the Amish, the reasonability or otherwise of which can seldom be established by naked reason as conventionally understood.

From what I have been arguing so far it follows that it is not enough to say that a person is critical; it is equally important to examine what is the ethical and political aim of his or her critique and the suppositions and presuppositions that any enterprise of critique carries. Likewise, it is equally important to see *how* criticism is pursued. That is, there are different ways, modes, and objectives of criticism. Returning to the Rushdie affair, it is important to ask, What was the goal of Rushdie's critique? Did Rushdie criticize Islam, as Ziauddin Sardar (2008) observed, "to destroy Islam"? Was his portrayal of the Prophet's life as a myth meant to render it dispensable as all myths are in the Enlightenment worldview (except its own; on which see Horkheimer and Adorno 2002)? In contrast, is Sardar's own critique of Rushdie "to reform and change Muslim behavior and understanding of Islam"?

An effective, meaningful critique without a sustained relation to the conceptual coordinates, "social imaginary,"[3] ethical and cultural templates of the tradition in which it is situated, and a conceptualization of the past and envisioning of a future with reference to a dynamic notion of solidarity and community rarely exists.

If the equation of critique with the secular and its opposition to the religious is intensely precarious and no longer tenable (Asad et al. 2009; cf. Gourgouris 2008), so is the dominant Enlightenment dualism between heart and reason, mind and body, intellect and affect. The truncated reason of Cartesian cogito does not resonate well with the Islamic conception of reason that is much broader, nondualistic, and holistic. And this is my third argument. In Islamic tradition, reason (*ʿaql*) is highly valued; however, it dwells with rather than banishes the cognate Islamic notion of *qalb* (heart) as well as revelation and prophecy—as the epigraph of Iqbal's couplet suggests (for details, see chap. 2). Far from being antagonistic to one another, they cohere in complex ways so that they often become complementary. The simultaneity and coexistence of heart, reason, and mind are evident in the prefaces of books that Urdu authors write. They appeal at once to the heart, mind, and reason of their readers. As Abul Kalam Azad (2004 [1968], 39) argued, the Qurʾān at once addresses the heart (*dil*) and mind (*dimāġh*) of its reader. In both Arabic and Urdu, instead of splitting them apart, the term *qalb* encapsulates intellect and feelings. The locus of intellect or reason, *qalb* is logically the fountainhead of human knowledge. Even for Sayyid Ahmad Khan (1907), arguably the greatest champion of rationalism and reason in nineteenth-century British India, the heart was the locus of doubt as well as satisfaction concerning philosophical arguments.[4] Viewed from the framework this book develops and pursues, John Walbridge's (2010, 3) proposition that "Islamic intellectual life has been characterized by reason in the service of a non-rational revealed code of conduct" falls flat for it continues to operate within the dualistic framework of the rational and nonrational.

Finally, I make a strong case for broadening and extending the practices of critique from the widely assumed but highly restrictive domain of the elite to ordinary subjects. I suggest that critique ought not to be the sole preserve of (salaried) professional intellectuals; nonintellectuals too enact and participate in the works of critique. Nor should it be lopsidedly limited to "texts." I share, in some ways, Antonio Gramsci's (1996, 9) observation that "all men are intellectuals." This does not mean, however, that critique by ordinary subjects and professional intellectuals is the same. Obviously, there are vital differences between the two—in terms of the function, source, degree of credibility, and audience, as well as the valence each has. It is worth quoting the qualification Gramsci introduces after this statement: "It can happen that everyone at some time fries a couple of eggs. . . . We don't necessarily say that everyone is a cook" (1996, 9). Much of what this book deals with is derived from textual sources and conversations with interlocutors (intellectuals—*ʿulema*) during my fieldwork. In chapter 7, I particularly shift my focus to pay attention to practices of critique by ordinary, unschooled subjects in their everyday lives.[5]

The rationale for focusing not simply on texts but also on the everyday lives of the unschooled subjects requires further explication. Criticism has been long identified with literature and its predominant field, literary studies. As Raymond Williams (1983, 84–86) notes in *Keywords*, criticism, especially from the seventeenth century on, was used for "commentary on literature" and for "the act of judging literature and writing which embodied this." The primacy of the literary and the aesthetics in Williams's elaboration of its usage is evident, inter alia, from reference to words such as "reader" and Lord Kames's *Elements of Criticism*. It persists even today. According to Jonathan Culler, "one of the most influential literary critics in North America" (Stanford University Press website 2006), "criticism is writing about lit. [literature], whether evaluative, interpretive, historical, or formal and technical" (Culler 2012, 317). So naturalized is this identification that in an essay on literary criticism, Richard Ohmann (1981) titled it "What Is Criticism?" rather than "What Is Literary Criticism?"

Due mainly to this identification, the focus has been squarely placed on "text." It was only in 2009 that to the meaning of literary criticism as "judging . . . a literary work" and "analysis of a text" (*Oxford English Dictionary* 2009b), the *Oxford English Dictionary* (2009a) added, "A non-textual subject regarded as open to analysis . . . using methods of literary criticism, semiotics, etc." Such is the backdrop to appreciate Gayatri Chakravorty Spivak's (1990, 168) observation that "I am a literary critic: the only thing empirical for me would be a short story." Pace Spivak (1990), Kalimuddin Ahmad (2006, 35), a noted Urdu literary critic, held that "literary criticism is just one among the countless forms of criticism." Before I might be misunderstood, let me clarify that I am not indifferent to aesthetic, rhetorical, or other aspects of a text (I find positivist texts unmusical). Nor do I maintain that literary criticism is necessarily apathetic to the non-, extra-, and supratextual. It is, however, the case that it primarily approaches them through the lens of literary texts rather than treating them as subjects of analysis in their own right (see Davis and Schleifer 1991; and Eagleton 2005 [1984]). My goal, therefore, is to restore critique to where it rightfully belongs: to life intertwined as it is with death. Muhammad Iqbal (2014, 37) reformulated Arnold to say: "Matthew Arnold defines poetry as criticism of life. That life is criticism of poetry is equally true." A further reformulation would read: Critique informs as much as it is informed by life (and death), poetry being one among many aspects of life that the separatist Enlightenment split into neat grooves. It is the totality of life and the comprehensiveness of critique—*tanqīd/naqd*—that I enunciate in chapter 7.

I imagine some readers may now smile, perhaps with a dash of irritation, and say, "Railing against limiting critique to texts by writing another text?" A full response to your objection, dare I say, awaits another text.

Having synoptically presented the fourfold propositions this book makes, in the remainder of the introduction I discuss Amartya Sen's (2005) *The Argumentative Indian*. This discussion is tailored to show the ways this book is theoretically and methodologically distinguished from Sen's. Sen talks about India; so do I. However, as will become clear from what follows, each of us talks about a different India—and quite differently.

◆ Amartya Sen and *The Argumentative Indian*

Critique is simply not the main subject of Sen's exposition. The contours and properties of what Sen calls "the argumentative Indian" are assumed throughout but seldom explained. Reasoning, skepticism, argument, debate, disputation, pluralism, heterodoxy, and tolerance are used, almost interchangeably and teleologically (e.g., Sen 2055, xii, xv, 3, 6, 12, 15–16, 26, 30, 35). Unlike what Reinhart Koselleck did with terms like *Legitimitat, Bund,* and *Stand* in the German traditions (see Ahmad 2009a), Sen doesn't chart out the genealogies of these terms. Also absent is the question of language. Sen does not consider the valence and meanings of these English terms vis-à-vis their analogous terms in Sanskrit, Hindi, Tamil, Malayalam, Marathi, Punjabi, or Bhojpuri. Not even the equivalent word for "reason" in Sanskrit, *hetu* (as in Matilal 2015 [1971], 96; and Monier-Williams 1963 [1898], 1304), appears in Sen's text to receive proper treatment. Nor do readers know how *hetu* is related to and different from *tarka* (argument), *vivāda* (debate), *manas* (mind), *ānvīkṣiki* (critical inquiry, and the like (see Ganeri 2003, 411, 416, 418; and Monier-Williams 1976). In a rush to undo the dominant Western view of Hindu philosophy as, following Bimal Matilal, "mystical, non-argumentative" (qtd. in Mohanty 1992, 402), Sen doesn't attend to such vital issues. Without demonstrating how they work, he (Sen 2005, 3) merely asserts that "we encounter [in the *Mahābḫārata* and *Rāmāyṇa*] masses of arguments and counterarguments spread over incessant debates and disputations."[6]

Sen's project is lavishly nationalist. He writes as an Indian (xvi) about India. Both the object and subject of writing is informed and produced by nationalism (so is perhaps the primary audience). Reviewing Sen's book, Ramachandra Guha (2005, 4420) in fact describes Sen as "the firm upholder of the freedom and integrity of an independent India." Who, one is curious to know, is the implied "breaker of the freedom and integrity of an independent India"?

Sen's book shows how his, and the Indian intelligentsia's, secular liberalism is accommodative to Muslims in the face of Hindutva's politics. That there is an Indian liberalism Sen takes for granted. He laudingly quotes Chris Bayly, who called Ram Mohan Roy (d. 1833) the "first Indian liberal" (Sen 2005, 32). No mention is made of Roy's hostility to Muslims and affability toward colonialism. Roy was aggrieved to have seen Hindustan "for several centuries subject to Mohammadan Rule, and the civil and religious rights of its *original* inhabitants being constantly trampled upon." Note that, to Roy, Hindus were the "original inhabitants" of India. This is how Roy welcomed colonialism: "Divine Providence at last, in its abundant mercy, stirred *up the English nation to break the yoke of those tyrants* and to receive the oppressed Natives of Bengal under its protection." As if this was insufficient, Roy went on, "Your dutiful subjects have *not viewed the English as a body of conquerors, but rather as deliverers, and look up to your Majesty not only as a Ruler, but also as a father and protector*" (qtd. in Dhar 1987, 26, 30; italics mine). Roy, called the father of modern India, thus bestowed the title of father on the British as the protectors of Hindus against

Muslims. Variations of this figure of the Muslim as invader, outsider, and outcast are amply present in modern India, exponents of Hindutva being only the most vocal. Such a rendering of Muslims in the protonationalist discourse of Roy, and its continuation in nationalist discourses later, signals how "European orientalism and Indian nationalism colluded" (Wolfe 2002, 374) to create Muslims as "Other."

Since the figure of the Muslim as Other is integral to Roy's, and India's, liberalism, as it is to Western liberalism, a child of the Enlightenment "shot through with Islamophobia" (Trumpbour 2003, 119), it is logical that Sen reproduces it even as he seemingly refutes it. In his third chapter, Sen writes of "Muslim conquerors who overran India." Barely distinct from Hindutva, Sen, a votary of liberalism, doesn't describe Muslim invaders as "individuals" but as a culture (on such a paradox almost intrinsic to liberalism, see Mehta 1999, 112): "The 'slash and burn' culture of the Muslim invaders, making bloody excursion to India, did, however, gradually give way to immigration into India and to settling into the country, leading to Indianization of Muslim rulers" (58). The premise of Muslims as immigrants and Hindus as native is thus central for both Roy and Sen. It is this Indianization of Muslims for which Sen identifies himself as an "integrationist," to stress "the need for integration [nationalization]" (x). Integration minimally supposes two entities—entity A, which needs to be integrated into another entity B. I ask, Who created these entities and for what purposes? What are the terms on which this integration is commanded by the likes of Sen? Does not the discourse of integration presuppose and enact symbolic violence (Bourdieu and Wacquant 1992)?

As Guha (2005, 4423; see below) notes, there are shared grounds between Hindutva's and Sen's view of history. Both view Indian culture serially and diachronically: from the Vedic age, to the eras of the Mahābhārata and Rāmāyṇa, Buddhism, Christianity, and Islam. Conceptualizing culture this way has profound implications, the explication of which is necessary. The difference between Hindutva and Sen's conceptualizations, however, is that while the former erases the Muslim period as dark, Sen aims to retain it by invoking the secularism of the sixteenth-century ruler Akbar who, along with the ancient ruler Ashoka, serves as hero of his prose. Another commonality is the conception of the Indian nation as flowing seamlessly from ancient to modern times—a point Guha also notes. Sen makes, as does Hindutva, an unbroken link between Ashoka and modern India. In brief, the eternalization of a nation! Contemporary India as a nation-state, however, is radically different from Ashoka's kingdom of the third century BC. Sen's concept of premodern India is also territorial—a point central for Hindutva. Grievously, he says, "The earlier conceptions of India as a country have had to undergo some cutbacks over the last century, through the Partition of India in 1947" (42)—this grief resembles Pakistan's (Van Schendel 2009) after the birth of Bangladesh, where Sen's family comes from. Which earlier conceptions of India does Sen refer to and what is the historicity of that India to the movement of nineteenth-century territorial nationalism? Does Sen's notion of history echo Henry Glassie's credo: "History is the essence of the idea of place" (qtd. in Glassberg 1996, 19)? Can history, as I submit, be also thought of as an idea related, but not hostage to, a retrospectively crafted nation-state?

A major weakness is Sen's neat distinction between "small" and "large" India: the former refers to Hindutva's India, the latter to a broad idea with a "heterodox past and pluralist present" (72). The advocates of large India, Sen implies, are the Congress Party. Such a distinction is no better than a textbook view. Historically, the boundary between the Congress Party and overtly Hindu nationalists has been fairly porous. The flow between the Congress Party and Hindu parties was smooth, as shown by the trajectories of leaders like Lajpat Rai, K. M. Munshi, S. P. Mookherjee, and Madanmohan Malaviya, who comfortably moved from the former to the latter and vice versa (Ahmad 2012, 484; Bhagavan 2008). In postcolonial India, too, one can see to and fro from "secular" parties to various Hindutva formations (Ahmad 2014c). Sen is silent about this regular flow. His treatment of the "Muslim question"—central to anticolonial struggle and postcolonial India—is at best under-discussed. So is the issue of why secularism—Sen's concern—was not inserted into the constitution by the Constituent Assembly with figures as important as B. R. Ambedkar, Jawaharlal Nehru, Sardar Patel, K. M. Munshi, and others. Why was it put in the constitution only in the 1970s?

Without going into further detail on Sen's text, let me state the point relevant to this book. The argumentative Indian Sen writes about is ultimately an argumentative Brahmin , as made explicit in sentences like, "I shall not enter here into the difficult question of the role Hindu tradition may have played in sustaining a dialogic culture and the tolerance of heterodoxy in India, with which this book is much concerned" (46). Before I get misunderstood, let me clarify that my issue with Sen is not his tracking of a tradition of argumentation in Hinduism—as a student of religion I indeed value it. The issue is that Sen renders Hindu tradition synonymous with India, the nation. He subsumes Muslims within the Hindu tradition, thereby rendering Muslims invisible. Muslims appear in Sen's text as a mere statistical group whose numerical size, in comparison to Muslims in Indonesia and Pakistan, he asserts more than once, providing no further analysis. Barring Akbar and Dara Shikoh here and

Ali Akbar Khan there, he develops a framework based on Hindu tradition to fit Muslims in it. Least noticed by reviewers of Sen's book is that while he relates argumentation among Hindus to their reliance on and in relation to religious traditions, in the case of his predominant reference to Akbar, debate and use of reason occur in spite of and indeed against tradition: in the very first chapter, he writes, "Akbar's overarching thesis that 'the pursuit of reason' rather than 'reliance on tradition' is . . ." (16; no citation given in original for single quotes). My point is in contrast to Mushirul Hasan's (1998, 1078) empirical complaint, twelve years after Partha Chatterjee's *Nationalist Thought and Colonial World*, that the latter mentioned Sayyid Ahmad Khan and his companions only peripherally. Nor does Sen discuss Sayyid Ahmad Khan (1817–98), the renowned "modernist" reformer and founder of what later became Aligarh Muslim University, or the philosopher Abul Kalam Azad, who grew up in Calcutta, launched his Urdu journals *Lisānus ṣidq* and *Al-hilāl* from there, and was also jailed there (Ahmad 2009c). In my view, the disregard of Sayyid Ahmad Khan, Abul Kalam Azad, and others is not primarily an omission or oversight. Muslims probably do not easily fit in the tradition of liberalism, instituted by Ram Mohan Roy and owned and elaborated by scholars like Amartya Sen. If Patrick Wolfe (2002, 373) is right in his reading of *A Critique of Postcolonial Reason*, the case of Spivak's text is similar. Wolfe detects "an effacement that results from her [Spivak's] own recapitulation of a colonizing (and, for that matter, communal) binarism." He continues: "For the figures in her scheme of things . . . are all non-Muslims." Wolfe titled his article-length review of Spivak "Can the Muslim Speak?"[7] Put differently, my argument is that Muslims are less a statistical group and more a framework, a tradition, a perspective for unpacking the drama of Indian modernity, which found no other way to deal with them but to reduce them to a minoritized statistical entity, or simply efface them.[8]

That Muslims have a tradition of inquiry and critique is not Sen's concern. When liberals such as Sen write about Muslims, it is less about Muslims themselves and more about how liberals like him want to see Muslims. Thus, in their article-length reviews of Sen, neither Ramachandra Guha (2005) nor Sabyasachi Bhattacharya (2005) ever mentions the key point I make here. In Guha's text, Muslims are mentioned twice (no Islam), each time tangentially. Guha takes the "liberal" Hindu assumption I critiqued as given. He detects parochialism in scholars like Sen for their obsession with Bengal and its description as "the crucible of Indian nationalist politics and the home . . . of . . . liberal consciousness itself" (4421). Making a territorial claim, Guha, located in "neutral Bangalore," wants to award this credit instead to Maharashtra. Guha further notes that Sen neglects the issues of languages. He observes how, from the 1920s, the organizations and units of the Congress Party got aligned along territorial-linguistic lines—Marathi, Kannada, and so on. After independence, language issues became volatile, leading to anti-Hindi campaigns and demands for the linguistic reorganization of states. Nowhere does Guha mention Urdu—a territorially dispersed language. I understand the points of such criticism based on region. How about a tradition uncontainable within the liberal premise of territory? What are the epistemological grounds for valorizing territorial units but not a cultural, tradition-bound formation beyond a given territory? Guha's criticism of Sen may look like shadow boxing, as neither interrogates the fundamentals and banality of the nation. The differences between them, if any, concern geography—north or south, east or west. Of several names Guha lists—Gandhi, N. K. Bose, D. R. Gadgil, D. P. Mukerji, and D. D. Kosambi—to say that Sen did not discuss them, none is a Muslim. He does not even mention Badruddin Tayab Ji from Maharashtra, which Guha presents as an alternative to Sen's Bengal. Guha terms these figures "proximate" to differentiate them from "distant" figures such as Ashoka. My point is that a distant figure is not simply one who lived long ago in history; it can also be a more recent one, such as Azad or Zakir Hussain (an educationist, translator of Plato's *Republic* into Urdu, and the third president of India; see Preckel 2008, 304), who is rendered distant and invisible by Guha. Likewise, in Bhattacharya's text there is no Muslim at all. He mentions Islam once, and then only in relation to medieval India. What about the present?

Sen writes of Indians that "we do like to speak" (3). But is not this speaking predicated on what an audience desires to hear? Is not that audience mainly a nation which is based on the assumption of who "we" are and who we don't want to be? Importantly, who is (dis)entitled to speak? In what language? What is considered legitimate and intimate, desirable and horrible, forbidden and mistaken in acts and themes of speech? Does not speaking also imply silencing? It is this silenced Muslim tradition of critique across the recent, imperially planted borders of the nation-state that *Religion as Critique* aims to lay bare. I don't take the bloody boundaries installed by national, regional, and international power elites as boundaries of knowledge, misrecognizing political boundaries as epistemological ones (Mamdani 2001, xii). When appropriate I refer to individuals, events, and shared traditions elsewhere—for instance, the Middle East, Africa, as well as the West.

◆ Design of Intervention

The first key argument sketched above is substantiated in chapter 2. To reiterate, it argues that the Enlightenment was an ethnic project and its conceptualization of reason was highly local as it pitted itself against a series of Others, Islam being one of them. My anthropological critique of the Enlightenment and Western philosophy builds on a number of works. For instance, feminist scholarship demonstrated the "maleness" of reason and philosophy generally (see Grimshaw 1986; Schott 2000). Genevieve Lloyd (1984) discussed the isomorphism between maleness and Western philosophy. In her call to gendering reason, Phyllis Rooney (1991, 98) contended that "it [reason] has propelled itself, not by the power of reason . . . but by the power of a [male] myth." Professing a "distinctive Afrocentric epistemology," black feminist scholarship went further to describe reason as "white" and "Eurocentric" (Collins 1989, 755–56). Scholars have also noted subtle and blatant racism in the philosophers of the Enlightenment—John Locke, David Hume, Kant, Voltaire, and others (see Bernasconi and Lott 2000; Eze 2002; Franklin 2002; Poliakov 1982). Evidently, these writings offer a powerful critique of universalism. A point less stressed is that the erasure of non-Western philosophy in Enlightenment thinking construed "universal" as only "to all," not "from all." By this I mean non-Westerners were construed as empirical objects, not thinking subjects. As it disregarded *from all*, Western universalism claiming that it is *for all* and *to all* could only be missionary-like, for the only option it leaves open for those not subscribing to or already within is to *convert*. The blueprint for conversion stemmed from the Enlightenment ideas of the "civilizational infantilism" of the non-West and the obligation to "better the world" (Mehta 1999, 70, 80).

Extending the argument of the previous chapter to the field of critique, chapter 3 unsettles the view that ancient Greece was where critique began and which later, through Europe in the nineteenth century onward, spread to the world, India included. To illustrate this contention, I build on the works of Martin Bernal, Michael Herzfeld, and John Keane, which interrogate the prevalent views of Greece as the modern West's primordial ancestor and birthplace of nearly everything modern and desirable—anthropology, democracy, critique, and so on. Here I also critique the thesis of Rémi Brague in his *Eccentric Culture: A Theory of Western Civilization* (2002). The objective of this chapter, therefore, is to draft an *alternative* genealogy of critique—*tanqīd/naqd*—in the Islamicate traditions (Lawrence 2003, 2009) of South Asia as expressed in the Urdu language. I examine the secularist and secularizing premise of Urdu literature and how it was designed as distinct from religion but aligned to territorial nationalism. I also discuss how the overriding idea of critique in Urdu is grossly skewed so as not to include nonliterary critique. At the heart of the alternative genealogy of critique is the premise that God Himself is the source of critique. The mission of the successive prophets God sent was to do reform (*iṣlāḥ*). At its core, to reform was to critique and to critique was to reform. In the "religious" texts and social practices of "traditional" *ʿulema* thus a different notion of critique emerges—a notion that doesn't reject the Greek, pre-Muhammad, or Western traditions but which simultaneously can't be subsumed within them. I trace elements of this genealogy through the Qurʾān, prophetic lives, and the early community constituted around Muhammad and his companions. Maududi and his interlocutors read, craft, elaborate, configure, update, and modify that tradition of critique. Rooted in the discursive traditions of Islam (Asad 1986b), what distinguishes this critique are its comprehensiveness and ethicality. To this end, I discuss how critique (*tanqīd/naqd*) as an enterprise is desirable and encouraged, whereas *tāʿeīb* (to find faults or defame one), *taḥqīr* (to disrespect), *tanqīṣ* (to find demerits), *taẓḥīk* (to mock), *takfīr* (to denounce), *taḵhfīf* (to minimize, to distort), *tardīd* (to refute), *tajhīl* (to show one as unlettered), *tʿarīf* (to shower undue praise on), and *takbīr* (to glorify) are not (though of course, context matters). The terminological specification of critique in Urdu and its differentiation with cognate but distinct (often conflated by nonspecialists) terms go to clarify the goals and parameters of *tanqīd/naqd*.

Part 1 of the book is devoted to the theoretical-conceptual mappings of critique in chapters 2 and 3. The four chapters in part 2 demonstrate critique in practice. Part 2 begins with an anthropological account of the key ideas of Maududi, the founder of Jamaat, in chapter 4. This chapter lays out facets of the conceptual frame and methods that inform Maududi's ideology. To this end, I first de-reify the hegemonic portrayals of Maududi as a "fundamentalist" and make the case for seeing him instead as a political thinker. Central to his exposition on Islam were the use of reason, critique, and *ijtihād* (using reason as opposed to imitation [*taqlīd*]; see chap. 4). To illustrate this point, the chapter dwells on his educational thought and critical evaluation of past scholars—ʿOmar bin Abdul Aziz, Imam Ghazali, Ibn Taymiyyah, Shaykh Ahmad Sirhindi, and Shah Valiullah and his successors. The final section outlines the metaphysical assumptions of Maududi's thought about cosmology, human nature, and civilization in order to locate the objective behind the formation of Jamaat-e-Islami. It addresses issues such as the meanings of Allah, the message of the Qurʾān, monotheism, prophecy, *jāhiliyat* (ignorance), and so on, to ask, What does Allah want from His followers in individual and collective domains? Here I also discuss Maududi's citations from the New Testament and references to Christ's life to argue that Muhammad's message and life resembled those of earlier prophets, including Jesus. Maududi held that his call for a polity resting on divine sovereignty echoed the teachings of prophets preceding Muhammad. Maududi's thought on this point—the primacy of God's sovereignty—was similar to those of the Protestant politician and thinker Abraham Kuyper (d. 1920) in the Netherlands, Catholics in Australia, as well as Robert Bellah's notion of civil religion in relation to the United States (see chapter 4).

The next two chapters describe multiple and diverse critiques of Maududi on two issues: his ideas about and activism for an Islamic state and his exposition on "the gender question." Anticipating a possible misunderstanding, it is worthwhile to point out that my use of critique does not mean that criticism of Maududi by others is a work of critique whereas Maududi's own writing is not. Maududi's corpus of writing (as outlined in chapter 4) is as much a work of critique as are the writings on, about, and against Maududi.

Chapter 5 discusses searching, comprehensive, and at times aggressive critiques of Maududi's understandings of the state. I focus on critiques by three "traditional" former Jamaat members: Manzur Nomani, Vahiduddin Khan, and Abul Hasan Ali Nadvi. I also discuss responses to their critiques by Amir Usmani (the editor of *Tajallī*) and two other Jamaat members. In the following section, I shift to critiques by five "modern" Jamaat sympathizers. This chapter combines "contextual studies" by anthropologists and "textual studies" by historians and humanists (Messick 1993). My aim is not simply to show that individuals critique Maududi—which I do—but equally to demonstrate how critique is undertaken. How ideas, sentiments, mental conditions, types of knowledge, forms of authority, language capacity, motivations, the (un)sayable, notions about the private and public, facial appearance, hair style, conceptions of home, intellectual suppositions, political power, readings of the past and future, tears, joy, and much else inform and are played out in the enterprise of critique. Any understanding of critique that fails to take into account this whole array of factors will remain superficial. This array of factors is nothing but life in its entirety, approximating Ludwig Wittgenstein's description of words as deeds and, therefore, life. To unpack critique is to enunciate the cultural milieu it relates to. Critique is connected to a form of life the full meaning of which presupposes and is inseparable from death.

The multiple and diverse critiques of Maududi on the state display neither an outright rejection nor a wholesale embracing of it. Critics of Maududi are ambivalent. Some agree with the spirit of his critical enterprise, considering it an important intervention at a specific historical moment, but they stress that its relevance in the future is skewed, even outdated. Others differentiate the universalist Maududi from the nationalist Maududi, to extend and revise the former to encompass concerns and aspirations of humanity beyond the divides of faith and ethnicity. For such critics, *Maqāṣid al-sharīʿā* (literally, aims of sharia; see chapter 5), among others, is the medium to pursue such a universalism. Yet others continue to underline the relevance of his ideas for a state by reinterpreting him differently. In such interpretations, Maududi made the simple point that any culture could barely survive, much less flourish, without an engagement with power. This was certainly true for a minority (and minoritized) culture in a majoritarian democracy. To them, Maududi was not irrelevant.

From the subject of the state, chapter 6 moves to vibrant critiques of Maududi's neopatriarchate. It begins by outlining Maududi's gender ideology by noting its Janus-like character. Arguably, he was the first thinker in India to open the door of his organization to women qua individuals. At the same time, however, his interpretation of Islam vis-à-vis women was harsh and regressive. I show how Maududi's position came to be criticized by people connected to Jamaat. I discuss critiques on issues such as veiling, women's participation in the public domain (including work and cinema), questions of eligibility to become head of state, studying in coeducational institutions, and issues of gender and knowledge. I also account for the factors enabling Maududi's critique. I conclude by discussing what such critiques of Maududi's neopatriarchate mean. Is it theoretically productive to describe such critiques as inaugurating an Islamic feminist discourse? Here, as elsewhere, I reflect on my own earlier understanding to signal a reassessment. The key contention here is that the diverse critiques of Maududi's position on women make it clear that Islam, contra assertions by many feminists, can also be a critical language for empowering women.

In the penultimate chapter, "The Mundane: Critique as Social-Cultural Practice," I shift the focus hitherto placed on critique by intellectuals to the domain of everyday lives and ordinary subjects. I show how immanent critique discussed so far has been put to work in one of the most outstanding mass movements for peace in history—the twentieth-century Ḳhudāī Ḳhidmatgār (servants of God), led by Khan Abdul Ghaffar Khan. I discuss the mechanisms of recruitment, themes, and means of mobilization and people's participation by focusing on the idiom and values of Islam central to Ḳhudāī Ḳhidmatgār. In particular, I discuss the role of mosques, reference to the Qur'ān, and employment of *ṣabr* (perseverance) in the pursuit of nonviolence and the struggle against British colonialism. The case of Ḳhudāī Ḳhidmatgār, launched in 1930, is important because the community from which this movement mainly drew its followers—the Pathans, with their segmentary social structure in the northwestern part of contemporary Pakistan—have historically been depicted, especially in colonial anthropology, as anything but intellectual and critical. I conclude the chapter with everyday critique in contemporary times using illustrations from my own fieldwork, as well as those of others. I focus on three significant proverbs. I show how by circulating "nonshifter" proverbs, social discourses—scholarly and popular alike—institute a particular regime of truth. While the first two proverbs ridicule *molvī* and *mullā*—both "theologians"—the third one introduces a "shifter" proverb to show a different reality, namely, how the religious poor and subalternated view the rich. Put pithily, the alternative portrait it presents is of a hawker as critic. The chapter gainfully utilizes Didier Fassin's differentiation between as well as connection of *reality* and *truth* as productive and tension-ridden at the same time.

In the epilogue, I offer a preliminary outline of a theory of critique. Engaging with Abdolkarim Soroush's theory of contraction and expansion (*qabz v bast*) in knowledge, I address the following questions. Is critique simply an intellectual-epistemological exercise? Or are there extraintellectual factors—anthropological, political, generational, technological, and so on? When and how does the boundary between things considered external and internal, permissible and undesirable, become sharp or porous? What roles do commoners and their practices have in shaping that boundary? My basic contention is that a more plausible theory of critique and change can't be only intellectual-epistemological; it should also account for mundane social-cultural practices, shaped by as well as shaping the political. To demonstrate this contention, I shed light on past and contemporary discussions about the permissibility of images and statues of living beings among *ʿulema*.

2
CRITIQUE
Western and/or Islamic

I confess that I am a bit tired of metaphysics. But whenever I happen to argue with people I find that their arguments are always based on certain propositions which they assume without criticism. I am, therefore, driven to examine the value of these propositions. The practical in all its shapes drives me back to the speculative.

—MUHAMMAD IQBAL (2014, 22)

Kant represents the brilliance of bucket thinking at its best (or worst).

—JOHN CAPUTO (2013, 42)

Liberalism's alleged universality is impugned in its descriptive proximity to ideas that claimed no such universality.

—UDAY MEHTA (1999, 69)

The distinction [between the universal and the particular] . . . ignores the particularity of the West itself.

—SALMAN SAYYID (1998, 388)

Let's move away from the tradition of modern writings.

Most contemporary discussions of the Enlightenment often begin with Kant's "What Is Aufklärung?" or Foucault's commentary on it. I instead begin with a quote from Edward Shils. According to the *Times* of London, Shils was "an intellectual's intellectual and scarcely a single corner of the Western cultural tradition has not benefited from the illumination afforded by his . . . pungent attention" (qtd. in *Chicago Chronicle* 1995). Shils belonged to a network of scholars—among them Daniel Bell, Seymour Lipset, and Raymond Aron—which mobilized intellectuals from both sides of the Atlantic to back the new post–World War II imperium presided over by the United States. To this end, in 1950, the Congress for Cultural Freedom (CCF) was founded to counter the USSR-backed peace movement. In its inaugural meeting in Berlin, the CCF stood to defend "intellectual freedom" and warned that "any indifference or neutrality" vis-à-vis totalitarianism "amounts to a betrayal of mankind and to the abdication of the free mind." The CCF and other such organizations had "connections . . . with the CIA." According to Shils, the CCF "stands in a tradition of intellectuals of a common outlook joined together in a common task—it is a product of the eighteenth century Enlightenment. I think it is not wrong to see its forerunners in the circle which produced the *Encyclopédie*" (qtd. in Scott-Smith 2010, 137, 139).[1]

Given that for Shils the Enlightenment was an insignia of the West in its war against communism in the bipolar post–World War II era, the Enlightenment is not merely philosophical, an attitude or an approach to knowledge. It is equally a party to the geopolitics of a binary definition of the New World Order (NWO) and its War on Terror (WOT). In 2006, Victor Hanson of Stanford University stated "that Enlightenment . . . [which] established the Western blueprint for a humane and ordered society" was under threat. He wrote, "What would a Socrates, Galileo, Descartes, or Locke believe of the present decay in Europe—that all their . . . courageous thinking . . . would have devolved into such cheap surrender to fanaticism?" Who were the threatening fanatics? "Islamic fanatics" was Hanson's reply. Curiously, in Hanson's hand the pope, who in accounts such as Luther's symbolized the Antichrist, became a friend of the Enlightenment as he admired Pope Benedict XVI's "courage to speak his conviction" (cf. Asad 2009, 21). Hanson's attribution of "conviction" to the pope is puzzling. It is largely a Protestant term, and Catholics usually give priority to practices and teachings rather than conviction (Asad 1993, 39; Asad 2012, 40). In the latter half of the nineteenth century, Sweden's Bishop Eric Fahlcrantz held that the "real conviction . . . exists in the true Lutherans," because "a Catholic can't have real conviction of the true validity of his confession" (qtd. in Werner and Harvard 2013, 232). Leaving aside that for Johann Wolfgang von Goethe (d. 1832) Irish Catholics were a "pack of dogs" (qtd. in Almond 2009, 179n49), in the formulations of sociology's fathers like Max Weber, Catholicism was "a form of polytheism" (Joas 2012, 19). That the Greek Orthodox and India's Syrian Christians don't matter (also in debates on secularism) is another matter. In a move similar to Hanson's, John Owen and Judd Owen posited that "modernity initiated by . . . the Enlightenment seems today . . . open to challenge." Secularism as a "central current in the Enlightenment legacy," they wrote, stood challenged by "radical Islam." For "peace . . . in the new global order" and for "Western foreign policy," the call by the Owens (2011, 7, 18, 14, 10, 5) was to spread Enlightenment "the world over" and make "reason" prevail over "irrationality."

In *Quadrant,* Paul Monk (2015) wrote that what Ayaan Hirsi Ali desired "is not the Reformation [of Islam]. It is the Enlightenment." She wanted "what a Locke or Voltaire called for in the seventeenth and eighteenth centuries: toleration, skepticism and civil authority over religion." This evolutionary scheme mimics that of Habermas (1987, 16–17), who presents the Reformation, Enlightenment, and French Revolution as successive, linear stages defining the modern age. Stressing the need to "engage in the struggle of ideas of our time," Monk concluded his essay as follows: "That's why we need a new Congress for Cultural Freedom [CCF]." Monk's call for a new CCF completes a full circle, returning as it does to Shils. If the Cold War needed a CCF, which Shils linked to the eighteenth-century Enlightenment, the NWO and its WOT need a *new* CCF informed by Voltaire and the Enlightenment.

It is clear how during the Cold War and the current NWO, the Enlightenment served as an ethnic marker of the West's identity. Was the eighteenth-century Enlightenment any different in terms of its Other? Scholars identify an array of Others against which the Enlightenment fought—faith, religion, fanaticism, superstition, prejudice, enthusiasm, tradition, custom, speculation, and so on (Pocock 1997; Hampson 2001). Missing from their analyses is Islam as an important Other against which the Enlightenment constituted and consolidated itself. This was most pronounced in none other than Immanuel Kant (d. 1804) himself—the star philosopher of the Enlightenment.[2] It is my contention that the Enlightenment was an ethnic project as Europe/the West constituted their identity in the name of reason and universalism against a series of others—internal and external—Islam being one of them. Rarely critical, anthropological accounts of the Enlightenment often read like eulogies to the Enlightenment (e.g., Eriksen and Nielsen 2015; Patterson 2009; Hastrup 2005). For instance, Kirsten Hastrup defends "a pragmatic Enlightenment" as a "vital counterpoint to current antienlightenment feelings, often found . . . in fundamentalist rhetoric of all kinds." Fundamentalists, she warns, "put an end to all dialogue"; they claim a "superior right to influence the history of other people," and their worldview is marked by "an epistemological closure" (Hastrup 2005, 147). As I show later, a superior right to influence others' history and epistemological closure attributed to fundamentalists is also part of the Enlightenment. In assigning exclusivity to "fundamentalism," Hastrup effaces the exclusivity internal to the Enlightenment. She thus ends up producing the binary categories of closure and openness without examining the condition that nurtures them. To an extent, my argument resonates with those of Bruce Kapferer (2007, 87, 85, 90) and Marshall Sahlins (1999), who subject the Enlightenment's reason and universality to critique, albeit differently. However, their focus is not religion, certainly not Islam. Nor do they suitably anthropologize the culture of the eighteenth-century Europe in which the Enlightenment emerged.[3] In some ways, Joan Vincent (2002, 5–6, 18) does. She identifies three worlds that Enlightenment thinkers inhabited: the tiny bourgeois class of print culture, militarized nationalism, and Europe's imperial expansion. In *The Anthropology of Politics*, she mentions Kant and even reproduces four paragraphs from his *Anthropology*, but without relating them to her own three worlds. For her the value of Kant's *Anthropology* lies in "fieldwork" (cf. below). Like Kapferer and Sahlins, she does not discuss religion.

Furthermore, I argue that the Enlightenment was not a break from Christianity as commonly understood but its reconfiguration whereby the West/Christianity/Europe enacted an immunity to protect itself from any critique while subjecting all others—"the Rest," as it were—to critique. *Immunitas* is connected to *communitas* (solidarity or cohesion)—interactionally, not oppositionally (Salvatore 2013). This immunity from critique is a major concern, which Anidjar's *Blood: A Critique of Christianity* addresses. As Anidjar asserts in other works, "Christianity exempts itself from critique" (2015b, 41) because "a critique of modernity will rarely take Christianity as its object" (2015a, 33). Using an anthropology of philosophy approach, I lay out this argument in the first part of this chapter. Here I dwell on both the German and French Enlightenments. In particular, I focus on Kant's *Anthropology* (1798) and *Physical Geography* (1801) (Malpas and Thiel 2011, 196). My overall thesis is that the Enlightenment is no more than a highly specific, local mode of critique and reasoning, which is by no means universal. Established binaries or dyads such as religious and secular, traditional and modern, rational and irrational—which crucially inform what constitutes critique—emanate from modernity, central to which is the construction of the category of the category (Caputo 2013). What is important, then, is not what such categories contain (for they can be invested with different significations at different times), but the very power of category-making at the disposal of modernity. The meanings with which categories are invested might vary; what does not vary is the boundary-making power of the categories. Thus Islam can be categorized as fatalist at one time and activist at another in the same way that the Enlightenment can be classified as Christian (Becker 1932) at one time and pagan at another (Gay 1996). In the second section, I dwell on important anthropological and related writings on Islam to show how they are reluctant to recognize critique in the Muslim tradition, and even hostile to such recognition, because of the Enlightenment's premise of critique being essentially against, not within and from, the religious Other.

In the final part of this chapter, I outline the possibility of analyzing Islam and reason as being interwoven. Building on Asad's conceptualization of Islam as a discursive tradition and his work on critique, here I show how immanent critique has been central to Islamic histories and cultures and stress its efficacy as a method of analysis. Against the standard narrative, according to which the Enlightenment marks a rupture from the past, I discuss how a reformulated idea of the "axial age"—inaugurating breakthrough and reflexivity much earlier than Enlightenment—will help better evaluate Islam as a critique. Set within this frame, critique emerges more as a duty than as the Enlightenment's rendition of it as a right (which, following Kant and when confronted with law, however, must abandon itself to submit to law). Furthermore, as the locus of faith as well as reason, in Islamic tradition the heart (*qalb*) is the ground for mediation, rather than confrontation, between them. That is, the dyads and binaries of modernity/the Enlightenment that fashion the category of the category tend to dissolve "into a spectrum of possibilities, not into a neat either/or classificatory judgment," to invoke Bruce Lawrence's (2009, 163) fitting phrase from a different context.

◆ The Enlightenment as Ethnicity

This subheading will possibly astonish many a reader. Predictably so! Given the naturalized, or what Edmund Husserl called sedimented (Hyder 2003) view that the Enlightenment is all about universality, some may ask, how can it be ethnic? Furthermore, is not ethnicity as a term employed to discuss things in the non-West or, to use a current vulgate, the Global South? When used in the West, does it not often refer to nonwhite immigrants? How can the Enlightenment as a philosophy with its insignia of reason and universalism be, then, ethnic? Neither philosophy nor anthropology alone address these questions. Anthropology of philosophy (thus of the Enlightenment) can. This entails, following Talal Asad (1997, 721; 2003, 22) and Michael Herzfeld (1997, 713), anthropologizing the West/Europe. However, to anthropologize the West as a region while remaining loyal to its conceptual arsenals is not the same as to anthropologize the Enlightenment, whose curiosity about the "strange" non-European world led to its very birth. Given that anthropology is "an Enlightenment discipline" (Kapferer 2007, 74), can it adequately anthropologize the Enlightenment that gave birth to it?

The literature on interactions between anthropology and philosophy is as scarce as the "distance" between the two fields vast. One stream of literature urges a dialogue between anthropology's emphasis on "particular, contextualized points of view" and philosophy's "ambition of generalizing point of view" (Pedersen and Liisberg 2015, 7, 3, 18). Another stream of literature too accepts this premise, if only by rejecting it: we are "not looking to philosophy to provide 'theory,'" as if anthropology lacked it. The goal of this stream is nevertheless distinct: to know "anthropology's philosophy" by examining how individual anthropologists engage with specific philosophers in their works (Das et al. 2014, 2, 24, 20). In this respect, "philosophical anthropology" is different. It refers to self-reflection by human beings to grasp themselves. The works of Max Scheler, Helmuth Plessner, Arnold Gehlen, Martin Heidegger, and others usually figure under this label (Wulf 2013, 307n1; Das et al. 2014, 25n1; Kuhns 1980).

My interest is not anthropology *and* philosophy. I am interested in the anthropology *of* philosophy. In *Philosophising in Mombasa*, Kai Kresse (2007, 11, 14, 13, 12) "introduces" and "develops" an anthropology of philosophy. Rightly noting that philosophy should be brought into the realm of anthropological inquiry, he views philosophy as a "social practice" that will "assist philosophy in extending its awareness of its own character and status." Kresse takes philosophy as "a human practice, responding to the common need for intellectual orientation that is at work in many different . . . contexts." With these premises, he studies the philosophical discourses of three Kenyan intellectuals in the Swahili context.

Kresse's premises are essentially Kantian. He begins with Kant's distinction between scholarly (*im Schulbegriff*) and worldly (*im Weltbegriff*) philosophy. The former is an institutionalized "system of knowledge" that trains thinkers; the latter addresses key questions of "necessary interest to everyone." In the worldly type, philosophy "can be learned only through practice and the use of one's reason." With this distinction, Kresse connects philosophy to anthropology by stating four questions central to Kant: "What can I know?" "What should I do?" "What may I hope for?" and "What is man?" These questions correspond to metaphysics, morality, religion, and anthropology, respectively.[4] Kant's philosophy helps Kresse "provide an orientation for an anthropology of philosophy." The task left, then, is to "use and apply them [Kant's passages] for our project, as both a rationale and method for an anthropology of philosophy" (Kresse 2007, 20–21).

What is striking in Kresse's otherwise laudable endeavor is that Kant's own philosophy is rarely treated as a social practice. He is summoned only philosophically, not anthropologically. He is the source of conceptual formulations through which Mombasa's intellectuals are anthropologized, while Kant's own philosophy is placed above anthropologization. Furthermore, he scarcely reflects on philosophy's ties with politics. Closing his "theoretical introduction," Kresse says that the subsequent chapters will be "documenting local philosophical discourse." But is documentation simply an application of Kantian postulates and distinctions in Kenya? If the Kenyan philosophical discourse is local, what is Kant's? Kresse is emphatic about Kant's universality: "[The] distinction that Kant has pointed at is . . . applicable to . . . any part of the world." Likewise René Descartes's *cogito ergo sum* "speaks to all of us." In contrast, Kresse (2007, 3, 15, 31, 22, 71) describes Sheikh Al-Amin Mazrui (d. 1947) "as a leading figure of a *regionally specific 'enlightenment'* movement" (italics mine). That an anthropologist delivers the judgment about universality is astonishing. Decades ago, Laura Bohannan (1966) ethnographically showed the folly of Shakespeare's universality based on "reason."[5] Unmindful of Bohannan, Kresse (2007, 15, 31, 22, 6) forges the universality of the Western Enlightenment throughout. Not even once, however, is there mention of Christianity in relation to the West's Enlightenment, whereas readers are told early on that the knowledge he dwells on is presented within "an Islamic framework." This staging of a secular-religious dichotomy is made clear in an earlier publication where he shows how Islamic reform in East Africa displays "rational principles," yet it can't be an "enlightenment movement" because "Islamic reform is incompatible with secularism" (Kresse 2003, 279). The binary opposition between Muslims/East Africa, on the one hand, and the secular/West/Europe, on the other, is thus on full display in Kresse's (2007, 11) prose, even where "we" and its geography are imprecise: "An anthropological investigation into philosophy provides *us* with insights . . . about . . . knowledge . . . *elsewhere* in the world, in social contexts very different from *our own*" (italics mine). Geography is construed culturally and culture geographically and both from the premise of a Western weltanschauung.

Pace Kresse, there can't be an anthropology of philosophy, I aver, without its grounding in power in a double sense: anthropology and philosophy of power and the operation of power within each discipline. If anthropology of power has mostly studied cultural differences and the (un)making of boundaries between two or more groups in the non-West, there is no reason why the gaze should not be shifted to Europe to examine its own ethnicity. If "ethnicity occurs when cultural differences are made relevant through interaction" (Eriksen 2001, 263), it follows that ethnicity is in full flow in terms of the West's enactment of being uniquely different in relation to Others.[6] If the drawing of boundaries by groups is central to ethnicity, with culture at its focal point, as

Fredrik Barth (1969) argued, ethnicity will *also* bear on philosophy as a cultural practice. My point is not that philosophy is reducible to ethnicity; my submission instead is that it is not entirely independent from ethnicity either. Richard Kuhns (1980, 732–33; see also Edel 1953) gestured earlier that "philosophical activities belong in the class of cultural events" or cultural "enactments." As for the second sense of power, philosophy's—especially, modern Western philosophy's—connection with power is impossible to ignore. Michael Dillon (1996, 28) contends that "Western political thought has been impelled by its metaphysical determination to secure the appropriate theoretical grounds and instrumental means by which security itself could be secured. The politics of Western thought has, therefore, been a security project in the fullest sense of the term."

The connection Dillon makes is not just political. At its core, it is metaphysical. Security in and of thought as certainty! To do philosophy is to secure an *arche*, to build principles and to create a ground. Gottfried Leibniz (1646–1716) drew an analogy between philosophizing and building a house. To build a house on sandy terrain one must keep digging until one finds "firm foundations." Similarly, "to establish . . . knowledge some fixed point is required, on which we can *safely* rest and from which we can set out without *fear*" (qtd. in Dillon 1996, 13; italics mine). The question, then, is, Where do insecurity and fear come from? That is, How is security in philosophy secured by way of nurturing *communitas* in a people? It is done, among others, through calls to expel and terminate that which is classified as the "foreign, strange . . . (and) outlandish" and without which the coherence of security—political-philosophical—remains insecure. Commenting on Dillon's book, Thomas Dumm (qtd. in Dillon 1996, ii) described security not as "a mere matter of geopolitical boundary maintenance, but as the dark heart of the western *logos*."

With this reformulated anthropology of philosophy, let's turn to Kant's Enlightenment as a project of security with boundaries. Kant sought to make philosophy "a science possessing the same universal validity as mathematics and physics" (Jaspers 1962 [1957], 135), to do a "Copernican revolution" in philosophy (Hogan 2010; Caputo 2013). Though Kant disagreed with Leibniz on many points, they were united in their hostility to Islam and search for a secure foundation, an edifice to philosophize from. In the preface to the first edition of the *Critique of Pure Reason*, Kant outlined a challenge to a rebuilding of metaphysics from those "nomads who abhor all permanent cultivation of the soil," for philosophical nomadism doesn't offer "a dwelling-place for permanent residence, *Wohnplatz*"[7] (qtd. in Malpas and Thiel 2011, 196). So, in the second edition, the stabilization of metaphysics is undertaken by erecting "the proper boundaries within which it can maintain itself" by thwarting "uncertainty" (Malpas and Thiel 2011, 196; see also Asad 2009; Caputo 2013, 40).

Noting Kant's "obsession with the limit, the boundary, the *Grenze*" to the extent that understanding itself is defined as "a land with many boundaries," Ian Almond (2009, 30) is one of the few scholars to connect Kant's philosophy to his statements as well as his silences about Islam and place it in a perspective that the vast literature on Kant has rarely done. Inspired by Edward Said's *Orientalism* (1995 [1978]), Almond identifies discussion of nomads in Kant, who wrote: "Those who have means to live—amply or poorly—consider themselves noble in comparison with those who have to work in order to live. The Arab, or Mongol, nurtures contempt for the town-dweller, and deems himself noble in comparison with him, as wandering about in the desert with one's horses and sheep is more entertainment than work" (qtd. in Almond 2009, 31).

Behind Kant's description of the Arab or Mongol as wandering about without working is his contrasting Protestant postulate of hard work, which sets his philosophical land apart from the Muslim-Arabs (or Mongols), "who abhor all permanent cultivation of the soil." Kant staged this contrast in his 1796 essay "On a Newly Raised Noble Tone of Philosophy"[8] to draw a boundary between rational, hardworking philosophers and irrational, enthusiastic mystagogues. The danger to philosophy is at once a danger to reason and to "Christian Europe," a term Kant uses in *Anthropology*. This boundary drawing aimed to protect philosophy from the "danger (Gefahr)" of "enthusiastic visions." In "What Does It Mean to Orient Oneself in Thinking?" (1786), Kant (1998 [1793], 6; 8–137, 11; 8–143) took thinking as the obverse of "enthusiasm" and not to use reason was to open the gate "to all enthusiasm, superstition and even to atheism." The figure assigned with the twin dangers—enthusiasm/zeal/fanaticism/sensuality and nomadism—was Islam and Prophet Muhammad (Almond 2009, 32). In Kant's 1765 "An Essay on the Illness of Head"—if he had died by then, there would be no Kantian philosophy (Jaspers 1962 [1957], 7)—he described Muhammad as a "zealot": "Zeal (Schwärmerei) leads the zealot to the external, led Mahomet [*sic*] onto his princely throne" (qtd. in Almond 2009, 33). In the *Critique of Practical Reason* (1788), the figure of Muhammad returns as a sign of unreason, nonsense, monstrosity, dream, or madness of imagination. Asking which interest is supreme—of practical or speculative reason—Kant (2002, 154–21) assured the primacy of the former as follows: "In fact, in case practical reason were presupposed as pathologically conditioned, i.e., as merely administering the interest of the inclinations under the sensible principle of happiness, this demand could not be made on speculative reason at all. *Mohammed's paradise* or the theosophists' and mystics' fusion with the deity, each [thinker] after his own mind, would thrust *their monstrosities upon reason,* and it would be just as well to have no reason at all as to surrender it in this way to all sorts of dreams" (italics mine).

In Almond's reading, Muhammad's paradise for Kant is a "scandalous blending of sacred and profane," a monstrosity threatening reason thereby making Islam anything but "a rational religion." Almond (2009, 36) writes, "If Islam is anything for Kant, it is the triumph of revelation over reason, of sublimity over accountability" and "an opiate, vision-ridden, sense-dominated, non-rational creed." Unsurprisingly, in *Religion within the Boundaries of Mere Reason* (1998 [1793], 185, 6–194), Kant dismisses (without explanation) the five pillars of Islam to initially say that *zakāt* (charity) pertained to "the moral good," but he later rejected it too on the ground that "in this faith almsgiving can well co-exist with extortion from others of things which are offered to God in the person of the poor." Extortion? Coercion (Almond 2009, 38; cf. Palmquist 2016, 483)? By whom? This judgment by Kant displays his prejudiced ignorance about *zakāt* and Islam; he describes the first of the five pillars as "washing." Like other rituals, *zakāt* qua *zakāt* is valid only if and when it is based on the *niyya* (intent) of the giver, thereby making it a voluntary contribution for the sake of Allah. This willingness thus separates *zakāt* from the forcible taxation regime of contemporary states (Hallaq 2013, 124). In the passage cited above, Islam is not the subject per se; it is mentioned only in contrast to Christianity to show how practices as means of grace in the latter directly bear on practical dispositions and concepts. Eight pages earlier, in a footnote, again by way of contrast with Christianity, Kant outlines the "character" and "trait" of other religions as follows: "Mohammedinism [*sic*] is distinguished by its *pride,* because it finds confirmation of its faith in victories and in subjugation of many peoples rather than in miracles, and because its devotional practices are all of a fierce kind." This footnote is explained in an additional footnote describing Muslims as "an ignorant though intelligent people" and the "fancy of its founder [*sic*]" that "he [Muhammad] alone had once again restored in the world the concept of God's unity" (Kant 1998 [1793], 177–78, 6:184–85; italics in original).[9] Readers see no source for Kant's claim. One may also ask, Can ignorance and intelligence logically coexist?

For a full anthropological appraisal of Kant's philosophy, we ought to go back to the fourth question Kresse lists and which, in Kant's own account, anthropology answers (Kuehn 2006, xii): What is a human being? Such is the goal of Kant's *Anthropology*. However, scholars on Kant are divided on its import. *Anthropology, Geography* (yet untranslated into English), and some other writings have been a "well-kept secret" (Louden 2000, vii). Kant scholars deem them irrelevant and unimportant to Kant's philosophy. However, recent scholarship stresses their salience. Scholars argue that *Anthropology*'s moral and practical goal is connected to Kant's idea of a cosmopolitan society of states as well as a virtue theory of cosmopolitanism. To one commentator, "anthropology completes metaphysics" (qtd. in Louden 2000, 67; see also Harvey 2011, 269, 275; and Kuehn 2006, xi–xii). Despite Kant's own view that metaphysics alone properly constitutes philosophy, he also held that there was no greater investigation than the knowledge of human beings. In the preface to *Anthropology*, Kant (2006 [1798], 3) put its task as the "investigation of what *he* as a free-acting being makes of himself."

Anthropology, which he lectured about for over two decades, sold more copies than any other book by Kant. It includes two parts: anthropological didactic and anthropological characteristic. The longer first part outlines a "regulative principle" for humans to graduate from childhood to maturity to reach a cosmopolitan society. I focus on the second part: "On the Way of Cognizing the Interior of the Human Being from the Interior." Racism and national types are stark in *Anthropology*. *Anthropology*, however, makes more sense when studied with *Geography*, where Kant wrote: "Humanity achieves its greatest perfection with the White race. The yellow Indians have somewhat less talent. The Negros are much inferior." People in hot lands are "exceptionally lazy" and "timid." And women in Burma felt proud that Europeans impregnated them (in Harvey 2011, 275–76).

David Harvey doesn't discuss religion or the connection that Kant forges between race and religion in *Anthropology*, which nationalizes "the character of the peoples." England and France are "the two *most civilized* peoples on earth." In a footnote, Kant says that he didn't mention Germany because—himself being a German—it would be "self-praise." About Spain, thus wrote Kant:

> The Spaniard, who arose from the mixture of European with Arabian (Moorish) blood, displays in his . . . behavior a certain *solemnity*; and even towards superiors . . . the peasant displays a consciousness of his own *dignity*. The Spanish grandeur . . . and the grandiloquence found even in their colloquial conversation point to a noble national pride. He is moderate and wholeheartedly devoted to the laws, especially those of his ancient religion.—This gravity also doesn't hinder him from enjoying himself on days of amusement. . . . This is the good side.
>
> The worse side is: he does not learn from foreigners; does not travel in order to get to know other peoples; remains centuries behind in the sciences; resists any reform; is proud of not having to work; is of a romantic

temperament of spirit, as the bullfight shows; is cruel, as the former *Auto Da Fé* proves; and shows in his taste an origin that is partly non-European. (2006 [1798], 218; italics in original)

Kant contrasts "good side" with "worse side," explaining the latter in terms of having a "partly non-European" origin. Who are the non-Europeans? The opening sentence answers: the Spaniard, "from the mixture of European with Arabian (Moorish) blood." That is, Muslim blood in the Spaniard is responsible for their "worse side." Turks are excluded from description because "nationals of European *Turkey never have* attained and *never will* attain what is necessary for the acquisition of a definite national character." Furthermore, only Europeans travel "to know human beings and their national character," not Turks and others, which "proves the limitedness in spirit of all others" (2006, 222, 215; italics in original). "Without freedom and without law," Turkey is uncultivated, that is, uncivilized (qtd. in Louden 2000, 91).

Turkey is mentioned again when Kant advises starting a conversation with "what is near and present." He suggests not mentioning the "news from Turkey" when one enters a room for it "over-exerts the powers of the imagination of those who don't see how the person has come to that topic." To expel Turkey from conversation was necessary because "the mind requires in all communication of thought a certain order" to agree "with the initiated imagination and the beginning, as well as the delivery" (Almond 2009, 29; Kant 2006 [1798], 69). Like nearly all references—important but sparse—to Islam/Muslims, this one too is in a footnote. Nevertheless, they demonstrate that Islam was a key cultural figure in relation to which Kant built his philosophy as security. The Orient must be kept out for it disoriented Kant, his philosophy as much as the culture he worked in and for. In *Lectures on Logic,* he wrote about the superiority of Western philosophy—a premise Max Weber (1992, xxxviii) later turned into a celebrated argument as a "peculiar rationalism of Western culture." By Kant's reasoning, Egypt's wisdom was "a mere child's play," Zoroaster's *Zend-Avesta* didn't contain "the slightest of philosophy," and Arabs only copied the Greeks through Aristotle (Kant 1992, 540, 27). Kresse's exclusive, uncritical reliance on Kant as "an orientation for an anthropology of philosophy," one is driven to conclude, is disorienting at best.

From my argument, it follows that Kant's call that "morals must be united with knowledge of humanity" (qtd. in Louden 2006, 354) is riddled with tensions. Not only is his notion of morality couched as universal distinctly local, in its application (especially, in *Anthropology* and *Geography*)[10] he fails to practice his own maxims about the use of reason in the *Critique of Judgment*—

unprejudiced thought, enlarged thought, and consistent thought (Reiss 1991 [1970], 254–55). Beyond the precinct of Europe and Protestant Christianity, he takes larger humanity as a mere object to which he can apply his particular philosophy. In a rush to secure knowledge *of* humanity, the idea of knowledge *from* humanity never arose. The erasure of non-Western philosophy construed universal as only "to all," not "from all." By this I mean precisely the philosophy such as that of Ghazali (d. 1111), who wandered in the desert for a full decade (Nomani 1901, 41), or Al-Beruni (d. 1048), who traveled to India to write an ethnography of Hindus—anthropology long before the Enlightenment (Ernst 2011; Al-Beruni 2002). Not only did Kant not leave Königsberg, he turned his limitation into a virtue. In *Anthropology*, he wrote that since Königsberg as a large commercial city was "the center of a kingdom," knowledge of "different languages and customs" could be acquired without traveling (2006, 4n4). Again, long before Kant, Saadi Shirazi (d. 1292), a Farsi poet, had philosophized that journeying broadened one's perspective.[11] In ancient Greece, *theoria* (from which theory is derived) meant seeing enriched by journeying (Brown 2005, 25; Miettinen 2012, 29). A deeper analysis thus shows that Kant's systematic erasure of non-European philosophy made his philosophy and reason missionary to offer only one option: conversion—either to Christianity, civilization, secularism, individualism, rationality, cosmopolitanism, and modernity, or to the Enlightenment (Ahmad and Turner 2015; see below).

So far I have focused on Germany and Kant, "the little school master" (Jaspers 1962 [1957], 3). It is time to shift to France, "the cradle of the Enlightenment," as christened in the *Encyclopedia of Anthropology* (Murphy and Visnovsky 2006, 818).

In "Islam and Arabs through the Eyes of *Encyclopédie*: The 'Other' as a Case of French Cultural Self-Criticism," Rebecca Joubin (2000) discusses reason in the French Enlightenment. She takes Voltaire (d. 1778), the baron d'Holbach, and other philosophers as the subject of her analysis. She analyses entries on reason and science vis-à-vis Islamic and Arab civilization in thirty-seven volumes of the *Encyclopédie* (published between 1777 and 1779). As proponents of "rational philosophy," she writes, philosophes of the Age of Reason "attacked Christian doctrine . . . derided" and "denounced" "Christian belief" and desired to "assault Christianity." However, readers are not given any citation to validate these claims. Due to a "climate of ideological suspicion," "official censorship," and fear of "persecution," she contends, instead of attacking Christianity, philosophes attacked Islam. As Islam was not the prime target of their attack, she continues, "the topos of the Oriental as Other" was a lens through which philosophes engaged "in cultural self-criticism as a key method of subterfuge to shield themselves from the watchful eyes of the censors" (Joubin 2000, 213n9, 197, 206, 207, 210).

Before accepting Joubin's argument, many questions arise: Of all religions, why did philosophes choose only Islam, especially because, we are told, they favored reason over religion in general? Institutionally, was the problem of eighteenth-century Christianity similar to Islam's? Or is the assumption that Islam is not *a* religion but *the* religion and, therefore, a critique of Islam is a critique of religion itself? Or are Islam and Christianity substitutable, implying no difference between the two? Can the specificity of Christianity be translated into a generality that in turn is typified singularly in Islam? What about the Kantian Enlightenment motto: "Have the *courage* to use your own understanding"? Why the deflection of courage from one culture or religion to another? Is it courage in the first place?

If attacking Islam was a cultural self-criticism of Christianity, can this mode of reasoning be extended to say that widespread racism against black people is indeed a cultural self-criticism of racist white power? To stay with Joubin's argument, one can imagine the following scenario. Some white intellectuals felt agitated against racism. However, because of fear of censorship and persecution, they didn't attack sources of white power. They instead attacked and critiqued black culture. In so doing, the white intellectuals in fact critiqued white power. An argument like this—flawed as it is—will amount to saying, by extension, that Islamophobia is not a prejudiced politics against Islam but indeed a critique of the cultures and polities Islamophobes hail from and desire to uphold.

Central to Joubin's contention is the basis of the secularity of Enlightenment philosophes. However, both reason and religion as categories remain beyond examination in Joubin's text. Contrary to the consensus view, Voltaire, as a representative of the philosophes, was not opposed to religion in itself. Indeed, he opposed atheism. Commenting on *Christianity Unveiled*, Voltaire said: "This book leads to an atheistic philosophy that I detest" (qtd. in Stephens 2014, 135). The doubt about elements of Christianity—which philosophes expressed in plenty—in no way means abandonment of faith or certainty because, after Wittgenstein (1958, 18e, 23e), "the game of doubting itself presupposes certainty" and "doubt comes after belief." Voltaire's "belief" or "certainty" was nothing else but "true Christianity." In critiquing the Church, clergy, and orthodoxy, his reference point was not reason stripped from tradition and religion, it was the "originary Christianity," "the times of the first Christians," and things that were "the opposite of the religion of Jesus" (Derrida 2002, 60). In the *Philosophical Dictionary*, he indeed affirmed his faith in

God and justice (Arkush 1993, 228; Williams 2012). Viewed from this perspective, Joubin's (2000, 198) inferential claim, that "given what is known about Voltaire's contempt for Christianity and considering the necessity of subterfuge to express any criticism of religion, it is *likely* that Voltaire was using Muhammad as a surrogate for Christ," collapses like a house of cards (italics in original).

What disturbed Voltaire most was violent intolerance among Christians. He attacked sectarianism. The famous *écrasez l'infâme* (crush the infamy) referred not so much to religion itself but to clashes in the name of sects, each of which claimed to own the truth. In *Dieu et les Hommes* he even counted the number of people killed, from the time of Constantine to his own present. Voltaire's agitation stemmed from his belief (certainly in his later life) that Jesus was a teacher of universal natural religion and tolerance (Arkush 1993, 234, 238). Like Kant in Germany, Voltaire too held that Christianity was the "sole 'moral' religion" (Derrida 2002, 60). It bears no repeating that the moral was already rational.

How do we, then, construe anti-Islam diatribe by the philosophes? First, let's list its contents. To Denis Diderot (d. 1784), editor-in-chief of the *Encyclopédie*, Muhammad was "the greatest enemy that human reason has ever known." He had "a lively and powerful eloquence," wrote the chevalier de Jaucourt (1704–80), but "stripped of reason and logic." Other philosophes regarded Islam not as a religion but as a "sect." Caliph/Imam Ali "held his reason captive under the yoke of prejudice." In Diderot's judgment, the Qurʾān was an "absurd, obscure, and dishonest book." To Abbé Edme Mallet, chapters in the Qurʾān had "ridiculous titles." Returning to Voltaire, in *Le Fanatisme, ou Mahomet le Prophète* (composed in 1736 and staged in 1741), he described Muhammad as an "imposter" (qtd. in Joubin 2000, 201, 203, 204, 205) and turned him into an archetype of fanaticism against which nearly all discourses of reason were conducted.[12] Secularist accounts of the Enlightenment and Voltaire mention that the play was banned in France. That the ban was lifted in 1845 at the behest of Pope Benedict XIV is often unmentioned. In fact, the pope consented to Voltaire's request to dedicate the play to him. Voltaire's letter to the pope stated that he had written it "in opposition to the founder of a false and barbarous sect [Islam]" (qtd. in Perchard 2015, 470). Of course, Voltaire (2000, 20–21) praised Islam for its tolerance of people of other faiths under Ottoman rule—as he also praised India under the Mughals. But this conditional praise was about the historical political sociology of Muslims, their theology and prophet remained fanatic, absurd, and false. The conditional praise of *zakāt* by an anonymous author in the thirty-sixth volume of the *Encyclopédie* likewise sounds problematic, as it is torn from the wider moral universe it belongs to. Neither the contributor nor Joubin (2000, 206–7) herself says how this act of "moral good," as Kant also saw it, but dismissed on the ground of being "coercive," is predicated on articles of faith. The surgical orientalist segregation between dealings (*muʿāmlāt*) and rituals (*ʿibādāt*) does not obtain in the Islamic tradition; one sustains the other (Hallaq 2013, 114–18). Seldom did even this conditional praise about *zakāt* or religious tolerance become part of public knowledge. Eventually, Voltaire's diatribe against Islam won in the same way the Christian calendar triumphed over the secular calendar of the French Revolution, thereby becoming the universal calendar (Perovic 2012, 126).

The diatribe against Islam by the French philosophes and encyclopedists was thus not mere window dressing aimed to attack Christianity. To say that Islam was a subterfuge is to lose sight of the whole argument about philosophy as ethnicity. The philosophes mobilized Islam to shape an ethnic identity of Europe/Christians as hostile to and distinct from Islam. Assigning the trope of reason to Christianity/Europe and that of fanaticism/unreason to Islam was an equally political-ethnic act. Reason and fanaticism/unreason were monumental categories through which the West's ethnic philosophy secured its coherence and identity. Like *Aufklärung* in Germany, the French Enlightenment, *les Lumières*, was "essentially Christian" (Derrida 2002, 59).[13] That is, *Aufklärung* and *les Lumières* were not a denunciation but an immanent critique of Christianity. Bellah's remark that Habermas is regarded as "the pope of European secularism" (qtd. in Calhoun, Mendieta, and VanAntwerpen 2013, back cover) can justifiably also be read as "the pope of European Christianity," because secularism, in many accounts, stemmed from logic exclusive to Christianity (see below). My reformulation of Bellah's remark echoes Nietzsche's description of Kant as a "cunning Christian" (qtd. in Godlove 2014, 1). Habermas, after all, is a Kantian (Ashenden and Owen 1999).

If the sharp religious-secular divide is no longer tenable, as recent scholarship argues (Asad 1993, 2003), the premise of a "secular" Enlightenment opposed to Christianity is likewise untenable. Many historians, philosophers, theologians, sociologists, and other scholars now recognize that the Enlightenment was not a condemnation of Christianity/religion. Nor was it a total break from Christianity (Barnett 2003; van Kley 2012; Gorski et al. 2012; Hudson 2005; Milbank 2013; Outram 2005; Van der Veer 2001). What the Enlightenment did was to reevaluate, not reject, Christianity. Unlike in the past when Kant was taken as a denier of God/religion (see Blond 1998), twelve contributors to a volume on Kant recently agreed that "*Kant's philosophy is religiously . . . affirmative*" (Firestone and Palmquist 2006, xx; italics in original). Similarly, it has been argued that the French Revolution was "the accomplishment (or fulfillment) of Christianity," and it was "Christianity's age of Reason" (Carson 2012, 163).

To maintain the secular-religious divide is equally tenuous vis-à-vis concepts like capitalism, democracy, individualism, secularism, and the state. Weber (1992, xxxviii) asked, "Why did not the scientific, the artistic, the political, or the economic development there [China and India] enter upon the path of rationalization which is peculiar to the Occident?" As for democracy, "Western Christendom has historically provided the womb within which modern democracy gestated" (de Gruchy 2004, 442).[14] And to Steve Bruce (2004, 19), "Protestantism was responsible for democracy." Louis Dumont (1985) traced the Christian beginnings of modern individualism to the teachings of Christ. What about secularism? Philosopher Charles Larmore (1996, 42) holds that "secularization is . . . the inner logic of Judeo-Christian monotheism." Peter Berger too held this view: "The very nature of Christianity . . . was the trigger for the secularization of Europe" (qtd. in Barker 2008, 5).[15] If so, since the "inner logics" and "nature" of religions other than Christianity and Judaism are different, for them to become secular will mean converting to Christianity, which is at the same time democracy, individualism, indeed, a civilization (the West). I read Peter Van der Veer's (1996) *Conversion to Modernities* along this line; as I do Mehta's (1999, 79, 81–82) description of liberalism as "evangelical," imbued with "tutorial . . . obsessions." Ultimately, conversion to modernity, progress, and Christianity are more or less the same thing. Finally, the state! Let's return to Weber (1992, xxxi): "The State itself . . . with a rational, written constitution, rationally-ordained law . . . is known only in the Occident." And that state, as Hobbes theorized it, was uniquely Christian. In the *Leviathan*, Hobbes proclaimed, "Jesus is the Christ" as a flag under which all Christians could unite, thereby making it the single article of dogma. Matters of religion other than the unifying dogma were allocated to the private domain. Hobbes's Commonwealth was thus not a rupture from Christianity: truth took on other forms to reside in "many locales from which it launches its various crusades" (Rasch 2009, 109). That is, Christianity remains the pivot—if only (in)visible—not only of Western discourse (including academic ones) about itself but equally for the non-West/non-Christians, because as the Protestant theologian-philologist Friedrich Schleiermacher (d. 1834) put it: Christianity is "the religion of religions" obliged to judge for "non-Christian others what they can think or say—or even whether they are capable of thinking and saying anything at all" (Keane 2000, 14).

Sociologist Rodney Stark (2006b) has brought all these elements together in a single book: *The Victory of Reason: How Christianity Led to Freedom, Capitalism, and Western Success*. In his formulation, "While the other world religions emphasized mystery and intuition, Christianity alone embraced reasoning and logic as the primary guide to religious truth." The uniqueness of Christianity extended to democracy: "It [democracy] all began with the New Testament." Not just democracy, but Western civilization itself "rests on [a] religious foundation." Modernity was no different: "Modernity arose only in Christian societies. Not in Asia. Not in Islam. Not in 'secular' society—there having been none." Globalization too is Christianity on a much vaster scale because "today Christianity is becoming globalized far more than is democracy, capitalism, or modernity" (Stark 2006a, 17, 19).

When and where, then, is Christianity—not simply as heritage—absent? To address this question is to see modernity differently. If for Habermas (1981, 9) modernity is the eighteenth-century project "by the philosophers of the Enlightenment for the rational organization of everyday social life," Anthony Giddens (1990) highlights its institutional aspects. Relevant to my purpose is the simple yet profound characterization by Caputo (2013, 90, 39): "We can define modernity as the construction of the category of the 'category.'" Modernity's "cunning innovation" of the category of the category resulted into "dividing our beliefs and practices up and setting up them apart from one another with analytic clarity." One can add that behind the category-making and act of division is an (in)visible Christianity, itself distributed, inter alia, through the binary categories of religious and secular. Christianity, then, is not only a "religion" but a "distributive order" that fashions domains and allocates spaces (Anidjar 2015a). Modernity thus becomes not a stage in the history of the West but the staging of these distributive categories: tradition versus modernity, religious versus secular, reason versus faith, civilized versus uncivilized, and so on (cf. Mitchell 2000). These categories are not filled with fixed referents, for they can change. What doesn't change is the very staging of those boundary-making categories.

In *The Heavenly City of the Eighteenth-Century Philosophers*, Carl Becker argued that notwithstanding their "engaging cynicism, their brave youthful blasphemies[,] ... there *is more of Christian philosophy in the writings of the Philosophes* than has yet been dreamt of" (1932, 31; italics mine). To Becker, "the *Philosophes* demolished the Heavenly City of St. Augustine only to rebuild it with more up-to-date materials." Fourteen year later, in *The Idea of History*, R. G. Collingwood (1985 [1946], 76), however, wrote that the Enlightenment was "a revolt not only against the power of institutional religion but against religion as such." Twenty-five years later, Peter Gay (1957, 188) reversed Becker's thesis to say that "the beautifully articulated machine of the *philosophes* is not a Christian but a pagan machine." In *The Living Enlightenment* (1996, 71), Gay decreed that the Enlightenment was "a secular revolution" external to Christianity. Gay and Becker agreed, however, that the Enlightenment was specific to the West. To take another example, in *Primitive Man as Philosopher*, Paul Radin (1927, 99), a pioneer of the anthropology of philosophy in a way, wrote that fatalism among the Malay "may be due to the influence of Mohammedanism [*sic*]." In contrast, Joseph Schacht (d. 1969) stated that Islam was a "religion of action" (qtd. in Masud 2006, 5).

A telling index of the staging of these dualistic categories was Western self-perception during the Cold War. In his 1949 lecture, George Thomas noted that the "*threat of secularism* to our civilization [has] made it necessary for us to find *our way back to the well-spring of faith*" (qtd. in Kavka 2012, 187; italics mine). Indeed, the Cold War itself was religious: "Christian Democracy versus Godless Communism." The threat of communism was equally "to Christian society as expressed in Western bloc democratic nations" (Bouma 2007, 190). The threat of godless communism led to the downplaying of differences within Christianity. It was against this backdrop that Will Herberg's *Protestant—Catholic—Jew: An Essay in American Religious Sociology* (1955) was welcomed as the onset of a pan-American identity (Bouma 2007, 190). It is after the USSR's collapse that the rhetoric of the "secular" on the part of the West and the United States intensified. To the question, "Why?," the answer is simple: in the Cold War, if the enemy was the "atheist/secular" USSR, the West could not also be secular. In the current new world order (NWO), since the enemy is religious/Islamic terrorism, the West can't be "religious." As Reinhard Schulze (2000, 27) aptly observes about Muslim societies, the dichotomy of tradition versus modernity persists "due to Western modernity's continuing need for a 'contrasting opposite' in order to understand [and define] itself."[16] In philosophy, categories of dichotomy produced are faith versus reason, revelation versus rationalism, or traditionalism versus rationalism (Martin, Woodward, and Atmaja 1997; Watt 1988). Binyamin Abrahamov's (1998, vii) position, if extreme, exemplifies it best: "Philosophy has not penetrated into wide circles of Muslims."

My argument so far has been that the Enlightenment and its reason were rooted in a distinctly local political anthropology. The Enlightenment's reason was a boundary-making and category-creating mo(ve)ment: civilized versus uncivilized, rational versus irrational, European/Western versus non-European, pure race versus mixed, traditional versus modern, reason versus fanaticism, and so on. Islam was an important Other in the matrix of that boundary making. In short, the Enlightenment was a local but gigantic project of ethnicity (cf. Casanova 2009, 218–22). If one more "proof" is required to consolidate my contention, it is the reaction to Reinhard Schulze's thesis, with which I will close this section. Schulze advanced a provocative argument: Muslims had their own Enlightenment. He argued that because autonomous agents of innovation and renewal were present in the eighteenth-century Islamic world, it could be described as an Islamic Enlightenment similar to the Western Enlightenment. Rudolph Peters (1990, 162) rejected Schulze's thesis straightaway. Peters's reason, in the precise sense of the Enlightenment's reason, was that to label expressions in the eighteenth-century Islamic world as "Enlightenment" is "confusing and would strip the concept of [Western] Enlightenment of its precise meaning." What Peters said without needing to say was plain enough: since the Enlightenment is Christian/Western, with the admission that Muslims also had an enlightenment the categories instituting modernity would evaporate into thin air, as would the ethnic boundaries the categories are invested with.

◆ Anthropology and Critique

My examination, demonstrating the complex, layered imbrication of Enlightenment philosophy, reason, and the secular with Christianity—despite the demotic view in the academy, not to mention that of mainstream media and social media—seems to tilt in favor of accounts such as Gay's and Collingwood's, rather than ones like Becker's. My point is not that Christianity was not critiqued. But it was not critiqued in the same way as Islam was—in the German Enlightenment as well as the French Enlightenment. Across multiple, and at times bitter, divides, Enlightenment philosophy took Christianity as a moral and rational religion. For Kant, Protestantism, unlike Judaism and Islam, was the consummate rational religion (Turner 2007). More important, while Islam was perceived as an adversary of reason, reason was depicted to dwell within Christianity. So was critique, a medium to institute reason in a world rampant with "unreason." It is probably because of this highly Christian/secularist investment in the concept and practice of critique that anthropologists working on Islam have shown reluctance, if not hostility, to using it. To illustrate this, I will discuss some ethnographic works, the choice of which is predicated upon diversity in their theoretical, methodological, and geographical anchoring, though I am also limited by considerations of space.

In his rich ethnography of the Gayo highlands of Sumatra, John Bowen (1993, 18, 8, 11, 324) chooses to name the intense exchange of arguments and reflective comments on rituals and practices by Muslims as "religious disputes," "debate and discussion," and "commentary," not as works of critique. Even the critical contributions of learned *ʿulema* of different persuasions in Gayo qualify as "debates" (ibid.: chap. 3) and as a "genealogy of divergent understandings" (as the first part of the book is christened), never as critique, because "[the Gayo] highlands modernism focused less on 'reason' (*ʿaql*) and more on the proper following of scripture." To take another Indonesian example, in discussing the thought of Abdurrahman Wahid (d. 2009) and Nurcholish Madjid (d. 2005) as an embodiment of what he called "neo-modernism," Greg Barton (1997) described them as "intellectual ulema." The premise—fundamental to Shils's (1972) secularist conceptualization of an intellectual—is that *ʿulema* as a group don't qualify as "intellectuals" because they don't engage with the Western intellectual canons. In contrast, both Wahid and Madjid were exceptions among *ʿulema*, because Wahid, in addition to being a lover of French cinema and soccer, read social theory and philosophy in English and French, while Madjid studied with Professor Fazlur Rahman at the University of Chicago. Hence Barton's description of them as "intellectual ulema"! At stake here is also the issue of translation. *ʿUlema* is wrongly translated as "clerics" or "theologians"; the correct translation is "scholar." Maududi called Aristotle and Plato *ʿulema* of Greece (see chap. 3, n. 20). It seems *ʿulema* has been overly religionized to rob it of its broader meanings. The same holds true for the adjective "Islamic" as used, for instance, by Dale Eickelman—"Islamic knowledge," "Islamic education"—and partly endorsed by Clifford Geertz (in his foreword to Eickelman's book; Geertz 1985). Before the rise of the West, categories like "Islamic art," "Islamic economics," or "Islamic law," however, didn't exist, and certainly not in the sense in which they came to be deployed after the nineteenth century. Sherman Jackson (2005, 154–55) observes that "the Western provenance of the modern neologism 'Islamic'" connotes "both geography and ethnicity" as a tool "to demarcate the boundary between the West and a particular set of 'others.'" Likewise Soroush maintains that premodern philosophers didn't call their philosophy "Islamic"; orientalists named it so (qtd. in Ahmad 2005, 26n9).

Michael Fischer and Mehdi Abedi's work is another case in point. By titling their book *Debating Muslims,* they imply that Muslims debate but don't critique because the reference of debate remains revelation. If this interpretation is plausible, it gains further salience because, before publishing *Debating Muslims,* Fischer (with George Marcus) had published *Anthropology as Cultural Critique.* Its objective was to rehabilitate the promise of anthropology as "a form of cultural critique." By this, they meant harnessing "the portraits of other cultural patterns to reflect self-critically on our own ways," to interrogate "common sense and make us reexamine our taken-for-granted assumptions" (Marcus and Fischer 1999, 1)—an idea flagged in *Mirror of Man* by Clyde Kluckhon in 1949 (Robertson 2002, 785) but unacknowledged in *Anthropology as Cultural Critique*. Marcus and Fischer make it unambiguous that critique is enacted by the anthropologist, not by the people the anthropologist works with. This is so because the anthropologist travels from one culture to another, and the aim of cultural critique is to "apply both the substantive results and epistemological lessons learned from ethnography *abroad* to a renewal of the critical function of anthropology as it is pursued . . . at *home*" (Marcus and Fischer 1999, 112; italics mine). That the notion of "home" and "abroad" is highly problematic, even containing seeds of violence (Ahmad 2013b), is a separate issue. Let me focus on the method Marcus and Fischer offer for cultural critique: it is defamiliarization in two ways. First, there is defamiliarization through cross-cultural juxtaposition. An example they give is Margaret Mead juxtaposing Samoan and U.S. cultures to critique the latter. The second type is defamiliarization by epistemological critique. They cite, among other works, Clifford Geertz's *Negara* as an example. By exploring Balinese politics, Geertz offers an epistemological critique of the very ways the modern West has conceptualized the political.

Marcus and Fischer seem to accord salutary weight to the second form—defamiliarization by epistemological critique. In *Debating Muslims*, Fischer and Abedi (1990, xxxi) state that their book addresses only the first form of cultural critique. Hence they describe their approach as one of critical hermeneutics, not of critique. Critical hermeneutics, they hold, furnishes the space for critique, but not the critique qua critique. The assumption is that the subjects of the book—as they discuss the Qur'ān, hadith, the ritual of the hajj, and so on—don't offer epistemological critique, for they operate within the framework of religion. For instance, in striving to preserve the originality of the oral Qur'ān, Muslims dismiss the salience of reason, *ʿaql* (105). That is, all that Muslims do is merely debate; they don't—or is it that they can't?—critique because they dismiss reason. However, it is possible to read reason vis-à-vis the preservation of originality differently. Might it be that it is not the dismissal of reason in itself but a different notion of reason that anthropology as an Enlightenment discipline is less familiar with?

A largely similar premise appears to be at work in Eickelman's (1985, 15, 13, 11, 33, 62, 134, 132) ethnography (presented as a "social biography") of "traditional" Moroccan intellectual life. Remarkably in a context when modernization theory dominated the scene, Eickelman studied the life of a traditional scholar not taken seriously by the Westernized ruling nationalist elites, who considered traditional scholars to be "a residual, disappearing category." In Abdallah Laroui's tripartite classification of Arab intellectuals, they were "the clerics, the religious intellectuals." To this end, Eickelman appropriately questioned Shils's modernist conceptualization of the intellectual who necessarily distrusted "tradition," thereby offering a rationale for his own inquiry. What is even more fascinating is that the ethnographer lets the reader know what he himself had "uncritically assumed" prior to the fieldwork: knowledge in Morocco was "essentially fixed," "remote from everyday life," and "artificial." Yet a secularist assumption assigning noncriticality to Islamic learning, similar to Walbridge's (2010, 3), appears in its third chapter. "Reason (*ʿaql*) is popularly conceived as a man's ability to discipline his nature in order to act in accord with the arbitrary code of conduct laid down by God and epitomized by such acts of communal obedience as the fast of Ramadan." Two pages later readers are told that "any attempt to explain meaning [of verses during memorization of the Qurʾān] was considered blasphemous and simply didn't occur." Blasphemous? On what ground? Elsewhere, Eickelman does say that the description of *ʿulema* by the nationalists as "non-rational" is incorrect. However, at the very point where discussion about reason could have been more fruitful, the anthropologist does not pursue it. Thus, when ʿAbd ar-Rahman, the main interlocutor, told the ethnographer that "to persuade a person irrevocably committed to a course of action to change his mind would display a lack of 'reason,'" and "'reasonable' men don't stand on absolute rights or wrongs," the latter didn't ask what "reason" and "reasonable" meant to the former. My point is this: neither reason nor critique in its own right is the subject of Eickelman's inquiry. His key concern, among others, is to document the transformation of knowledge in a rural setting from mnemonic to new forms like writing and print.

In this respect, Magnus Marsden's (2005, 8, 10, 11, 29, 87–88, 113–14) work in Pakistan's Chitral region (in a village and a small town) is markedly distinct, especially because "intellectual creativity, emotional modes, ethics and morality, and personhood" are at the center of his monograph. He justifiably observes that anthropologists have "only partially explored" these "dimensions of Muslim life." He aims to unsettle the common assumption that Muslims lives are "intellectually barren" and villages "are places of non-thought." He instead brings to readers' attention the "life of the mind" as lived in Chitral. Based on nearly eight years of fieldwork, Marsden's is a rare book, at least in studies of South Asia, in foregrounding intellect and the life of the mind as a proper subject of ethnography. To also see commoners and the barely educated as intellectuals, engaged in what Marsden calls a "culture of debate," is to go past Shils's notion of an intellectual. In the culture of debate, Marsden demonstrates how his informants used concepts such as heart (*hardi*), mind (*zehn*), brain (*dimāġh*), rational intellect (*ʿaql*), the emotional carnal soul (*nafs*), and so on. In discussions, those fortunate to have received higher education referred to Ibn Khaldun as much as to Jean-Jacques Rousseau. Marsden also dwells on the moods—emotionality, anger, extremeness—that mark such debates. In contrast to an "open-minded person," someone refusing to heed the viewpoints of others is, as one of his informants described, "something of an intellectual donkey."

Like in Bowen and in Fischer and Abedi discussed above, critique is largely absent from Marsden's (2005, 35, 113, 114, 1) text. People engage in "critical discussion," articulate "critical" voices, and scrutinize "doctrines in contentious ways," but such activities in and of themselves don't constitute "critique." Marden instead calls them "debate [*baḥaṡ*]," a word that appears in the title of his fourth chapter: "The Play of the Mind: Debating Village Muslims." The reason for this is perhaps the Enlightenment notion of critique as being opposed to religion in general and the fact that in the Enlightenment and subsequent philosophical tradition, Islam was the significant object, not agent, of critique. The subtitle of Marsden's book is *Muslim Religious Experience in Pakistan's North-West Frontier Province*. Curiously, Marsden describes the rich debate he observed as opposed to "Islamic reform," without specifying what it meant to him or his informants. Elsewhere, readers are given a sense of geography but not its detailed genealogical details: "attempts made by Islamizing Muslim reformers and purifiers from Pakistan and beyond." Early on in the text, on page 8, Islamization is placed in scare quotes. So what were the debates for, if not reform (see chap. 3)?

From the perspective of this book, Marsden (2005, 30) does not adequately relate the conversations he had to the textual and philosophical traditions—whether Islamic or Western/Christian. To clarify, I don't maintain the old-fashioned binary between "folk" and "scriptural" traditions. My point is that it is precisely at the intersection of both that a comprehensive portrait of life (and death) emerges in full bloom. Importantly, Marsden's temporal frame appears hugely skewed—some might even say seduced—by a presentism that stretches back to the past only lamely. He writes that the "importance of self-consciousness and self-examination in the study of Muslim thought has deep historical roots . . . and is related . . . to the effects of colonialism." To reduce self-consciousness and self-examination to the effects of colonialism is a typical Enlightenment trope, as it posits reflexivity and modernity as concurrent. To Giddens (1990, 39), "what is characteristic of modernity is . . . the presumption of wholesale reflexivity." As I show below, reflexivity was a property of the axial age, nearly a millennium before the so-called Age of Enlightenment and Reason.

◆ Reconfiguring the Axial Age: Critique before the Enlightenment

As a conscious practice, or vocation, critique is almost unanimously regarded as a sign of the Enlightenment (Kontopoulos 1995, 6). "Our age is, in especial degree the age of criticism, and," wrote Kant (2007, 37n3), "to criticism everything must submit." In his 1784 essay "What Is Aufklärung?," Kant characterized the Enlightenment as "man's release from the self-incurred tutelage" and "the freedom to make public one's use of reason at every point" (29, 31). In my reading, Kant's essay is concerned with the religious Europe of his time, where he found people (mostly non-Protestants) not using their own reason and submitting themselves to the tutelage of priests or what he called "outside directions." His age being the age of criticism,[17] everything had to submit to criticism and reason. Like Kant, Voltaire also showed immense faith in criticism: as the tenth Muse, criticism was "to rid the world of unreason" (qtd. in Koselleck 1988 [1959], 114). As we saw in the preceding section, Kant and several other philosophers took Christianity (in contrast to other religions, especially, Judaism and Islam) as already rational. It is unclear from his essay, however, whom Kant (2007, 35) meant by "we" when he asked, "Do we now live in an *enlightened age*?" (italics in original).

Nearly two centuries later, in "What Is Critique?," Foucault commented on Kant's essay. Equating critique with Kant's notion of the Enlightenment, he observed that the cultural form of critique was "born in Europe" and that a critical attitude was a "specific attitude in the West" (Foucault 1996, 384, 386, 385). To Foucault, Reformation was the first critical movement. Nowhere in the essay, delivered as a lecture in 1978, does Foucault mention practices of critique in Muslim cultures and histories. The implication of such a position is not ambiguous. Critique is seemingly not part of non-Western traditions, including Muslim ones. It probably couldn't have been. Foucault construed critique as "the art of not being governed so much." The mission of the critic was to enact "desubjugation" in the wake of an all-pervasive governmentalization of European lives from the sixteenth century onward, when the state took on pastoral power to regulate every sphere of life, including the intimate zones of sexuality and care (see also Butler 2003). The function of the critic was to critique the rationalization of lives conducted under the flag of reason. Against

Kantian universalism, Foucault thus argued that a critic was a "specific intellectual" and that "one dimension of criticism for the specific intellectual is the critique of universality per se" (qtd. in Caputo and Yount 1993, 8).

My purpose is not to depict Foucault as an orientalist (or to devalue his work, for I myself have utilized it elsewhere, including in this book). I simply aim to point out this specific similarity between Kant and Foucault. Despite difference between the two, both took modern Europe/reformed Christianity as the precinct for the birth of critique.

However, to see the modern age as the age of criticism, as both Kant and Foucault did, is to celebrate the "us modern." Criticism as a practice is probably as old as humans themselves. It may, therefore, be flawed to think of critique and reflexivity as the sole property of the Enlightenment and modernity (Walzer 1988). If we can't decipher the contour of critique in premodern times, it is unwise to assume there was none. The Buddha was a critic of his times. His teachings and practices contested the foundation of the hierarchical social order legitimized by the divine logic of *jati* (caste division). Those at the bottom of the caste hierarchy were thus drawn to Buddhism (Ambedkar 2003; Fitzgerald 1999; Guru 1991; Singh 1972, 45).[18] If the Buddha was a critic, so were the prophets Mūsā (Moses) and ʿIsā (Jesus), in whose tradition Prophet Muhammad was placed. Contra the near consensus among non-Muslims—not only among orientalists by any means (and in part also shared by some Muslims)—that Muhammad was the founder of Islam (e.g., see Bosworth 1976, 1; cf. Ernst 2004, 10), Muslims hold that he did not bring any new religion. He only renewed what had been God's religion (*dīn*) from the beginning. The reformulation of new interest in Karl Jaspers's notion of the axial age will empower readers to comprehend my proposition better.

Used first by Jaspers in 1949 (Joas 2012), the "axial age" (also called "axial time," "axial period," and "pivotal age") refers to the period from 800 to 200 BC, which saw the rise of the Buddha and the growth of the Upanishads in India,[19] Confucianism in China, the prophets in Palestine, and the Hellenic philosophers in Greece. For Jaspers, the axial age, not modernity or the Enlightenment, marked a rupture with the past. It was in the axial age that man, "as we know him today," he postulated, "came into being." There is no reason not to expand the temporal frame of Jaspers's "crypto-Protestant model" (Van Ess 2006, 234) to include Christianity and Islam, as Ian Morris and Karen Armstrong do in some ways (Bellah 2005; Boy and Torpey 2013; Casanova 2012; Salvatore 2007; Thomassen 2010; Van Ess 2006).[20] As a matter of fact, it doesn't require expanding provided we locate Islam in the tradition of the prophet Abraham, as Hans Küng, a Catholic scholar, did (Van Ess 2006, 233–34).

In Maududi's discourse, as in the Islamic tradition generally, Adam was the first human God created. He was also the first prophet. God sent His message through a series of prophets whose exact number is hard to determine. Abraham, Moses, and Christ were all prophets; so was Muhammad. As descendants of Adam spread to different parts of the world to form different "communities [*qavmēñ*],"God sent a prophet to each community. The religion of all prophets was the same.[21] Many of these prophets were tortured, exiled, or killed; but they continued to spread the message. Using quasi-evolutionary language, Maududi (1939, 47) wrote that as civilization advanced (*taraqqī*) in trade and technology and "the species of humans [*nauʿ-e-insānī*] began to mature into adulthood [*sinn-e balūġh*]," it became possible to send the same message to the whole of humanity. Humanity reached such a stage in civilization "around 2,000–2,500 years ago" when Allah sent Prophet Muhammad (570–632 AD), marking the conclusion of the long chain of prophets. Though Maududi didn't use the term "axial age," its connotation is discernable in terms of a societal transformation accompanying the axial age, with reflexivity and critique of rulership as its signature (Wittrock 2012, 104–13). Arnaldo Momigliano spoke of the axial age as an "age of criticism" (qtd. in Joas 2012, 11; Turner 2016, 147). In Qurʾānic terms, the mission of all prophets was to do reform (*iṣlāḥ*). And integral to the prophetic mission of *iṣlāḥ* was critique. To reform was indeed to critique and vice versa. This mission of reform resonated well with what the Talmud and the Bible say. The prophets of Bani Israel (children of Israel) endeavored to reform the social orders of ṭheir time and "mounted full-blown critique [*tanqīd*] of the wrong leadership" (Khursheed Ahmad 1991, 18). Prophet Mūsā's (Moses) delivery of the message of monotheism to the pharaoh was a critique par excellence. To Maududi (1927, 11), the Buddha was a determined figure who did reform (*iṣlāḥ*) of Brahmanism. The mission of reform and critique was continued by the prophet ʿIsā (Jesus). In formulating the goal of Jamaat-e-Islami, Maududi cited the New Testament. In his view, Muhammad only carried forward the mission of Jesus (see chap. 4).

◆ Islam as Critique

In 1969, Robert Bellah (1991, 152) described Muhammad's message as "too modern to succeed [in its own time]."[22] He could have used any other term, but Bellah preferred to use the then-reigning language of modernization. This critical enterprise of Muhammad didn't end with his demise. An ordinary woman did not hesitate to question and reprimand Caliph ʿOmar during his public address on what she regarded as his mistaken judgment (Shaz 2006,

122). The exile of Abu Zar Ghaffari (d. 652), a companion of Prophet Muhammad, to what is now Syria was a consequence of his critique of growing tendencies among the ruling elites to amass wealth. In refusing to have any personal savings—contrary to what we under capitalism take as self-evident—and leading an ascetic life, Ghaffari offered an embodied critique of the violent asymmetry of the Arabian social order (Shariati 1979; Rahnema 2007). Muslims hold that since Muhammad was the final prophet, the mission of reform and the renewal of God's message, after Muhammad's death, lay with the *'ulema*, regarded as heirs to the prophets. Advice (*naṣīḥa*) was one fundamental medium, among others, of reform and renewal, directed at commoners as much as at those in power.

Scholars like Joseph Schacht, J. N. D. Anderson, H. A. R. Gibb, and Montgomery Watt maintain that critical approaches such as Ghaffari's did not last long. Around the close of Islam's third century, so goes the argument, the gate of *ijtihād* got shut down. Wael Hallaq (1984, 1, 9) shows the fallacy of such a view. Drawing on sources from subsequent centuries, he demonstrates the constant employment of "human reason" in the ongoing process of *ijtihād*, "the exertion of mental energy in the search of a[n] . . . opinion."[23] As Hallaq's focus is on the category of jurists, an example from the category of nonjurists is in order. In sixteenth-century India, proponents of the Raushaniya movement asked, Why can we pray only in Arabic when God understands any language?[24] Clearly, they used reason to critique what they regarded as incomprehensible. Interestingly, followers of this movement considered their leader as *pīr-e-raushan*, leader of the light (Tariq Ahmed 1982). This line of argument can be further pursued if we pay attention to the new science of *Adab al baḥaṡ* (the science of rational argumentation) Arab intellectuals had developed by the end of the thirteenth century. *Adab* means both "rules" and "etiquette," the latter making politeness a precondition for any debate. While differentiating debate from dialectic (*jadal*), *Adab al baḥaṡ* discussed what constituted a question and how to pose different types of questions, including their order (*tartīb*). For these scholars, reasoning and use of dialectic emanated from God Himself as enunciated in the Qur'ān. Utilizing Greek philosophy, in particular Aristotle, *Adab al baḥaṡ* delineated the nature of proof (*dalīl/burhān*) and causes (*'illa'*) necessary for a proposition to be valid. Contra Larry Miller (1984), whom I rely on for discussion of *Adab al baḥaṡ*, Salah El-Sheikh (2003, 30, 24) contends that rational discourse among Muslims owes less to extraneous Greek influences—which (neo-)Orientalists routinely stress—and more to endogenous factors, including the Qur'ān. In particular, El-Sheik discusses the *sura al-mujādlah*, "The Dialogue or the Dialectic." He interprets it as addressing "the organization and institutions of rational debate on public affairs" and how assemblies (*al-majālis*) were integral to such a debate.

In response to Alexandre Deleyre's question of whether Muhammad was a fanatic or an impostor, and his conclusion that he was foremost a fanatic and second an impostor (Joubin 2000, 205), practitioners of *Adab al baḥaṡ* would have pointed to the nature of that question as restrictive (*ḥajr*) as opposed to nonrestrictive (*tafvīd*). And Shams al-Din Muhammad bin Ashraf al-Husaini al-Samarqandi, who coined *Adab al baḥaṡ* and expanded the provisions of "objections," would have asked, "We don't grant (that it is so); why could it not be otherwise?" And Al-Juwaini might have detected *fasād al-vaẓ*ʿ (false construction) in Deleyre's question, and argued to turn back "the construction by means of that which necessitates the falsification of construction" (qtd. in Miller 1984, 118).

Through my discussion in the preceding pages, I argue for the case of immanent critique, which will help us recognize and analyze the practices of critique in Muslim cultures and histories. It follows that immanent critique is what Michael Walzer (1987, 1988) calls "connected" criticism. It is connected to the ethos of a culture even as it seeks to question it; it is connected to the tradition even as its goal may be to reconfigure it. It is a criticism from and of an ethical standpoint with a mooring in a given tradition that is neither monolithic nor static. Because of such an anchoring, it departs from the Kantian notion of critique. In Kant's claim, reason was "autonomous." It was predicated upon no outside but itself. John Rawls (1993, 100) puts it lucidly: "Kant is the historical source of the idea that reason, both theoretical and practical, is self-originating and self-authenticating." Immanent critique, I propose and elucidate in this book, thus builds on the work of Alasdair MacIntyre, who justifiably suspects any claim for the autonomy of reason. He describes it as an "illusion to suppose that there is some neutral standing ground, some locus of rationality as such, which can afford rational resources sufficient for enquiry independent of all traditions. Those who have maintained otherwise either have covertly been adopting the standpoint of a tradition and deceiving themselves and perhaps others into supposing that theirs was just such a neutral ground or else have simply been in error" (MacIntyre 1988, 367).

As this quote shows, critical inquiry presupposes a tradition and historical anchoring. In Islam it is this form of immanent critique that has been the most dominant, and possibly also the most effective. Immanent critique, I discuss, is not peculiar to Islam; any good, effective critique—"religious" or "secular"—is by necessity immanent.[25] I also don't subscribe to the categorical wedge driven between a "hermeneutic" approach to and a "practice-based" model of immanent critique (Stahl 2013), for hermeneutic presupposes practice in the same way as some notion of hermeneutic is already at work in any conception of practice. Similarly, to posit that a tradition- or context-bound critique is "weak," whereas a context-transcending (is that possible?) and so-called universal critique is "strong" (Honneth 2009, 44), may be tantamount to ethnocentrism disguised as universalism, entailing bloody "intervention"—as witnessed in the recent and remote pasts—at home and abroad alike.

A word or two about the efficacy of immanent critique as a method or analytical tool is in order here. As a method and a mode of knowledge, it doesn't simply allow us to go beyond Western stereotypes according to which Islam is inimical to criticism and debate; it also enables us to ask a series of interlocking questions: Why is critique being made? Who is making it and for what purposes? What is the condition which facilitates or hampers the practices of critique? What are the anthropological coordinates and power configurations—local, national, transnational, and global—under which practices of immanent critique, of this or that variety, are undertaken? What are the streams of critiques and how do they, with their respective ideologies, utopias, and social capital, interact with one another? How do they define and use tradition? How is the boundary drawn between "self" and "other"? How and why are networks of critics forged, maintained, or severed? To this end, what are the resources harnessed for dissemination, persuasion, and resistance? Immanent critique as a method will also empower students of anthropology, social sciences, and other disciplines to explore many sites of criticism—literature and arts, collective movements and mobilizations, print culture and mass media, humor and laughter, versions of histories and visions of futures, politics of inclusion and exclusion, the articulations of cultures as a gendered reality, and so on. In disciplinary terms, such an endeavor entails a skillful interdisciplinary intervention. A disciplinary promiscuity, in short.

An arguably influential and pioneering illustration of immanent critique in anthropology is the work of Talal Asad. In his inspirational book *Genealogies of Religion*, Asad (1993, 203, 208, 207, 211) urges us to take into serious consideration "forms of criticism" that "are integral to many non-Enlightenment" societies. In so doing, he also points out a basic tension in Kant—and by extension in liberal thinking. The motto in "What Is Aufklärung?" that "to criticism everything must submit" ultimately stands banished, for when faced with public criticism, on the one hand, and obedience to law, on the other, it is the latter Kant sanctifies.[26] Concerned with exploring the dynamic of "reasoned criticism" in non-Enlightenment societies, Asad persuasively shows how through the medium of *naṣīḥa* (advice), the young *ʿulema* (in the wake of the first Gulf

War) offered engaged critique of the Saudi Arabian state and society. For these young ʿ*ulema* as well as Asad, far from being antithetical to each other, Islam and critique indeed inform each other. Such "morally corrective criticism" aimed at undertaking the work of reform (*iṣlāḥ*). Though Asad doesn't use the term *iṣlāḥ*, its meaning permeates the text. Asad's call to pay attention to criticism integral to non-Enlightenment traditions is already a monumental departure from the established doxa. He does not see non-Western and Muslim societies in terms of the "presence" of a thing called x in the West and its "absence" in Arab/Muslim social formation as does Mona Abousenna, secretary general of the Averroes and Enlightenment International Society of Egypt. In "The Absence of Enlightenment in Arabic Culture," published in the journal *Think: Philosophy for Everyone*, she cited Kant to say that "human reason is autonomous, and being autonomous is being critical." She called for rationality "to defend human civilization from the irrationality and destructiveness of all kinds of fundamentalisms and terrorism." To achieve this goal, the key question for her was, "How does this [Kant's Enlightenment] apply to contemporary Arabic culture?" (Abousenna 2006, 12). The conclusion is straightforward: Kant has already supplied the answer; Arabs/Muslims must only apply it. That is, thinking belongs to Kant, only its implementation to Egyptians/Arabs/Muslims. More important, in urging scholars to study criticism integral to non-Enlightenment societies, Asad does not take Europe as a model and thereby beckons to a possible universe of discourse: a counterpoint to the dominant view that "there is not much alternative left but to adhere to the universal values of [the] Enlightenment" (Abaza 2007, 22). Asad concludes by arguing that the asymmetrical world order and the placement of the Middle East in that (dis)order limit the scope and forms of criticism among Muslims.[27]

In discussing "tradition-guided reasoning," Asad (1993, 211, 215) also notes, tellingly, a significant difference between the Enlightenment notion of critique as a "right" and Muslims' conceptualization and practice of criticizing political authority as a "duty." There is another difference I want to highlight. Unlike in Enlightenment thinking, with its focus on reason, in Islamic tradition the focus is on *qalb* (heart), which is the locus of reason or intellect (ʿ*aql*). Recently, in what many may consider a daring critique, John Milbank described Habermas as "already outdated." Noting the increasing salience of religion in theorization as well as in life, he offered a significantly different reading of the Enlightenment, which "at bottom . . . still retains a Christian coloring." Based on a revisionist reading of David Hume, "the defender of Church establishment," Milbank placed a greater significance on "feeling." For Milbank, feeling is an intermediate category between faith and reason, enabling him to overcome the Habermasian divide between faith and reason. I got drawn to this call to "feeling" and expected some discussion of the heart. But it does not figure in Milbank's prose. The two times I noticed the word, it was used differently: "denial of internal relations lies at the heart of Hume's thought" and "heart of the natural order" (Milbank 2013, 340, 334, 339, 336, 346).

In Islamic philosophical tradition, the highly valued intellect or reason (*ʿaql*) is not an independent entity in its own right; it dwells in and constitutes the heart (Arabic: *qalb*; Urdu/Farsi: *dil*). It is better to first render explicit the assumptions behind discourse on the heart and reason. In Hallaq's (2013, 129–30) reading of Ghazali, human nature is in itself predisposed toward neither good nor ill. Endowed with four potentialities—*sabʿiyya, bahimīyya, shaytanīyya*, and *rabbanīyya* (aggressive, beastly, satanic, and divine, respectively)—knowledge and training make human nature what it becomes by (dis)employing these potentialities. The domains where these potentialities dwell are different. While the first three reside in the *nafs* (soul), the last one lies in the domain of the heart, which the Qurʾān takes as "the center of human awareness and intelligence" (Chittick 2011, 14). The heart signifies one's innermost purity aligned with, not unhooked from, exercise of the mind or reason, for the latter itself dwells in the heart.[28] According to Arabic dictionaries, *qalb* denotes "one's innermost core, which includes both intellect and feelings" (Haj 2002, 350–52; Ramadan 2004, 14). In short, the Islamic notion of *qalb* is far more holistic and complex than the truncated reason of Cartesian cogito. Unlike the Enlightenment dualism between heart and reason, mind and body, intellect and affect, in Islam, the Arabic and Urdu term *qalb* encapsulates both intellect and feelings. William Chittick (2011, 14) calls this approach in Islam a "nondual understandings of things"; calling it "antidualistic" might not be inappropriate. If understood so, the statement in the *Brill Encyclopedia of Islam*, second edition (Vadet 2012), that "while *ʿaql*, 'intellect,' has no place in the vocabulary of the Qurʾān, *qalb* is very frequently employed" is grossly misleading. The word *ʿaql* appears in the verb form many times in the Qurʾān as, for instance, *afalā taʿqilūn*. The appearance of *ʿaql* in the verbal form indeed has a greater significance in that for the Qurʾān the issue is not of its presence or absence but how it is used or not used or how to deploy it better (Kocabas 1987). This interdependence between the heart and reason to the point of inseparability between them is not just a philosophical postulate; anthropologists such as Marsden (2005) have also observed it ethnographically. This interdependence implies the sheer nonrelevance of the dualistic tension that Leo Strauss posed between Jerusalem and Athens—symbolizing faith and reason, respectively (Tarcov and Pangle 1987, 910). As Josef Van Ess (2006, 235) noted,

"Muslims never speculated about the tension between knowledge and belief." Yet Western knowledge/philosophy continued to see Islam as representing a "dilemma" between reason and revelation (Arberry 2008 [1957], 7). In one sense, Renan's comment on Ghazali illustrated it best, or worst: he described Ghazali as an enemy of philosophy. The tradition, set by Renan, of describing Ghazali as an opponent of philosophy continued for generations. In *Revelation and Reason in Islam*, A. J. Arberry (2008 [1957], 61) opined that Ghazali delivered "the fatal blow to philosophy in Islam." Nearly thirty years later, Oliver Leaman (2002 [1985]) stuck to this tradition, calling the first part of his book "Al-Ghazali's Attack on Philosophy." This was, however, at a radical variance with the self-perception of philosophers like India's Shibli Nomani (1901, 56), who, as early as 1907, held that Ghazali indeed "offered justification in favor of philosophy."[29] In schematic thought like that of Abrahamov (1998, vii), "tradition causes continuity, and hence stability," whereas "reason causes change, and hence instability." Do not the continuity and stability in Western thought about Ghazali from Renan to the present, then, mean absence of "reason" in the Western/Orientalist traditions?[30]

Unlike Leo Strauss's allusion to a profound tension between Jerusalem and Athens (faith and reason), what flourished in Hijaz was antidualism. An alternative genealogy of critique with reference to Hijaz is long overdue, and it is a task undertaken in the next chapter.

3
THE MODES
Another Genealogy of Critique

> The book before you is a modest attempt in the same direction [of critique (*tanqīd*)] that Mavlana Maududi has adopted. Excuse me, the rule of one-way traffic doesn't apply to intellectual-scientific critique, investigation for the quest for the beneficial and virtuous and the results of thought and study. If this were to apply to the world of thought and writing, the human mind would become dull, intellectual activities paralyzed, initiative for reform, renewal, and the perennial quest for the betterment of the *umma* [community] closed. Critique is such a benevolent tree, its roots planted in soil and its branches open to the sky; with God's approval it continues to bear fruit.
>
> —ABUL HASAN ALI NADVI (1980, 29–30)

The principal aim of this chapter is to chart out an *alternative* genealogy of critique—*tanqīd, intiqād, naqd*—in Islamicate traditions of South Asia as expressed in the Urdu language.[1] In the first part, I examine accounts of critique in Urdu, nearly all of which relate to literary criticism. Here I engage with authoritative works on criticism by scholars such as Shamsur Rahman Faruqi, Gopi Chand Narang, Vazir Agha, and others to argue that its predominant rendition is secularist-secularizing and nationalist-nationalizing—a process traceable to and visible from the early twentieth century onward as a result of colonial modernity. I critique the dominant accounts of literary critique on three points. First, given that it is a child of Westernizing modernity and therefore secularist, it not only does not engage with religion but also shows religion as its own obverse—sometimes implicitly, sometimes explicitly. This literary criticism also embraces the borders of political nationalism. Second, the notion of critique in Urdu literary criticism is grossly limiting, failing to include critique outside the iron wall it has built to separate itself from the nonliterary. Third, I question the hegemonic pedigree of literary criticism as beginning in ancient Greece and brought by colonizing Britain (Europe) to nineteenth-century India and beyond. I argue that such a pedigree is an ideological topos no longer able to sustain itself. To make this contention, I draw on the works of Martin Bernal, Michael Herzfeld, and John Keane, which unsettle the doxa that Greece was the citadel of ancient civilization and nearly everything modern or European (that is, desirable and valuable) began there, including anthropology, democracy, and critique. Here I discuss the paradox that modern Greece, whose ancestors are considered to be the intellectual-spiritual forefathers of the West, itself does not yet belong to the West/Europe.

Based on these triple critiques, in the second section, I chart out an alternative genealogy of critique emanating from traditions of Islam. This notion of critique goes past the limiting field of literature and broadens itself to include culture, society, politics, and more. Here I show how in the circles of "traditional" *ʿulema* (scholars) and the "religious" texts they author a different notion of critique is at work—a notion that does not reject the Greek, pre-Muhammad, or Western traditions but which at the same time refuses to be contained within and by them. In this genealogy, critique doesn't stand against religion; rather, it emanates from God. Here I trace key elements of this genealogy through the Qurʾān, the lives of various prophets, the Sunna, and in the early community constituted around Muhammad and his companions. I discuss how Maududi, his interlocutors, and his critics read, craft, elaborate, configure, update, and modify what I call an alternative genealogy. Rooted in the discursive traditions of Islam (Asad 1986b), the hallmarks of this alternative notion of critique are its totality, or the wholeness (not neat separation) within which it works, and the comprehensive morality that undergirds it. Here, thoughts and actions appear as a coordinated ensemble whereby one sustains the other. By virtue of these features, this critique is neither nonpurposive nor "neutral." Furthermore, it is as much about life as it is about death, death being only a continuation of life here and now.

◆ Critique—*Tanqīd/Naqd*—in Urdu

In contemporary Urdu, the most often used word for critique is *tanqīd*. Shamsur Rahman Faruqi (2004, 247), modern Urdu's most celebrated critic, traces its first usage back to 1910 and the writer Mehdi Ifadi (d. 1921). This attribution is incorrect, however. In 1904, Haji Mohammad Khan (1971) had already used *tanqīd* in an article in *Aligarh Monthly*, where it occurred no fewer than a dozen times.[2] That same year *Lisānuṣṣidq* (1904, 12–13), a journal edited by Abul Kalam Azad, also used *tanqīd*, in a review of Altaf Hussain Hali's biography of Sayyid Ahmad Khan. The issues of temporal accuracy and who used *tanqīd* first need not detain us here. Before *tanqīd* became the hegemonic term, *intiqād* was also used. For example, Neyaz Fatehpuri (d. 1966) titled a collection of his critical essays *intiqādiyāt*. Along with *intiqād*, *naqd* was also used (e.g., see Kalimuddin Ahmad 2006 [1940s],[3] 35; Nomani 1970a, 65, 67; Nomani 1970b, 147; Sajjad 1979, 25). Faruqi is right to say that *tanqīd* is most commonly used; however, he is wrong to say that *intiqād* and *naqd* have "nearly disappeared," for they continue to be used (e.g., Ansari 1994, 10; Bari 1997, 41; Chishti 2012, 7; Husain 1965, 219; Mehdi 1999, 38, 92; and Quadri n.d.), though with less frequency than *tanqīd*. Important to note is Faruqi's assumption that *tanqīd* is an invention of Urdu (thus unique to India), for this word is absent both in Farsi and Arabic. In Arabic and Farsi, the words used for criticism are *naqd* and *intiqād*.[4] Faruqi's prose thus shows an acute anxiety to distance Urdu from Arabic and Farsi. I argue that the key source of that anxiety is literary nationalism.

This anxiety is greater in Faruqi's *The Secret Mirror: Essays on Urdu Poetry* (1981), which helps us comprehend the discussion better. In it he argues that the Urdu *ghazal* is "an expression of the Indian mind and part of the poetic tradition of the Indian heartland." Noting that it is the "mind"—not Indian themes, like the mango grove and dusty plain the Anglo-Indian poets wrote about but that did not appeal to Indians—that makes poetry Indian, he avers that Indian Farsi poets were distinct from Iranian poets "in temperament, in attitude to life and the universe." Whereas the "Iranian mind . . . loves simplification, . . . [it] doesn't feel at home with the complexity and verbal conceits," writes Faruqi, "the essence of Indian style has been . . . love for the baroque, ambiguity, a close verbal texture with much word-play." He continues: "The Iranian is essentially outward-looking and fights shy of abstract thought in poetry," while "the Indian mind is endowed with a "tendency to speculate" (1981, 15–16, 24–25, 19, 33). This Indian mind is expressed in Urdu *ghazal* too, which succeeded Farsi poetry. "In the crucible of Urdu *ghazal*," Faruqi asserts, "Indian and Islamic elements fuse into a true Indo-Islamic consciousness." As an example "in our country," Faruqi discusses Urdu *ghazal*'s preoccupation with life after death with a wide variety of speculation: "There is life after death; there is no life after death; there is no death; there is no life therefore no death either; there is rebirth after death; there is rebirth but in a different form; there is a cycle of life and death with each being an aspect of the other" (19). From this presumed fusion, Faruqi concludes that while "Ghalib or Momin or even Yagana would have resented the idea of standing in the Indian or Hindu tradition, . . . Mir and Insha might have been delighted" (33). Note that for Faruqi India equals Hindu. Note also that Faruqi describes the so-called fusion not as lesser or greater but as "true" and thereby logically false. Whether or not this fusion leaves any room for literary pluralism is a separate matter. A different facet of what I call the literary nationalism of Faruqi is manifest in the remarks of Abdul Halim Sharar (1860–1926), himself an Urdu writer. In an essay on the development of Urdu prose, Sharar (2009, 202) wrote that the "Qur'ān was in the national language."

That Faruqi mimics, if unconsciously, the American-style anthropology of the 1940s and 1950s—especially of Ruth Benedict, Margaret Mead, and Rhoda Métraux (Fabian 1983, 46–52; Silverman 2005, 295–96)—engaged frantically as it was in producing "national character," "national personalities," and "national identities," is striking. As an anthropologist, I distrust claims of ethnicizing and nationalizing the mind—Iranian, Indian, or Western. Raphael Patai's *The Arab Mind*, published eight years before Faruqi's *The Secret Mirror*, also belonged to this genre (Ahmad 2015f). Importantly, in Faruqi's formulation India/Indian functions as a perfect substitute for Hindu, which is posited as indigenous in contrast to Islam as alien. He doesn't write "Indian *and* Hindu"; rather, it is "Indian *or* Hindu tradition" (italics mine). Of course, he also assumes that Urdu poets are only Muslim. Is this really the case? There have been and are many great Hindu poets who wrote in Urdu. And they learned Hinduism by reading its religious texts in Urdu. Gulzar Dehlvi—whose nonliterary name is Anand Mohan Zutshi (b. 1926)—is one among many examples.[5] My point is that Faruqi's move first renders Islam alien and then seeks to indigenize it in the only way his nationalism allows—by assuming that the link between Hinduism and Islam is a one-way street. Faruqi is thus not averse to religion per se; he is averse to a religion that he inscribes as foreign and deficient in complexity and speculation.

Faruqi's aversion, even hostility, to religion becomes glaring in his discussion of Altaf Hussain Hali (1837–1914), whose *Muqaddamah-e-shaʿr-v-shāʿrī* is regarded by most scholars (e.g., Suroor 2011, 143) as the first book of criticism in Urdu. Others, such as Vazir Agha (2011, 158), however, dispute this, saying that it was Husain Azad (1830–1910), not Hali, who wrote the first Urdu criticism. Faruqi too contests this consensus, albeit differently. To him, in *Muqaddamah-e-shaʿr-v-shāʿrī* neither *tanqīd* nor *intiqād* figures even once. This alone doesn't disqualify Hali as being the founder of criticism, however. The disqualification comes from the fact, as Faruqi avers, that even Hali didn't consider himself to be a critic. Evidence? Faruqi cites the concluding passage of *Muqaddamah-e-shaʿr-v-shāʿrī*: "If because of human frailty I have written anything that hurts my fellow countrymen, with all humility I seek their apology." Faruqi (2004, 250) concludes that Hali wrote this because he didn't regard himself as a critic. As I show below, Faruqi could reach such a conclusion only by staging a secularist notion of *adab* (literature) torn apart from the wider Islamic notion of *adab* that is marked, to cite Barbara Metcalf (1984, 4), by its "radical comprehensiveness" addressing "all domains of life." To Metcalf, *adab* is "key to central religious concepts of South Asian Islam." Let me quote Ira Lapidus (1984, 38–39), who brings to light its full meaning:

> In its pre-Islamic Arabic usage it [*adab*] referred to the norms of correct behavior inherited from one's ancestors. With . . . Islam it came to apply to the ethical and practical norms that regulated the life of a good Muslim. In the eighth and ninth centuries *adab* referred to the etiquette appropriate to the aristocrats and courtiers. . . . Urbanity, aristocratic learning, refined manners, cultivated conversation and good taste constituted the *adab* of the gentleman, scribe and courtiers. The term also applied to the knowledge necessary to the offices of scribes, vizier, judge, and to the learning and correct behavior of the scholar and Sufi. . . . *Adab* meant the proper upbringing of the children. The word also acquired a more strictly intellectual and literary meaning, as knowledge of poetry, language, and ethical and political works, selected from the Arab, the Greek and the Iranian past. Thus *adab* was used throughout the classical era . . . to imply learning and knowledge acquired for the sake of right living. It was a concept of what a person should know, be, and do to perfect the art of living.

Drawing on, among other sources, the Qur'ān, Lapidus further explains the meaning of *adab* through a series of associated concepts, *ʿilm*, *īmān*, and *taṣdīq* in particular. What both Laipdus and Metcalf contend is that *adab* is simultaneously about the inner self and about external deeds or the world, and that *adab* as literature can properly be construed only in relation to the moral universe, which this concept denotes in its comprehensive usage. Rather than appreciate this comprehensive meaning of *adab*, which Hali's apology reflected, Faruqi, I contend, (mis)reads it as an absence of criticism in Hali.

What Faruqi chose not to tell his readers is that just after the cited passage, Hali referred to the Qur'ān. Invoking chapter 11, verse 114, "lo, good deeds annul ill deeds" (Marmaduke Pickthall's translation), he notes that humans have instead devised a different principle: ill deeds annul good deeds. Alluding to his readers' human frailty, like his own, which he acknowledged, Hali said that if the reader identified only the flaws in his book he would still consider himself fortunate. Hali's text is interspersed with such comprehensive ideas of *adab* in his discussion of what Faruqi and his ilk consider purely literary matters. The Qurʾān, God, and Islamic figures appear in several places in *Muqaddamah-e-shaʿr-v-shāʿrī*: for example, in discussion of the differences between the poetry of John Milton and Ibn Rashiq as well as in discourse on how and why poetry should be preserved from lies and exaggeration (Hali 1998, 95–101).

Thus, pace Faruqi, rather than being bereft of critique, Hali's text shows a different concept of critique that secularist accounts of literary critics such as Faruqi's and many others' can either only misunderstand or suppress, or both. As a practitioner of *adab* (literature), Hali is also enmeshed in a more comprehensive idea of *adab* bequeathed by the Islamicate tradition. Faruqi's elision of the Islamicate tradition is not a personal[6] oversight, for it emanates from a specific conception of *adab* as a secular enterprise, which Faruqi shares with his rivals as much as with his sympathizers (Agha 2011; Ansari 1968; Barelvi 1970; Husain 1965; Husain 1983; Suroor 2011), who together constitute and define the dominant history of what Urdu literary criticism is.

Adab, as literature, moral code, and cultivation of self and society, is common to Arabic and Urdu/Farsi, as Lapidus and Metcalf demonstrate. Both in India and the Arab world and, therefore, in Urdu and Arabic traditions, the separation between the literary and the moral occurred as a result of Westernizing modernity, which Elias Khoury termed "a child of the colonial relation" (qtd. in Sacks 2007, 35). In his Beirut lecture "Ḳhuṭba fī adab al-ʿArab," delivered before "a gathering of Europeans and Arabs," Butrus al-Bustani (d. 1883) secularized the notion of *adab* as not only separate from but also in opposition to "religious science." Subsequent figures like Ahmad Faris al-Shidyaq imitated him by solidifying that notion (Hallaq 2014; Sacks 2007). Such a notion of *adab*, fully emergent only in the early twentieth century, was enabled by a violent work of distribution—central to the political theology of colonialism—to arrive at "literature as secularization, secularization as separation" (Sacks 2007, 34; also see Viswanathan 2008). Through its English and French rendition, *adab* thereby became almost denuded of its earlier comprehensive meaning and reduced to a "secular" domain distinct from the so-called religious one. Since in Hali's usage this secularist separation doesn't exist, it is only logical for Faruqi to reject Hali as a critic. In a sentence reeking of sarcasm, Faruqi (2004, 247) writes that Hali might have been a "reformer, preacher," but he was not a critic. Faruqi is not alone in this view. In his 1941 account of the development of Urdu prose, Abdul Qadir (2009, 219) defined it in opposition to religion as follows: "Before the nineteenth century there was hardly any prose literature in Urdu" because "earlier prose writings were either religious tracts or books of old-world stories."[7]

This secularization mission at work in Urdu, as far as I know, has not interrogated the very theology that constituted the English literature that Urdu was mobilized to model itself on. The teaching of English literature, instituted in India before the United Kingdom, was not divorced from Christianity; indeed in some ways it functioned as an ancillary arm of the missionaries. English literature was not just literature; it was held to be "imbued with the spirit of Christianity." Notwithstanding the colonial establishment's platitudes of religious neutrality, Charles Trevelyan, president of the General Council of Public Instruction and brother-in-law of Lord Macaulay, did not hesitate to say, "Without ever looking into the Bible[,] . . . natives [Indians] must come to a considerable knowledge of it merely from reading English literature." The same Trevelyan wanted Arabs/Muslims to read Greek and Roman literature. Despising their pride in their own literature and language, Trevelyan held that if Muslims had "made themselves familiar with Greek and Roman literature they might have suspected that their caliph was a traitor and their prophet an imposter" (qtd. in Viswanathan 1989, 94, 132). Such is the context that informs Talal Asad's (1993, 287–89) observation, as I understand it, that the post-Enlightenment literary scene marked neither a continuity with premodern Christianity nor a complete break from it but reflected a resignification in which "literature can fill the role previously performed by religious textuality" or become a "substitute religiosity," a "source of spirituality," and even "the truth of life."

Nearly all accounts of critique in Urdu, as indicated above, are limited to literature, mostly to poetry, and largely to *ghazal*.[8] In Faruqi's (2010, 36) account in *Ṣurat v mʿānā sokhan*, to critique is (1) "to describe the merits and demerits of a literary work/piece" and (2) to "formulate such statements about literary works that can be universally applicable to those literary works which are of the same nature or of the same genre." As is obvious, he limits *naqd/tanqīd* to the literary/artistic realm. Elsewhere he states, "Wherever there is art/literature [*fann*], there will be critique" (2004, 12). In my reading, one of the defining features of Faruqi's writings on critique is this dictatorship of *fann*. *Fann* is to be judged on its own merits by "isolating itself from the rest" and "solitarily analyzing and studying it" (2004, 5, 314). This exclusive inwardness leads him to focus on its internal dynamics alone and oppose, almost violently, any "external" criteria. My description of Faruqi's approach to critique as the dictatorship of *fann* is probably partly a reaction to the position of Marxists, prominent among them being Ehtesham Husain (1965, chap. 16), who held that *fann* must be at the service of the masses. The secondarity in Marxism thus acquired primacy in Faruqi's enterprise. Long after the fall of the USSR and the decline of Marxism on the Indian literary scene, he is reluctant to appreciate even a minimalist sociological approach to literature. Faruqi's position is in part perhaps also a rebellion against (some might say the slaughter of) his own previous self. In the 1950s, he had proclaimed, "You can't deny that the relations between life and literature are unbreakable" and "Today we are ready to accept only that literature which propagates a philosophy of life or at least possesses psychological and moral values" (qtd. in Usmani 1999, 30).

It is not that Faruqi is oblivious to the cultural, civilizational, and social aspects of literature. At times he recognizes the salience of these elements, especially as highlighted by Hasan Askari (1919–78), who is marginalized in the Urdu canons because in the latter phase of his career he became "a traditionalist in matters of religion and culture" (Farooqi 2004, 176). However, Faruqi advocates a path where everything nonliterary must be subordinated to what he deems literary. It is one thing to underscore the salience of the literary but quite another to dismiss the nonliterary altogether or use it as a criterion to judge what is fit for criticism or not. As an underground poet, I am well aware of the pitfalls of reductionism of poetry or art—be it anthropological-sociological, historical, or political. At the same time, a position such as Faruqi's leads only to a dead end, because his premise is separatist—he continually separates A from B, B from C, and all three from one another. Thus his move to separate poetry from philosophy and vice versa (itself a reformist move similar to Hali's) in such sentences as this: "Those who want to learn philosophy through poetry are . . . cowardly" (2004, 7). To begin with, I know of no one who takes poetry as a replacement for philosophy as an institutionalized and disciplinary knowledge. Faruqi's straw man is, to say the least, weak. Importantly, how can it be denied that to many readers (myself included) the poetry of Ghalib, Iqbal, Jameel Mazhari, Rumi, and Hafiz offers philosophical reflections and aesthetic bliss at the same time? Before I am misunderstood, let me clarify that my point is not to see different fields as one and the same; but it is surely to see them as connected as opposed to neatly demarcated or sealed off from one another. My inquiry is directed not to this or that specific domain of life defined as a watertight compartment but to life itself insofar as life and death are interlinked. And it is here that I find Faruqi's conceptualization of critique seriously crippling to the pursuit of my aims.

Rejecting the connections between life and literature (*adab*) and critique and life, Faruqi (2010, 13) contends that such claims have arisen because of an "inferiority complex." As he wants to seal off literature from nonliterature and life at large,[9] he likewise aims to limit critique to literature alone. This notion of critique enjoys an almost universal consensus in Urdu writings. The only notable exception is probably Kalimuddin Ahmad (1909–83), a well-known and controversial critic. Though writing about literary critique, he offered a comprehensive notion of critique that is relevant to my goal:

> Without *tanqīd* [critique] life is impossible in the same way as we would die if we stopped breathing. . . . Each and every domain of life feels its power and impact. . . . There is hardly a moment in life when we don't make critical [*tanqīdī*] judgments. . . . Everywhere and in everything it is our critical capacity that guides us. Whether a judge or a thief, a commoner or a trader, a scientist or a craftsman, a lawyer or a doctor, a soldier or a philosopher, even a prostitute, all are steeped in critique [*naqd v intiqād*] and the success of each depends on whether or not the person correctly employs his or her critical capacity and integrity.
>
> For a long time *tanqīd* has been used in limited and specialized senses. Until now it has been confined to the realm of literary critique alone. Therefore, whenever it is presented in its comprehensive meaning it is necessarily perceived as something extraordinary. Literary critique is just one among the countless other forms of critique, though it is probably the highest one. (Kalimuddin Ahmad 2006, 34–35)

My recourse to Kalimuddin Ahmad is purposive. I aim to go past the restrictive notion of critique as developed by Faruqi, "the T. S. Eliot of Urdu criticism" (Tompkins 2013). This by no means implies my agreement with other aspects of Ahmad's thought, such as his description of *ghazal* as "semibarbaric" (Mazhari 2013; Samiuddin 2007, 20). I invoke Ahmad only to support my contention that the idea and practice of critique are equally relevant and important to social, cultural, and political realms. Indeed, Ahmad (2006, 39) held that specialization in knowledge is a compulsion, for all branches of knowledge are interrelated in the same way that life can't be divided into endless tiny grooves.

The final element of consensus is that critique originated in Greece. Many books open with the names of Socrates, *Soqrāṯ* (d. 399 BC), Plato, *Aflāṯūn* (d. 347 BC), and Aristotle, *Arasṯū* (d. 322 BC). Having emerged in Greece, so goes the story, critique was transferred to India as a result of Western/British rule. The journey begins in the nineteenth century but is traced back to seventeenth- and eighteenth-century Europe (Akhtar 2014; Ansari 1968; Barelvi 1970; Faruqi 2010, 2004; Husain 1965; Hasan n.d.; Nomani 1970a; Suroor 2011). Much discussion revolves around literary figures like Matthew Arnold (1822–88), F. R. Leavis (1895–1978), I. A. Richards (1893–1979), T. S. Eliot (1888–1965), and so on. Kalimuddin Ahmad studied in the United Kingdom and attended Richards's lectures. Ahmad credited Leavis with making him a critic (Mazhari 2013, 50).

After the names of British literary figures appear the names of Urdu ones, some of whom I have already discussed—for example, Hali and Azad. The year 1857—when the first unsuccessful anticolonial resistance took place—appears as a benchmark in whose aftermath much discussion unfolds.

Vazir Agha's (2011) *Tanqīd avr jadīd Urdu tanqīd* exemplifies best the linearity of this narrative with specific geographies. Divided in two, the first section of the book is titled "Tanqīd." Its three chapters offer a background to critique, a discussion of critique in the West, and a long summary derived from the first two chapters. The focus in this section is squarely on the origin and development of critique in the West; here there is no conceptual mention of the non-West. The second section, titled "Jadīd Urdu tanqīd [modern Urdu critique]," is composed of five chapters delineating the background of critique in Urdu, its beginning, its temporal perspective, its spatial perspective, and critique in modern Urdu. In Agha's narrative, critique begins in Greece and the West (where the non-West is absent); hence he places it in a section tightly separated from the next one, where critique in Urdu develops only because and under the influence of the West. Nurul Hasan Naqvi's ([1990] 2013, 7) *Fann-e-tanqīd v tanqīd negārī* treads the same path, even as Agha began with the observation that the first human on Earth might have had the capacity to critique.

◆ Elements of an Alternative Genealogy

This temporally fixed, territorially unified, thematically enclosed, and linear pedigree (in contradistinction to genealogy as developed by Nietzsche; see Nietzsche 2003; Foucault 1972; and Geuss 1999) of critique that Agha rehearses has rarely been questioned. Two scholars who have done so tangentially are Salim Akhtar and Arifa Subh Khan, the latter relying on the former's *Tanqīdī dabistān*, published in 1973. Khan shifts the locus of the beginning of critique from Greece to 1000 years earlier in ancient Egypt. To support this claim, Khan (2009, 35, 70), marshalling Akhtar, cites a passage from Khakheperresenb. Khan dates the text of Khakheperresenb, who lived in Pharaonic Egypt, to 1990 BC (cf. Krystal 2002, 30, which dates it to 2000 BC). Leaving aside that Khan (2009, 70) elsewhere in the same book contrarily repeats the consensus that "the real origin of Urdu critique is . . . Greek critique," she doesn't say what one achieves, analytically, by predating critique to Khakheperresenb. If the objective is to prove that the Egyptians were far ahead of the Greeks, that is far from laudatory. Giambattista Vico (d. 1744) warned us long ago that all nations have had "the foolish conceit of having been ahead of all the others in discovering the good things of human life and of having memories of their affairs that go back to the beginning of the world" (qtd. in Herzfeld 1987, vi). In my view, an interrogation of the topos of Greece as the locus classicus of critique should be undertaken to examine the very idea of the "West," the identity of which is predicated on producing the category of the "non-West," often assumed and asked to imitate the West in order to join the march of "civilization."

In his influential and unsurprisingly contested *Black Athena*[10]—a planned tetralogy of which three volumes have been published (in 1987, 1991, and 2006)—Martin Bernal examined the "origins of ancient Greece," which, Herzfeld (1987, 25) notes, is considered to be the site of "European aboriginality" or the "primordial ancestor" of the West/Europe. Bernal's aim was not only to "rethink the fundamental bases of 'Western Civilization' but also to recognize the penetration of racism and 'conventional chauvinism' into all our historiography, or philosophy of writing history." He sought to "lessen European arrogance and to attack myths of [the West's] purity" (qtd. in Cohen 1993, 21). The epigraph of the introduction to volume 3 reads, "Mixture is the ultimate engine of growth in society" (Bernal 2006, 1). Bernal's thesis was categorical. There are two models of the origins of Greece: the Ancient and the Aryan. The Ancient model, based on classical Greeks' accounts, held that their forefathers lived happily until "people from Egypt and Phoenicians arrived . . . and introduced civilization." To Bernal, this model prevailed until the Aryan model was introduced in the late eighteenth century, according to which "Greek civilization is the product of conquest from the north by . . . Aryans." Thus, German scholars from the late eighteenth century began to contend that "the Greeks had invented philosophy." The Aryan model aimed to eradicate the "unanimous opinion" that the Greeks had "learned philosophy from the Egyptians" (Bernal, qtd. in Cohen 1993, 1). According to Bernal, the triumph of the Aryan model was due to external factors: "Romanticism, the revival of Christianity, and . . . a persisting racism (ibid., 2)."

Bernal the historian's challenging thesis is supported, if perversely, by Herzfeld the anthropologist's ethnographic work on modern Greece. Though many educated Greeks were outraged by Bernal's thesis that Hellenic culture is and was influenced by Afro-Asian templates (Herzfeld 2002, 917), others held that Greeks "have either never attained or never desired" a European identity (Herzfeld 1987, 18). Herodotus, "the first anthropologist"[11] in one account, himself was far from sure if "Scythians—a buffer zone between Greeks and true barbarians—were truly European in a cultural or even a geographical sense." Importantly, in the nineteenth century western Europeans saw Greece as an "outpost of the Orient." Herzfeld (1987, 19, 54, 55) tellingly captures this paradox: "Greece . . . was a child of its antique past, one that has failed to mature in the manner of the West."

If philosophy was not born in Greece/the West, as new accounts tell us, neither was democracy. The assumption that democracy was born in Athens is plainly false. In *The Life and Death of Democracy,* Keane questions the doxa by arguing that the candle of assembly-based democracy was lit first in the "East," in areas constituting present-day Syria, Iraq, and Iran—a point also made by Jack Goody (2006, 288). From there it spread westward to Athens. The Greeks didn't invent democracy; they plagiarized it. The claim that democracy emerged in Greece and, therefore, as "something unique to the West," writes Keane (2009, x–xi), was made as a "sign of its [Western] superiority over the 'barbarism' of the East."

The purpose of the preceding pages is not to suggest that Greece made no contributions to civilizational flourishing but to destabilize its sacralized ancestry, linearity, and fixity woven into a Eurocentric project of domination. Similarly, Europeans were not the only ones to engage with and benefit from Greek heritage and philosophy. Commenting that philosophers such as Charles Taylor, Alasdair MacIntyre, and Charles Larmore limited themselves to the "so-called European tradition," Hallaq (2013, 5, 173n17) instructively adds, "'so-called' because Plato and Aristotle were no more 'European' than they were 'Islamic,' a matter evident to any scholar of Islam." In fact, Muslim philosophers engaged with Greek philosophy so thoroughly that they christened Aristotle "the first teacher, *muʿallim al-avval*" (Alwishah and Hays 2015, 1), al-Farabi (d. 950) being the second one (Mahdi 2001, 125).[12] And long before Western domination, Mulla Wajhi (1953, 7), a seventeenth-century Indian writer, described Sultan Abdullah (r. 1626–72) of Deccan as a "disciple of Aflāṭūn in *ḥikmāt* [philosophy]." Though well-known, it is worth recalling that Europe's rise was enabled by the adoption of scholarship and scientific research advanced by the Arabs. Based on Robert Briffault's *The Making of Humanity* (1911), Muhammad Iqbal (1934, 123–25), among others, articulated this viewpoint long ago. As for Europe's interests in classical philosophy, those too were translated into Latin "from the Arabic and they were accompanied by translations of Aristotle's Muslim commentators" (MacIntyre 2009, 43).

Acknowledging Muslims' engagement with Greek philosophy, Rémi Brague, a French philosopher, however, makes a curious argument. In *Eccentric Culture: A Theory of Western Civilization,* Brague asks if there is something unique about the European culture in relation to Islam. Setting aside the nature of this question, he answers it as follows. Europe's distinction vis-à-vis Islam lies in the ways each has treated the foreign (the other) "cultural heritage" (Brague 2002, 93, 107) preceding Islam and Christianity. By cultural heritage, he means the intellectual and literary accomplishments of Greek and Latin scholars. For Brague, what is important is not only the content of classical philosophy but also the Greek and Latin media through which the heritage was articulated. He argues that Christian Europe had the Bible in Latin, not in Hebrew. Likewise, the sources of European culture lay in another exteriority—Greek philosophy. Central to this process of appropriation of the other by Europe/Christianity was what he calls "inclusion." The other was included without destroying it. That is, the other was appropriated both in its contents and its media. The Muslims' approach, however, was marked by what he calls "digestion." Digestion appropriates the other by absorbing the contents and casting off the form or medium. Muslims engaged with the other by assimilating the contents of Greek philosophy but remained uninterested in its form, the Greek language. Philosopher Avicenna didn't make commentary on Aristotelian science as this would entail retaining the original Greek. He paraphrased and rewrote the original (and thus killed it). Aristotelianism became synonymous with Avicennism. As a result, maintains Brague, whereas Greek and Latin survived Christianity, Muslims' belief in the Qurʾān as a miracle led them to digest both languages, thereby eliminating the other.

Brague's thesis raises many issues. Prior to Islam and Christianity, there were cultures other than Greek. Why, for example, would Egyptian, Phoenician, Buddhist, or Hindu religion/philosophy fall outside "cultural heritage"? How about Chinese philosophy (Goody 2006, 37)? What power is at play in Brague's notion of cultural heritage? Is it anthropological? What is Europe? What goal are Brague's philosophical gestures tailored for? Is not Brague's question (that is, thesis) ethnic/nationalist at its core, formulated to institute and assert Europe's distinctiveness/superiority vis-à-vis Islam (see chap. 2)?

To buttress his claim, Brague cites Friedrich Schlegel: "The Arabs are . . . annihilators among the nations. The mania they had of erasing the originals . . . when the translation was finished characterizes the spirit of their philosophy. . . . For the barbarian is indeed he who is at the same time anti-classical and anti-progressive." Having cited and mobilized Schlegel for his argument, Brague (2002, 104–5) rushes to clarify that Schlegel's "value judgment" can be detached from "fact." Can there be an irony greater than this that Brague, whose entire argument is built on the inseparability between medium and content (that is, Christians kept both while Muslims took only the latter), announces, almost in a panic, the surgical separability between "value judgment" and "fact"?

◆ ◆ ◆

So far, in the second section of this chapter, I have interrogated the standard doxa of critique, which invariably traces its origin to ancient Greece. I have showed inconsistency, paradox, and multiple erasures in the doxa by also including antistandard accounts of the origins of democracy in Greece as well as deeper tensions in the self-perception of modern Greeks vis-à-vis whether or not they are European/Western. I then argued that Christians/Europeans were not the only ones to engage with Greek heritage and philosophy. I argued that Brague's contention that Christian/European engagement with Greek heritage, in contrast to Muslim engagement of the same, was unique is broadly of a piece that establishes Western superiority vis-à-vis Muslims/the non-West as barbarians—a line of thought Bernal, Keane, and Herzfeld contested for its Eurocentrism so as to pave the way for scripting a democratic narrative of the world and its cultures. Having liberated the notion of critique from an inevitable and linear pedigree to the West—at the same time cognizant of power at its disposal to monopolize its self-representation—the stage is now set to write an alternative genealogy of critique.

◆ Religion and Literature: Believing Ghalib

I began this chapter by showing how the dominant historiographies saw the onset of Urdu literature and criticism as a secular enterprise unhooked from and in opposition to the comprehensive premodern notion of *adab*. On the margins of this dominant historiography, however, rests, if precariously, a strand that disavows such a separation. Pejoratively called *mullā* (fundamentalist/conservative) *adab* and looked down upon by their secular counterparts, litterateurs on this margin read history and the present differently. Religion is a central but by no means the only element of their counternarratives. The emic term for their own enterprise is "constructive literature [*tāʿmīrī adab*]." The works of some who don't subscribe to this label may still resonate with the framework of constructive literature.[13]

For constructive literature's proponents, literature is connected to religion. But this is not to say that religion is literature and literature is religion (see below). To them, all religious books of the world *also* have literary merits: the Rāmāyaṇa, Mahābẖārata, Taurēt (Torah), Injīl (Gospel), or Qur'ān (Sajjad 1994, 96; Usmani 1999, 38). Furthermore, seldom is any great literature delinked from spiritual goals, moral imperatives, or Sufi influence. The respective visions of religion and the notion of morality permeate the literary works of figures as diverse as Hassan Bin Sabit, Hafiz, Rumi, Jami, Sadi, Firdausi, Tulsi, Kabir, Mir, Ghalib, Iqbal, Hasrat, and Faani. Given the connection between religion and literature, they reject the nomenclature "religious prose" that is often used to describe the prose, inter alia, of Sir Sayyid Ahmad Khan (1817–98), Shibli Nomani (d. 1914), Abul Kalam Azad (d. 1958), and Maududi. If their prose is merely religious, asks Abdul Mughni (1981, 79), then what constitutes literary prose?

In the history of Urdu literature, Burhanuddin Jaanam's (mid-sixteenth-century) *Kalimatul haqāʾq* (Matthews 1993 , 83; Mohamed 1968, 52–53) stands excluded as prose on account of its religious theme (Quadri n.d., 1; also see Azmi n.d.), whereas Mulla Wajhi's *Sabras* of 1635 (Haq 1953, 5) is taken as the first work of prose because of its "nonreligious" nature. Wajhi was a scholar and Sufi; his prose was interspersed with Arabic, Farsi, Gujarati, Marathi, Sanskrit, and words from Hindi and Urdu. To Quadri, it is too easy to wedge a rupture between Wajhi's "religious" thought and his "nonreligious" work. Wajhi's story about beauty and love, the theme of *Sabras*, is prefaced with a religious idiom and anchored in a divine framework, as is his *Tājul haqāʾq*, which explicitly deals with "morals and Sufism" (Haq 1953, 4). At stake here is thus the very notion of religion, which secularist accounts of Urdu literature presuppose and disown in a single brushstroke. In this account, religion equals orthodoxy, immobility, intolerance, and narrowness. While these features are assumed to be common to all religions, Islam as an "alien" religion typifies the commonality. If Muslims speak of humanity, practice tolerance toward other faiths, or express doubts, they can't be orthodox Muslims; they must be *Indian* Muslims. That is, Muslim "fanaticism"—a standard trope in British/orientalist literature shared by Indian scholars (Almond 2015), including some Muslims—is lessened only by the syncretic culture of India, central to which is Hinduism (Ahmad 2017). This assumption is fundamental to the celebration of Asadullah Khan Ghalib, who is tolerant not because of Islam, but in spite of Islam.

In *The Famous Ghalib*, Ralph Russell (2015), a well-known Western interpreter of Ghalib, writes, "[Ghalib] uses one of the central tenets of Islam—belief in the oneness of God—but he turns it into a call for humanity to transcend religious divisions." As readers may have already noticed, Russell presumes that monotheism opposes humanity and from there proceeds to describe Ghalib's greatness with the conjunction "but." This gigantic "but" says more about Russell's premise than about Ghalib's. Elsewhere he says that "Hinduism was particularly unacceptable to orthodox Muslims" (Russell 2015, 91). Were Al-Beruni and Abul Kalam Azad not orthodox to see Hinduism differently from what Russell allocates to the orthodox (without evidence, of course)? The *Encyclopedia of Islam* (Brill) is considered more explicit: "He [Ghalib] was not even passionately concerned with the Muslim religion, and his broad and tolerant attitude in this respect is shown in a letter to Munshī Hargopāl Tāfta, to whom he writes: 'I hold all human beings, Muslim, Hindu or Christian, dear to me, and regard them as my brothers'" (Bausani 2012).

Ghalib's broadmindedness, emanating from his distance with Islam,[14] is partly also explained in terms of his confession to be a wine-drinker. Thus, like Russell, Alessandro Bausani can see Ghalib's tolerance toward various faiths only because he is projected as far removed from Islam, not because of Islam. Gopi Chand Narang, a noted critic, also holds such a view of Ghalib: "Although Ghalib came from outside [central Asia], the reality is that Ghalib's nature was made from the soil of India." Narang continues: "His independence, broad-mindedness, and religious cosmopolitanism are deeply connected to Indian culture and mind." As evidence, Narang cites Ghalib's respect for festivals of other faiths. After quoting one of Ghalib's couplets, Narang (2002, 1, 7, 10) stresses that "this couplet has been composed especially for India." India is presented as uniquely multireligious, as if the rest of the world, including the "outside" Ghalib came from, was monoreligious. Narang cites a quartet to show how Ghalib loved India. It is unclear to me if Ghalib's notions of love and India are the same as Narang's, for Ghalib predates political, majoritarian nationalism. Whatever the differences between Faruqi and Narang might be on other issues, the nationalization of poetry and externalization of Islam make them intimately united. In the hands of Narang, Faruqi's "Indian mind" gets made in the "soil of India." Mediated by religion, the mind is soiled and the soil mentalized, and both ultimately are nationalized.

However, Abdul Mughni, a sympathizer of constructive literature, read Ghalib and religion alternatively. Ghalib's broadmindedness, he argued, reflected his attachment to, not departure from, religion. Contra the consensus that he was a *rind*, Mughni read him as a *qalandar*. Though Mughni didn't elaborate its meanings, it is worth noting that *rind* in Farsi and Urdu means not only "wine-drinker" but also "unbridled," one whose outward action is defective but whose inner self (*bāṯin*) is fine (*Fīrozulloghāt* 2014, 761). And *bāṯin* is the center of one's worldview—how one comprehends the universe, the place of humans, the meanings of life and death, and relations among humans, nonhumans, and nature at large. Religion is not simply about rituals, dos and don'ts. Followers of a religion endeavor to approximate its ideals. But not all individuals succeed, or to the same degree. In the case of some intellectuals and poets, their worldview and personal actions may diverge. To single out specific acts, to isolate certain couplets and read them as a negation of religion, results from a crooked understanding of humans, religion, and poetic metaphors. Ghalib's

(1993, 167–68) *ghazal* with wine (*ḥavas-e-nā'ye v nōsh*), taste for lust (*lazzat-e-kām v dehen*), and so on are more a confession of his own frailty than a worship thereof. In fact, Ghalib notes the ephemerality of such desires to underline the salience of eternity after death. The entire *ghazal*, argues Mughni (1988), is *naṣiḥat* (moral advice) exemplifying the old Farsi adage *Man na kardam, shumā ḥuzr be kunīd* (I could not refrain, but you should refrain from such undesirable things). Such acts as Ghalib himself admits do not dislodge his faith, for he also famously mused, "With what face, Ghalib, will you go to the Kaaba? Don't you have a sense of shame?"

This doesn't mean a believer doesn't doubt—there is hardly any atheist evacuated of all beliefs or any believer without any doubts. Ghalib is no exception. The vacillation between Kaaba and church (*kalīsa*) is as much an expression of Ghalib's personal doubt as it is of the massive turmoil in Indian civilization following British conquest in 1857, which Ghalib witnessed as a disempowered poet-philosopher. Even in the face of a "more systematic reign of terror" by the British, culminating in Delhi as "the city of the dead" and the "destruction of Hindustan" (Pritchett 1994, 19, 21; Bell 2004), Ghalib didn't abandon hope for a civilization in ruins. He continued writing a love story stained with blood even after his hands had been chopped off. Many of his couplets show how for the sake of freedom he even desired to sacrifice life, life gifted by God. For Ghalib, to continue to keep the lamp of that civilization lit was as sacred as the Kaaba itself, to the extent that the struggle engaged in by a Brahmin with firm faith is as laudatory as the struggle by a Muslim: hence his plea that a priest who died in his temple be buried in the Kaaba. In poetic moves such as these Ghalib indeed enacted Islam to show the oneness of humanity as children of Adam and Eve. In Ghalib, thought flowers into poetic beauty, and beauty pledges loyalty to the civilizational pathos he philosophically sought to address. His poetry is a mainspring of both aesthetic bliss (*musarrat*) and philosophy (*baṣīrat*) (Mughni 1988, 37, 41–42).

For the proponents of constructive literature—contra, for instance, Faruqi (1981, 106), who regards Iqbal's "philosophical" works as poor, even impoverished—aesthetics and philosophy are not oppositional entities; they can and often they do go together. To Sajjad, one such proponent, aesthetic expression undoubtedly is central to any literature. However, he reminds his readers that it is disconnected from neither thought nor the divine: "Allah is beautiful [*ḥasīn*] and He loves beauty" (Sajjad 1981, 94; see also Sajjad 1994, 116). A key distinction usually made between the literary and the nonliterary is that the former privileges "how it is said" (*oslūb*, aesthetic expression) over "what is said" (*mavād*, content). However, this privileging does not work uniformly across all genres. Abul Kalam Qasmi (1981, 36–37) observes that while it is more appropriate for poetry, in a short story (*afsānā*) content is no less important. Qasmi's point permeates the framework of constructive literature, if only in an accentuated, and at times perverse, way.

If content/thought/philosophy and aesthetics, literature, and religion are not as neatly separate or separable as the purist partisans of literature hold, for the proponents of constructive literature nor are religion and critique. In fact, for them critique is rooted in and emanates from religion, and its locus is neither Greece nor the West but God Himself. It is to this genealogy that we turn to complete the task of this chapter. Here I will draw on the writings of Maududi, his sympathizers, and those who critiqued him.

◆ Divine Critique

The successive prophets Allah sent were critics of their respective social orders. All these prophets—from Adam through Nūḥ (Noah), Ibrāhīm (Abraham), Yusuf (Joseph), ʿIsā (Jesus), Mūsā (Moses), and up to Muhammad—brought the same message of Allah. The Qurʾān describes the mission of all prophets as that of enacting reform (*iṣlāḥ*). Thus in the Qurʾān (11, 88), the prophet Shuʿayb stated, "I desire only *al-iṣlāḥ* as far as I am able" (qtd. in Ahmad 2015d, 147; Al-Musleh 2007). Integral to the prophetic mission of *iṣlāḥ* was critique. To reform was indeed to critique and vice versa.[15] This mission is also acknowledged in the Talmud and the Bible, the study of which reveals that the prophets of Bani Israel (Children of Israel) endeavored to reform the social orders of their time and "mounted a full-blown critique [*tanqīd*] of the wrong leadership" (Khursheed Ahmad 1991, 18). The prophet Mūsā's very act of going to the pharaoh to deliver the message of monotheism and secure freedom for the children of Israel from the pharaoh's tyranny was a critique par excellence. So was his reply to the pharaoh: "And [as for] that favor of which thou so tauntingly remind me—[was it not] due to thy having enslaved the children of Israel?" (Maududi 1982, 36, 42; Muhammad Asad's translation). The subsequent reform initiative by ʿOzair (Ezra) was precisely to renew Mūsā's message. The prophet Isā continued the work of reform and critique by confirming and renewing the same message as Mūsā.[16] So did Prophet Muhammad (Maududi 1982, 151–52, 168–69).

Prophet Muhammad never made a claim that he founded a new religion. Islam, therefore, didn't begin in the seventh century. He claimed that he had brought the "same religion which the prophets Isā, Mūsā, Ibrāhīm, and Nūḥ had brought" (Maududi 1982, 548–49). Also, he didn't claim that the teachings of the prophets Isā and Mūsā were thoroughly eliminated, only that the complete message was lost or forgotten. Prophet Muhammad thus sought to renew the old message through reform and critique. He critiqued the prevalent tenets, practices, and traditions of the Meccan social order not to dissolve but to reconfigure them in accordance with the earlier message of God. If Jews opposed Muhammad, they did so not because he negated the teaching of Moses but because he confirmed the truth of Christianity as well. Likewise, if Christians opposed Muhammad they did so because he also endorsed the teaching of Moses. Prophet Muhammad didn't ask people of other religions to jettison their respective faiths but to get back to and rescue the authentic teachings of their own religions because their message, when revealed, was the same. He didn't introduce a new religion; he reminded people of what was already there (Azad 2004 [1968], 433–34). And as the pharaoh rejected Moses's message in the name of sticking to the ways of "our fathers," so did the chiefs of Mecca vis-à-vis Muhammad's message.

Clearly, in this conceptual scheme, God Himself is not—can never be—the subject of critique. How about the prophets? The constitution of Jamaat, as Maududi (1942, 173) determined it, outlined an obligatory expectation on the part of the person joining it that she or he "does not make anyone except Allah's Prophet [*rasūl*] the yardstick [*me'ār*] of truth [*ḥaq*], does not consider any one above critique [*tanqīd*], and is not engaged in the mental enslavement of anyone." This constitutional clause notwithstanding, many held that some parts of Maududi's writings were tantamount to critiquing the prophets too (Yusuf 1999 [1964], 77). This became a matter of heated controversy, and thousands of pages were written as *tanqīd*, by opponents as well as partisans of Maududi and Jamaat-e-Islami.

In responding to the doubt expressed by a reader of *Tarjumānul Qur'ān* about the story of the prophet Dāūd (David) mentioned in the Qur'ān (sura Ṣ, 38), Maududi (1938, 56–57), having offered various other explanations, gives his own:

> These individuals probably haven't thought about this matter—that in fact the notion of innocence [*'iṣmat*] of prophets doesn't concern their personas but the responsibilities of prophethood that Allah has protected them from errors and mistakes [*k̲h̲aṭāoñ avr lag̲h̲zishōñ*]. Otherwise, if the protection from Allah is lifted mistakes can be committed by prophets too, in the same way as ordinary Muslims do. This is a delicate point that

> by lifting His protection Allah has let one or two mistakes be committed by every prophet [*nabī*] so that people don't consider prophets as God and they know that prophets are human.

Husain Ahmad Madni, a noted scholar of Deoband, sharply critiqued the above statement, questioning if Maududi and his organization were Muslims in the first place: "To what extent is this creed [of Maududi], . . . where in the statement 'every prophet' also includes Prophet Muhammad and it is believed that Allah lifted His protection from each prophet and allowed some mistakes to happen in accordance with the principle and creed of Islam? In such a situation no prophet could remain the yardstick of truth. . . . Tell me, if this disagreement is fundamental or peripheral, and tell me, if Jamaat-e-Islami and its founder are Muslims or not!" (qtd. in Yusuf 1999 [1964], 74).

From the passage in the constitution of Jamaat I cited earlier, some critics of Maududi also deduced that the companions (*ṣaḥābā*) of Prophet Muhammad were not above critique either. Thus the charge against Jamaat and Maududi included that they denied the prophets' innocence and did not place Muhammad's companions above critique. Maududi's and his sympathizers' responses were twofold. First, the innocence of prophets related to their protection from *m'āṣī* such as lies, disbelief, and other major sins. This does not include *zallāt* (in Arabic), which approximates in Urdu as *laghzish* and *ghalaṭī* (minor errors and mistakes). Furthermore, this distinction is not new, as many reputed *'ulema* of yore maintained it and also held that prophets were prone to errors and mistakes. However, whenever such mistakes happened, the Qur'ān testifies that Allah immediately corrected them by way of *iṣlāḥ*[17] (through revelation, *vaḥī*), because He sent the prophets as a model for humans to emulate. Thus the goal of the reform-cum-critique (*iṣlāḥ*) for which Allah sent His prophets also applies to the prophets themselves when they committed such mistakes, including those of an *ijtīhādī* (adjective from *ijtīhād*) nature (Maududi 1944, 21–22; Maududi 1951, 85; 1954, 291–92, 298–99; Yusuf 1999 [1964], 44–68). As for critique of the companions, Maududi reiterated that no humans, nonprophets including the companions, were above critique. Affirming his respect for the companions, he stressed that the approach of scholars who concealed their mistakes or didn't discuss them was unreasonable, for it went against justice and scholarly investigation (Maududi 2001a, 284). More important, he observed that his critics did not sufficiently understand what *tanqīd* meant. They took it to mean discovering demerits in a person or his or her work. But the correct meaning of critique, as the learned know, is to assess and to evaluate: *jāñchnā/parakhnā* (Maududi 1956a, 186–87).

Naqd, the Arabic word from which *tanqīd* is derived, also means "cash." In Arabic dictionaries, as in Arabic proverbs, it originally meant to examine to determine whether a currency (*dirham/dīnār*) is genuine or counterfeit. That is, to discern the genuine from the fake. In Urdu this meaning is also retained: to determine if a coin is genuine or counterfeit (*kẖaḍē avr kẖōtē meṅ tamīz karnā*). However, in some Arabic proverbs, it is also used in the sense of demerit/defect/defamation, *ʿēb* (Nadvi 1990, 27–29; Matin 2001, 18–20; Mehdi 1999, 17–19; Yusuf 1999 [1964], 199–200). This specific meaning has nearly no acceptability in modern Urdu usage (even though some might pursue the second meaning in the guise of the first one). As I am concerned here with critique and religion, it is important to explore if the Qurʾān stipulates principles about critique, and, if so, how.

In his book-length critique of Maududi, Vahiduddin Khan, an erstwhile member of India's Jamaat whom we will meet in chapter 5, takes the Qurʾān as a source of and inspiration for critique. Justifying his critique in the preface to second edition of his book, he cites verse twenty-six of the *sura sajda* and refers to Abdullah Ibn Abbas, for whom وَالْغَوْا فِيهِ was similar to *ʿēb* in its plural. In light of Abbas's translation, Khan (1995 [1963]: 12) observes that there are two modes of expressing one's viewpoint: (1) through critique (*tanqīd*) and (2) by finding fault or defaming someone (*tāʿeīb*). The mode of *tanqīd*—to assess and reject a viewpoint based on clear arguments—is Islamic. The mode of *tāʿeīb* is, however, clearly anti-Islamic; in the eyes of the Qurʾān it is the way of the disbelievers.

Shahnavaz Faruqi (2014), a sympathizer of Maududi, however, differentiates *tanqīd* from other associated practices: *tanqīṣ* (to search for demerits or defects), *taḥqīr* (to show someone in a poor light), *tazḥīk* (to mock), and *takfīr* (to declare someone a disbeliever). He rejects the term *tanqīd* for most reactions against Maududi because if they were genuine critiques, he notes, they would have advanced thought. To Faruqi, they were less critique and more *tanqīṣ*, *taḥqīr*, *tazḥīk*, and *takfīr*. All these forms of responses, including *tāʿeīb*—popularly but erroneously construed as critique—are against the spirit and tradition of Islam. In particular, the Qurʾān (*sura Ḥujrāt*, 12) disapproves of seeking to find fault in others and indulging in backbiting. Many sayings of Prophet Muhammad condemn finding *ʿēb* in others (Yusuf 1999 [1964], 201–3, 246). In this category also falls *takhfīf*, misrepresenting a complex viewpoint by deleting or reducing it to a singular standpoint that the commentator aims to critique. Amir Usmani (1920–75), a scholar of Deoband, editor of the journal *Tajallī* and an ardent defender of Maududi (see chap. 6), wrote a critique of Sayyid Ahmad Bijnauri, a senior fellow Deobandi. In his interpretation of the *sura Nūr*, Bij-

TABLE 1 Forms of intervention and their status

PRACTICE APPROVED OF BY ISLAM	
Tanqīd	critique/criticism
PRACTICES DISAPPROVED OF BY ISLAM	
Tāʿeīb	to find fault with or defame a person
Taḥqīr	to disrespect
Tanqīṣ	to find demerits
Tażḥīk	to mock
Takfīr	to denounce
Taḳhfīf	to minimize, to distort
*Tardīd**	to refute
*Tajhīl**	to show a person to be unlettered
Tʿarīf	to shower only praise on
Takbīr	to glorify

*See chapter 5.

nauri had charged Maududi with *tafarrud*, introducing a position that defies that of the majority of scholars. To Usmani, Bijnauri practiced *taḳhfīf*, for Maududi didn't claim to invent a new position. He outlined three existing positions and went on to say that "this is the third position and also a reasonable one" (which he endorsed). Another instance of *taḳhfīf* is found when Bijnauri cited Shabbir Usmani, a noted Pakistani scholar, on other issues but didn't cite him on the very issue that formed the basis of *tafarrud* against Maududi because, he notes, Shabbir Usmani's position was similar to Maududi's (Usmani 1973, 44–49). To Aslam Qasmi (2011, 14, 43), *tanqīd* is a middle line between *tanqīs* and *tʿarīf* (praise).

This obviously raises the crucial issue of what constitutes the basis on which to categorize a specific work as critique. Put differently, what is the center or paradigm (Hallaq 2013, 7) that critique presupposes and within which it conducts its activities?

The answer is sharia—the Qurʾān and Sunna. The legitimacy, desirability, motive, function, mode, and goal of critique ought to speak to the yardstick (*meʿār*) of truth (*ḥaq*), which sharia ultimately is (Maududi 1976b, 179–80; 1956, 186–91). And in sharia no human is above critique. Indeed, for Mufti Yusuf, a

Pakistani sympathizer of Maududi, even Khiẓr, no ordinary human being, is not above critique. *Sura Kahf* (18, 60–82) includes the famous story of Khiẓr and the prophet Mūsā. Though commentators disagree whether Khiẓr was a prophet or not, there is near unanimity that he was surely unlike any other human, as he was unique in possessing knowledge of the unseen, or *ghayb* (Albayrak 2003). Some hold that Khiẓr possessed certain knowledge (*ʿilm*) that even the prophet Mūsā lacked. Yet Mūsā "made critique [*tanqīd*] of Khiẓr right in his face." Even when the terms of friendship were breached, Mūsā didn't give up his critique of Khiẓr (Yusuf 1999 [1964], 211–12).[18] Though not clearly stated, Yusuf implies that Mūsā's critique of Khiẓr sprang from the yardstick of his own sharia[19] and the fact that Allah had sent the Torah through Mūsā.

The principles and practices of critique discussed above were also fully at work more recently than the story of Mūsā and Khiẓr. During the time of Prophet Muhammad and thereafter, vigorous and lively forms of critique ensued; indeed, there was a culture of critique. In place of four, once Muhammad offered only two units (*rikʿat*) of prayer. A companion asked him, "Have the units of prayer been reduced or was there a lapse on your part?" He verified it from others and completed the remaining two units. Prophet Muhammad pleasantly embraced critique. His companions also critiqued one another. To a questioner, Abu Musa Ashari described the details of how to divide inheritance in the case of a death. He also advised the questioner to consult Abdullah Bin Saud, who might endorse Ashari's view. Instead Saud critiqued it, arguing that endorsing it would amount to deviation from Prophet Muhammad's teaching. A more-often mentioned case is the exchange between Caliph ʿOmar and an ordinary woman who had no qualms in questioning and reprimanding him during his public address on what she regarded as his mistaken judgement. In the mosque in Medina she disagreed with and questioned ʿOmar's decision to place a cap on a dowry (of 400 dirhams, Maududi 2001a, 94). ʿOmar withdrew his decision in light of the woman's Qurʾān-based objection. Interesting to note is that the incident took place inside the mosque, with full attendance, and the person critiquing the caliph was a woman, a mere commoner. Not only did ʿOmar admit his fault, he also applauded his critic: "The people are more knowledgeable about the law than is ʿOmar" (qtd. in Stowasser 2001, 107). In another account, ʿOmar said, "A woman debated with ʿOmar and she won" (qtd. in Nadvi 1980, 26–27). In such critical exchanges gender was no barrier, nor were age and relations. Abdullah, ʿOmar's son, disagreed with and rejected his father's opinion on a specific aspect of the hajj and *ʿomra* in favor of Prophet Muhammad's position (Yusuf 1999 [1964], 219–20).

In acts of critique, however, it is not sufficient simply to state that what one thinks is more appropriate and correct. If the goal of critique is to reform (*iṣlāḥ*), then the manner in which critique is executed is no less important, for on it rests the likelihood of the intended reform. Prophet Muhammad's grandsons Hasan and Husain noticed that an aged person didn't correctly perform his ablution. Instead of telling him that his method was incorrect, they asked, "Uncle, could you judge which of the two of us does ablution properly?" The old man watched both the brothers perform their ablutions as they had seen their father Ali and grandfather do. When they had finished, the old man remarked, "Both of you did better than I did" (Gulen 2013). It is apt to call the act of critique by Hasan and Husain *tanqīd* by *tamśīl* (exemplification, perhaps even embodiment).

Forms of critique such as these and others not only continued but flourished. In response to a specific question, which expressed astonishment at the kind of critique he was engaged in, Maududi wondered if ever there was a time when critique had been considered illegitimate. "Pick up any book in the vast literature of *fiqh*," he advised the questioner, and "you will find thousands of examples of critique" (qtd. in Yusuf 1999 [1964], 298). Maududi's point was not limited to books. He saw critique in full flower in the social-political order presided over by Prophet Muhammad and his immediate successors. Of the many distinct features of that polity, an important one was "the complete freedom of critique [*tanqīd*] and freedom of expression," for it was an "elected caliphate" permeated with "the spirit of democracy" (Maududi 1960, 328, 3, 2001, 94). This in itself was possible because the caliphs were at once accountable and accessible to the people. People posed questions to those in power, not only through "a notice to the *shūra* committee [*Parliament*]" but five times each day when they appeared in the mosque and faced people. Every Friday, as well as during annual prayers, they had direct discussions with people. Day and night and without bodyguards, the caliphs visited the bazaar. On all such occasions, "everyone had the freedom to critique and hold them accountable." This freedom to critique was not a favor granted to the people by the rulers; it was a right gifted by Islam. The caliphs' thatched houses were not set apart from the public; they lived amid the common people. Caliph Usman faced the harshest criticism. In response, he issued public clarifications. Even when death threats were made against him, Caliph Ali embraced them as criticism, taking no action unless people tried to act on those threats (Maududi 2001a, 93–95, 1960, 328–32).

The martyrdom of Imam Husain was momentous not solely because of personal reason. His sacrifice and its salience were for the sake of a principle. Likewise, Yazid too represented a principle. The battle between Husain and

Yazid was indeed a battle between the elected caliphate and the initial monarchy, between freedom of thought and the silencing of it. It was the silencing of critique and freedom of thought in the form of monarchy associated with the policy of Yazid, Maududi observed, which began the downfall of that ideal polity. Yazid inaugurated a massive change in power-sharing: acquiring power through *bay'ah* (oath of allegiance) was changed into acquiring *bay'ah* through power. Freedom of thought and critique were stifled. Sycophancy replaced the recognition of merit and ability. People who stood for freedom of thought (*āzād ḵhayāl lōg*) were slowly expelled and silenced. *ʿUlema* who questioned such practices were punished, for example Imam Mālik, who was flogged and whose arms were amputated from his shoulders (Maududi 1960, 327–30).

Yet *ʿulema* (scholars)[20] such as Imam Malik continued the work of critique. This is not to say that some *ʿulema*, either willingly or under duress, didn't acquiesce to power, shunning their task of critique. But those who continued their work connected it to their roles as heirs of the prophets as a hadith stipulates. It is to the enactment and fulfilment of this role that Abul Hasan Ali Nadvi (1914–99), an ex-Jamaat member quoted in this chapter's epigraph (see also chap. 5), related his critique of Maududi. Crucial to the roles of *ʿulema* is the promotion of *maʿrūf* (right) and prohibition of *munkar* (wrong). So pivotal is this role that speaking truth to power has been described as a greater jihad. Stipulating the role of *ʿulema* as critics, Nadvi simultaneously invoked the "pre-Islamic poets" (Pellat 2012) of Ḥamāsa. What this demonstrates is that for Nadvi and many others, borrowing, citing, and benefiting from what is deemed as "non-Islamic" is not problematic. It also shows the continuing, though less intense, fallacy that Islam is particularly hostile to poetry and that a poet is as the antithesis of a prophet. This contention, made based on specific readings of certain hadith and the *sura shuʿraʾ*, misses the point according to which "a prophet is only a practical poet" (Matin 2001, 41–46; O'Donnell 2011; Sajjad 1994, 96, 111).

Nadvi's stress on the role of *ʿulema* as critics allows us to read the history of critique from a radically different perspective. If one of the roles of *ʿulema* has been to work for the promotion of *maʿrūf* and prohibition of *munkar* and thereby engage in acts of critique, then surely critique began neither with the rise of the West nor with the publication of Hali's *Muqaddamah-e-shaʿr-v-shāʿrī* in the nineteenth century. It began much earlier. So far I have elucidated the theological postulates and prophetic stories as the basis, source, and inspiration for critique. Two modern examples will be relevant here.

In histories of critique in South Asia seldom do we hear or read about Shaykh Ziauddin Makhdum, an Indian scholar who lived in the sixteenth century in the Malabar region of India. Confronted with an early phase of mercantile capitalism by the colonizing Portuguese, Makhdum composed *Tuḥfatul Mujāhidīn* in Arabic. In it, he showed how Malabari social formations had been radically affected by the Portuguese intrusion, including through the building of forts. Makhdum exhorted local inhabitants—Hindus, Muslims, and people of other faiths—to come together for jihad to resist the Portuguese. Makhdum's (2006) quasi-anthropological text is a critique of the Malabar political order as much as the Portuguese encroachment (cf. Dale 1988). If viewed from the framework I outline here, works of scholars like Shah Valiullah (1703–62) are equally works of critique. His *Ḥujjat Allāh al Bāligha* and *Moshāhidāt v maʿārif* and several other works in Arabic and Farsi are not mere theology (and its branches) as conventionally understood. They are works of critique, but we have not recognized them yet as such.

Critique is not only about life—almost an obsession in the Western intellectual traditions. It is also, if not equally, about death, which, believers hold, inaugurates a new life. If the task of critique and the role of critics are connected to observance of *maʿrūf* and *munkar* mentioned in the Qurʾān, they can't be disassociated from death, a central theme in the Qurʾān. Vahiduddin Khan (1995 [1963], 343), a critic of Jamaat and Maududi whom I earlier quoted, concluded his book with the invocation of the Judgment Day, when each and every human being will stand in front of God and truth will reveal itself in its entirety. Likewise, Manzur Nomani (1998, 158), one of the prominent Deoband *ʿulema* who wrote a critique of Maududi (see chap. 5), concluded his book as follows: "Whatever I have written I have done not to elicit a reply [from Jamaat] but, given my old age and impending death, with the hope for reform. . . . Further than this, the affair rests with Allah!" My aim is to note that death, no less than life, informs critique.

In the chapter to follow we discuss at length how critique worked in Maududi's enterprise—in his enormous scholarship as well as in his activism during and after the formation of Jamaat-e-Islami.

PART II
Illustration

4
THE MESSAGE
A Critical Enterprise

> I hold such views about Islam not because I was born into a Muslim family. . . . I had no attraction for that Islam which I found in the immediate Muslim society. After acquiring a capacity for critique and research [*tanqīd v taḥqīq*] the first thing I did was to throw off the belt [*qalādāh*],[1] of that spiritless religiosity which I had inherited.
>
> —MAUDUDI (1942, 14–16)

In conversations with historians, I have noted their inclination to stress continuity when we discuss a contemporary event or process. In contrast, anthropologists, sociologists, and political scientists are fond of announcing rupture from the past and using phrases such as "radical break," "momentous rupture," "notable shift," and so on. In Melbourne in 2009, I had a fruitful discussion with David Pritchard on contemporary democracy—the context being the U.S.-led invasions of Afghanistan and Iraq. As we discussed George W. Bush's Manichean language, Pritchard, a historian of classical Athens, suggested that Bush's language had much continuity with that of ancient Greece. He advised me to read the funeral oration of Pericles (495–429 BC), a prominent Athenian politician.[2] I read Pericles's oration online and found merit in Pritchard's advice. Yet, as an anthropologist/sociologist who values a historically informed narrative and is least seduced by presentism, I thought there was something *new* about the contemporary Western democracy.

My unease with either of the disciplinary orientations—sociology/anthropology and history—in some ways echoes the debate between Georges Gurvitch and Fernand Braudel. For Gurvitch, a sociologist at the Sorbonne, discontinuity and novelty were important. For instance, the Russian Revolution of 1917, which Gurvitch witnessed as a young man, was a decisive moment puncturing continuity. It heralded discontinuity, which he described in terms of erratic times as opposed to enduring times of continuity (Harris 2004; Hodges 2010). Though influenced by Gurvitch, Braudel held that his theorization was antihistoricist for he (wrongly) saw the present as "a more or less autonomous reality." "There can be no science," Braudel proclaimed, "without historical continuity" (qtd. in Harris 2004, 163, 164, 161). True to his commitment to continuity, Braudel averred that the French Revolution, like the Russian Revolution, didn't inaugurate a break. Olivia Harris (2004, 164) sums up the differences between Braudel and Gurvitch: "Sociology uses the data of history to show the discontinuity of social types. . . . History constructs continuity in order to bridge the ruptures identified by sociology." In the rest of her essay, Harris shows how Braudel's *longue durée* at times admitted rupture. He didn't reject discontinuity *tout court*; rather, he found it rare. Two such breaks in European history were the Neolithic and Industrial Revolutions. Importantly, Harris (2004, 172) also shows how Braudel saw his own work as marking a rupture, for he maintained that "to its author, every work seems revolutionary" and that "ideas advance . . . by ruptures."

The issue of continuity and rupture is at the center of our understandings of Islamic/Islamicate civilization in general and the revival, or what is now called "Islamism," in particular. Whereas sociologists/anthropologists and political scientists often write about it in terms of a break with the past, even a betrayal of history and tradition, orientalists and historians, usually of premodern times, often stress the continuity of and similarity with the past. An apt example of the former is Olivier Roy (1994, viii), who wrote, "Beginning in the 1930s, Hasan al-Banna . . . and Abul-Ala Maududi, the creator of the Indo-Pakistani Jamaat-e-Islami party, introduced a *new* movement of thought that endeavored to define Islam primarily as a political system, in keeping with the major ideologies of the twentieth century" (italics mine). To describe what Roy thinks of as "new," he uses words like "break" and "rupture." Thus, he writes, "Islamism was created both along the lines of and as a *break* from the *salafiyya*." He continues, "The Islamists engage in a social and political re-reading of the Qur'ān . . . made possible precisely by the *distortion of the Muslim tradition*." In so doing, Islamists, Roy (1994, 35, 40) asserts, institute a rupture with tradition: "The Islamist contribution (or *rupture*) with respect to the tradition consists in applying this theological concept to society, whereas previously it was related exclusively to God" (italics mine). The identification of rupture here is grounded in the distinction that while pre-Islamist Muslim tradition restricted theology to the domain of God, Islamists extend it to society. Historically, such a claim is hard to sustain, however. Pre-Islamist theological notions and practices very much impacted society, if by society we mean social relations constituted around trade, social exchange, marriage, property, family relations, gift-giving, the meanings and practices of life and death, and so on. Also, Roy's conceptualization of both God and society—undemarcated as they remain—seems to be very specific, implying no traffic between the two. It is not that Roy is entirely unmindful of classical tradition—elsewhere his text recognizes it, if only fleetingly—but he nonetheless theorizes it as a rupture. In a similar vein, political scientist Nazih Ayubi (1991, 3) avers that "political Islam is a new invention." Mark that it is not just an invention, but a *new* invention that "doesn't represent a 'going back' to any situation that existed in the past or to any theory that was formulated in the past." Mohammed Ayoob (2008, 2), another political scientist, sees Islamism as an "invention of tradition" and its employment of religious vocabulary as the "instrumentalization of Islam." This resonates with the anthropological reading by Fischer and Abedi (1990), who view Islamism as a surface phenomenon arising from deeper structural disparities. For Ayoob, as well as for Fischer and Abedi, the vocabulary of Islam is no more than an accidental medium expressing something else—economic discontent, institutional dislocation, and the legacy of colonial history. The question is: Is Islam a language which merely *expresses* or does it also *constitute* that something?

In a valuable critique of such works, Ovamir Anjum (2011, 46) urges scholars to pay simultaneous attention to contemporary context, premodern formations, and the tradition of Islam: "A proper understanding of what is called Islamism . . . is not possible without a serious engagement with the classical tradition of Islamic political thought and history. . . . More specifically, since contemporary Islamic groups persistently draw on various classical Islamic visions of a normative political order, and since the very memories and desires of the people in the Islamic world are shaped by and recorded in that tradition, continued examination of that tradition remains indispensable. In arguing this, I argue for an epistemic continuity between the pre-colonial and contemporary periods in the Islamic world." I find this suggestion important (it is more appropriate to speak of epistemic connection than continuity, perhaps). But actualizing it would require a diversity of expertise and labor. An individual possessing multiple disciplinary skills about premodern and modern formations—intellectual, social-political, and religious—is not easy to find. My own training as a sociologist and anthropologist restricts me from pursuing this task, especially in relation to premodern history and the largely Arabic-based textual corpus. Yet, here I wish to pursue it. Working on this book has forced me to take the Islamic discursive tradition more seriously and in its own right than I did in my earlier works (Ahmad 2009a, 2009b). Maududi, his followers, and their critics draw on, pledge their allegiance to, and work within as well as expand and critique that historical tradition, which needs to be recognized. As this chapter and subsequent ones will demonstrate, the critique I discuss shows moments of ruptures but, as MacIntyre (1988, 356) noted, "some core of shared belief, constitutive of allegiance to the tradition, has to survive every rupture." Notably, the issue of rupture and continuity is constitutive of and emanates from the very critiques I discuss; it is not a label imposed from without.

In order to grasp Maududi's message, that is, his understanding of the prophetic message, this chapter lays out facets of the larger frame and methods that undergird his thought. It begins by dereifying hegemonic depictions of Maududi as a "fundamentalist" and viewing him instead as a political thinker. Next it demonstrates how the use of reason, critique, and *ijtihād* were basic to his exposition on Islam. To demonstrate their centrality, I focus on his educational thought and his critical evaluation of contributions from past *ʿulema*—ʿOmar bin Abdul Aziz, Imam Ghazali, Ibn Taymiyyah, Shaykh Ahmad Sirhindi, and Shah Valiullah and his successors. In the final section, I describe the metaphysical assumptions of Maududi's thought about cosmology, human nature, and civilization, so as to situate the goal of Jamaat-e-Islami, namely, the formation of a polity inspired by God's teaching that he first called "Allah's rule." Here I also discuss Maududi's citations from the New Testament and reference to Christ's life to show how Muhammad's message resembled that of earlier prophets, including Jesus. This outline of Maududi's thought is purposive, as it highlights elements that his critics found controversial. If my account appears "sympathetic" to some readers, this is simply because my aim is to first describe Maududi's thought (as far as possible in his own words) before subjecting it to multiple critiques in the chapters to follow.

◆ Maududi Dereified

Any discussion of Maududi ought to begin by noting that his views were far from monolithic and static. "Indeed, there is not a single Mawdudi" (Ahmad 2013a, 334). The writings of young and early Maududi are significantly different from those of late Maududi, as there are differences, perhaps even tensions, between early and late Maududi.[3] The year 1937 is a watershed because under the Government of India Act of 1935, for the first time elections were held to form provincial governments. The 1937 elections, not based on the adult franchise, were crucial as they unveiled the challenges and problems of democracy in a multireligious polity and the minoritization[4] of Muslims, a process linked to a democracy that is only national-territorial. In the 1930s, two formations had emerged as almost hegemonic on the Indian political scene: the Indian National Congress (formed in 1885; hereafter "the Congress") and the Muslim League, a party established in 1906. In 1941, Maududi founded Jamaat to contest the vision of Muslim politics represented by both the League and Jamiatul Ulema-e-Hind (JUH), an organization of Deoband *ʿulema* formed in 1919, of which Maududi had been an ardent sympathizer. In the 1920s and subsequently, the JUH and the Congress forged an alliance. Initially, Maududi supported the Congress and published biographies of Mohandas Gandhi and Madanmohan Malaviya (Maududi 1992 [1919]), Hindu nationalist leaders. He served as editor of *Muslim*, the Urdu organ of the JUH. Maududi grew disenchanted, however, with the Congress's nationalism, which, he held, favored Hindus and marginalized Muslims and their culture. Another reason for his distrust of nationalism was the breakup along nationalist lines of the Ottoman Empire at the hands of colonial Western powers. Dismayed, Maududi quit the JUH-Congress alliance. In 1928, he left Delhi for Hyderabad. He turned to the study of Islam. Maududi concluded that the reason for Muslims' decline lay in the corruption of an authentic Islam, for the propagation of which he took over the editorship of the Urdu journal *Tarjumānul Qurʾān* in 1932. It was after the 1937 election and the subsequent formation of provincial ministries by the Congress that Maududi's ideology fully crystallized. He equated the policy of the ministries with heralding a "Hindu raj" (Maududi 1938, 61, 148–52).[5] He criticized the ministries not only for marginalizing Muslims but also for gradually making them Hindu.

Across the ideological divide, academics and social scientists (Bukay 2007; Kramer 1993; Voll 2007; Whine 2001), including philosophers (e.g., Blond and Pabst 2005), not to mention journalists, hurriedly cite Maududi's later writings as proof of Muslims' hostility to democracy as manifest in his notion of theo-democracy. Since their project is to "theologize" Maududi, they rarely mention his writings on economy, where he critiqued colonialism for impoverishing India. To Maududi (1990a, 104), the exploitation of Indian labor and the working poor was not a national issue; it was part of global colonialism, the leitmotif of which was the "pursuit of self-interests by the capitalists." Highlighting the wider economic gap between the ruler and the ruled in India, in an article published in 1920 he compared the annual salaries of the viceroy of India (£16,720), the prime ministers of the United Kingdom (£5,000), Japan (£1,231), and Italy (£1,000), and the presidents of the United States (£15,625), Argentina (£6,000), Chile (£2,062), and Portugal (£2,600) (Maududi 1990b, 107–9). Decrying the racial inequity, he asked why the monthly salary of a married white (*gorā*) soldier was ₹206 (if single, ₹150) whereas an Indian (*hindustaānī*) soldier got a mere ₹42? Such being the pathetic condition of laborers (*mazdūr*), Maududi supported the formation, in 1920, of the All India Trade Union Congress under the leadership of Lala Lajpat Rai (1865–1928). In *Tāj* (Jabalpur), Maududi wrote a detailed article in which he described Rai's selection as "highly appropriate." Noting that history is often written by the victors, he showed the contradictions in colonialism's promise of benevolence. While the British rulers kept propagating the message that their rule over India was a series of favors to help India develop, he asked why India was so poor and why, between 1877 and 1900, 15 million Indians—half of the total population of Britain—perished (1990c, 155). In greater detail and with hard data, he showed how Britain deindustrialized India and how its mischievous trade policy kept India poor. He also discussed the British East India Company and the deception, division, and coercion with which it had transformed itself from a trading to a ruling company (1990c, 156). In these writings, Maududi was not discussing "Islamic economics"; he was writing about political economy.

It is only logical, then, for those whose project is to theologize Maududi to stress his idea of theodemocracy but rarely ask how and why Maududi got to that idea. He was driven to theodemocracy because the Congress didn't differentiate Indian nationalism from Hindu nationalism. He opposed the pervasive move, with strong backing from within the "secular" Congress, of rendering "Hindu nationalism and Indian nationalism coterminous."[6] Theodemocracy, I suggest, is not the obverse of democracy. On the contrary, one type of theodemocracy packaged as a democracy fashions another type of theodemocracy. It was the majoritarian, assimilationist democracy of the Congress, especially the anti-Muslim practices of the 1937 ministries, which drove him to theodemocracy. In 1938, he wrote:

> The real issue is not if the political system . . . should proceed along the path of democracy, because no sane person can disagree with the spirit of democracy. . . . The spirit of democracy and this specific notion of democracy based on the principle of a single community should not be conflated. . . . It is assumed that because of a shared geography . . . we Hindus, Muslims, Untouchables, Sikhs, Christians are a single community and thus the grammar of democracy should be such that the state should be run by the wish of the majority community. Based on this ideology, the constitution has been framed. . . . Such a situation has made Hindu nationalism and Indian nationalism coterminous. . . . In contrast to Hindus, our condition

> is such that under this [democratic] system our community aspirations remain unfulfilled; rather they are . . . squashed because we are in a minority. (Maududi 1938, 204–6)

That the theodemocracy of the majority passes as democracy is evident, inter alia, in the insertion in the constitution of India of the state's role in banning beef and the endorsement thereof by the Supreme Court of India. Many states in India had banned beef earlier; Maharashtra did it in 2014 (BBC 2015). In 2004, the right-wing Bharatiya Janata Party (BJP) government introduced a bill asking for the prosecution of persons breaking the prohibition on cow slaughter under the Prevention of Terrorism Act (POTA) of 2002 (Chigateri 2008, 16). Such is the truth behind secular democracy.

My aim in reproducing the long quote above is not simply to show that Maududi supported democracy but also to underline his critique of democracy. However, his critique does not follow the lines "secular" scholars claim, namely, that he is a fundamentalist opposed to democracy. His critique instead resides in political theory proper. One of my aims is to read him as a political theorist. In *Musalmān avr maujudah seyasī kashmakash*, volume 2, from which I drew the quote, he presented problems facing minorities in Europe (and the United States and United Kingdom) and the failure of democracy to satisfactorily address them. Citing works in English, he showed how majoritarian democracies with a unitary, hegemonic notion of nation dominated minorities and gradually eliminated their distinctiveness. He cited the example of the former Czechoslovakia, where domination by the Czech majority (more educated and wealthier) over the Slovak minority (less educated, more religious, and largely rural) led to the latter's demand for *"autonomous self-government."* He also discussed the condition of the German-speaking minority in Czechoslovakia. There, the majority dominated the minorities, thereby "depriving them of their democratic right to rule" (Maududi 1938, 104–5). The rights of minorities given in the Czechoslovak constitution didn't prevent their subordination to the majority.[7] He also cited the example of the new state of Yugoslavia comprising Serbs, Croats, and Slovenes (and other minorities) and the religious pluralism—Orthodox, Catholic, and Muslims—that characterized it. Maududi noted with anguish how under the garb of the Yugoslav nation, the Serbs imposed their own culture over all others, replacing the agreed principle of federation with a unitary, strong center. Yugoslavia's "national democratic state" aimed to destroy every sign of the nationality (*qaumīat*) of different minorities.[8] He also gave the example of Switzerland, where the seven Catholic states were attacked by free thinkers and forced into a confederation. The 1848 constitution concentrated power at the center to weaken the autonomy of the states in order for the majority "to exercise its own will and principles over the minority." The example of Britain had a direct bearing on India. To Maududi, the identity of Great Britain was not the identity of Scotland, Wales, and Ireland but England's suppression of them. He also highlighted the persecution of Catholics, Jews, and others at the hands of the Anglican majority. Through coercive power and material and spiritual domination over other nations and religious groups of Great Britain, the English created "one country, one nation," which nationalists like Nehru cherished as an ideal. Maududi, therefore, held that "the mind of Nehru, though born in India, was made in England" and flavored too with Russian communism. With a dash of sarcasm, he continued, "Despite living in the midst of Indians, like an American tourist Nehru only views them superficially." In Nehru's persona Maududi saw an embodiment of the evolution of political and democratic institutions introduced by the imperial power from 1861 onward. To Maududi, all the constitutional developments introduced between 1861 and 1935 were made with the goal of keeping Britain as the model of democracy for India. Britain and its rulers, therefore, "lacked independent, creative reasoning [*ijtihādī ṣalāḥiat*] to formulate principles specific to each condition" (92). It was owing to this historical and institutional dynamic that in India not only did "the majority community/nation increasingly become more and more powerful but, worse, it also began to think of political domination over the minority as its natural and moral right" (93). In Nehru, Maududi saw shadows of majoritarian Serbian nationalism. Citing the Serbs' rejection of the Croats' demand for an autonomous province, Maududi asked, "Doesn't it look exactly as if Jawaharlal Lal Nehru was making a speech?" (107–8, 113, 92–93, 132).

Maududi's criticism of Nehru with a comparative empirical-historical account of nationalism and democracy in Europe and India, I suggest, is by no means a rejection of democracy but only its radicalization toward the path of being beneficial to all, the minority as much as the majority. Arguably, Maududi was one of the first to plead for the introduction of the people's right to recall an elected representative. "To make democracy effective, the method of referendum should be adopted and voters should also have the right," Maududi (1938, 219) demanded, "to recall those representatives who have lost the people's . . . confidence [*eʿtamād*]" because voters should not become "slaves to those they have elected."

With this antilinear and democratic reading of Maududi, and recognizing the complexity and shifts in his thought, in what follows I outline the basic theological-political features on which he crafted the ideology of Islamism and sought to spearhead his organization, Jamaat-e-Islami, along those lines. To pursue this task, first we should be familiar with the larger frame and methods that informed Maududi's thought.

◆ Frame and Method: The Permanence of *Ijtihād* and *ʿAql*

Critique was central to the objective and method Maududi employed to study Islam. Indeed, his choice of Islam, or his re-turn to Islam, was itself born out of a critical, comparative investigation of Islam and other worldviews. Maududi made his own judgment. He expected the same from his readers—Muslims and non-Muslims. In a passage that may surprise many, Maududi (1942, 15) wrote, "I invite not only non-Muslims but also Muslims to Islam." The most effective medium of Maududi's critical enterprise was *Tarjumānul Qur'ān*, the monthly journal he edited. As Maududi (1939, ii) put it, the mission of *Tarjumānul Qur'ān* was "to critique from a Qur'ānic viewpoint those thoughts and principles of civilization [*tahzīb v tamaddun*] that are spreading in the world, to interpret the principles of the Qur'ān and Sunna in the fields of philosophy, science, politics, economics, civilization, society, everything, and to apply those principles to the conditions of the modern age."

Roy's contention that revivalists like Hasan al-Banna and Maududi "define Islam primarily as a political system, in keeping with the major ideologies of the twentieth century" is thus less than original, as Maududi himself stated it. Interpreting the contemporary age from an Islamic framework is not contradictory. It is only logical.

Reading the above quote, one may, however, argue that while Maududi sought to critique the prevalent ideologies from "a Qur'ānic viewpoint," his own understanding of Islam was anything but critical. That is, he held his view of Islam because he was born into a Muslim family. However, the full biographical quote below hardly supports this:

> I hold such views about Islam not because I was born into a Muslim family and thus have a favorable inborn attitude toward Islam. I can't speak for my friends, but I am certain for myself that I had no attraction for the Islam I found in the immediate Muslim society. After acquiring a capacity for critique and research [*tanqīd v taḥqīq*], the first thing I did was to throw off the belt [*qalādāh*] of the spiritless religiosity I had inherited. If Islam was the name of the religion that is prevalent among Muslims now, then I would have joined the groups of apostates and the irreligious because I have no inclination toward a Nazi philosophy based on ancestor wor-

ship as the basis for pursuing a purely nationalist life. But the thing that kept me from the path of apostasy or accepting any other worldview [*maslak*] and made me a Muslim again was the study of the Qurʾān and the life of Prophet Muhammad. The study of the Qurʾān and the life of Prophet Muhammad made me aware of the real value of humanism; it familiarized me with that consciousness of liberty, the height of which can't be grasped or reached by the concept of even the greatest liberal and revolutionary of the world; it presented to me a map of individual beautiful life and collective justice such as I had never seen before, . . . and this very thing convinced me that this Islamic system is also instituted by that Judge [*ḥakīm*] Who created the earth and heaven with justice and truth [*ʿadl v ḥaq*].

In reality I am a new Muslim. After due thought and examination, I have pledged my faith in this *maslak* [worldview, i.e., Islam], to which my heart and mind bear witness, that there is no better way for humanity's welfare and virtue than this [Islam].[9] I invite not only non-Muslims but also Muslims to Islam. Through this invitation my aim is not to preserve and perpetuate the so-called Muslim society that stands far removed from Islam. Rather this invitation is directed toward the elimination of the injustice and tyranny that pervade the world. Let us eliminate deification [*ḳhudāī*] of human over human and build a new world on the model of the Qurʾān, where human qua human enjoys honor [*sharf*], dignity [*ʿizzat*], liberty [*ḥurrīyat*], equality [*masāvāt*], justice [*ʿadl*], and goodness/beauty [*iḥsān*]. (Maududi 1942, 14–16)

Maududi's emphasis, even insistence, on presenting and interpreting Islam as a matter of conscious choice rather than as an article of inherited faith or culture is best expressed in the terms he employed to refer to two categories of Muslims—conscious (*shōʿūrī*), or pure (*ḳhāliṣ*), Muslims (1942, 122; 1937, 71), on the one hand, and census (*mardumshumārī*), or born (*naslī*), Muslims, on the other (1942, 47, 92, 107–8, 178; 1959b, 226, 246; 1991, 51). Maududi himself probably exemplified the former best. "For years, I have made a critical and investigative [*tanqīdī v taḥqīqī*] study of Islam. . . . I have also investigated other collective systems of the world and have compared them with Islam. This entire study, research, and inquiry has convinced me that the happiness and virtue of humanity lie in embracing Islam" (1942, 14).[10] Maududi could read English. He also tried to learn German. According to Abdulhaq Ansari (2003, 522), Maududi "turned to Western thought, and devoted a full five years to the study of major works in philosophy, political science, history, and sociology." He had bought the entire set of the *Encyclopedia Britannica* (Maherulqadri 1990). In

Maududi's writings, especially those after his turn to Islamism, the obverse of a "conscious Muslim" is a "census Muslim," a term strikingly colonial in origin.

As a policy of imperial management, the British introduced various mechanisms to map, measure, and classify land, natural resources, and the botanical world, including human beings. The British census, first introduced in 1871, enumerated Indians, among others, along the lines of caste and religion (Appadurai 1996; Cohn 1996). The census counted those as Muslims who described themselves so—this resembles the definition by Wilfred Cantwell Smith (1946, 304): "Any person who calls himself a Muslim" is a Muslim. In Maududi's reading, such Muslims were Muslims simply because they were born into Muslim families; very few among them had chosen Islam. Census Muslims, to Maududi, could be found among "traditionalists" as well as "modernists." Referring to the traditionalists, he asked, "What would be more shameful for a *reason-bearing* person than having no other argument [*dalīl*] except that he holds a particular creed [*ʿaqīda*] simply because his father and grandfather too held it?" (1959b, 235; italics mine). So central to Maududi was the conscious choice of Islam that the Jamaat constitution (formulated in 1941) specified the criteria of membership—open to "every person (man or woman) of any race, nation, and resident in any part of the world"—to be a conscious recitation and internalization of the *kalima ṭayyiba*: "I bear witness that there is no god but Allah; I bear witness that Muhammad is Allah's messenger." The constitution went on to say that "a person will not be admitted to Jamaat on the assumption that he or she is born to a Muslim family, his or her name is Muslim, and thus he or she is necessarily a Muslim." In contrast, anyone born in a non-Muslim family would be given membership if he or she recited and internalized the meaning of the *kalima ṭayyiba* (1942, 177–78). As regards modernist Muslims imitating the West, Maududi judged them as follows: "If they adopt certain methods and ways just because they are prevalent among contemporary dominant nations, it only shows that their mind has lost the autonomous capacity to think and to differentiate what is correct [*ṣaḥīḥ*] from what is incorrect [*ghalaṭ*]" (1959b, 235).

It follows that Maududi regarded *taqlīd* (imitation) as an obstacle to (re)interpreting Islam. This does not mean that he accepted wholesale the stance of modernists. Not shackled by *taqlīd*, they unreflectively allowed, presumably under the banner of reason (*ʿaql*), adoption of nearly everything associated with the West. Their folly, as Maududi saw it, was not to relate themselves to, or even bypass, the discursive Islamic tradition that recognizes, encourages, and deploys reason in its own right. The critique of *taqlīd* indeed informs the entire corpus of Maududi's writings. So opposed was he to *taqlīd* that he wrote,

"In my view, for a scholar [*ṣāḥib-e-ʿilm*] *taqlīd* is illegitimate [*nājāʾz*] and sin [*gunāh*]" (Maududi 1956b, 266). Quoting this sentence, a reader asked him if this did not imply disrespect to such scholars as Abdul Qadir Jilani, Ghazali, Shah Valiullah, and so on. Clarifying that a single sentence could not be taken as full exposition by him on the issue of *taqlīd,* Maududi differentiated *taqlīd* from *ittebāʿ*: whereas the former means to follow someone's words and deeds irrespective of arguments, the latter means following someone on the basis of argument—*taqlīd* is for the commoner (*ʿāmī*); *ittebāʿ* is for the scholar (*ʿālim*). The four imams themselves held that their *taqlīd* was legitimate only when and as long as their position was backed by argument (*dalīl*). The differentiation between the commoner and the scholar on this issue was not introduced by Maududi; it is part of a tradition in place well before modernity. Thus viewed, following the position or practice of an eighth- or seventeenth-century scholar is not *taqlīd* in itself as long as it can be demonstrated by argument in consonance with sharia. However, following such a position will be classified as *taqlīd* if it lacks supporting argument. All forms and types of *taqlīd* are thus not blind adherence; only those that lack rationales.[11]

With this comprehensive notion of *taqlīd* laid down, I will present Maududi's critique of it. To illustrate this I will examine his writing on the need for a new education system and his critical evaluation of revivalist movements.

His article "New Education System" was delivered as a lecture in 1941 at Nadwat al-Ulama (hereafter Nadwa), a college in Lucknow. While applauding the reforms under discussion during the 1930s, he warned that mere patchwork would do no good in the present. Mocking the "progressivism [*rōshan-ḵhayālī*]" of those wanting to give English education to madrasa graduates, he stressed that this novelty had already become old. The need was not to replace a few old books with new ones. He argued for "total revolutionary reforms." To him, there was an organic link between knowledge and "leadership [*imāmat*]." It was the superiority of knowledge that made Egypt, Greece, and Europe world leaders in different epochs of history (1991, 56–57). Almost unmindful of any divine role, he asserted that whosoever possessed the most superior knowledge, whether atheist or believer, would become the leader—a point critiqued at length by Israr Alam (1990).

Maududi identified three sources of knowledge in the Qurʾān: aural (*samʿa*), observational (*baṣar*), and the ability to deduce results from the first two—to think in general—(*fūvād* [heart, as in *sura isra*ʾ, 36]). However, he emphasized *baṣar* and *fūvād* (1991, 57–58). It was the suspension of *baṣar* and *fūvād* among Muslims and the accomplishments of Europe precisely in those two domains in the preceding three centuries that led to Europe's marching ahead while Muslims lagged behind. In his view, all centers of education in the Muslim world continued making the "mistake [*ghalaṯī*]" of not excelling in *baṣar* and *fūvād*. Even the reforms by Lucknow's Nadwa and Cairo's Jamiʿa al-Azhar, Maududi held, did not go far enough: *baṣar* and *fūvād* remained paralyzed in those two premier institutions (1991, 60). Elsewhere he wrote that such an attitude was akin to "suspending reason [*ʿaql*], closing one's eyes, and imitating others—whether one's father, grandfather, or one's contemporary" (1959b, 222). Pleading for renunciation of "blind imitation," he stressed the need for constant thinking, because "what was proper in days of yore becomes improper in the present." To this end, he saw an urgent necessity for new books for the alternative education system he envisaged: "In particular, on principles and rulings of *fiqh*, Islamic economics, sociological principles of Islam and *ḥikmat* of the Qurʾān there is an urgent need for writing modern books, as the old books are no longer relevant for teaching. People of *ijtihād* may find good materials in them, but teaching them exactly as they are to students of the contemporary age is absolutely useless" (1991, 40). Maududi urged the recasting of teaching to appeal to the "minds and psychology of boys and girls of this age" (38). Dissatisfied with available books, he wrote, "For this purpose you will not get a ready-made syllabus; you have to make everything anew" (18). To many, what appeared unusual in Maududi's scheme was the direct teaching of the Qurʾān and its application to the problems of the world. "To understand the Qurʾān there is no need for any of its interpretation [*tafsīr*]—an accomplished and high-level professor who has deeply studied the Qurʾān and possesses the skills to impart its teaching following a modern model can generate the necessary capability among intermediate-level students to comprehend the Qurʾān" (38). Evidently, learning Arabic was important to meeting this goal.[12]

Against *taqlīd*, Maududi (1991, 13–14) proposed *ijtihād* in restructuring the education system: "A real leader and reformer is one who adopts, subject to time and occasions, the most proper ways of using his power of *ijtihād*." Elsewhere he observed that *ijtihād* was not a temporary mechanism but an enduring principle of Islam (1942, 18). Maududi's call for *ijtihād* was most pronounced in his ninety-one-page article "Tajdīd-v-aḥyāē dīn" ("The Renewal and Revival of Religion," 1940–41). Its subtitle was "A Critical [*tanqīdī*] Analysis of the Works of Umma's Renewers."[13] At the outset Maududi stated that in the minds of most readers the burden of devotion was so gripping that the mere mention of honorific titles like "Imam" or *mujaddid* in a name might impede any "assessment with freedom and fairness." He, therefore, urged for adoption of standards of investigation and research to go past the "poetic language of devotion" (18). Due to uncritical devotion (*ʿaqīdatmandī*), people simply know that certain individuals were *mujaddid*; they don't know who is *mujaddid*, in what capacity, and in what ways their work qualifies as that of a *mujaddid*. To Maududi, *tajdīd* means rescuing Islam from *jāhiliyat* and to make it shine again (19). Juxtaposing Islam and *jāhiliyat*, he identified three types of *jāhiliyat*: pure (*ḳhāliṣ*), polytheistic (*mushrikāna*), and ascetic (*rāhibāna*). Relevant to note here is that since Islam holds that there would be no prophet after Muhammad, whose mission it was to institute an Islamic civilization and polity, the task of renewing Islam fell on *ʿulema*, heirs to the prophets (41).[14] But not every endeavor by *ʿulema* qualifies as *tajdīd*.[15] Maududi differentiated *mujaddid* from *mutajaddid*. If someone attempts a renewal by amalgamating the dominant *jāhiliyat* and Islam, he is generally called *mujaddid*. However, in reality he is *mutajaddid*. The work of *tajdīd* is to purify Islam of *jāhiliyat* and to relive it in its pure form, *ḳhāliṣ ṣūrat* (38–39). Maududi identified the following criteria of a *mujaddid*:

> Correct identification of one's condition and environment;
> Recommendations of reform [*islāḥ*] in order to establish Islam collectively;
> Assessment of one's own capability for reform and the ways to accomplish it;
> Attempts to initiate a mental-intellectual revolution;
> Practical attempts to institute Islam and moral reforms;
> *Ijtihād fiddīn*: to understand Islam's universal principles to determine change;
> Defensive struggles;
> Revival of the Islamic system called *ḳhilāfat ila minhāje nabuvat*; and
> To bring about changes at a collective, translocal level. (Maududi 1940–41, 40–41)

Based on those criteria, no one had acquired the title of a perfect (*kāmil*) *mujaddid*; only ʿOmar bin Abdul Aziz came close. Every subsequent *mujaddid* worked in one or a few of these areas. The role of the *kāmil mujaddid*, to Maududi, was reserved for Imam Mehdi, mentioned in a hadith. Imam Mehdi would establish a robust system where the spirit of Islam would be at its pinnacle, as would be "*scientific* progress" (1940–41, 45). With the role of *kāmil mujaddid* set for Imam Mehdi, all others have been partial (*juzvī*) *mujaddid*. Maududi's article was a critical assessment of five such major *mujaddid*: ʿOmar bin Abdul Aziz (682–720), Imam Ghazali (1058–1111), Ibn Taymiyya (1263–1328), Shaykh Ahmad Sirhindi (1564–1624), and Shah Valiullah (1703–62) and his successors. In less than two pages he mentioned the founders of four schools (*madāhib*):

Imam Hanifa (d. 767), Imam Malik (d. 795), Imam al-Shafi (d. 820), and Imam Hanbal (d. 855).

Maududi's assessment of ʿOmar bin Abdul Aziz was positive; Aziz reintroduced the spirit of Islam absent during the time of his predecessor. He abolished the hierarchy between the royal family and common people. He canceled the illegal taxes imposed by the Ummayad. He corrected the injustices meted out to non-Muslims by restoring their places of worship and occupied lands. Though a caliph, he lived as a beggar. He was determined to change the royal rule by an elective caliphate. But ʿOmar's reign lasted only for two-and-a-half years as he was poisoned to death (at age thirty-nine), after which power went into the hands of *jāhiliyat* as the Ummayad, Abbasids, and later Turkish kings became rulers. Subsequently, the spring of *ijtihād* had run dry and the disease of fossilized imitation (*taqlīd-e-jāmid*) had become widespread (Maududi 1940–41, 53). Imam Gazali studied Greek philosophy, under the influence of which many *ʿulema* unfamiliar with the rational sciences had introduced unreasonable (*ghayr mʿaqūl*) premises as part of the articles of faith used to prove the truth of Islam. To this end, Ghazali offered reasoned interpretation (*mʿāqūl tʿābīr*). Considering unconscious religiosity to be unnecessary, he demonstrated how the triviality of sectarian differences impeded efforts to broaden the compass of Islam. He opposed fossilized imitation and rekindled the spirit of *ijtihād*. He critiqued the rotten education system that separated worldly from religious science. He "freely critiqued" the unjust deeds of the sultans, urging people not to bow to injustice but to "independently critique" the sultans (57). Maududi detected three weaknesses in Ghazali: his knowledge of hadith was imperfect; his mind was overwhelmed by reason (*ʿaql kā tasalluṭ*); and he leaned toward Sufism (*taṣavvuf*) more than necessary.[16]

Ibn Taymiyya, according to Maududi, was a more effective *mujaddid* than Ghazali. Owing to *taqlīd-e-jāmid*, the differences among various schools had reached the status of a permanent religion (*dīn*). Taymiyya critiqued such un-Islamic differences by stressing the commonalities among them. He established arguments more reasoned (*mʿāqūl*) than Ghazali's. The influence of Ghazali and Ibn Taymiyya impacted Europe. Above all, Taymiyya practiced and showed the ways of conducting *ijtihād* following the pattern of Islam's early era (*qurūn-e-ōlā*). The path of *ijtihād* was thus renewed, also for the benefit of common people. So opposed was Ibn Taymiyya to *taqlīd* that his critique (*tanqīd*) didn't spare even the most revered and most feared. His only shortcoming was his failure to launch a transformative movement (Maududi 1940–41, 59–62).

Ahmad Sirhindi's (1564–1624) role as a *mujaddid* was spectacular because he spoke against the *jāhiliyat* of his time, mainly the one introduced by Emperor

Jalaluddin Akbar (1542–1605) under the banner of his invention *dīn-e-ilāhī*. For various reasons, many *ʿulema* also legitimized it; some even described Akbar as "Allah's shadow" (Maududi 1940–41, 64). In his court, Akbar introduced the custom of bowing down before the emperor; many *ʿulema* and Sufis practiced this custom. In the royal palace, the sun was worshipped four times a day.[17] Interest, alcohol, and betting were made halal (meaning "permissible/permitted" and not simply applied to food). Marriage with maternal and paternal cousins was prohibited. Akbar's official historian, Abul Fazal, mocked Islamic rituals. To Maududi, Sirhindi's achievement lay in his fight against the prevalent *fitna* and his solitary struggle for the revival even as he faced imprisonment (63–68).

The bulk of Maududi's article discussed Shah Valiullah, whom S. M. Ikram (1964, 263) described as "the greatest Islamic scholar India ever produced." Born eighty years after Sirhindi, Valiullah's work was remarkable for having been composed in a time of moral collapse and political chaos. Calling Valiullah's time "dark," Maududi (1940–41, 69–71) wondered how a man raised in such an era emerged as a "free thinker [*āzād ḳhayāl mufakkir*]" to break the yoke of "imitative knowledge [*taqlīdī ʿilm*] and centuries-old prejudices" and judge issues from the "framework of research and *ijtihād*." As a *mujaddid*, Valiullah's accomplishment related to "critique and research [*tanqīd v tanqīḥ*] and restructuring [*tʿāmīr*]." In Maududi's view, Valiullah was the first to critically differentiate the history of Islam from the history of Muslims. Valiullah identified two causes of decline: the degeneration of the caliphate into a kingship; and the "death of the spirit of *ijtihād* and dominance of imitation [*taqlīd-e-jāmid*]." Critiquing the *jāhiliyat* of his time, he aimed to reinstitute Islam through his scholarly works. As regards his contribution to the restructuring, he was eclectic, balanced, and nonpartisan in a situation rife with endless conflicts along the lines of *firqa*, *madhab*, and so on. He embodied tolerance and moderation. That was why he appeared as Hanafi here, Shafai there; Maliki here and Hanbali there (82). He opened a new door of inquiry, stressing that "*ijtihād* is compulsory [*farẓ*] in every age." Valiullah, to Maududi, was "a man of such powerful reason [*ʿaqlīat*]" that in some respects, his contributions surpassed Ghazali's (84–86).

Barely half a century after Valiullah's death, a movement with an aim exactly like Valiullah's appeared on the scene. Shah Abdul Aziz (1746–1823), Valiullah's son and successor, continued his mission. His disciple Sayyid Ahmed Brelvi (1782–1831) strove to replace the alien colonial polity with an indigenous one. Shah Abdul Aziz's nephew, Shah Ismail, and his son-in-law, Maulvi Abdul Hai, became Sayyid Ahmad's followers. All three wrote along the lines charted by Valiullah. Eventually, they failed in their mission, which was centered in the North West Frontier Province (NWFP), currently in Pakistan.[18] It is Maududi's analysis of the failure of that movement, on the one hand, and the success of the British formation of what Maududi called a "*jāhiliyi* state," on the other, that concerns us here. To Maududi, the reasons for the failure were three.

First, from Sirhindi up to the successors of Valiullah, reformer-leaders could not adequately assess "the disease among Muslims concerning Sufism." Clarifying that he favored the "real Sufism of Islam [*Islām kā aṣalī taṣavvf*]," he stated that Valiullah's successors adopted the medium of the prevalent Sufism to mobilize followers. But the prevalent Sufism could not cure the moral disease it had generated. Such Sufism was like opium, making Muslims fall into a slumber. The relationship between a spiritual master (*pīr*; Arabic, *murshid*) and disciple (*murīd*) was such that it led followers to mental slavery to their *murshid*, paralyzing their power of critique and independent knowledge. It drove them from the tangible world to the world of magic and wonderment (*ṯalismāt avr ʿajā'bāt*).

Second, Maududi (1940–41, 92–93) argued, reformer-leaders should have first initiated a moral and mental revolution so that the local people understood the Islamic system better.

Third, the British succeeded whereas Muslims failed in "their own home" due to a lag between intellectual development in Europe and in India. In the age of Shah Valiullah, Shah Abdul Aziz, and Shah Ismail, Europe, having woken up from the slumber of medievalism, had produced scientists and philosophers and created new knowledge, revolutionizing the world. In India Shah Valiullah and his followers produced only a few books, whereas in Europe library after library was created. Maududi offered a long list of philosophers and scientists whose contribution made Europe a world power: Jöns Berzelius, Johann Gottlieb Fichte, Luigi Galvani, G. W. F. Hegel, Auguste Comte, Antoine Lavoisier, John Stuart Mill, François Quesnay, Anne Robert Jacques Turgot, Adam Smith, Thomas Malthus, Jean-Jacques Rousseau, Voltaire, Montesquieu, Thomas Paine, Charles Darwin, Johann Wolfgang von Goethe, Johann Gottfried Herder, Gotthold Ephraim Lessing, and so on. Comparing their contributions to those of Indians, he concluded that the latter's were negligible (Maududi 1940–41, 94–95). He wondered why Valiullah and his successors did not send a delegation of enlightened *ʿulema* (scholars; see chap. 3, n. 20) to Europe to learn new knowledge and methods (Maududi 1940–41, 97). Maududi concluded that the work of *tajdīd* required not simply the knowledge of religious sciences but a comprehensive, all-inclusive movement, efficient in modern sciences and informing every domain of life.

> Now the work of renewal entails new power of *ijtihād*. The insight of *ijtihād* available to Shah Valiullah or his preceding renewers and *mujtahedīn* [those doing *ijtihād*] is not adequate for the contemporary challenges. The new *jāhiliyat* has arrived with countless new resources creating countless new problems that didn't even fleetingly touch the minds of Valiullah and other ancients [*qudama*]. . . . Thus the Qur'ān and Sunna are the only sources of guidance for the pursuit of which there is a need for permanent power of *ijtihād* that is not tied to the knowledge and path of any of the preceding *mujtahedīn* but doesn't shy away from benefiting from all. (Maududi 1940–41, 98)

The aim of the foregoing pages was to demonstrate not only how Maududi's oeuvre critiqued blind imitation and stressed continuous *ijtihād* but also to identify the mechanisms through which he sought to conduct it. A sentence that captures this dynamic well is found in the Jamaat constitution before the explication of its goal as an obligatory expectation of one who joined the Jamaat: "Does not make anyone except Allah's Prophet [*rasūl*] the yardstick of truth [*ḥaq*], does not consider any one above critique, is not engaged in the mental enslavement of anyone" (Maududi 1942, 173). Before I close this section, I want to mention another key element of Maududi's reading of Islam. For him, Islam was not a religion as generally understood in the modern West as well as by those considered traditionalists and modernists among Muslims themselves. He saw it as a civilization and a system of life—logical, harmonious, and practical.

From his long article "The Renewal and Revival of Religion," it may appear that Maududi didn't consider Valiullah relevant to his own time. This would be a hasty reading. Maududi (1940–41, 85) was at once indebted to and critical of Valiullah. He acknowledged that Valiullah was the first major thinker to rationally present Islam as a system. For Maududi (1959b, 304), Islam is not merely a set of creeds; it is "a detailed *scheme* for the entire life of humans." Creeds, rituals, worship, principles, and rules of practical life synthetically form an indivisible whole: "Creed is the heart [*qalb*] of Islam; the specific *attitude of mind*, view of life, *goal of life*, and *standard of values* which emanate from that creed are its mind [*dimāgh*]" (ibid., 305). In his 1943 lecture (later published as *Dīn-e-ḥaq*) delivered at Jamia Millia Islamia (a well-known university in Delhi), he stressed the wholeness of life and argued that the division of life into compartments was a feature of *jāhiliyat* (Maududi 1997 [1943], 11). Islam, Maududi held, is a system (*neẓām*)—a notion common among, though not limited to, Islamists.

To Maududi, Islam is also a distinct civilization. In his book *Islamic Civilization: Its Principles and Sources*, first published[19] in 1955, he acknowledged that cross-cultural influences did impact Islamic civilization. However, he stressed that cross-cultural influences such as those between Islamic, Greek, and Roman civilizations were manifest in features and appearance. In its *aṣl* (foundation), Islamic civilization is distinct (Maududi 1977a, 8). Fine arts, sciences, literature, material objects, architecture, social practices, and types of political arrangements per se don't constitute a civilization; they are rather its manifestations. The foundation of a civilization is essentially conceptual and spiritual, with metaphysical postulates.[20] It is to these metaphysical postulates that we turn now to see how Maududi offered a reason-based explanation thereof.

◆ The Postulates

To map out the postulates of Maududi's thought spread across several thousand pages is far from easy. His magnum opus, *Tafhīmul Qur'ān*, an interpretation of the Qur'ān, alone is six volumes (begun in 1942 and completed in 1972, it was translated into several languages). Familiarizing ourselves with these general postulates, however, will help us better understand his positions on a number of issues this book deals with. Before I proceed, let me clarify that I do not presuppose that identifying generality is a substitute to specificity of all sorts.

The best place to start is with Maududi's (1939) book *Risāla'-e-dīnīyāt*,[21] which he wrote prior to forming Jamaat-e-Islami. *Risāla'-e-dīnīyāt* was meant for upper-level high school students or freshmen in tertiary education. Subsequently, it was adopted as a textbook by several institutions, mostly nontraditional. The specificity of *Risāla'-e-dīnīyāt* was, however, not just the lucidity of its style or its audience (young readers). What distinguished it was its mode of argumentation. Though it was directed more to readers' reason (*ʿaql*), the appeal to their heart (*dil*) was not absent because, as we saw earlier, reason and heart constitute an integrated assemblage. This point is made clear when we compare *Risāla'-e-dīnīyāt* to *Tāʿlīmul islām* (a four-part book in question-and-answer format). Written by Mufti Muhammad Kifayatullah (1875–1952), a noted Deoband scholar, freedom fighter, and important JUH leader, *Tāʿlīmul islām* was also addressed to children and on the syllabi of many madrasas (Moʿizuddin Qasmi 2000, 139). Like *Risāla'-e-dīnīyāt*, it was translated into many languages. So widely used was this textbook that in a condolence meeting of Kifayatullah in Delhi, two boys were heard saying, "Mufti sahib of *Tāʿlīmul islām* is no more" (Ikhlaq Qasmi 2000, 15). The difference between *Tāʿlīmul islām* and *Risālaʾ-e-dīnīyāt*, however, is profound. Whereas *Tāʿlīmul islām* takes for granted that its readers are believers, *Risālaʾ-e-dīnīyāt* does not (except with qualifications; see below). *Tāʿlīmul islām* assumes that offering prayer is obligatory. Therefore, it offers copious details about how to do prayer. For instance, it outlines details about when the water used for ablution becomes impure. It tells readers that when a bird, cat, chicken, pigeon, or rat falls and dies in water, that water is unsuitable for ablution. However, when creatures like fish or frogs—which are born and live in water—die in water, that water does not become impure (Kifayatullah n.d., 2:28–29). In short, *Tāʿlīmul islām* is rich in details regarding the performance of rituals, but it says little about *why* these rituals are important and *why* one should perform them.

The premise of *Risālaʾ-e-dīnīyāt* is different. To Maududi, the way to conduct rituals and issues of the purity of water for ablution are of not prime concern; what concerns him is faith (*ʿaqīda*). He wants his readers not simply to know what Islam is and what it enjoins but why Islam enjoins what it does. Does Islam want its believers to just accept certain creeds, or does it also offer argument (*dalīl*) for the reasonability and truth of those creeds? In the preface to *Risālaʾ-e-dīnīyāt*, Maududi writes that the procedures of prayer will be useful to those who want to pray. However, for those not wanting to pray, it is useless to tell them how to pray. Therefore, it is important to first spell out what indeed is prayer, why it has been made obligatory, and what are its advantages (Maududi 1939, 7). This explanatory framework based on reason is precisely what distinguished Maududi's approach from that of several others. Also notable is the selection of examples. Stressing why mere verbal proclamation of لا إله إلا الله ("There is no God but Allah") is insufficient, he contends that it must be understood fully to find a place inside one's heart and change one's thoughts and actions. Otherwise this proclamation will be similar to a person suffering from fever uttering "quinine" a million times rather than taking a pill (66). It was this quality of Maududi's prose that attracted skeptics and atheists, within as well as outside of the Muslim community, to his writings, like Zain Abdullah (2014, 26), professor of religion at Temple University. On reading Maududi's *Risālaʾ-e-dīnīyāt*, Abdullah, born in Detroit to a nonwhite family, "immediately decided to become Muslim."

Central to Maududi's reading of Islam is the contention that it is a universal religion neither confined to any geography, race, caste, ethnicity, nation, or community (*qaum*) nor associated with any specific individual. This is how he opened *Risālaʾ-e-dīnīyāt*:

> Each religion in the world is either named after its founder or the community in which it was born. For instance, Christianity is called so because its founder was *ḥaẓrat ʿIsā* [Christ]. Buddhism is named after its founder, Mahatma Buddha. Zoroastrianism is named after its founder, Zoroaster. The Jewish religion was born in a specific tribe.... However, the distinction of Islam is that it is not linked to an individual or community; its name denotes a specific feature embodied in the meaning of the word *Islam*. This name itself shows that this religion is not an invention of a person nor is it associated with a community. Islam has no relation with an individual, country, or community. Islam's aim is to simply generate its features among people. The truthful and virtuous people with this feature in every age and every community were all "Muslim," and they are and will be Muslim in future. (Maududi 1939, 9–10)

The last sentence in the quote revolves around the word *fiṯrat* (in Arabic *fiṯra*).[22] Translated and construed as "nature" (Bowker 2003), "natural disposition" (Ashur 2007, 80), "primordial nature" (Nasr 2004, 6), "natural predisposition" (Izutsu 1964, 112), and "innate human nature" (Sachedina 2001, 73), it is by no means a simple term. Its precise meaning has long been an issue of much debate. Based on the Qur'ān and hadith, scholars hold that every infant is born a Muslim (Maududi 1952, 97–100). That is, God creates every human being predisposed to recognizing one God. Due mainly, inter alia, to customs, social upbringing, and certain cultural prevalence, some humans subsequently fail to recognize the oneness of God and His message, for *kufr* is nothing else but to veil this very truth. Going by this account, as Maududi meant above, all who upheld monotheism before the revelation of the Qurʾān were already Muslims. In Islamic-Arabic vocabulary *fiṯrat*, then, means a sort of primordial orientation or an inclination (Anjum 2012, 221)[23] to the recognition of the oneness of God, also referred to as *fāṯir* (creator) in the Qurʾān. The verbal form of *fiṯrat* is *faṭara* which means "to create" (Esposito 2003, 87). Becoming a Muslim is thus to intentionally recognize and come to what is already there within every human being. Such was the discursive theology within which, Maududi (1939, 24), like his predecessors, described Islam as a "natural [*fiṯrī*] religion of humans."

In the course of rewriting this chapter in the summer of 2015 in Melbourne, I met a Sikh taxi driver with a master's degree from an Indian university. He liked discussing matters of religion. I asked him how Sikhism viewed nature, especially in relation to an infant. To him, every infant is born a Sikh. It is society that makes the child a non-Sikh. In this taxi driver's view, Hindus are only partially right in believing that every infant is born Hindu (because he is made Muslim by interfering with nature through circumcision). Sikhism, he continued, is pure nature for, unlike Hinduism, it prohibits any interference in the natural growth of an infant as it also disallows even the shaving and cutting of hair.[24]

The notion of *fiṭrat* that Maududi drew from the tradition of Islam thus should not be misconstrued with mere biological features or visible bodily markers. Importantly, it also does not presuppose any original sin; humans (*insān*) are not posited as sinful, that is, as beings for whom the message of heaven was sent "to heal the wound of the original sin" (Nasr 2004, 6; Schimmel 1992, 32). Primordial nature presupposes and requires human endeavor for its affirmation. A child born into a Muslim family thus does not automatically become a Muslim, for he or she is required to certify the prophetic message (Maududi 1952, 100). The notion of *fiṭrat* should also not be taken to signify humans' inability to change themselves on the ground that what they do they do because of their *fiṭrat*. In response to a question of whether "humans' *fiṭrat* can be changed through human efforts or if humans are helpless in this respect," Maududi clarified that the primordial *fiṭrat* was endowed with the will to change itself. That the questioner himself realized that he had certain weaknesses meant that he could overcome them and reach the point of balance, *ʿetadāl* (Maududi 1959a, 51).[25]

A fuller understanding of *fiṭrat*, however, entails an outline of broader Islamic cosmology, itself anchored in *fiṭrat*, which Maududi also expounded. This will better equip readers to locate Maududi's project and to see later in this book the interface of continuity and differences with the understandings of Islam by others—predecessors and/or contemporaries.

Fundamental to Maududi's understanding of cosmology is that the whole universe, humans included, did not come into being by accident. At work is a divine power who created everything, from the tiniest specks of dust to the splendid galaxies of the heavens. He created *jamādāt* (stones, minerals, fossils, inorganic nature at large), *nabātāt* (grass, trees, leaves, and flora), and *ḥayvanāt* (kingdom *animalia*). What distinguishes humans from the rest of Allah's creation is that they are endowed with reason (*ʿaql*) and enjoined to interact with the entirety of His creation in a just way so as to fulfill His will. The nonhuman world is not simply at the disposal of humans to be used as the latter wish; rather, humans are to interact with it in accord with Allah's goal of creating a virtuous world where peace (*amn*) and justice (*ʿadl*) reign supreme. Islam discourages caging birds. One can use flowers and fruit, but Islam dislikes the destruction of trees and plants. Transcending the world of *nabātāt*, endowed as it is with life, Islam entails respect for even nonliving things. It prohibits the waste of water. The whole universe is based on a definite order whereby everything is assigned a specific place in the grand scheme. The heavenly bodies, the moon and the stars, are woven together in a majestic order to follow the laws ordained for them. It is the same in the human world, which also follows the *fiṭrat* of Islam. In accordance with Islam's codes and regulations, a human is born, breathes, and receives water, food, and energy. Each beat of a human heart, the circulation of blood in the body, and every act of breathing follows a pattern. Each organ of the human body—from the tiniest cell to the heart and brain—is regulated by laws set for them. As Islam means submission to Allah, the whole universe (*kā'nāt*)—the stars, moon, sun, earth, water, light, trees, stones, and animals—is divine for it follows the laws of Allah. Even a person who doesn't recognize God or associates others with Him, is in accordance with his or her own *fiṭrat* a Muslim because that person's birth, growth, and death invariably follow the divine regulations.[26] *Kufr* (denial) is to deliberately conceal this very *fiṭrat* whereby a human, because of his or her lack of knowledge, inadequate use of reason, or sheer naivety, fails to recognize Allah. This failure opens the door to *ẕulm*, oppression (Maududi 1939, 10–13).

It should be evident by now that this cosmology distinguishes between the domains of *takvīnī* and *tashrīʿī*. In the former, every nonhuman creation unintentionally bears witness to Allah. Humans qua biological beings, Muslims or not, also follow Allah. In the latter domain, pertaining as it does to the human world, humans have the freedom to follow or not follow Allah. How do humans know what Allah wants them to follow, however? Revelation (*vaḥī*) is key to knowing (Maududi 1942, 174–77).[27]

It is through the prophets that Allah sent His message. The medium through which God sent His message is *vaḥī*, and the book with the message is Allah's book. Humans possessing reason and scientific capability ponder over and analyze the virtuous life of Prophet Muhammad and his teaching. It is reason that leads humans to embrace his teachings and the heart that bears witness to it. This is the act of professing faith, *īmān* (Maududi 1939, 31–38). Allah created Adam (ʿĀdam) first. Adam was the first human as well as the first prophet to impart Islam's teaching to his children. The good among Adam's descendants followed His path; the others did not. Over time, descendants of Adam spread to different parts of the world, forming themselves into different "communities [*qaumēñ*]." Allah then began to send prophets to every part of the world—India, China, Iraq, Egypt, Africa, and Europe. The religion of every prophet was one: Islam. So was its spirit: monotheism, virtuous acts, peace, and belief in the hereafter. Those prophets were tortured, exiled, and even killed; but they persisted in their mission and won many followers. However, after their deaths, their followers began to forget or tamper with their message. Yet aspects of the truth, like ideas of God and a hereafter, survived.

With the passage of time and advancement (*taraqqī*) of civilization in trade and technology, it became possible to send the same message to all of humankind at the same time. Such a stage in the human civilization began to unfold "around 2,000–2,500 years ago," when "the species of humans [*nauʿ-e insānī*] began to mature into adulthood [*sinn-e balūgh*]" and Allah sent his final messenger, Prophet Muhammad (Maududi 1939, 47). Readers may notice similarities as well as differences between Maududi and Kant (2007 [1784]) on what constituted the Enlightenment (*Aufklärung*), and when it began, for both discussed the immaturity of mankind, though differently.

Prophet Muhammad reminded the world of the forgotten teaching of monotheism. He was truthful. He didn't speak in a harsh tone; his language was sweetness at its pinnacle. He was honest in dealings and transactions. Such was his honesty that people gave him their possessions for safe keeping. The whole community trusted him so much that they conferred the title of trustworthy (*amīn*) on him. So delicate was his heart that it beat for the sufferings and hardships of everyone. He helped orphans and widows. He fed paupers and the hungry. He was a generous host to travelers. He didn't hurt anyone; instead he underwent sufferings for the sake of others. He didn't bow his head in front of anyone except Allah. He was offered power in exchange for refraining from spreading God's message; politely, he turned it down. In a span of twenty-three years, his piety, gentleness, exemplary ethical standards, and teachings turned foes into friends. When bestowed with victory, he didn't take revenge against his enemies; he forgave even those who had killed his uncle and chewed his liver. To those who had tortured him and thrown stones at him, he offered forgiveness. Every promise he made he kept. When granted success and power, he continued to lead the simple life of a beggar. He slept on a mere rug. He ate like impoverished person; on some occasions, he had nothing to eat. While engaged in social affairs, he worshipped for hours during the night. To the Arabs, who were engaged in perpetual fights, he showed paths to reconciliation and amity. Preaching and practicing truth, equality, and justice, he stressed that all were humans (*insān*). Greatness and gentleness resided neither in power nor in wealth, skin color, appearance, ancestral traditions, or birth. For, following death, when humans appear before God, faith and virtuous deeds alone will matter (Maududi 1939, chaps. 3–4).

The rituals of worship—prayer, fasting, *zakāt*, and the hajj—are the means by which humans prepare to face Allah in His court (*ʿadālat*). These rituals connect this life and the hereafter. When performed with the realization of their proper aims, these rituals shape the entirety of human lives, individually and collectively. Helping the poor, feeding the hungry, and attending to the sick are also acts of worship, if done to please God rather than to secure selfish interests or fame. Likewise, undertaking employment is also a form of worship if performed with honesty and free from bribes and corruption. The daily prayers attest to and renew faith in God, His messenger, and belief in the hereafter. They serve as a foundation for the cultivation and consolidation of the self. They purify the self, enhance the spirit, reform morals, and induce acts of virtue. In prayers with no loud recitations, no other person knows what one recites or does not. Yet the person praying knows that God sees everything. Those who earnestly pray will recall God's message and His guidance in every act they do, not just in rituals.

Fasting is an annual ritual to seek the Almighty's favor by purifying one's *nafs*. Fear and love of Allah is generated and reaffirmed throughout the month, manifesting as it does in the enactment of high morals and splendid deeds as well as abstinence from sinful acts. Thus lying is *ḥarām*—not only during the month of fasting—because it harms others as well as defiles one's own *nafs*. Fasting trains individuals to recognize and practice patience (*ṣabr*). It enables one to endure suffering and hardships (*maṣā'b*). To fast is to tame and control temptations for the sake of the Almighty. The 2.5 percent of their wealth that Muslims are obliged to give away doesn't go to Allah, for He does not need it. This prescription exists to purify wealth and win divine rewards in return. The rewards, however, don't go to those who give for worldly reasons, such as fame, societal approval, or pride; or to those who expect thanks in return. Giving must be done in such a way that it remains anonymous. Wealth is not to be worshipped; nor is to be concentrated. It is to be spent to please God so that humans overpower their own selfishness and narrow-heartedness. To give *zakāt* is to sacrifice love for wealth for the sake of love for Allah. *Zakāt* aims to eliminate tendencies of wealth-worship so as to create a just, egalitarian, and healthy society. Anyone not paying *zakāt* is a *ẕālim* (an oppressor). The final ritual, the hajj—obligatory to complete once in a lifetime for those who can afford it—is to visit the house of Allah built by the prophet Ibrahīm to worship Him. To perform the hajj is to purify one's heart (*dil*), control desires of *nafs*, inculcate the language of purity, and present oneself, in a fakir's dress, in the house of Allah with total humility and respect. The hajj is the embodiment par excellence of humans' love for God, for they leave the affairs of the world, relatives, and friends behind to perform it. Before undertaking the hajj, however, one should receive the consent of one's aged parents and arrange for their care in one's absence. The hajj is as much an expression of love for Allah by humans as it is an expression of universality, unity, and love among humans transcending geography, nationality, race, color, and language (Maududi 1939, 103–17).

In rituals as in other domains of life, *fiqh*—the body, principles, and postulates of knowledge to study the Qur'ān and hadith—is concerned with the exterior and outwardly appearance (*ẓāhir*). That which concerns affairs of heart (*dil*), *bāṯin*, is *taṣvvuf* (Sufism). While *fiqh* evaluates if one's action and deeds are right or wrong, harmful or beneficial, *taṣvvuf* assesses whether those deeds and acts are sincere, truthful, and if one's heart is free from malice, prejudice, and the seduction of immediacy. The interior and the exterior inform each other to constitute a balanced equation. *Taṣvvuf* is indeed the byword for love (*ʿishq*) of Allah and his prophet, which complements rather than contradicts *fiqh* (Maududi 1939, 125–28).

◆ The Aims

In setting the goal of Jamaat-e-Islami, Maududi linked that aim to the teachings and missions of all prophets, not only Muhammad. All prophets—*ḥaẓrat* Nūḥ (Noah), Ibrāhīm (Abraham), ʿIsā (Jesus), Mūsā (Moses), Shoʿaib, Ṣāleḥ Hūd—brought the message of the same *dīn* (religion). However, the *sharīʿat* of each prophet was somewhat different. Maududi used *sharīʿat*, literally "path" or "way," to mean, inter alia, modes of worship and fasting, principles of sociality, mutual dealings, regulations about what is *ḥarām* and what is halal, rules about marriage and inheritance, and so on. With the conclusion of prophecy in the figure of Prophet Muhammad, Allah made his *sharīʿat* prevail over the previous ones, for his prophethood is not limited to one country or nation but extends to the whole of humanity. The differences among the prophets' *sharīʿat*, however, don't mean difference in *dīn*, which has been the same (Maududi 1939, 64–65, 121–22). But what was the mission of the prophets Allah sent?

Though this question is addressed in *Risālaʾ-e-dīnīyāt*, a fuller elaboration occurs in Maududi's 1939 article "Political Perspective of Islam," (1972) in which he argued that the mission of all prophets was to establish Allah's sovereignty on earth. That is, Allah wanted to eliminate the godhood of humans over humans and establish His sovereignty. By Allah's sovereignty, Maududi meant sovereignty not only in the metaphysical world (*takvīnī*) but equally in the social-political world (*tashrīʿī*).[28] For this reason, the temporal power, the king, opposed the prophet. To *firʿaun* (the pharaoh), who had announced to Egypt's populace that he was their God (*rab/ilah*), Moses preached the worship of the one true God. In Maududi's reading, the same was the case for the prophet Ibrāhīm vis-à-vis the king of Babel who held power (*ḥukūmat*). Before citing examples of other prophets, Maududi discussed at length how the modern states had acquired sweeping and unbridled power similar to that previously attributed to God. He asked,

> Is the Political Bureau of the USSR not god for the inhabitants of the USSR? Is Stalin not their god? Is there any village and farm where the image of Stalin is not present? Do you know how the Soviet system was inaugurated [*bismillāh*] in the part of Poland recently occupied by the USSR? Thousands of photos of Stalin were installed in village after village so that people could become familiar with their God [Stalin] after which they were initiated into the Bolshevik religion [*dīn*]. Why is such importance given to one individual? Why is one individual being imposed on the minds and spirits of millions of people? . . . This is how a human becomes god over other humans.
>
> Likewise look at Italy where the grand Fascist council is the assembly of gods, Mussolini being their greatest god. In Germany the leader of the Nazi party is god and Hitler the god of gods. Despite being a democracy, in the figures of directors of the Bank of England and a few wealthy people, the United Kingdom has its own god. In the United States, a few Wall Street capitalists have become gods of the whole country. (Maududi 1972 [1939], 16–17)

Returning to theology, Maududi (1939, 23) stated that the message of all prophets was to worship none other than Allah and proclaim that He is the only *ilah*, equally in the social-political domain. In short, the message of all prophets was to establish a virtuous state. This state would be a "theodemocracy." It would be *theo* in that its sources of law would be God, but it wouldn't be like Europe's theocracy or papacy because, Islam knowing no priestly class, it would be run by the community of Muslims. Under an Islamic state, paramountcy and sovereignty would belong to God and executive power to every member of the community. This theodemocracy, Maududi argued, was closer to democracy, even though proponents of democracy vigorously denied it. He found the claim of popular sovereignty dubious because elections authorized only a few people to rule. And in elections only those become successful who—through their wealth, chicanery, shrewdness, and propaganda—fool people into making them their *ilah*, not for the benefit of people but for the benefit of their own selfish and class interests. "This is the state of democracy," Maududi (1972[1939], 27) opined, "in America, the United Kingdom, and all those countries that claim to be a paradise of democracy."

In a chapter titled "How an Islamic Government Is Established," in the third volume of *Musalmān avr mavjuda seyāsī kashmakash* (hereafter *Kashmakash*), published in 1942,[29] Maududi underlined the mission of all prophets in terms described above, to say that the exact and elaborate details of how earlier prophets accomplished it are far from available as the Qurʾān offers only some indications thereto. Yet some statements of the prophet Christ (*ʿIsāʿ ʿlaihissalām*) did shed light on how an Islamic movement was conducted in its early stage. To demonstrate this claim, while Maududi drew heavily on the life of Prophet Muhammad to offer a full scheme, he thought it necessary to add an appendix to the chapter that explained, with citations from the New Testament, how the prophet ʿIsāʿ's statements were a "brief, effective manifesto of *ḥukumat-e-ilāhiya*," a phrase that occurs in the first constitution of Jamaat as its goal, "*ḥukumat-e-ilāhiya kā qeyām* [the establishment of God's Rule]" (1942, 155, 173). In Maududi's reading, to the people of Palestine, *ʿIsāʿ ʿlaihissalām* (Christ) gave the invitation of *ḥukumat-e-ilāhiya*. The seven-page appendix gives numerous citations from the New Testament to drive home this specific point. To this end, Maududi cited several passages, which I list in the same order as in the original (by Maududi): Mark (32–28:12), Luke (8:4), Matthew (10:9:6), Matthew (39–34:11, 24:16, 22–21, 10, 18–16:10), Luke (33–26, 14), Matthew (41–39: 15, 28:110, 19–20: 6, 24–33: 6, 7:7, 28–30:11), Luke (25–26:22), Matthew (28: 23, 15–21, 22), and Luke (23:1–23). By citing these passages, Maududi demonstrated that *ʿIsāʿ ʿlaihissalām* (Jesus) did not simply preach a religion; he aimed to change the whole of civilization and politics (*tamaddun v seyāsat*). Citing passages from the New Testament, Maududi concluded that they resembled the Meccan passages in the Qurʾān as well as Meccan hadith (1942, 151–57).

If only briefly, we ought to also note multiple similarities between the thought of Christian thinkers and secular scholars, on the one hand, and those of Maududi, on the other. The Protestant Dutch thinker-politician Abraham Kuyper (d. 1920) famously said, "No man has the right to rule over another man. . . . Authority over men can't arise from men. . . . All authority of governments on earth originates from the sovereignty of God." To Kuyper, this was the teaching of Christianity/Calvinism that democracy violates (in Ahmad 2011b, 466). And in the Catholic tradition, Australian Catholics, just before World War II, held that the "government derives its authority from the community and the community derives it from God" (Murtagh 1946, 2, 18). And here is one more example, an academic one! "In American political theory," writes Robert Bellah, "sovereignty rests, of course, with the people, but implicitly, and often explicitly, the ultimate sovereignty has been attributed to God." "This is the meaning of the motto, 'In God we trust' as well as the inclusion of the phrase 'under God' in the pledge to the flag" (qtd. in Ahmad 2011b, 466).

In the next chapters we will see how other Muslim scholars and intellectuals critiqued Maududi on a number of positions and issues, including his conceptualization of an Islamic state emanating from the prophetic mission.

5
THE STATE
(In)dispensable, Desirable, Revisable?

> Readers bear witness to the fact that on the issue of critique [*naqd v naẓar*] we are neither stingy nor lazy. . . . Therefore, in the name of Allah, today we open the gate of critique [on Vahiduddin Khan's book].
>
> —AMIR USMANI (1965, 99–100), editor of *Tajallī*

This chapter ideationally deals with the searching, comprehensive, and at times aggressive critiques of Maududi on the issues of religion and the state. The nature and forms of these critiques are diverse. So are their actors. I focus on critiques by two groups: former Jamaat members and Jamaat sympathizers. These categorizations are for analytical ease. I distinguish between former members who no longer identify themselves with Jamaat in any way and those who do, however so loosely and conditionally. I place the latter with Jamaat sympathizers, in part also because critiques of Maududi conceptually converge with those of sympathizers.

In the first part of this chapter, I discuss critiques of Maududi and his notion of the state by three former Jamaat members: Manzur Nomani (1905–97), Vahiduddin Khan (b. 1925), and Abul Hasan Ali Nadvi (1914–99). Of the three, Nomani and Nadvi are *ʿulema* educated in two "traditional" and reputed universities of Islamic learning in the state of Uttar Pradesh: Darul Uloom (hereafter Deoband), located in Deoband, which Nomani attended, and Nadvatul Ulema, in Lucknow, where Nadvi was educated. Khan's education is also regarded as "traditional," but he did not attend such a reputed institution. I also discuss responses to their critiques by scholars from and aligned with Jamaat. One such scholar was Amir Usmani (d. 1975), a graduate of Deoband and editor of *Tajallī*. I also briefly explore responses from two Jamaat members. In the second part of this chapter, I dwell on critiques of Maududi by five Jamaat sympathizers whose educational capital is different from that of the former Jamaat members in that they were not trained or educated entirely and/or only in "traditional" institutions. Many of them were self-educated in Islam and Arabic and also held degrees from modern universities. As this chapter lays out the range and depth of ideas on critique, in two cases I break from my analytical categories of ex-Jamaat members and Jamaat sympathizers. For instance, I include an existing member (viewed by a few members as anti-Jamaat) because his ideas resonate with those of the sympathizers.

This chapter weaves together ethnographic data and textual-literary sources. Though some anthropologists continue to distinguish the ethnographic from the textual (often privileging the former over the latter), during fieldwork my interlocutors asked such questions as, "Have you read this book?" and "So, how did you find that book"? Or they told me a book was hard to find but offered to put me in touch with the right bookshop. In short, fieldwork for this book went beyond Bronislaw Malinowski's (1922, 18) insistence on recording *"the imponderabilia of actual life"* (italics in original). During my fieldwork, texts were no less real in life than the Malinowskian "social life around the village fires." The division between the "contextual studies" of anthropologists and the "textual studies" of historians and humanists is puerile, as Brinkley Messick (1993, 2) rightly notes. What I am also concerned with is "the play of the mind" and the "life of the mind" (Marsden 2005, 85) evident in texts as an activity in its own right rather than reductively viewing it as separate from "behavior" in so-called actual life. Indifference, annoyance, disappointment, optimism, and joy emanate from as well as are embodied in textual as much as material lives.

Contra the Enlightenment's self-congratulatory account by several of its partisans, the mind rarely works entirely on its own. Culture and tradition tend and cultivate minds as much as minds tend and cultivate culture and tradition. Here my aim is not only to show that individuals critique Maududi and his thought but equally to demonstrate how the work of critique is undertaken. How ideas, sentiments, mental conditions, types of knowledge, forms of authority, language capacity, motivations, the (un)sayable, notions about private and public, facial expression, hairstyle, conceptions of home, intellectual suppositions, political power, readings of past and future, tears, joy, and much else inform and are played out in the enterprise of critique. An understanding of critique that fails to take into account this whole array of factors will be superficial at best. This array of factors is nothing else but life in its entirety, approximating as it does Wittgenstein's description of words as deeds and, therefore, life. To recognize critique as I discuss it is to grasp the cultural milieu to which it relates. Reason and doubt don't dislodge belief for, to remain with Wittgenstein (1980 [1977], 46e, 85e, 23e), "doubt comes after belief." Pursuing Talal Asad's (1993, 290) insight, let us restore critique, often (mis)taken as the singular triumph of mind or of intellect of some kind, to where it belongs: "life" as "essentially itself." In connecting critique and reason to life—as opposed to a "Kantian reason view[ing] . . . itself as the supreme authority which produces itself and thereby man" (Jaspers 1962 [1957], 97)—we shouldn't ignore death. Asad's short phrase contains enough to mean, or so it seems to me, life as essentially death. That is, critique is connected to a form of life the full meaning of which is inseparable from death.

The multiple and diverse critiques of Maududi's view of the state neither outright reject nor entirely embrace it. Critics of Maududi display considerable ambivalence on this specific aspect as well as on his thought more broadly speaking. Some agree with the spirit of Maududi's critical enterprise, considering it an important intervention at a specific historical moment, but they stress that its relevance in the present and future is limited. Others differentiate the universal Maududi from the nationalist Maududi, extending and revising the former to encompass concerns and aspirations of humanity beyond the divides of faith and ethnicity. For such critics, *Maqāṣid al-sharīʿā* is the medium to pursue such a universalism. Still others continue to underline the relevance of his idea of what a state should be by reinterpreting him quite differently. In such interpretations, as a thinker Maududi made the simple point that a culture could scarcely survive, much less flourish, without engaging with power. This was certainly true for a minority (and minoritized) culture in a majoritarian democracy. Thus viewed, Maududi was no less relevant for the present than for the future.

The critiques discussed in this chapter also demonstrate how specific issues get connected to the larger social, cultural, and political world, including the life of the person under discussion. However, there is no unanimity about if and to what degree someone's personal life should be imbricated in public discussion. No less significantly, the diverse critiques elaborated in this chapter point to the etiquette and principles of critique. What types of information qualify to be included or relied upon in a critique? Can an author's intention be discussed? If so, how should that intention be deciphered? Is moral advice also a critique? What does critique in general aim for? Should seniority or juniority matter in acts of critique? Do anger and arrogance annihilate the intellectual equality necessary for a proper critical exchange? Does writing critique presuppose responsibility? To what extent does the thought being critiqued as well as the thought of the critic mark continuity or rupture with past understandings?

◆ Rupture and Continuity

The themes of the three critiques of Maududi by ex-Jamaat members and the responses thereto that I address in this section are far from singular. They address a variety of themes: for instance, competence in Arabic, the length of a man's beard, and hairstyle. However, a key concern underlining these diverse themes is the issue of continuity with the authoritative tradition and its maintenance. The issues of continuity and tradition, discussed in chapter 4, were central to Maududi's own conceptualization of Islam.

Maulana Manzur Nomani (1905–97),[1] a graduate of Deoband and a founding member of Jamaat, was one of the first to leave the group (Nomani 1998, 16–17, 36–37). In his self-account *Mavlānā Mavdūdī kē sāth̲ mērī refāqat kī sarguzasht avr ab mērā mavqif* (*The Tale of My Friendship with Maulana Maududi and My Current Stand*; hereafter *The Tale*), published in 1980, Nomani recounted how attracted he was initially to Maududi's writings in *Tarjumānul Qur'ān*. He admired Maududi's convincing critiques of orientalists' scholarship on Islam. Nomani, who in 1934 had launched his own journal, *Al-Furqān*, used to receive *Tarjumānul Qur'ān* in exchange. So enamored was he of Maududi that he often reproduced the latter's articles in his own journal. Later he invited Maududi to write on Shah Valiullah in *Al-Furqān*, an essay Nomani later published as a booklet. A "lover [*'āshiq*]" of *Tarjumānul Qur'ān*, he established a correspondence with Maududi. As the epistolary relationship between the two men grew, Nomani traveled to Delhi to meet Maududi. In 1941, when Jamaat was founded in Lahore, Nomani joined as a founding member. If his tale is to be believed, others within Jamaat considered Nomani as second only to Maududi (22, 35–36, 25). In 1942, Nomani left Jamaat. A notice in *Al-Furqān* stated that Nomani's reasons for disassociation from Jamaat were not "ideological [*usūlī*]" but concerned "a few things of an individual nature." He clarified that his separation didn't mean disagreement with Jamaat's "fundamental goal," which he continued to regard as "correct" (22, 35–36, 25, 68–69). *The Tale* in fact fondly recalled the days of the Ḳhilāfat movement of the early 1920s and how as a student Nomani felt as if in India, especially in Uttar Pradesh, an Islamic government (*Islāmī ḥukūmat*) was already in place. The Ḳhilāfat movement boycotted British institutions and established alternative courts, including Islamic ones. In Mau, Uttar Pradesh, where Nomani was then based, he recollected that both Hindus and Muslims took their cases to Islamic courts (15–16). Recalling the 1936 elections and the formation of the first ever government by the Congress, he also noted how people like him realized that the future "democratic, na-

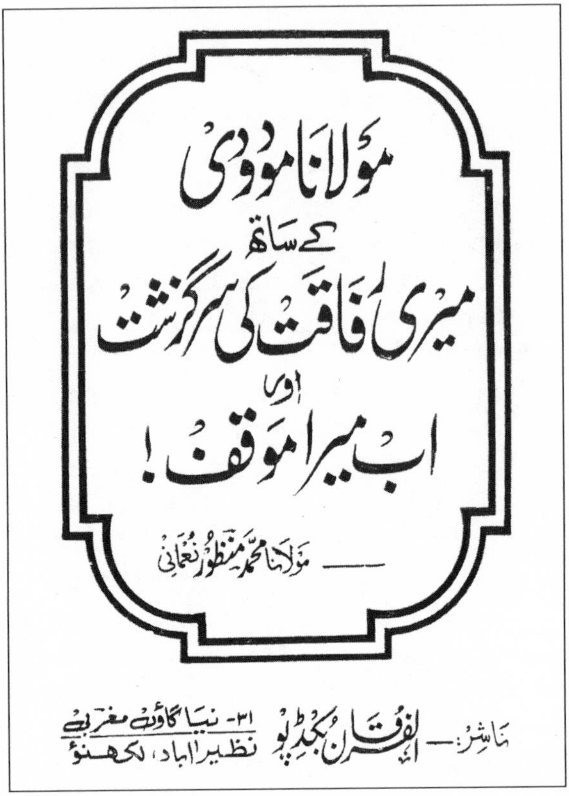

Cover of Manzur Nomani's book, 1980.
Used with permission by Maulana Yahya Nomani Sahib.

tional government" of India would create dangers for the desires, aspirations, and cultural identity of Muslims (15–16, 23–24).

What Nomani published as a book in 1980 was planned as a series of articles to appear in *Al-Furqān* in 1979. However, Nomani postponed its publication upon hearing the news of Maududi's demise in that year. In the joint issue of November–December 1979, Nomani published the first installment. While I cite the book derived from articles in *Al-Furqān*, it is important to note that Nomani had already published parts of his critique, in 1958, which had been met with countercritiques.[2] One such critical response came from Amir Usmani (1920–75)—poet, critic, and editor of an influential Urdu monthly, *Tajallī*, which he launched in 1949 from Deoband and continued to edit until his death (*Bazmesukhan.com* 2015). An admirer of Maududi, Usmani had not joined Jamaat, however. Usmani was a graduate of Deoband and it was important to him that on the cover of *Tajallī* he be identified as "Editor, Amir Usmani,

Cover of Tajallī, *November 1966, stating its editor's designation.*

a graduate of Deoband." *Tajallī* was known as one of the few "independent" journals to support Maududi. The other response came from Abullais Islahi Nadvi (hereafter Abullais), first *amīr* of Jamaat in independent India, who led Jamaat from 1948 to 1972 and again from 1981 till his death in 1990. Born in 1913 and educated at Nadvatul Ulema (Lucknow) and Madarsatul Islah (Azamgarh), Abullais published his response in *Zindegī*, the Urdu organ of India's Jamaat, in 1958.

As I have noted, Nomani's critique was not about principles but instead related to Maududi's life as a leader. Nomani's (1998, 26–27, 38, ii) central points of criticism were two: (1) Maududi's beard was short and his hair cut in an English style, and (2) in Maududi's home (*g̱har*) a young male cook was allowed to flout *pardāh* (distance to be maintained between men and women) while performing his duties. Nomani grouped the two points under the banner of sharia's injunctions (*aḥkām*). As for elements in his first point, Nomani noticed them when he met Maududi in Delhi. The second "came to his knowledge" when he stayed with Maududi and other Jamaat members on the campus of Darul Islam (in Pathankot, Gurdaspur, currently in the Indian Punjab). On the initiative of Neyaz Ali and the poet Muhammad Iqbal, Darul Islam was established, in March 1938, as an endowed research institute that Maududi was invited to lead. However, owing to some differences (on which, see Azam 2010, 186–99), in January 1939 Maududi left Darul Islam for Lahore (Nasr 1996, 34–39). After Jamaat's formation in August 1941, its headquarters shifted back, in June 1942 (Nasr 1994, 23; cf. Baghpati 1979, 73), from Lahore to Darul Islam. Nomani stayed with Maududi for "two, three days" (Nomani 1998, 32) in 1938. He did not specify the duration of his 1942 stay.[3]

When Nomani met Maududi first, he was "jolted" to see that his beard was too short. He was also aghast at Maududi's "Western/English hair [*angrēzī bāl*]," a description whose meaning Nomani never clarified. During his stay at Darul Islam, Nomani found Maududi's beard still short. Nomani's insistence that Maududi have a long beard in consonance with what the former regarded as the correct interpretation of sharia was premised on the belief that if a leader's life didn't match his message (*dʿāvat*), the movement could not gather momentum; and if it did by virtue of the power of pen, it wouldn't succeed in its goal of reform. The oral exchange between Maududi and Nomani (as the latter recorded and I paraphrase below) is as follows:

NOMANI: Tell me clearly, do you observe sharia's injunctions [*aḥkām-e-sharīʿat*]?

MAUDUDI: To the extent it is possible and I want to observe them.

NOMANI: Do you consider it [pointing toward Maududi's short beard] legitimate [*jāʾez*] to keep your beard this short?

MAUDUDI: I don't consider it *ḥaram* or illegitimate [*nājāʾez*]. In my view, a beard should be long enough to be noticeable from a distance and the fist-length beard is Sunna.

NOMANI: Books of *fiqh* state that a beard shorter than fist-length is *nājāʾez* and there is a consensus among scholars over it.

MAUDUDI: Books of the Hanbali school state that a shorter beard is also *jāʾez* (legitimate).

NOMANI: Your beard is too short [invoking hadith and *fuqaha* without naming them]. In my view, and from the viewpoint of hadith as well, there is no justification for it.

MAUDUDI: You are right; I should reform it.

NOMANI: Don't you consider it [pointing toward Maududi's hair] a problem [*maẕāʾeqā*] to have such hair?

MAUDUDI: Do you think it is *qazzʿ* [prohibited in hadith]?

NOMANI: I don't say it is *qazzʿ*. However, to wear such hair is the way of the nonvirtuous [*ghair ṣāleḥīn*].[4]

MAUDUDI: You are right about this as well. I will reform it.

Nomani (1998, 38–41, 48–49) concluded his version of conversation with Maududi by noting that "I also inquired about many other things concerning his personal life and he comfortably addressed them." It was after this conversation that Nomani agreed to attend the foundational meeting of Jamaat in 1941, where he proposed Maududi as its *amīr* (president). Six months later, when Nomani went to Lahore to attend another meeting, he was saddened to see none of the desired changes in Maududi's appearance. With the shift of Jamaat's office from Lahore back to Pathankot, Maududi moved to Pathankot. So did Nomani. Hardly had Nomani spent a week there that he came to know things concerning *aḥkām-e-sharīʿāt*. In his 1958 critique, he mentioned, without naming it, "the problem in Maududi's home [*ghar*]." In 1980, he was more precise:

> Only two, four days after my stay, probably through a friend, it came to my knowledge that Maulana's [Maududi's] chef (who was young) cooks inside the women's section of the house [*zanānḳhānā*] and that there is no *pardāh* [veiling] with him [by his wife] and that it is casting a bad impression on friends residing at Darul Islam. . . . At first my heart and mind refused to believe it. . . . However, ultimately it turned out to be true. This incident jolted and shook me. Probably this might have been due to the fact that it was inconceivable in the environment in which I had grown that even a minimum standard of piety and religiosity would allow it. (Nomani 1998, 53–54n1)[5]

So saddened was Nomani that he wept in privacy. He wrote letters to two of his friends within Jamaat to seek their advice. Receiving no reply, Nomani "unveiled his secret" to a friend at Darul Islam who shared his concern. At this friend's advice, he wrote a ten- to twelve-page letter listing his complaints to Maududi, who replied in less than ten hours. This reply didn't lessen Nomani's restlessness. He decided to leave Jamaat (pro-Jamaat writers state that Jamaat expelled Nomani; Saeed 1998, 31).[6]

Amir Usmani (2002, 20) wrote a countercritique of Nomani in the June 1958 issue of *Tajallī*. Usmani began by asserting that he would not undertake a thorough "critique" of Nomani's article because it didn't raise any "scholarly issue." A key target of his critique was Nomani's "style of expression," for this style flouted the moral limits recognized by every civilized morality, not only that of Islam. What Usmani really meant was the issue of "home." But if home was mentioned, he contended, it should have been with all of the details because central to critique were transparency and a full presentation of the issue at stake so that "the court of reason and justice could judge" what the truth was.

> Apparently, Maulana Nomani is displaying caution and piety: look, despite being an opponent I kept the secret of "home" and didn't even cite the letter [to Maududi]. However, he has also clearly mentioned his impressions in such a way that readers are left free to nurse their worst speculations. . . . This is dishonesty, not piety. . . . Ethics and justice demand that those deeds of Maulana Maududi and the issues concerning his home which he [Nomani] presents as a charge sheet should have been described in detail and with precision so that readers could judge on their own if things construed as crime to a frightening extent are factually so or if they are simply a result of Nomani's state of mind or his distinct worldview. (Usmani 2002, 38–39)

A significant portion of *The Tale* critiques Maududi's position on women's participation in politics. The first part of *The Tale* ends with Nomani's leaving Jamaat and includes events up to 1942. In part 2, spanning eighty-six pages, he includes events to 1965. Of this, twenty-five pages are devoted to opposing Maududi's support for the presidential candidacy of Pakistan's Fatima Jinnah. In early 1965, during his dictatorship (1958–69), the Sandhurst-trained General Muhammad Ayub Khan of Pakistan staged sham elections to legitimize his rule. Propounding "basic democracy," Khan desired to see Pakistan "as organized as her army" (qtd. in Sayeed 1961, 251). Comprising five tiers of government, of which only the local level, called "union councils," were elected by the people, Khan's was a militarized model of indirect elections. Only "Basic Democrats," those elected to the councils, were entitled to choose the president. Political parties, Jamaat included, came together under the banner of Combined Opposition Parties (COP) to defeat Khan's dictatorship. Against Khan, the COP fielded Fatima Jinnah, sister of Pakistan's founder, Muhammad Ali Jinnah. Chaudhury Muhammad Ali of the COP met Maududi in jail to seek his approval (Nasr 1994, 155). Maududi's backing of Fatima Jinnah,[7] however, contradicted his earlier position that Islam did not allow a woman to be a legislator, let alone a head of state (see chap. 6). While advocating equal voting rights for men and women, Maududi considered it illegitimate for women to stand for Parliament. Addressing a meeting of women in Montgomery (currently Sahiwal, a town in the Pakistani Punjab), in 1950, he had asserted that while women should form their own associations and "unbiasedly critique the government," it was "not legitimate [*jā'ez*] that women become members of the Parliament" (Maududi 1976a, 153). Fifteen years later Maududi argued that a woman could become a political premier: "While the sanctity [*ḥurmat*] of some things deemed as *ḥarām* by sharia is categorical, eternal, and can't be changed under any circumstance, the sanctity of some other things is such that under necessity it can change. Now it is clear that the prohibition to make a woman *amīr* does not belong to the same genre of sanctity that is eternal and categorical" (qtd. in Nomani 1998, 118).

To Nomani, Maududi's support for Jinnah based on sharia was not only an endorsement of *ḥarām* but also an appeal to people to approve that *ḥarām*. Furthermore, Maududi's support was not a contextual step, for it opened, Nomani feared, "a wide gate of *fitna* in *dīn* [Islam] till the end of the world." The primary reason for this, Nomani (1998, 120–21, 75) underscored, was that Jamaat was led by "modern educated people" unfamiliar with, even disrespectful of, scholars preceding Maududi and their reliance on Maududi's writings alone. Abullais (2002, 131), whom I mentioned earlier, critiqued Nomani for delivering his judgment without saying anything about the method used to reach the judgment (*ṭarīqa' istembāṯ*). He reasoned that Nomani's judgment would be valid if he knew how many of the modern educated members had no other education (that is, no other nonmodern, traditional education) at all and how many of them had some. It was also possible that many of them had acquired that education through self-study. Had he done this investigation (*taḥqīq*), Nomani would have been able to categorize Jamaat members accordingly. This alone would not have been sufficient, however. The next step entailed, Abullais argued, determining how each category of people viewed Maududi and scholars preceding him, and if the view of each was correct. To Abullais (2002, 132–33), Nomani's "categorical judgement" was devoid of evidence, investigation, and necessary differentiation among Jamaat members.

Another important point in part 2 of *The Tale* was Nomani's (1998, 122, 118, 76) view that Maududi and Jamaat had deviated from their earlier path and now were "only concerned with the pursuit of power," for in Pakistan they contested elections and adopted policies similar to other political parties even if they "went against Islamic principles." Nomani sarcastically described Jamaat members participating in elections as "election mujahedin." In that observation Usmani (2002, 88–92), however, saw Nomani's "innocence and deceit." From the very beginning, he argued, Jamaat stood for a shift of power from the corrupt to the virtuous. Usmani found it astonishing that "like political tricksters and ignorant scholars," even a "reliable scholar" like Nomani construed power as a "forbidden tree," forgetting that in itself power was not necessarily bad. As for Jamaat's participation in elections and its adoption of policies similar to those of other parties, Usmani asked if Nomani meant that instead of participating in elections, the Pakistani Jamaat should have embraced an underground method, as terrorist organizations do, or should have kept itself aloof from elections to maintain its identity as a religious organization. On this point, Abullais's response to Nomani was different from Usmani's. Stressing that Nomani's article appeared in the wake of a crisis within Pakistan's Jamaat, he emphasized that the controversies over whether the Pakistani Jamaat should participate in elections or remain focused on reform[8] (India's Jamaat then didn't participate in elections) were "internal matters of the Pakistani Jamaat." Abullasi (2002, 108) continued, "For us [India's Jamaat] there is neither a need for nor any benefit in" discussing them. As Nomani had commented about Pakistan's Jamaat, based on his conversations with ex-members during his trip to Pakistan (in 1957), Abullais wondered about the nature of those conversations. To cite people's views expressed in private conversations, he averred, went against ethics and etiquette (*adab*). Furthermore, he found Nomani's mention of "reliable sources," without reference and specification, problematic. Usmani also wondered about the timing of and motive behind the publication of Nomani's article. Call it a coincidence or miracle, Usmani noted, but whenever the Indian government cracked down on Jamaat, Nomani's pen swung into action against Jamaat.[9]

Unlike Nomani, whose early criticism of Maududi and Jamaat concerned beards, hair, and women, Vahiduddin Khan's was predominantly conceptual. Born in 1925 in Azamgarh, Khan joined Jamaat soon after Partition and worked for ten years, also becoming a member of the Central Advisory Council (*markazī majlis-e-shūra*), Jamaat's most powerful elected executive body. From 1956 until his resignation, he worked in its research and writing department, which allowed him to do extensive study. Khan resigned in 1963 and published his critique: *Tʿābīr kī ghalaṭī* (*The Folly of Interpretation*, hereafter *The Folly*). His dissatisfaction with Jamaat ideology, as *The Folly* records, began in the late 1950s, following his immersion in the Qurʾān (Khan 1995 [1963]: 23). It is hard to separate his critique of Jamaat from the crisis of the mid-1950s, however. Of its 344 pages, 114 documented Khan's oral and written communication with Jamaat scholars and leaders, including Maududi (those communications comprise twenty-three pages). Khan first aired his discontent in conversation with Jamaat leaders, who advised him to write it down, promising to reply. The written reply didn't satisfy Khan, who sent his text, in June 1962, to Maududi in Pakistan. Initially inclined to respond, Maududi later chose not to: "Your text is like a book. . . . From introductory notes [and elsewhere], I feel the issue concerns not only a few objections. Rather, your study has taken you in a direction opposite to that which my study has taken me. Given this, it seems a bit vain that you and I get embroiled in a debate. . . . If you have come to the conclusion that I have entirely misunderstood Islam [*dīn*], then disassociate yourself from that viewpoint and positively begin propagating what you deem correct. However, if you consider it necessary to demonstrate mistakes in my interpretation I have no objection. You may publish your book" (qtd. in Khan 1995 [1963], 114).

When Khan insisted on a reply from Maududi, the latter again refused, noting its fruitlessness, telling Khan that, in the "text you talk to me by placing yourself in a higher position" and "your style of dialogue assumes that one who doesn't accept your viewpoint is ignorant and unwise." Maududi also opined that Khan's study was "highly defective," and rather than "fully grasp my position," Khan made a "wrong interpretation" of it. Khan admitted that his style might be aggressive but said his sole aim was the "quest of truth." Maududi reread the text to reiterate his earlier judgment, pleading with Khan to read his own text from a "critical perspective." Maududi also felt that Khan would be satisfied with no less than an "admission of mistake [*ʿetrāf-e-ḳhaṭā*]" by him (qtd. in Khan 1995 [1963], 118, 121, 134). Khan concluded the communication as follows: "This text of mine is being published against my wishes. I am probably right to say that Maududi—not I—is responsible for it." From the introduction to Khan's book it is evident that Maududi was at least partly right, for in it Khan stated his objective as follows: "It is rather necessary that the correct interpretation [of Islam] be presented by first mounting a direct critique [*tanqīd*] on its earlier interpretation proving it wrong [*ghalaṭ*]." So preoccupied was Khan with the correctness of his own position and the incorrectness of Maududi's that he could not visualize another possibility. When a Jamaat leader told Khan that he agreed with the "*spirit*" but disagreed with the "*tone*" of his text and said that "though there is a difference between yours and Maududi's interpretation," nevertheless "both are also correct," Khan (1995 [1963], 132, 17, 30) found this utterly incomprehensible.

After the communication section I just discussed, *The Folly* has three additional sections. The first of these aimed to critique the basis of Maududi's ideology, showing that it was political and incorrect, since "in its favor there is no categorical verse [*āyā*] in the whole Qurʾān" (142). The second section dwelled on the consequences of that incorrect ideology. In the third section, Khan outlined the "correct notion" of Islam. My focus is on the first section.

According to Khan, Maududi's prime contribution lay in the realm of philosophy of religion (*ḥikmat-e-dīn*),[10] distinct from *fiqh*. *Fiqh* is about practical details and rules relating, for instance, to how the hajj should be performed; *ḥikmat* is the explication of an overall rationale for the hajj. Compared to *fiqh*, there was only a small body of work on the philosophy of religion, Valiullah's *Ḥujjat Allāh al Bāligha* being the most prominent example. To Khan, Maududi's contribution was a philosophical explication of Islam as an "*interrelated whole*." He found *ḥikmat* among different elements (*ajzāʾ*) of Islam, connecting them all to present the whole as a comprehensive *niẓām*—Islam as a way of life. Against its compartmentalization, Maududi presented Islam as a unity encompassing metaphysical, individual, and collective life, central to which is politics and a movement to enact that politics (Khan 1995 [1963], 138–40, 159–63).

Khan took Maududi's *Four Basic Terms of the Qurʾān* (*Qurʾān kī chār bunyādī iṣṭelāḥēñ*; hereafter *Iṣṭelāḥēñ*) as exemplification of his ideology. In it, Maududi had argued that to know the "authentic objective" of the Qurʾān was to grasp the "real and total" meanings of *ilah* (Allah), *rabb* (Lord), *ʿibādat* (worship), and *dīn* (religion). To Maududi, while their meanings were correctly understood at the time of the Qurʾān's revelation and in the generation after Prophet Muhammad, in subsequent centuries the real meanings of those terms got lost. Khan's first objection was to Maududi's claim of discontinuity in comprehension of the meanings. Contra Maududi, he saw continuity, *tasalsul* (on which see Graham 1993), from Prophet Muhammad's time until now. In preserved written records of the past, if the meanings Maududi attributed to those terms were absent, Khan argued, this meant that those meanings were attempts of the present. Khan's (1995 [1963], 149, 140) critique identified three fundamental problems in *Iṣṭelāḥēñ*.

> Equalization of the real [*aṣl*] with the additional and contextual [*iẓāfī, taqāẓa*];
> To render what is contextual as real and then attribute other things to it; and
> To present what is an additional aspect of Islam as the real message of the Qurʾān.

For Khan, the real in Islam meant not "believing in God as an ideological basis for a specific way of life [*ẓābṭa-e-ḥayāt*]" but a "deep attachment between God and humans," generating a "psychological condition when a human feels extreme love [*ḥubb-e-shadīd*] for God." According to Khan, in Maududi's rendition the weaving of the four Qurʾānic terms into a whole led to the eclipse of "the real." If Maududi's argumentation was based on establishing proximity and continuity between the metaphysical (*takvīnī*) and the worldly (*tashrīʿī*) (see chap. 4), Khan's (1995 [1963], 153–54, 221–25, 216) was the reverse: demonstrating distance and discontinuity. "To be religious," Khan argued, "is neither a political nor a civilizational matter" but instead an "absolutely personal affair" whereby an individual surrenders himself to God. In precisely this sense, he went on, the prophet Ibrāhīm was a Muslim (196). In disagreement with Maududi (1965), who held that أَقِيمُو الدِّين in the Qur'ān (e.g., *sura shūrā*, 13) meant establishing *dīn* (Islam) in its entirety, including social, political, and civic domains, Khan argued that it meant that which was common among the teachings of all prophets: monotheism, belief in the hereafter, and prophecy. To buttress his thesis, he cited *tafsīr* of scholars from the Arab world as well as from the subcontinent. He clarified, however, that he didn't expel collective and civilizational aspects from the ambit of *dīn*; he simply did not deem it obligatory (*farẓ*), as Maududi and his ilk did. He concluded that "the pages of the Qur'ān are unfamiliar with" the notion "that Allah has asked us to establish a political and civilizational [*tamaddunī*] *niẓām*."

Khan repeatedly said that his critique didn't mean that he considered the political irrelevant or un-Islamic. He wrote, "There is no doubt that in one sense *dīn* is state and *niẓām*" (193) and "it is absolutely right that Islam has its own way of life and the Prophet has also established a government [*ḥūkūmat*]." Once he even said that "if an Islamic government is established here, I will surely be happy" (254). Khan's primary critique, then, was that establishing a government was neither the real demand of Islam nor the mission of its believers (nor was it the message of the prophets). Like Egypt's Ali Ar-Raziq (1982) and Muhammad Said Al-Ashmawy (1998, 78; also see Tayob 2010, chap. 5), he stated that if it were so, it would have surely been mentioned in the Qur'ān (256). Power is a gift (*'ṭyā*) from Allah, Khan observed, not the mission of Muslims (Khan 1995 [1963], 168).

Khan, over twenty years younger than Maududi, did not personally know Maududi. In contrast, our third critic (in this section), Abul Hasan Ali Nadvi (1914–99), a scholar of global renown who became the rector of Nadvatul Ulema in 1961, knew him. He met Maududi first in August 1939 and maintained postal contact with him thereafter. Like Nomani, Nadvi was influenced by Maududi's *Tarjumānul Qur'ān*. In 1940, Maududi had sought Nadvi's advice about the Arabic translation of his book, *Pardāh* (see chap. 6). In January 1941, Nadvi invited Maududi to deliver a talk at Nadvatul Ulema. When Jamaat was formed, Nadvi joined and led the group in Lucknow, where he was based (Nadvi 2000a, 242, 2000b, 268–69, 273). Three years later he resigned. In Nadvi's account, he made this decision based on his experience with "individuals of Jamaat." Without offering details and precise sources, Nadvi held that these individuals (1) gradually began to think that no one had understood Islam better than Maududi did, (2) became fearless in speaking their thoughts vis-à-vis the religious circles (*dīnī ḥalqōñ*), and (3) didn't show adequate perfection in their piety and spirituality. Though impressed by his writings, in lived interactions he did not feel spiritually attracted to Maududi. Nadvi nonetheless continued his ties with Maududi and Jamaat and didn't air his critique until 1979, when he published *ʿAṣr-e-ḥāẓīr mēñ dīn kī tafhīm v tashrīḥ*.

For Nadvi (1980, 21), the reason for publishing this book was his commitment to *naṣīḥat* (advice)—a concept basic to moral theology. In an illuminating essay on Saudi Arabia, Talal Asad (1993, chap. 6) showed how modes of criticism and reasoning worked in a non-Enlightenment milieu. Unlike Asad and the actors in his prose, Nadvi saw *naṣīḥat* and *tanqīd/naqd* as linked. To Nadvi, criticism was rarely adversarial, intertwined as it was with *naṣīḥat*. To do critique that is constructive, positive, and noncombative, Nadvi noted, was far from easy. Terming it exceptional, he admitted that his own book on the Qadianis lacked these features for it was a refutation (*radd*) (Nadvi 1980, 22–23). When Nadvi published his book, he sent a copy to Maududi, who replied: "I received a copy of your new book. . . . I thank you for critiquing what you consider apprehensible in my thought. You have also done a frank critique of what you think might harm *dīn* and its followers. I have never considered myself beyond critique nor do I take it negatively. However, it is not necessary that I take every critique [*tanqīd*] as just and accept apprehensions [*khadshāt*] and doubts [*andēshōñ*] described by my critics as correct" (qtd. in Nadvi 2000b, 279–80).

Most elements of Nadvi's critique of Maududi as *andēshā* and *naṣīḥat* were already articulated, though differently, by Nomani[11] and Khan. Importantly, Nadvi had written the foreword to Nomani's book, and they were friends. Like Nomani, Nadvi also believed that modern, educated Muslims, more than traditional ones, felt attracted to Maududi. And like Khan, Nadvi also mounted his critique largely based on *Iṣṭelāḥēñ*. Stressing continuity rather than rupture, Nadvi argued that if the meanings of the four Qurʾānic terms became clear again only in the mid-twentieth century, as Maududi's claim implied, then, it raised doubts about the intellectual capability of the entire *umma* not to have understood them for that long (Nadvi 1980, 34–36). For him, continuity persisted in meanings as well as in practice (*ʿamal*). He cited Hassan Ismail al-Hudaybi (d. 1973), the Muslim Brotherhood's guide who had critiqued Maududi, as showing unbroken continuity (44). Clarifying that he didn't doubt Maududi's intention, he sharply disagreed with Maududi's exposition of the term *rabb*, which equated it with political "*sovereignty*." Nadvi mentioned that his friend Qutub (influenced by Maududi) interpreted Islam similarly. To critique both Maududi and Qutub, Nadvi again cited al-Hudaybi, who contended that divine sovereignty didn't mean humans had no freedom to legislate. Excluding the forbidden, Islam allowed freedom in most areas such as health, education, town planning, irrigation, traffic control, and so on (66–68). Like Nomani and Khan, Nadvi argued that Maududi ignored the spiritual dimension of Islam manifest in love (*moḥabbat*) and beauty (*jamāl*) of the divine (70). To Nadvi as well, power and state were not the foremost aim of *dīn*, simply a means (107–10). Nadvi concluded by appealing, especially to Jamaat, that "rather than take it as harsh they should express joy over this critique," for it was offered as an invitation to think beyond their exclusive circle so that they constructively related themselves to the wider society (126–28).

◆ Forceful Arguments

In 1965, *Tajallī* published a special double issue on Khan's book. The issue, titled "Critique Number [*tanqīd nambar*],"[12] contained four articles. The first, six pages long, was an excerpt from Maududi's *Tafhīmul Qur'ān* explicating the notion of أَقِيمُو الدِّيْنَ; the second was a fourteen-page letter by Sadruddin Islahi, a key intellectual mentioned in Khan's text as tasked by Jamaat with writing a response to Khan's critique; and the third was a twenty-one-page article on the concept of *dīn*, reproduced from *Fārān*, a journal published from Karachi. The final article (twenty-six pages) was by the editor himself. Amir Usmani had had no plan to review Khan's book, as it had "barely any impact either on scholars or commoners" and hence it was not Usmani's "religious duty" to critique it. In scholarly terms, he also found it weak. But when he learned that some people of Deoband planned to publicize Khan's book, he decided to open "the gates of critique [*naqd v naẓar*]."[13] Asking his audience to read his "partial" critique along with other articles, he began with a long quote from Khan detailing his psychological condition on 7 March 1963 (at 1:00 p.m.) while doing research on Maududi's *Iṣṭelāḥēñ*. With no one else in the library and surrounded by books, Khan stood up to shelve a volume of the *tafsīr* by Muhammad Ibn Jarir al-Tabari (839–923). Weak from continuous study, however, he fainted. When he recovered, he felt that "to have an exchange of ideas with early scholars of Islam [*aslāf-e-umma*] I had gone too far and felt tired. Despite this weakness I felt happy that I came to know their viewpoints, and now I am in a position to confidently refute the concept under discussion [Maududi's reading of Islam] on their behalf. It seemed as if the entire shelves of books are spirits [*rūḥēñ*] of *aslāf* standing behind me and I am proceeding with my weak hands and trembling feet for defense on their behalf. So happy I felt that my hunger, thirst,

Special issue "Critique Number" of Tajallī, *February–March 1965.*

and tiredness disappeared and I continued my study till sunset" (Khan 1995 [1963], 15).

With this quote Usmani showed that the intellectual and logical aspects of Khan's mind, as Khan himself described, were under the spell of speculation and imagination (*vahm v ḳhayāl*). Usmani asked what if not imagination and speculation were the spirits of *aslāf* that convinced Khan of the correctness of his own position? Furthermore, can one expect a serious thinker to consider as the foundation of his thought (and regard as right) something that emanated from his physical fragility? In Usmani's view, before beginning his research Khan had already decided that *aslāf* backed his position. Usmani's main target was not Khan's psychological state, however. With "forceful arguments [*dalā'l-e-qāherā*]," he aimed to show that Khan's knowledge of Arabic was defective. Khan had learned Arabic in a nonsystematic, informal way; he was insufficiently familiar with its grammar, morphology, syntax, and terminology. As a result, his translation of Arabic text was faulty. Against Maududi, who wrote that "the word *ʿibādat* was derived from *ʿabd*, Khan (1995 [1963], 185) argued that "ʿ*ibādat* was not derived from *ʿabd*; on the contrary *ʿabd* is derived from *ʿibādat*." Usmani (1965, 121, 105, 104) found this claim peculiar, as no dictionary supported it. He wished Khan had consulted a scholar more knowledgeable than himself about Arabic. Usmani enumerated fifteen such mistakes. As I am not qualified to discuss linguistic and grammatical issues, I will focus on other aspects of Usmani's critique. In Usmani's reading, Maududi's contention that Islam viewed political and civilizational issues in the framework of divine guidance was in consonance with tradition. Likewise, he held that there was nothing new in Maududi's contention that the notion of *rabb* encompassed the metaphysical as well as the worldly domains. He found Khan's claim that his argument was in line with that of all earlier interpreters of the Qurʾān unsustainable. He cited *Tafsīr al-manār* and Shabbir Ahmad Usmani's *tafsīr* (see Zaman 2012, 47, 286) to show that neither of them drew a sharp line between the metaphysical (*takvīnī*) and worldly (*tashrīʿī*) (Usmani 1965, 104, 108, 114, 123). Khan reached a different conclusion than Maududi, Usmani argued, simply because Khan lacked a "command over Arabic." Usmani concluded the linguistic part of his critique by inviting to readers to verify the mistakes he identified in Khan's book with any knowledgeable scholar not biased against Jamaat. In addition to the fifteen mistakes, Usmani held that Khan's concept of Islam was too personalized. Usmani called it "ascetic [*rahbānī*]." It was monodirectional, extremist, and thereby bereft of *tavāzun* (balance), which he considered to be the most delicate issue in Islam.

In the same issue of *Tajallī*, Muhammad Navaz critiqued not so much what Usmani viewed as ascetic in Khan's concept of Islam but a glaring contradiction at the very foundation of Khan's critique. Khan's distinction between the real (*aṣl*), on the one hand, and the additional and contextual (*taqāẓa, iẓāfī*), on the other, Navaz (1965, 79, 72–76, 77) argued, had no sanction in either the Qurʾān or hadith. Viewing them as a connected whole, Navaz averred that the heart and the spiritual were no less important than the political or the legal in Maududi's corpus. Agreeing with Khan that if Maududi erased the spiritual and matters of the heart it would be "an unforgivable mistake," he then asked if Maududi really did so. He gave citation after citation from Maududi's writings to demonstrate the salience of the spiritual and personal. He wondered why Khan exclusively relied on Maududi's *Iṣṭelāḥēñ* and not his other writings, noting that even *Iṣṭelāḥēñ* didn't argue what Khan attributed to it. To Navaz, Khan's critique was mere wordplay, for a careful reader would notice that after repeatedly stating that Maududi was wrong, Khan said exactly what Maududi had said: "I would have no objection if it was said that *dīn*, in accordance with its list of *aḥkām*, is the name of everything concerning different aspects of individual and collective life for which the Prophet instructed throughout his prophecy. From this angle, the word *dīn* is the title for the entire Islamic *aḥkām*. There is consensus on this matter and there is no question of any disagreement with it" (Khan 1995 [1963], 202).

If this was an accepted matter, Navaz asked, why did Khan waste nearly 100 pages saying that Maududi was wrong? Did not Khan in the passage cited mean that Islam included the personal and the individual as much as the political—a position upheld by Maududi? Navaz concluded that Khan's "critique was a manifestation of his intellectual confusion of staggering proportions." He continued, "The method of his [Khan's] critique is that he first attributes a specific thing to Maulana Maududi and then he enhances it with a notion of his own in order to mount a critique against his own self-created notion. However, when his mental anger becomes inclined to moderation, he repeats in a style specific to him what Maududi has already said" (Navaz 1965, 85).

Sadruddin Islahi[14] (1916–98, hereafter Sadruddin), another contributor to *Tajallī*, focused on a different aspect. Considered to be "the pen of Jamaat" in independent India by some of my interlocutors, he wrote a response to Khan's critique on behalf of Jamaat. His contribution to *Tajallī* touched on many aspects of Khan's book. My interest is in the communication between him and Khan. According to Sadruddin, of the seventeen people Khan spoke with in person (mentioned in the book), none certified the accounts of their conversation as Khan reported them. Some felt that their intentions were distorted; others held that things attributed to them in print had been taken out of context, either due to faulty memory or, possibly, willfully. Still others felt that words had been consciously omitted to give a specific color to the conversation (Sadruddin 1965, 58). Presenting his own case, Sadruddin wrote that he had at least three meetings with Khan (of which two were fairly long), but Khan mentioned only one short meeting.

It is important to look at the career behind the text that eventually became Khan's book. In Sadruddin's account, Khan's first text was about twenty pages long, on top of which Sadruddin wrote a three-page critical note and had an hour-long discussion with Khan. Some months later, Khan's text had grown to fifty pages with the addition of new issues and the revision of old discussions. Later the text become a "voluminous book" (Sadruddin 1965, 54). At the request of Jamaat, Sadruddin wrote a response of twenty-five pages, which Khan (1995 [1963], 35, 38) found "highly defective [*nāqiṣ*]," leading to no change in his earlier position. Khan wrote a summary response to Sadruddin, to which the latter responded, saying that if his earlier arguments seemed unconvincing to Khan there was no need for further correspondence. At that point Khan indicated his plan to write a more detailed response to Sadruddin, provided he promised a reply. Sadruddin said he would read the response before deciding whether it was appropriate to reply. There was no further communication between them.

In his contribution to *Tajallī*, Sadruddin explained why he did not reply. He also felt that Khan wrote his text while placing himself at an unusual height of intellect, thereby precluding a judicious understanding. Khan also doubted the piety, integrity, and intention of all except himself. Sadruddin cited passages with page numbers to prove his point. He found Khan's counterresponse to his own reply to be a work not of critique (*tanqīd*) but of refutation (*tardīd*), wherein Khan had mocked (*taẓḥīk*) him to show him as unlearned (*tajhīl*). Moreover, he guessed that Khan's aim was not to reach a true understanding but to gather the necessary materials and weapons to mount an attack on Jamaat by publishing his book. Immediately after writing the sentence that Khan's goal was not to reach an understanding but to gather materials for attacking Jamaat, Sadruddin added, "May God forgive me; I could not protect myself from that ill thought." Echoing Usmani, he felt that Khan did not have the necessary competence in Arabic to construe complex texts, as his discussion of the concept of *dīn* demonstrated. Khan had included parts of Sadruddin's reply in his book, which the latter found objectionable. Citing a long passage from his reply, he showed how Khan misled readers by only including part of the passage in his book. Sadruddin (1965, 63, 58, 53–57) wished that Khan had reproduced his entire reply and then critiqued it. He noted similar examples in Khan's communication with other Jamaat members.

In the preface to the 1995 edition of his book (which I reference here), Khan stated that some responded to his critique. Omitting Navaz and Sadruddin, he mentioned only Usmani, dismissing his critique as a "mockery [*masḳharāpan*]." He also published a rejoinder—"Critique or Mockery"—to Usmani.[15] Khan went on to say that though Usmani lived for another ten years after the publication of his rejoinder, he maintained a silence and did not write about *Tʿābīr kī ghalaṭī*. Khan concluded that probably Usmani "had realized his mistake" and, to compensate for it, in 1966 in *Tajallī* he employed all adjectives at his disposal to praise Khan's new book: *Mazhab avr jadīd challenge*. Usmani certainly praised it. But he also included a note (which Khan didn't mention) to readers, recalling his earlier critique of Khan: "Never forget that our endorsement or opposition is not predicated on personality. . . . Our agreement and disagreement, softness and harshness are all for the sake of truth [*ḥaqq*]. When we had earlier said openly that by writing *T'ābīr kī ghalaṯī* Vaḥīduddīn Ḳhān's pen met with errors and misguidance, we had done so not because of our ill will to his personality, in the same way we don't praise his new book because of his personality but due to the *ḥaqq* in it" (Usmani 1965, 9).

When I met Khan to discuss his critique, he advised me to first read his book (which I had done). He was firm in his view that Maududi was wrong and he right. When I asked him how his critique differed from others', he stressed that his was the only one that critiqued the very foundation of Maududi's thought (*fikr*): Manzur Nomani, Israr Ahmad (see chap. 5, n. 8), Kausar Niazi[16] (1934–94), Amin Ahsan (1904–97; see chap. 5, n. 22), and many others had articulated only small disagreements and their focus was on problems in the implementation of the ideology, not its foundational (in)correctness. In our hour-long meeting, he described himself as "secular," by which he meant that he hated no one and treated people of all faiths equally and with kindness. He claimed that he was "the only secular person in India" for, when invited, he attended meetings of the Rashtriya Swayamsewak Sangh (RSS), an organization formed in 1925 to establish a Hindu state. He likened attending such meetings to propagating Prophet Muhammad's message. He asked me if I knew that some Muslims also called him a "*sarkārī* [government] . . . or . . . *z'āfranī* [denoting the saffron flag of the RSS] *mavlānā*."[17] Nothing was more misleading, he clarified, than allegations such as these. He also claimed that he had turned down an offer from the BJP to make him a member of Parliament. Likewise, he had also declined an offer to become Delhi's governor.

◆ Recovering Universalism

As in the previous section, here the themes of critique of Maududi are multiple as the entry points of different critics are diverse. Clearly, their biographical trajectories are as important as their educational capital and social moorings, as well as their individual and collective visions of the past and future in the ways they formulate, articulate, and conduct their criticism. However, if there is a single thread that connects their multilayered responses it is their advancement of a universalism whose resources they find in Islam as well as in Maududi, though not adequately enough in the latter. If in some cases the catalog of that universalism is *Maqāṣid al-Sharia*, in others it is the designation of India as neither *Dārul Kufr* nor *Dārul Islām* but as *Dārul farōgh-e-insānīyat* (abode of flourishing for humanity), and in yet other cases it remains less than named.

Halfway through my fieldwork, a Jamaat critic advised me to meet Akram Zurti. Over eighty years old, Zurti had retired as a reader from Aligarh Muslim

University (AMU). In 1940, he had heard Maududi deliver a speech at AMU. This speech transformed Zurti into a Jamaat member. In the mid-1960s, however, he resigned. Among many reasons for his resignation, Jamaat's reduction of Islam to Muslims as a mere statistical community was the most important. In this reduction, Zurti saw the erosion of Islam's universalism. All the interlocutors I discuss in this section related themselves to and acknowledged Zurti as an articulator of this line of thought. While some did explicitly, others did implicitly. That Zurti was quite senior to them was important to that acknowledgment. Zurti's respectability was also due in part to his life approximating a *qalandar*, a person preoccupied with philosophy of the universe but least desirous of worldly success and recognition. Unlike many others who read less but wrote and published more, Zurti's case was the reverse. For Zurti, to study was to know God. To educate was at the same time to de-educate oneself. It was through these dual processes that he liberated himself from the prison (*ḥesār sē nikalnā*) he had been placed into by his father, a hard-line follower of Ahl-e-ḥadīs̤ school and an *ʿālim* of Gujarat in his own right.

> I was so prejudiced vis-à-vis Bohras [a branch in Shiism], groups other than Ahl-e-ḥadīs̤, and also Hindus. My father thought that only his *maslak* was right. Through sustained self-study I developed critical resources to craft my own understanding and find the truth. I read texts of all major religions. I also read the Gita and I like Arjun. . . . When I began to live away from my father, I stopped praying. My father used to beat me if I didn't pray. I told myself: if I pray under duress it will be far from genuine and purely for Allah. It was through self-study that later I began to pray without fear of any human and due to urge from within. . . . I have long studied the Qurʾān on its own. The Islam that emerges from my study of the Qurʾān is radically different from the Islam most Muslims practice and talk about. . . . There is a need to de-Muslimize the Qur'ān.

Zurti recited a couplet from Maulana Rum (in Urdu he is known more as Rum than Rumi) to elucidate what it means to know God and what He wants: "Tū barāēy vaṣl kardan āmadī [To connect, you have come] / Nēy barāēy faṣl kardan āmadī [Not to separate, you have come]."[18] He asked me to explain it, so I did. "I didn't expect someone based in a Western university to know Farsi. Do you know Arabic?" he asked. "Only elementary-level," I replied. "If you can't understand the Qurʾān in its original language," he said, "our conversation won't be fruitful." I felt ashamed. "You must learn Arabic soon," Zurti said as if to invite a promise from me.

Returning to the couplet, he elaborated that Allah, surprised at the prophet

Mūsā's response to the shepherd, reminded Mūsā that he was sent to connect people, not to separate them. This connection is grounded in the very idea of *dīn* (religion). In *sura an-naṣr,* Allah calls it *dīn-Allāh* (Allah's religion). Unfortunately, some Muslims, including some *ʿulema,* describe Islam as *dīn-e-Muḥammadī,* Muhammad's religion. Central to Allah's religion are *āfāqīat* (universalism) and justice (*ʿadl*). Critique (*tanqīd*) is a method and mode of knowledge deployed to determine what is universal and just, the permanent principles of the Qurʾān. In *sura mujādilah,* a woman critiques and argues with Prophet Muhammad for delivering a judgment about divorce she thought was grossly unfair. She later complained to Allah, who through revelation overruled Prophet Muhammad's judgment. The Prophet judged the issue of divorce based on prevalent customs, whereas Allah judged it on the principle of *āfāqīat,* which means, inter alia, defining who is a mother.[19] According to Zurti, when assessed from the perspective of the Qurʾān and its universalism, many *aḥādīṡ* (plural of *ḥadīṡ,* or hadith) become doubtful: "Everything that contradicts the Qurʾān Muslims ought to disown." In the collection by Imam Bukhari and Imam Muslim, he continued, there is a hadith: "Don't take the initiative in greeting Jews and Christians." To Zurti, this negates Qurʾānic universalism; for in *sura an-nisa* (86), God says, "Whenever you are greeted, you should do better than others." In Zurti's reading of this verse, it means taking the initiative to greet others, whatever their faith. Contrary narratives, Zurti held, were made to instill tribal pride and dilute Qurʾānic universalism.

According to Zurti, Maududi certainly had the intellectual ability and critical capacity to decipher Qurʾānic universalism and justice—and in many of his early writings he actually did so—but in later years Maududi trod a different path. He was only half-familiar with science. Instead of reading the divine signs correctly and universally, he attributed to them his own narrow views and the prevalent notions of the age. Every sentence of the Qurʾān is called an *āyāh* (symbol) precisely because it requires understanding and reason for its explication. Allah wants us to argue, critique, and find what is beneficial to humanity using our own reason. He gave humans complete freedom about how to rule as long as the affairs of the state are in line with Qurʾānic universalism, justice, and morality (*akhlāq*). Maududi's writings on an Islamic state tell readers that under an Islamic state humans would have no freedom to make laws. Their role would only be to implement laws that ignorant theologians made centuries ago. Maududi misunderstood the meaning of "divine sovereignty," equating it with God's government. There can never be God's government; government is always by humans. The state run by universalist Muslims would be like any other government; its *differentia specifica,* however, would be the principles guiding it. The Qurʾān gives the principles; the delineation and practical details are left open to humans to consider in light of those principles.

In Zurti's view, Maududi's idealization of the caliphate was overenthusiastic. The election of the first caliph, Abu Bakr, was imperfect. He should have drafted a constitution to set the criteria for elections as well as the conditions under which a ruler could be changed. Bakr should have arranged to acquire a copy of Solon's (630–560 BC) constitution from Greece to assess its merits and demerits. Solon's denial of rights to slaves was clearly antiuniversalist, but some of his ideas could have been creatively adapted to the Arabian context. A committee of experts (appointed by Bakr) should have drafted a new constitution articulating Qurʾānic universalism and justice to stem the chaos that followed. It was due to this lack of any constitutional provision ensuring the mutual consultation the Qurʾān so firmly advocates that Bakr, disregarding the opinions of Prophet Muhammad's companions, decided to undertake jihad against those who refused to pay *zakāt*. To Zurti, those who refused to pay *zakāt* did so not for lack of piety; instead, as members of non-Quraish collectivities, they refused it to protest being denied any say in the formation of the government (*ḥūkūmat sāzī*).

I met three more individuals whose views broadly echoed Zurti's line of thought. Rahmat Bedar was one. Trained as an economist, he taught at AMU. In the late 1970s, Bedar went to Saudi Arabia and subsequently to the United States, where his children lived. A member of Jamaat, he had been on its national *shūra* for decades. While most within Jamaat considered him an influential thinker, a few within and outside the organization regarded him as anti-Jamaat. This contradictory positioning of Bedar resembled, in some ways, the description of Australian Catholic University (ACU) by some as Anti-Catholic University.

Like Zurti, Bedar regarded the Qurʾān as the only authentic (*mustanad*) source. When I met him, he was studying the subject of *Maqāṣid al-Sharīʿā*. He gave me a copy of his bibliography with around thirty references in Arabic[20] and five in English.[21] It was through the lens of his interest in *Maqāṣid al-Sharīʿā* that the conversation about critique, the state, and Maududi ensued. To Bedar, Maududi was an important thinker of the past; but what mattered more were the present and future, about which he found the works of Tariq Ramadan and Rachid Ghannouchi more valuable than Maududi's. Bedar was concerned more with economic matters, to which Islamic movements paid inadequate attention even as a hadith stated that poverty turned a person away from God. Economy, understood conventionally as "national economy," was less relevant in the face of globalization and the increasing financialization of the economy. If national economy needed a reconceptualization, so did the notion of the world split into Muslim and non-Muslim. A significant number of Muslims lived in the non-Muslim world (one-third of the total Muslim population), especially in the West, as did a significant number of non-Muslims in the Muslim world. Denying non-Muslims in Muslim-majority societies the rights Muslims enjoyed in non-Muslim-majority societies was simply unfair, necessitating as it did a radical revision of *fiqh* developed in medieval times under a different context. Furthermore, Muslims in the Arab world as well as on the subcontinent rarely took into account the contributions and condition of Muslims in Southeast Asia, notably in Indonesia, Malaysia, Singapore, and Thailand. Any thinker's ideas, Maududi's included, ought to be assessed, Bedar urged, if they were relevant to the changed circumstances of our times, when global warming, hunger and poverty, the weaponization of economies, and water scarcity impact all of humankind. To Bedar, Maududi's exposition on the state was important. But what would that state be and what would it do in practice beyond the mere rhetoric of a state based on "divine sovereignty"? Who would shape its policies and how? Would it be universal in its reach or would it be ethnic to serve a specific community?

Such questions were at the heart of *Maqāṣid al-Sharīʿā*, a theme on which Maududi rarely elaborated. Relevant to the future was Maududi's espousal of universalism and his critique of Muslim nationalism. To Bedar, Maududi's critique of the Muslim League, that the League had made Islam and nationalism into substitutes for each other, was correct. Thus Maududi's presentation of Islam as an ideational template of universal values and principles beyond a Ram Das (a Hindu) or an Allah Bakhsh (a Muslim), as he presented it in his *Ḵhuṭ̤bāt*, was exemplary. But he vacillated between universalism and nationalism; in his later life he veered more toward the latter. Moreover, despite the independent critical mind he displayed in his early life, Maududi remained a follower of a specific *fiqh*, of Imam Hanifa. This prevented him from separating *fiqh* from sharia and identifying the universal aims of the latter.

The renewed interest in *Maqāṣid al-Sharīʿā* was precisely to determine its larger aims, which preoccupation with the particularities of *fiqh* obscured. A specific ruling of sharia was not the same as the objectives of sharia, and in some cases the former might even negate the latter. When asked why he did not offer a textual citation to support his argument about the necessity for determining *Maqāṣid al-Sharīʿā*, al-Juwayni replied, I always keep in mind the objective and spirit of sharia and draw conclusions from what I see and understand. Ishaq al-Shatibi (d. 1388) made an important contribution by asserting that there were many domains in which *ijtihād* could be carried forward by ordinary Muslims, not only *ʿulema*, for it did not require knowing Arabic. If one was familiar with *Maqāṣid al-Sharīʿā* through Arabic sources, its application and amplification required knowledge of the world through reason (*ʿaql*), not Arabic per se. To Bedar, *Maqāṣid al-Sharīʿā* in the twenty-first century and beyond must address the concerns and aspirations of people of all faiths, not just Muslims. When asked who the best among humans is, Prophet Muhammad replied, "One who is first in benefiting all human beings." Several passages in the Qurʾān (*shuʿraʾ*, 182; *ʿarāf*, 85; *Ṣ*, 26; *hadīd*, 25; and others) underlined the goal of benefiting humanity by practicing and establishing justice, including the fairness of weight and measurement in transactions. Philosophers thus far had identified the aims of *Maqasid al-Sharīʿā* as protection of (1) religion (*dīn*), (2) life (*jān*), (3) reason and intellect (*ʿaql*), (4) progeny (*nasl*), and (5) property (*māl*). Bedar wanted to broaden it by adding the following:

Pursuit of human dignity and decency;
Provision of fundamental freedom;
Establishment of justice;
Sustenance of all and elimination of poverty;
Social security and peace;
Decrease in the growing gap between the rich and the poor; and
Mutual cooperation at international levels.

Naqi Rahman, who held a PhD in chemistry from a top university in India and was once a Jamaat sympathizer, expressed similar ideas. Without using the terminology of *Maqāṣid al-Sharīʿā* Rahman critiqued Maududi for phrasing Jamaat's goal as *iqāmat-e-dīn*, the establishment of religion (which replaced the earlier phrase *ḥukumat-e-ilāhiya*). From the universal paradigm of the Qurʾān, he argued, the goal of a movement should not be *iqāmat-e-dīn* but rather the establishment of justice (*iqāmat-e-ʿadl v inṣāf*), which religion stood for. Since the central message of the Qurʾān vis-à-vis public life is justice for all, regardless of faith, Muslims and Jamaat likewise should strive for universal justice. Thus viewed, the women's liberation movement, which sought equality under the law, was already Islamic. Rahman distinguished women's liberation from feminist movements. He termed the latter as glorification of *nafs* and negative in the long run for societal balance. To Rahman, if women's liberation movements were Islamic, then it followed that the imposition of *jizyā* on non-Muslims by Muslim rulers was wrong. The justification for that imposition was human, not divine; the Qurʾān did not sanction any such ruling.

In this context, the account given by Ijaz Akbar, who taught at AMU for over two decades, was both similar and different. He grew up in a Jamaat environment, as his father was a member. Many non-Jamaat people considered Akbar to be a Jamaat loyalist, but this was decidedly untrue. Akbar was a relentless critic of Jamaat. In Jamaat's philosophy he saw only a pale shadow of philosophy but no comprehensive philosophy in its own right. If Plato, Hume, and Kant figured in his conversation, so did Al-Farabi, Ibn Sina, Ghazali, and other thinkers. For Akbar, religious philosophy was different from modern philosophy in that it had to ground itself in the divine. For Muslims, the Qur'ān and reason are two fundamental sources needed to understand and live in the world. In Akbar's view, the Qur'ān asked its readers and listeners to think, reason, and reflect. Without grounding in science and philosophy, therefore, there could be no adequate comprehension of the Qur'ān. Thinking with reason, practically more than speculatively, was continual. To stop thinking was to intellectually die. Muslim monarchical polities were politically places of *shirk* because they suppressed thinking as enjoined by the Qur'ān. Continual thinking was no less relevant to sharia. People tended to forget, Akbar noted, that the sharia of *ḥaẓrat* ʿIsā was contextual, as was Mūsā's. As there would be no prophet after Muhammad, Muslims must continually rethink issues of practical and policy concerns, while being attentive to the universal and permanent principles of the Qur'ān—justice and monotheism. The *ʿulema* looked at the Qur'ān arithmetically (only once does it mention arithmetic, in relation to inheritance) rather than philosophically and universally, key concerns for Akbar.

The problem with later Maududi, Akbar maintained, was that he nearly stopped thinking. On issues such as women's rights (more below) he reasserted *fiqh* positions over two centuries old (see chap. 6); as he did vis-à-vis people of other faiths, disregarding their equality. For Akbar, a universal reading of the Qur'ān indicates that the state must be secular (which does not mean that it should deny religion) in treating people of many faiths equally. India's constitution, he observed, was already Islamic in many ways. If the addressee of the Qur'ān is not Muslims alone but people in general, logically there cannot be multiple standards of justice. Akbar found it illogical that while a non-Muslim could embrace Islam, a Muslim embracing another religion would be subject to scrutiny or punishment.

To substantiate his point about continual rethinking, Akbar referred to the case of water becoming impure (and hence unsuitable for ablution) when an animal fell in a well. Books of *fiqh* continued to state that forty buckets of water should be taken out of the well to make it pure, whereas science had found a more suitable answer. Chemicals could be added to the water to purify it more quickly and efficiently. Likewise, in cases of rape, Akbar said, *ʿulema* continued to insist on two eyewitnesses before a rapist could be punished. This too was illogical; it was also antiwomen and in fact against Qur᾿ānic justice. Since rape rarely happened in public, producing two witnesses was almost impossible. Why did *ʿulema* oppose DNA testing as evidence in such matters? Akbar cited a few cases from Pakistan where women, unable to produce witnesses, were themselves punished, while the rapists were let free. The courts that freed rapists ruled on the basis of sharia. Does not this injustice by the courts, he asked, go against the justice central to the Qur᾿ān?

As the first phase of my fieldwork finished in Aligarh, I moved to Delhi where I met Maghfur, the director of an institute focused on research, publications, and public talks about marginalized Indians, particularly Muslims. Speakers and participants invited to its programs included Muslims, Hindus, Christians, and Buddhists. Maghfur came under the influence of Jamaat and the writings of Maududi while earning his master's in economics during the 1970s. In 1974, he also attended a regional congress of Jamaat in Delhi. He was equally, if not more, influenced by the books of Amin Ahsan (1904–97), especially those written before Ahsan left Jamaat. In particular, he liked his writings on monotheism and the purification and cultivation of self.[22] Maghfur interacted with the Jamaat circle then, as he did occasionally at the time of my fieldwork. He never joined Jamaat.

It took many phone calls before he agreed to meet with me. In the initial phase of our first meeting, he was more a listener than a speaker. He asked many questions about my research and about me. To Maghfur, Maududi was a key figure who cleared the layers of dust clouding the understandings of authentic Islam. He was a genius. But he was a man of his time and space. And only prophets are beyond time and space. For humans who are not prophets, there is no direct divine message instructing them to do or stop doing something. Mistakes by humans are of two types: natural and deliberate. Natural (*fiṭrī*) mistakes relate to new works in circumstances unwitnessed in the past. If Maududi was a genius in some respects, he made natural mistakes in others. Maududi's achievement lay in presenting Islam to people like Maghfur in a systematic, rational way. Most *ʿulema* of the nineteenth and twentieth centuries had interpreted Islam aspectually; Maududi did it comprehensively. To Maghfur, Maududi identified the spirit of Islam that connected to the economy as much as to society, culture, and politics. Above all, he offered a methodology to think about Islam and the modern world while embracing both. Contra Vahiduddin Khan (discussed above) and others, Maghfur considered Maududi's books like *Ḳhilāfat v mulūkīat* and *Tajdīd v aḥyā-e-dīn* to be works of methodology.

When I interrupted Maghfur to ask for his views on Maududi's idea of the state, he ignored my question to stress Maududi's major achievement. Maududi was one of the few thinkers of the twentieth century, Maghfur said, to present Islam in its original form. Neither ethnicity, nationality, or geography nor tribal loyalty, sectarian fence, or racial bond interested Islam. Islam stood above those ascriptive affiliations as a set of principles and values addressing the whole of humankind. The identification of the universal principles together with a workable methodology geared to the task of that identification distinguished Maududi from his contemporaries and predecessors. And critique was central to both. When I raised the issue of the state again, he advised me to reserve this "delicate [*bārīk*]" issue for our next meeting.

In our subsequent meeting, which began after dusk, Maghfur was ready to discuss the state. As many academics do, he first laid out the larger premises of his views. To evaluate a thinker is to be alert to yesterday, today, and tomorrow. Maududi's context was British colonialism and the fight against it (independence). Of the many schools of thought present then, three were prominent: nationalists (Congress), Hindu revivalists, and the Muslim League. Bal Gangadhar Tilak (1856–1920), Gandhi, and Nehru belonged to the Congress, whereas Keshav Baliram Hedgewar (1889–1940) and S. P. Mookherjee (1901–53) belonged to the Hindu revivalist camp. The line between them was rarely well-demarcated, though. Muhammad Ali Jinnah began as a Congress leader and later shifted to the Muslim League (for some time he belonged to both). Individuals such as Subhash Chandra Bose (1897–1945) and his followers aimed to secure independence by force and violence. Maududi appeared on the scene to present his own view of a state based on Islamic principles. Much of this was no more than an intellectual sketch. He neither specified the modes of people's participation in politics nor sufficiently visualized what would happen to Muslims after independence and Partition. More important, as independence approached, the universal principles of Islam that Maududi had elaborated earlier, especially during the 1930s, began to fade. Though earlier he had correctly dis-identified Islam with nationalism of any hue, around 1947, and certainly later in Pakistan, he himself began to act more like a nationalist than a universalist. The general conceptualization of a state based on Islamic principles was right in Maghfur's view; Maududi's specific rendition of it was not. It was discriminatory and dignity-defying. Maududi's view that women could not lead the state and that non-Muslims would be debarred from its key positions was plainly wrong. Maududi saw an Islamic state as mere implementer of existing laws handed down over generations by specific interpreters of sharia, without sufficiently taking into account time and space.

To this end, Maghfur cited two examples. During a severe drought Caliph ʿOmar abrogated the rule of cutting off a thief's hand—a provision derived from the Qurʾān. What this showed was that ʿOmar interpreted the divine message in accordance with the requirements of the time, namely, the conditions of drought. What mattered to him was not merely the act of theft but also the condition necessitating it. In this respect, ʿOmar's was the correct step. But in others, he made mistakes. In some narrations, it is mentioned that once he crossed a fence to find some people drinking alcohol in privacy. They objected to ʿOmar's act, reminding him that the Qurʾān guaranteed the sanctity of privacy and it did not allow one to secretively cross someone's fence.

It was ʿOmar's democratic thinking, Maghfur averred, that led to the abrogation of cutting off a thief's hand, for in drought conditions more people were likely to resort to theft. But his crossing the fence was undemocratic because an ideal democracy guaranteed a citizen's privacy. To Maghfur, democracy was not an invention of the West; it developed out of a *"common heritage"* of all peoples and faiths. In principle, democracy allowed people of diverse faiths to present their own views and contest those of others. In this sense, India's constitution was close to the Islamic principle even though its source was not divine. Neither Prophet Muhammad nor Allah is for Muslims alone. If so, Muslims should democratically desire justice for themselves as well as for Hindus. In Maghfur's view, defending a neighbor—whether Christian, Hindu, Muslim, or Sikh—under attack by an armed robber or usurper was also jihad. Fighting against a Muslim who had bonded laborers was likewise jihad, which Hindus too could join. Irrespective of their faiths, all those who spoke against the Emergency imposed by Indira Gandhi in 1975 were engaged in jihad, for the restoration of democracy and the constitution was at stake. Maghfur qualified that he did not endorse every act and form of democracy. Theoretically, it was possible that in a democracy the majority could decide to prohibit monotheism or the practice of *zakāt*. If a democracy so decided, he cautioned, that would be tyrannical.

At the time of our conversation, Nandigram was much-discussed in the media. In this town in West Bengal, police had shot dead scores of villagers who had been protesting against the acquisition of their land by the state to develop it as a "special economic zone (SEZ)." Most of the poor villagers inhabiting the SEZ were Muslims and lower-caste Hindus (*EPW* 2007; Sen 2008). Nandigram prominently figured in Maghfur's discourse. He viewed the fight and sacrifices by the poor in Nandigram as no less than a jihad. Invoking *sura at-tīn* (4), Maghfur argued that human qualities (*sharf*) cannot flourish in the absence of freedom and dignity. While freedom meant freedom to think and choose, including religious freedom, without critical knowledge, secure housing, and economic rights there won't be dignity. An ideal Muslim would speak for the dignity of all, not of Muslims alone. Only a state that envisioned and embodied such universal principles would qualify as duly Islamic.

If Maududi's detour from his own early universalism was tragic, observed Maghfur, far more tragic was the canonization of Maududi by his followers and the near abandonment of the critical enterprise Maududi himself upheld. Neither in Pakistan nor in India were most followers of Maududi engaged in original thinking. That veneration of Maududi now resembled a cult among his followers testified to another fact. These followers remained in the age of Muhammad Ali Jauhar (1878–1931), Maududi, and Gandhi—an age marked by charismatic individual leaders. Ours is the age, Maghfur remarked, of collective leadership. The final part of our discussion was about the religious status of India as discussed in some postprophetic medieval literature. Neither *Dārul Kufr* nor *Dārul Islām*, India, Maghfur said, is *Dārul farōġh-e-insānīyat* (abode of flourishing for humanity).

By the time we finished our conversation, it was almost midnight. As I took my leave, I was loudly greeted in the streets by stray (read: free) dogs. The next day, I had a meeting with Muhammad Burhan, in the same locality where Maghfur lived.

There were many commonalities between Maghfur and Burhan in their interpretations of Maududi. There were also some differences, however. Given that Sufism (*taṣavvuf*) was enmeshed in the psyche of the subcontinent, Maududi's criticism of it, in Burhan's view, was immoderately harsh and its tenor unwise. Had his approach toward *taṣavvuf* been a bit wiser he might have emerged as a consensual intellectual leader of all.[23] To Burhan, there was also an irony at work. The outside world continued to view Jamaat and Maududi as opposed to *taṣavvuf*, whereas scholars within the Indian Jamaat had written articles and books critiquing Maududi (politely) for his unbalanced, incorrect view of *taṣavvuf*. Uruj Qadri (d. 1986) was one such scholar who critiqued Maududi on this point in his book *Taṣavvuf kī chār aham kītābēñ* (*Four Important Books of Sufism*). In his later writings, Sadruddin (discussed above) also critiqued Maududi for overstressing the political and not adequately accounting for spirituality within Islam; he did so without naming Maududi. To make matters even more complicated, in Pakistan, Jamaat and Maududi himself forged an alliance with people oriented toward Sufism. Maududi the writer was not the same as Maududi the activist. According to Burhan, in Maududi's discourse and praxis *qalb* (heart) and *vijdān*—central as they are to Sufism—were often ignored and reason alone crowned, even as sixty-seven *āyāhs* of the Qur'ān deal with *qalb*. This neglect of *qalb* went hand in hand with celebrating the personality of Maududi (*shakhṣīat parastī*). Some Jamaat members even wore their caps in the same way as Maududi. Critical thinking, especially thinking critical of Maududi, was, Burhan held, rarely appreciated, much less encouraged.

◆ Exceptions of the State

On finishing my meeting with Akbar in Aligarh, I went to the Dodhpur roundabout where, at a tea stall, I ran into Adil. I had met Adil during my doctoral fieldwork. On learning that I was in Aligarh for a new research project, he asked me whom I had met so far. I mentioned Akbar. "You should also meet the nonmisguided people like me," he said smilingly. A Jamaat member, Adil was considered conservative. In his own self-perception, though inside Jamaat, he considered himself an outsider, especially vis-à-vis people like Bedar and Akbar. A retired schoolteacher, Adil was not as educated as my other interlocutors were. He did not speak English; he'd had a "traditional" education. But he was a voracious reader, knowledgeable about the world through whatever was available in Urdu, and occasionally in Hindi too.

To Adil, Maududi continued to be important. Assuming that I was modernist-secularist, he suggested that I read Maududi afresh by replacing "religion" with "culture" wherever it occurred in his writings. Maududi's fundamental thesis (*d'āvā*), as he saw it, was that any culture by itself would not adequately survive, much less flourish, without some support from power. People like Manzur Nomani and Vahiduddin Khan are wrong, he claimed, to say that Maududi was interested solely in power. Maududi was interested foremost in culture; power, or the state, was no more than secondary. Maududi's thesis, Adil averred, seems only more valid in post-1947 India. He mentioned many examples to buttress his point. It was due to state policy that Urdu as a language and culture were almost dead in India. There were hardly any functioning Urdu-medium schools in the whole state of Uttar Pradesh (UP). The defamiliarization of younger generations of Muslims with Urdu as a result of state policy had already made most young Muslims unfamiliar with Islam, as Urdu was their main language. The power of the contemporary (*maujūda*) state was, he said, far more pervasive than its predecessors: the British (*angrēzī*) and pre-British states he described as *shakhṣī ḥukūmat*. It is power which determined rights, he asserted, not rights power.

"The Indian Constitution gives fundamental rights that can't be abrogated by any *ḥukūmat* [government]," I countered. He took out a piece of paper from the right pocket of his *kurtā*, looked at it carefully and tore it into pieces. "What you call fundamental rights [*bunyādī ḥuqūq*], my brother, is like this piece of paper." States could always take those rights away and seldom could you do anything, for you were left to yourself. If you had experienced curfew as I have so many times, he continued, you would know that the fundamental rights of movement, gathering, and freedom of expression are canceled during a curfew. Maududi's point was that in the face of opposition by the state, a powerless community or culture could not safeguard itself even when those fundamental rights existed. Every law (*qānūn*) had its own provision of exception (*istis̱nā*) whereby it could cancel itself to wield what was ultimately bare brute power. In many states bordering India's Northeast as well as in Kashmir, exceptional laws (*istis̱nāī qavānīn*) were almost permanent. In Egypt, exceptional laws introduced by Anwar el-Sādāt continue even today. International law apparently did not allow for the invasion of a country, yet the United States, the United Kingdom, and others invaded Iraq, claiming an exception to international law because they asserted that Saddam Hussain possessed weapons of mass destruction. "Please don't mistake me for a supporter of Saddam Hussain. He was a *ẕālim*. I give the example of the invasion of Iraq to demonstrate that every law has an exception which can be used to justify whatever the powerful decide." After listening to Adil, I grew more interested in the states of exception adumbrated by Carl Schmitt and Giorgio Agamben, both foreign to Adil. I had heard their names only after I moved to Amsterdam in early 2001.

Continuing his exposition, Adil said that people like Akbar might have sung a eulogy (*qaṣīda*) about democracy to me. In his view, Maududi was not against democracy per se but against a specific democracy prevalent in India. In democracy it was the power of the majority that ultimately mattered. The nonmajority can certainly vote in a democracy, but they can't decide the shape and the contents of a law. And if one was allowed to vote but not decide, what was the worth of that democracy? As it operated in India, democracy was a way to make law; since law had exceptions, logically democracy also had exceptions. It was not that exceptions had to be inbuilt in every law. At times, a law in writing could be without exception, but in practice it was used and applied only in exceptional cases as chosen by the state and based on the majority's whims. "Have you looked at the cases of terrorism [*dahshatgardī*] and who are the people jailed or reported in the media as terrorists?" he asked me, then answered his own question: "Almost 100 percent of them are Muslims. This is how democracy renders Muslims as an exception." Democracy and the majority decided what was "natural" and "national," Adil continued. "As a minority I can certainly vote, but as a majority they can veto whatever I vote for." Gloomily he observed, "With a full beard and in a Muslim dress, whenever I go to government offices, markets, courts, railway stations, bus stands, or simply walk on the roads, my appearance, identity, even the pronunciation of certain sounds specific to Urdu letters, are viewed, increasingly so in the past two decades, as abnormal, whereas the identity and appearance of the majority always appear and are promoted as national and natural. You know English, and you are more educated than I am and you live in the West; tell me, can I overcome what others regard as my abnormality by continuing to vote in elections?"

Remaining with the stratum of intellectuals and the educated such as Adil (and using printed sources), we turn to the issue of gender equality in the next chapter to see facets of multiple critiques of Maududi's Janus-like neopatriarchate.

6

THE DIFFERENCE

Women and (In)equality

Without doubt, owing to their oppressive selfishness, men have always made such a judgment [that women are more deceitful and cleverer than men in organizing acts of impiety]. However, this is not the judgment of the Qurʾān. Everywhere it has discussed men and women with equality; nowhere has it made any distinction between men and women vis-à-vis their virtues/merits [*fazāʾl*] and orientation/nature [*ḳhaṣāʾl*].

—ABUL KALAM AZAD (n.d.b, 83)

Freedom for Muslim women is freedom for half of society. Women can't be free as long as men are not free. And both men and women can become free only when they follow God's guidance.

—ABDULHALIM ABU SHAQQA (n.d., 15)

On 20 February 2007, Ghulam Sarvar killed Zille Huma in full public view while the latter was meeting workers of the Muslim League party. The murder took place in Gujranwala, seventy kilometers (forty-three miles) from Lahore, capital of the Pakistani province of Punjab. Aged thirty-six and the mother of two children, Huma was Punjab's social welfare minister. With a master's degree in political science, Huma had joined the League and recruited 10,000 women to the party. She then became the president of the Gujranwala district unit of the League. She did not accept any government security guards; she held that she was inimical to none. In 2005, when the Punjab government for the first time held a women's marathon, Huma played a key role in its organization.

The day Huma was killed was her wedding anniversary.

Sarvar reportedly justified his act as jihad but later disavowed it. According to a BBC (2007) report, Sarvar killed her because he opposed "rule by women."

He went to the 2005 marathon with a pistol to kill girls participating in it, for he had been told that they would be wearing only knickers. But he did not fire any shots as he found them properly dressed. Aged forty-five and the father of nine children, Sarvar ran a hardware shop in Gujranwala. He had earned his matriculation degree from PB Model School and later studied at religious seminaries. Unaffiliated with any organization, Sarvar belonged to a family that followed the Ahl-e-ḥadīṡ school of thought. In police custody after killing her, he reportedly offered prayer giving thanks for her death. Within twenty-eight days of the killing, the court sentenced Sarvar to death. He died in jail under mysterious circumstances (Adil 2007; BBC 2007; Salman 2007; *Urdu Point* 2007).

Huma's chilling murder and its popular rendition in South Asia and beyond trod a familiar path: "Told you so: another example of Islam's subjugation of women!" (Ishtiaq Ahmed 2011; Zia 2015). The implication of such a rendition is that for women to regain freedom and rights, they should exit, almost by necessity, the faith and tradition they adhere to or identify with. This rendition is also scholarly, rooted in the West's modernization theory, which aimed to paint the world in its own image by producing a non-West allegedly mired in heteronomy and devoid of autonomy. Despite critiques, much of the scholarship on Islam and the "woman question" continues to be driven by a modernization paradigm. A classic example is the assumption that not only Islamist movements but also Islam itself stand against women's equality. Articulated variously under the flags of Islamic "religion," "culture," or "tradition," it is held that Islam is the signature cause of women's plight. From an atheistic framework, Bronwyn Winter (2001b) argues that Islam and Islamist movements (she conflates them) have irredeemably chained women. She asks, Is Islam not "a primary cultural means of ensuring men's political domination of women?" (33). She rejects any progressive reading of Islam, claiming that the Qurʾān (like other holy texts) is inherently "oppressive to women" (Winter 2001a, 12; see also Sahgal and Yuval-Davis 1992). Critical of Islamic feminists' project of developing nonpatriarchal readings of sources of Islamic authority (see, e.g., Badran 2002; Mirza 2005; and Moghadam 2002), Haidah Moghissi (1999, 140) also contends that gender equality is "diametrically opposed to the basic principles of Islam" and that "no amount of twisting . . . can reconcile the Qurʾānic injunctions . . . with . . . gender equality" (see also Karmi 1996, 79). Likewise, Shaharzad Mojab (2005, 325) avers that Islamic feminism "is a compromise with patriarchy."

Several assumptions animate such arguments. To begin with, these writers reify Islam. If, for Winter, Islam is the primary cultural means of women's domination, for Ghada Karmi masculine rule is fundamental to the Qur'ānic view of society. For Moghissi, gender equality is alien to Islam because Islam has an essence, "basic principles," in her words, that clashes with feminism. These feminist scholar-writers also gloss over many forms of mutation that Islamist movements have historically undergone.

The aims of this chapter are two. First, I show how Maududi's followers in India and elsewhere critique a neopatriarchate such as that proposed by Maududi. Their critique demonstrates the folly of a position such as Winter's and others who assume that Islam has an essence antithetical to women's rights. This chapter shows that a nonpatriarchal reading of Islam is plausible, indeed even thriving. The critique I present resonates with emergent work on Muslim women (e.g., Abu-Lughod 2013, 1998; Afary 1997; Sadaf Ahmad 2009; Leila Ahmed 1992, 1986; Hassan 2001, 1991a, 1991b; Iqtidar 2011, Mahmood 2005; Mernissi 1993, 1985; Moghadam 2002; Engineer 1998; and Fernea 1998). It is my contention that it is not Islam qua Islam that legitimates the gender hierarchy but the person making the interpretation thereof and the historical-political formations in which it is undertaken. Thus Ubaidullah Sindhi (d. 1944), a Deoband theologian, quoted *sura aṣṣaf* 9 from the Qur'ān to argue for a communist revolution. Maududi, Jamaat's founder, quoted the same sura to debunk communism and call instead for establishing Allah's Kingdom (Ahmad 2009b, 70). Without multiplying examples, I stress that it is wrong to assume that the Qur'ān is predisposed against women.

Let me clarify that I don't wish to be taken as a religious determinist. I hold that a specific, socially dominant reading of Islam is one among many factors shaping Muslim lives (see Imtiaz Ahmed 1983, Leila Ahmed 1992; Abu-Lughod 1998; and Jeffery 1979). Yet, my concern in this chapter, as throughout this book, is culture informed by religion. Thus contra Lila Abu-Lughod (2013, 6, 30–35), who, in *Do Muslim Women Still Need Saving?*, appears to dismiss any cultural factor—thereby "writing against culture"—in understanding and explaining women's multiple disempowerments at the hands of global, regional, national, and local powers, I suggest that culture/religion is *also* crucial. However, the culture or religion I write about is not the culture or religion that the reigning metropolitan imperial formations and its cultural brokers—or, to invoke Pierre Bourdieu and Loïc Wacquant (1999, 54n19), "mercenary intellectuals"—in the Global South adequately know or want to know. As I read her, Abu-Lughod writes "against culture" as imagined and crafted by the global elites for a specific purpose. This by no means implies an outright dismissal of "culture" or "religion" as understood by its practitioners themselves. That is, how the practitioners of that tradition and faith themselves view, read, critique, and shape—provisionally as they do—that culture should also be accorded due recognition. Put differently, this chapter demonstrates how the educated and intellectuals connected to Jamaat think about women. What are the modes of reasoning in the enactment of that thought? How do they view and reason women's condition and Islam? How are cultural, historical, and religious resources employed in thinking about women? Who constitutes and what gets counted as religious authority in thinking and debating about women's rights? What suppositions and assumptions work in debates about women?

My second argument is that to impose, as Winter does, a blanket label of "right-wing" on all Islamist movements is misleading.[1] Such a label simplifies the complexity of Islamism. In *Prophet and the Proletariat* (2002 [1999]), Chris Harman argues that Islamism also has a progressive language—now shrill, now mild. During the first Gulf War, to the anxiety of Saudi Arabia, Islamists in many countries protested against the invasion of Iraq.[2] Harman concludes that Islamism is "a response to the ravages of imperialism" (6). The label "right-wing" is flawed on another count: Islamist movements lack a uniform and unifying character. The nature of Islamism in Iran, for example, is different from that in Egypt (Bayat 1998). Such differences become certainly substantial in the case of India where Muslims, in 2015, numbered 172.2 million, constituting 14.23 percent of the total population (*The Hindu* 2015). Though Islamists are too insignificant to bear upon the country's wider social-political landscape, the larger Muslim community in which they function is significant. The issue is not simply demography, however. Indian Muslims have been makers of and participants in a democratic polity. In some ways, this political feature of Indian democracy eludes the Muslim-majority societies of the "Islamic heartland," the Middle East (on why the Middle East has been "de-democratized," see Ahmad 2011b and 2011a). For example, while the post-1979 Iranian state forces women to veil, the Turkish state long forbade veiling in public institutions. By contrast, the Indian state leaves veiling/wearing of the scarf by women to the volition of its citizens. More recently, however, the scene seems to be changing as the Supreme Court of India, in 2015, endorsed the decision of an educational body to ban students with scarves from appearing for entrance exams to medical colleges (Nair 2015). To continue to describe all Islamic movements as "right-wing" is to miss their radical transformation, such as that of Jamaat, which I discuss here (for more on this, see Ahmad 2009b). A vital facet of Jamaat's transformation is its changing discourse on gender.[3] Building on Michel-Rolph Trouillot's *Silencing the Past* (1995), I contend that an important factor catalyzing change was practice both within the Islamist arena and in the larger world Islamists inhabit. The language through which this critical—and potentially transformative—discourse was articulated was the language of religion.

In the first part of this chapter, I discuss the Janus-faced character of Jamaat's gender ideology as laid down by its founder, Maududi. Arguably, he was the first thinker in India to open the door of his organization to women qua individuals. At the same time, he stipulated harsh rules for women. For instance, he argued that if women stepped out of the home they must be veiled from head to toe. In the second part, I show how Maududi's position came to be critiqued by people connected to Jamaat. I discuss critiques on issues such as veiling, women's participation in the public domain (including work and cinema), questions of eligibility to become head of state, studying in coeducational institutions, rendering women scholars of the past invisible, and issues of gender and knowledge. In the final part, I account for the factors behind this change. I conclude by discussing what such critiques of Maududi's neopatriarchate entail. Is it analytically useful and theoretically productive to describe such critiques as inaugurating an Islamic feminist discourse?

◆ Maududi's Janus-Like Neopatriarchate

In order to account for Jamaat's changing discourse on women, it is crucial to historically situate Maududi's expositions on women in the wider context of Jamaat's formation in colonial India. As I have already discussed the historical context of Jamaat's formation in chapter 4, I will focus here on how women figured in Jamaat's weltanschauung.

To Maududi, a reigning sign of Islam's contamination was the "moral degradation" of women. His treatise *Pardāh* (*The Veil*) argued that women's freedom had led to the decline of many a nation.[4] Praising the Greek nation, he lamented that its latter degeneration was caused when women began to participate in the public domain and hedonism grew pervasive. The ultimate sign of Greece's immorality was its worship of Aphrodite, goddess of love (1953, 12). The modern West was on the same path of immorality, he observed.[5]

Maududi saw a similar scenario unfolding in colonial India, especially among Westernized Muslims.[6] He attacked the League for flouting sharia limits on women. In his view, there was no difference between the Congress and the League in their respective stances toward gender issues. Both held an antisharia approach to women. He noted that unveiled women were the "candles of the party" in meetings of the League in the same way Hindu women were in meetings of the Congress (qtd. in Ahmad 2005, 70). Maududi

(1953, 91) called Muslim men like those in the League "true believers in the religion of the West." He cited an Urdu story, *Repentance*, written by a man.[7] In it, a young, unmarried girl falls in love with a man. They end up making love and she gets pregnant. Once pregnant, the fear of sin haunts her. She asks herself, "Sin? I have committed sin, never. I am not repentant at all. I am again ready to do that. . . . What is chastity? Only virginity? Or sanctity of thought? I am no longer a virgin, but have I lost my chastity? . . . I am not worried about whatever harm cruel society wants to inflict on me. . . . My heart says that I have done right. . . . Why should I, then, behave as a thief? Why should I not announce it to the world that I have done this and it is right?" (1953, 93–94).

With such quotations, Maududi showed how Muslim men mimicked "Western culture [*firangī tahzīb*]." He described Western culture as an "epidemic" (1959, 201). Like Westerners, such men promoted values antithetical to sharia. They encouraged women to step outside of their "natural" space: home. Maududi singled out women's visibility in public arenas—councils, bazaars, colleges, theaters, restaurants, etc.—as the greatest threat to morality. Art, literature, music, film, dance, and the use of makeup by women: all were shrieking signs of immorality (1953, 1959b). Though men embraced the "epidemic" before women did, the embrace by the latter was lethal, for Maududi regarded *ḥarem* (women) as the last shelter wherein Islam preserved its culture. In his usage, *ḥarem* meant both "women" and "space." Stressing its spatial import, he wrote: "*ḥarem* is indeed the mightiest fortress of Islamic culture, built so that Islam could seek shelter there if it was ever defeated" (1959b, 201). He lamented that even this fortress was no longer safe from the "epidemic."

Maududi's endeavors to protect the fortress resonate with those of wider reform movements (see Devji 1994; and Metcalf 1992). Indeed, as Chatterjee (1993) notes, Hindu reform movements also advanced the logic of protecting the inner domain (women) from the external intrusion of "the West." Given the invasion of *ḥarem* by Westernization, Maududi devoted two-thirds of *The Veil* to outlining mechanisms for safeguarding the fortress of what he called Islamic culture. This position of Maududi, also held by several others writing under subjugation in South Asia and elsewhere, only indicates how much it was enmeshed in the logic of colonial hegemony. Clearly, women held coveted, high positions of power in different parts of the world in the precolonial era. For example, in the eighth century Khayzuran governed the Muslim polity under the reign of Abbasid caliphs. During the eleventh century, Malika Asma Bint Shihab al-Sulayhiyya and Malika Arwa Bint Ahmad al-Sulayhiyya occupied the throne in Yemen. Two centuries later, in the thirteenth century, Razia Sultana ruled in India. In the fourteenth century, three women (Sultana

Khadija, Sultana Miriam, and Sultana Fatima) ruled over the Maldives. In the sixteenth and seventeenth centuries in Southeast Asia, many Muslim women held power. For instance, during the sixteenth century, Patani, a Malay Muslim kingdom now in Thailand, was ruled successively by four women. From 1641 to 1699, four successive Muslim queens ruled the kingdom of Ache in Indonesia. Themselves pious, these queens enjoyed a wider legitimacy in their rule from Islamic authorities. Their reigns saw considerable religious-cultural and scholarly flourishing. The Dutch trader Jacob de Roy, who lived in Ache in the seventeenth century, called the kingdom a "republic" (Khan 2010, 6; *Oxford Islamic Studies Online* 2012).

Oblivious of examples from history when women in different parts of the world ruled, Maududi's concern was to protect the fortress under colonial domination. Before I come to the specifics of his mechanisms, let me outline the general principles. The origin of the universe and its purpose are the axioms of Maududi's ideology. As the creator of the universe, Allah made humans, like other creations, in a pair. He endowed each pair with "natural sexual attraction." But unlike other creations, which possess limited attraction (solely to perpetuate themselves), humans have an unlimited capacity for attraction. Humans' goal is neither simple self-perpetuation nor pursuit of pleasure. Maududi (1977b, 93) viewed pleasure-oriented sex as a subversion of the divine, condemning contraceptives and birth control as impediments to the very survival of the human species. According to Maududi (1953, 109), "nature [*fiṭrat*]" wanted humans to fashion a "pious civilization." The foundation of that civilization is the heterosexual family. To sustain the family beyond sheer functionality, nature instilled in women the merits of beauty, sacrifice, and shame, to attract men. As Maududi saw it, the plan of nature was to fashion an order free from chaos (*fitna*). He presented this as a balanced path between the sexual anarchy of the modern West and the women-degrading stances of medieval Christianity and Hinduism (see below).

The position of women is central to this pious civilization. Quoting the Qur'ānic verse *sura an-nisā'* 6, Maududi argued that Allah made men rulers (*qauvām*) over women. A man thus has the authority to rule over his wife and children. He invoked a hadith to state that anyone who disturbed such an ordering of the family would not be dear to Prophet Muhammad (1953, 176–78). To maintain the ordering of the family, Allah also divided spheres of work for men and women. The provision of a woman's livelihood was the job of her husband and the woman's "natural domain" was the home. She was, therefore, not allowed to travel unless accompanied by a *maḥram* (a man she's forbidden to marry, for example, her brother or father; antonym: *ghair maḥram*). In a case of dire necessity she might go out; however, this was an exceptional concession, not an everyday occurrence.

Behind Maududi's insistence on woman's confinement to the home lay the belief that her entry into the public domain caused immorality such as that which, he believed, had led to the fall of a once-mighty power like Greece. He saw the woman's body as a source of *fitna* and destructive to nature's wish for a pious civilization. Outside of her home and in the presence of *ghair maḥram*, the sight of an unveiled woman is a visual sin inevitably inciting a sexual storm in men, which in turn prefaces the ultimate sin—copulation.[8] To one refusing such causality Maududi (1953, 234) asked if they would also deny that "the lava beneath the smoke of the volcano on the mountain is not restless to come out." Since there was a sinister volcanic power in the female body, women's bodies were a threat to a pious civilization. Precisely for this reason Allah, Maududi argued, contained the volcano by limiting women to the home. According to him, Islam at most allowed a woman to unveil only her face and palms. Even in the presence of *maḥram* in the home, she was obliged to observe this norm. A pious woman in the era of Prophet Muhammad, Maududi noted, covered herself from head to toe by wearing a niqab. She also wore gloves to cover her palms. Further, a woman's voice, gait, and smell, not to speak of her gaze, were all *fitna*. He also described photographs and drawn images of living beings as *ḥarām*. "All pictures. . ." he wrote, "will remain *ḥarām*" (1999, 125). He made no difference between a woman and her photograph, for the consequence of both was chaos. Music and films were likewise illegitimate (Maududi 1963, 438; Ahmad 2008). There was no question of a woman acting in a film.

Legitimizing the separation of men and women, Maududi called coeducation "poison." "Howsoever acceptable gender-mixed education may be to non-Muslims, from the Islamic viewpoint it is destructive" (qtd. in Ayaz Islahi, 1997, 108). Like the reformists Nazir Ahmad and Ashraf Ali Thanawi before him, Maududi recognized the need for women's education. But he considered the only proper education to be that which made her a perfect mother and housewife. Only exceptionally bright women could study nondomestic sciences, provided they didn't transgress sharia. Importantly, Maududi regarded, as did Kant[9] (2006 [1798]), women as inferior to men. He thought it "impossible that even a single person of the stature of Aristotle, Avicenna, Kant, Hegel . . . would be born in the fair sex" (Maududi 1953 [1940], 148). The reason was biological: nature had made woman suitable for nurturing and domesticity, not for intellectual pursuits. Like patriarchs in other religious and secular traditions, he offered, inter alia, menstruation and pregnancy as reasons for the domesticity of woman (138–50).[10]

Maududi didn't allow women to hold any decisive political role. In his view, women (like men) should have the right to vote, but they could not be elected to positions of power. Addressing a meeting of women in the Montgomery district of the Punjab in 1950, Maududi (1976a, 153) stated, "Women should only vote for virtuous and morally good men." Like many before him, he believed that it would spell disaster if a woman became a ruler. He quoted a hadith in which Prophet Muhammad said: "A nation which handed over its affairs [of state] to a woman would never prosper." When asked why Islam forbade a woman to lead in politics, Maududi justified it as follows: "The present-day assemblies ... control the whole of national politics. As such their status is ... that of a *qavvām* [ruler] over the whole republic. ... In *sūra annisāʾ* ... Allah clearly assigns the status of *qavvām* to men." Preempting the objection that the said verse dealt with the domestic domain, he went on to argue that if Allah did not make a woman ruler inside the home how could He allow her to rule a republic, "a collection of millions of homes?" (qtd. in Azmi 1999, 206). To strengthen his point, Maududi quoted the Qurʾānic verse, *al-aḥzāb* 4, to say that Allah commanded women to remain in the home. Rejecting the view that Allah's command was specific to Muhammad's family and did not apply to common women, he asked, "Does Allah want to see each Muslim home other than the Prophet's steeped in indecency?" (qtd. in Nomani 1998, 113).[11]

From the above outline, one might say that Maududi's gender ideology was a plain replay of patriarchy. Such a view will be simplistic, however. Following Hisham Sharabi (in Kazemi 2000, 455), I will instead call it "neopatriarchy," a reworked version of the traditional patriarchate in a modern context. And precisely because of the radically new context of its articulation, what may appear as a reassertion of patriarchy and tradition is indeed, in some important ways, also a departure from, even a subversion of, tradition. Below, I show how Maududi used Islam to at once contest and shape, if not institute, tradition.

Muslim women began participating in modern politics in the early twentieth century (Jalal 1991; McDonough 2002). They held their first conference in 1915. Bi Ammi, mother of the Ali brothers, was, in 1917, one of the first women to address a public meeting. Women's participation increased, as did the League's political mobilization[12] (Jalal 1991; Willmer 1996). The rationale for their participation, however, scarcely stemmed from sustained scriptural sources or theological reasoning. Organizations like the Jamiatul Ulema-e-Hind (see *Dastūr asāsī jamīʿatulʿulemā hind* n.d.) and the Tablighi Jamaat, which based their agenda on Islam, had no formal provision for recruiting women. Jamaat was the first to grant membership to women qua individuals and on the basis of the Qurʾān and hadith. Stipulating membership criteria, Jamaat stated that any person, "whether a man or woman," could become a member if he or she agreed to work for its goal ("Dastūr Jamāʿt-e-Islāmī" 1942, 177). Granting membership to women was a clear departure from tradition, because the very idea of a party like Jamaat was nearly alien to premodern polity (Tilly 1984), as was the notion of a formalized constitution. Social movements are themselves "an invention of the modern age" (Tarrow 1998, 2). It is in this sense that the female leader Razia Sultana's rule during the Sultanate period belongs to a different catalog. It was not only membership that set Jamaat apart from most other organizations of the time. The role it assigned to women was a departure from convention and customs. The Jamaat constitution obligated women members to spread its ideology to their families. It urged them to "disobey the commands of their husbands and guardians if such commands were sins against Allah" ("Dastūr Jamāʿt-e-Islāmī" 1942, 183).[13] Clearly, this call to disobey husbands and guardians defied tradition, which obliged women to obey them. In the same 1950 Montgomery address to women (referred to above) where he opposed the election of women to assemblies and parliaments, Maududi (1976, 153) desired that "women form their own associations and unbiasedly critique the government." Half a century after this pronouncement by Maududi, women members of Jamaat-e-Islami now run for office and are members of Pakistan's national assembly. One such member is Samia Raheel Qazi, daughter of Qazi Hussain Ahmed, who led Jamaat as its *amīr* from 1987 to 2009. Raheel Qazi was elected to the Pakistan National Assembly in 2002. Though she didn't always support what many would regard as progressive legislation about women, she did defy Maududi's neopatriarchate when she endorsed the position that Islam didn't require women to cover their face, hands, and feet. Interestingly, Qazi herself wore a full face veil (Ahmad 2013c; Jamal 2013; NDTV 2015; Weiss 2014).

It is precisely in this sense that Maududi's exposition on women is disabling and enabling at the same time. To reduce it to either disempowerment or empowerment is to lose sight of the Janus-faced character of Islamism in general and Maududi's exposition in particular.

◆ Neopatriarchate in Its Place: Multiple Critiques

The innovation of allowing membership to women notwithstanding, Jamaat's constitution obligated them to observe sharia, and it was this aspect of its ideology that became dominant. After Partition, Maududi left for Pakistan. The Indian Jamaat, however, followed its founder and his neopatriarchal prescriptions. In 1951, its organ, *Zindegī*, depicted the horrors India would face if Communists captured the state and listed several benefits if "God-worshippers" came to rule. One basic merit, *Zindegī* wrote, would be that gender mixing would become a "serious crime" and "women will remain women and men will remain men" (qtd. in Ahmad 2005, 278). *Zindegī* urged women to accept that there was a "clear difference in the physical, mental makeup of men and women which can't be eliminated" (May 1961, 54). In 1964, it reproduced each of Maududi's neopatriarchal arguments (August 1964, 20–32). Further, Jamaat resolved to fight dance, music, obscenity, and birth control (*Jamāʿt islāmī hin kī policy avr program* 1964, 10). As late as 1980, it forbade wearing lipstick outside the home (*Zindegī* September 1980, 48). Most Jamaat members continued to stick to Maududi. But from the 1980s onward, dissenting voices began to emerge from within. In the 1990s, they grew stronger to form a new, antiorthodox language. Below I will discuss these forms of reasoning and critique as they appear within both Jamaat and its student wing, the Student Islamic Organization (SIO). I will also discuss one heated debate on veiling in *Zindegī-e-nav*.[14] I will close this section with a discussion of the links between gender and knowledge as voiced by a former SIO activist running a nongovernmental organization at the time of my fieldwork.

Let me begin with Akram Zurti, whom we met in chapter 5. Initially influenced by Maududi, Zurti subsequently became a sustained critic. In Zurti's view, the Qur'ān is a book of ethics (*akhlāq*) and justice (*ʿadl*) for all of humanity, regardless of religious divides. Jamaat had, by contrast, turned it into a book for Muslims as an ethnic group. Thus, Zurti lamented, in the early 1960s when riots broke out in India, Jamaat sided with Muslim victims even if they were rapists, liars, and hypocrites. To Zurti, this stance was un-Islamic: rather than speaking for humanity Jamaat defended Muslims as an ethnic and statistical group. By backing Urdu-speaking West Pakistan against Bengali-speaking East Pakistan in the 1971 war, in Zurti's narrative, the Pakistani Jamaat further degenerated, coming to equate Islam with one language.

By ethics, Zurti meant what was morally good: love, kindness, and care for the poor. So pivotal is ethics to the Qur'ān that it calls prayer "fraud" if the person praying disregards compassion. Zurti cited *sura al-māʿūn*, where Allah chides worshippers who are unkind to their fellows. For Zurti, the Qur'ān is also a call to action, at the heart of which lies the obligation to command *māʿrūf* and forbid *munkar*. The words *māʿrūf* and *munkar* are taken to mean "right" and "wrong."[15] In Zurti's reading, these terms had different meanings, also containing a methodology of their own. For a thing to qualify as *māʿrūf*, it should (1) be popular (*māʿrūf*) and acceptable (*maqbūl*); (2) it should accord with Allah's feature (*ṣifat*): justice and compassion; and (3) it should hold up to reason. As Islam is dynamic, Zurti further stressed, with societal change the notion of *mā'rūf* would also change. He defined *munkar* as the "other" of *mā'rūf*. As he considered Islam a religion for humanity, *mā'rūf* was beyond religious borders. He held that in the modern West several ideas of *mā'rūf* had developed: human rights, democracy, freedom, and women's rights. So had ideas of *munkar*: slavery and colonial pillage, for instance. According to Zurti, it was Muslims' duty to embrace *mā'rūf* and shun *munkar*. He argued that a woman could become prime minister. Contra Maududi, he didn't consider women to be intellectually inferior. The writer-activist Arundhati Roy, he said, is brighter than many men. He lamented that Muslims had not produced a Roy (whose talk at AMU in early 2004 was a major event). In Zurti's view, women were also entitled to equal shares in property. Today, he continued, women's education, including in coeducational institutions, and their participation in the public domain were *mā'rūf*. In India, if they choose they could also uncover their head and wear a short-sleeved blouse, as both were *mā'rūf*. Rejecting popular practices of the age, he warned, would run against the Qur'ānic call to command and embrace *mā'rūf*.

In Zurti's account, Maududi confined women to the home because he took an ethnic, not a universalist, approach to Islam. Had Maududi's approach been universal, he would have welcomed Western *mā'rūf* about women. According to Zurti, Maududi also ignored justice—a feature (*ṣifat*) of Allah. As Allah desires justice, Zurti contended, how could He deny women the right to run a state? Maududi, despite his questioning of many conventional theological positions, remained a *muqallid*, an imitator (see chap. 4, on *taqlīd*). In Zurti's view, Maududi had the potential to be a *mujaddid* (renewer), but he ended up defending patriarchy. He called Maududi's commentary on the Qur'ān, *Tafhīmul Qur'ān*, a piece of "sheer ignorance [*nirī jāhlīat*]." He lamented that no one—from Ibn-e-Taymiyya down to Maududi—understood the Qur'ān well because commentators had thus far interpreted it through the hazy lenses of mostly distorted hadith and medieval jurisprudence. The sole authentic book was the Qur'ān, the writing of whose commentary, in its own terms, was his mission.

When I asked him if he had published his thoughts, Zurti sadly told me that owing to his advanced age he could not write any more. Whenever ideas came to him, he recorded them on cassette tapes. He had employed a PhD student from AMU to transcribe the recordings and read the transcriptions aloud to him for further reflections. He was hopeful that one day his views would appear in print. In one of several sessions I had with him, he urged me to also meet Sultan Ahmad Islahi, whom he often mentioned.

In the Islamist arena, Islahi was a contested figure. Some admired him for his novelty; others attacked him for diluting Jamaat's ideology. To his detractors, he was moody and provocative. He critiqued Maududi, they alleged, to equal himself to Maududi's stature. He was also seen as someone who promoted "obscene" things, for in one book (see below) he freely discussed the subject of sex. Born in 1951, Islahi was educated at Madrasatul Islah (in Azamgarh), a seminary initially receptive to Maududi.[16] Islahi also held key leadership roles in Jamaat. He was, however, foremost a writer. He had authored twenty books. Among other issues, it was his unusual view on women that was a point of debate, especially among young Islamists.

Bemoaning deviation from Maududi's ideology, one Jamaat hard-liner told me that people like Islahi were responsible for it. In this critic's opinion, Islahi justified unveiling, dancing, and singing. This critic asked me, rather angrily, what people would think of Jamaat when Islahi offered Islamic justifications for going against what the critic deemed to be the consensus in sharia over the issue of women's veiling. In such allegations, however, Islahi saw the play of masculine power rather than true concern about Islam. Men's obsession with women's veiling, he argued, ignored the fact that Islam also had codes for men. Prophet Muhammad forbade a handsome man to roam unnecessarily in the streets. Rarely did any of the *ʿulema*, however, cite that hadith to issue a fatwa (opinion) against men. The wearing of tight jeans, which show the crest and trough of a man's body and hamper the ritual of prayer (*namāz*), is likewise un-Islamic. But *ʿulema* do not prohibit it as they fear the wrath of men. They always focus on female dressing, however, because women are easy targets. In Islahi's opinion, his critics misconstrued the nature of Islam. It is "a soft [*narm*], flexible [*lachakdār*] religion." Excluding the categorically forbidden, he held that sharia was flexible enough to swim with the age, and women's issues were no exception. Islahi told me that his critics also didn't understand the principles of sharia. The early jurists (*fuqhā*) did not reject *māʿrūf*—by which he meant local traditions and culture. If a *māʿrūf* didn't directly clash with the spirit and fundamentals of Islam, most jurists accepted it. Thus, in Africa, they not only sanctioned dance and music but some also took part in them.

To fully comprehend Islahi's argument, let me turn to his forty-three-page article (1997) in a journal from AMU. Given Islahi's unorthodox position, the editor added a disclaimer that the journal didn't agree with all of the arguments. Titled "Modern Media and Islam" and supplemented by over ninety references (mostly Arabic), the article was written with the realization that despite attempts at reform, the media could not be purified of songs or women's voices and images, and that these were indispensable to contemporary life. Islahi's objective, then, was to find a rationale for women to participate in these arenas, notably in the domain of film. The maxim of Islahi's analysis was that Islam is "a soft, flexible, and natural religion [*fiṭrī dīn*]." As may be evident, he used *fiṭrat* differently than Maududi had done. While the latter used it to limit women to the home, Islahi used it to pave the way for their participation outside the home. In marked contrast to Maududi, he did not consider veiling (*niqāb*) Islamic. Citing works by Imam Hanifa and others, Islahi argued that Islam permitted a woman to unveil her face, hands, arms, and feet. She could also work outside the home; indeed, such was the case in Islam's early era. Asma, the daughter of Caliph Abu Bakr, worked in the field nine miles from Medina. She collected fodder for animals and carried it on her head. If Asma worked outside of the home, Islahi argued, today women could certainly work in fields, offices, and schools. The veil, for him, was more a status symbol of the elite (*shorfā*) than a tenet of sharia. Islahi's (1997, 67–68) specific aim, as stated above, was to explore whether a woman may also act, dance, and sing in films.

According to Islahi, a woman may certainly act in films. To argue this, he invoked canonical texts not discussed here due to lack of space as well as my inadequate knowledge of Arabic. I will focus on his conclusions and argumentation. To argue for woman's acting, Islahi first proposed that her coactors be *maḥram*, preferably her husband. However, since shooting for a film never happens in seclusion, in the presence of *maḥram* she could also act with *ghair maḥram*. In this setting, Islahi believed, the chances of romance while filming would be nonexistent. Islahi's next concern was the extent to which a woman could show her body. Sharia allowed a woman to show her face, palms, hands, arms, and feet; the question was whether she could reveal other parts of her body. In Islahi's view, she could on the following ground: Islam makes a distinction between "slaves" and "free women" and had different provisions of *satr* for both. *Satr* means the part of body which must not be revealed. A man's *satr* is generally from navel to knee, but there is not full consensus; for instance, Imam Hanifa didn't include the navel. In the eyes of sharia, *satr* for all men and for female slaves was the same, except that for the latter it also included the back and the belly. Stating that while he had no wish to revive slavery, if a free woman wanted to use the provision of a slave and thus show other parts of her body, Islahi argued that it wouldn't be un-Islamic. She could even touch a believing man. In a country like India, if such a provision was denied to her, Islahi feared, she might leave Islam itself. Allowing her to show the parts of body that a slave was entitled to show, he mused, was a lesser evil than apostasy. Islahi argued that women could also sing, as the Qur'ān did not forbid music and singing. He did not regard woman's voice as *fitna*, as Maududi did. If necessary, women could also dance in films. Preempting counterresponses from critics to his position, Islahi (1997, 68–73, 80) went on to argue that if a hadith on music and singing was taken literally, then a Muslim should become a renouncer because the Prophet once described the world as a curse, *lʿānat*.

Like Islahi's article, his book *Sex in Islam* also departed radically from Maududi's ideology of neopatriarchate. The book covers a variety of issues. I will deal with only some of its themes. As I have noted, for Maududi, sex for pleasure was illegitimate. The only purpose of sex was to procreate, in order to fashion a pious civilization. Islahi (2000 [1994], 240–47), by contrast, argued that pleasure in itself was equally Islamic. Unlike Maududi, he also saw no problem in using contraceptives. Indeed for Islahi, the issue was not its legitimacy but the terms of its usage. If a woman didn't want pregnancy, her husband could not force her. If he did, Islahi argued, she could take him to court (309–10). The book in fact taught readers how to use contraceptives so as to maximize pleasure and minimize risk. It also critiqued masculinity. As an example, Islahi cited the attitude of husbands on their wedding night when, to prove their "manliness" and subdue their wives, they indulged in repeated sexual intercourse (204–5). Such an attitude, Islahi argued, is un-Islamic. He also approvingly discussed the practice of going on a honeymoon. But some readers took as especially obscene was the graphic detail with which he spelled out Islamically legitimate modes of intercourse, which he called "Islamic positions [*āsan*]" (221). The Sanskrit text on sex, *kokḫ shāstra*, mentions eighty-four *āsans* of intercourse. Based on experiences with his clients, Keval Dhar, a sexologist, argues that only six were practical. Islam, Islahi noted, approves eleven *āsan*.

The young activists of the SIO also questioned Maududi's neopatriarchate. Of the twenty-eight SIO members at AMU in 2002, Jamal was quite distinctive. His father was a member of Jamaat, which he had joined after a long association with the Communist Party. Jamal had his early education in a gender-mixed government school. On joining Jamaat, Jamal's father sent his son to Jāmiʿatul Falāḥ, the Jamaat madrasa in Azamgarh, for further study. Jamal did not feel at home at Falāḥ. He critiqued his teachers and friends for their "orthodox," "theocratic" views. Here is one example. In class, a teacher argued that the Qurʾān said that women should be subordinate to men. Jamal asked what the rationale was. The teacher responded that it was "woman's nature" and that was why they had always worked within the home. Jamal argued back, saying that there was no such thing as "woman's nature" and that if educated, women too could excel. He asked, What about women such as Razia Sultana, Rani Lakshmi Bai (who fought against the British), and Sarojni Naidu (a leader of the anticolonial movement)? Jamal told me that he did not get "rational" answers. He was not convinced either by Maududi's argument that Islam prohibited a woman to be head of state. Like his brother, also an SIO activist, he believed that a woman could surely become a head of state. As a student at Falāḥ, Jamal's brother had written his final-year essay arguing why Islam allowed a woman to become prime minister.

Such intense debates as Jamal had at Falāḥ were also articulated in the Jamaat organ, *Zindegī-e-nav* (hereafter *ZN*). *ZN* discussed the veil, the ultimate symbol of Islam's "bigotry." In February 2002, it published an article "Muslim Society and the Issue of Veiling" by Abdurrahman Alkaf, a Jamaat intellectual, which unleashed a fierce debate. Educated at Ṡānavī Darsgāh, a higher studies institute founded by Jamaat in 1949, Alkaf was based in Sana, Yemen. His article delegitimized the notion of veiling as an Islamic requirement. Quoting *sura Iḥzāb,* he argued that Allah's command to women to remain in the home was specific to Prophet Muhammad's wives and not meant for women in general. Given such a clear Qurʾānic order, he wondered why all interpreters, including Maududi, were "adamant on" turning the specific into the general (*ZN* February 2002, 19). In Alkaf's view, there was no command for women to remain in the home or to be veiled (27–29). Women were required to cover only their "head, neck, chest, and nothing else." He called veiling an "invention of man" having "no place in the divine laws" (2002, 32). Calling for "justice" for women, he stated that it was the "antisharia manliness of men," and not the Qurʾān, which prevented women from participating in economic activities outside of the home.

Alkaf's article elicited strong reactions. From March through June 2002, *ZN* carried a dozen responses, mostly negative. One of the fiercest came from a Bombay woman, Farzana Tabassum. Describing his argument as the result of an "apologetic mind" under the influence of a "mesmerizing and glittering Western civilization," she refuted him point by point (*ZN*, 2002 March, 71).[17] In so doing, she repeatedly invoked Maududi. In Tabassum's opinion, Alkaf's attempt was "contemptible" because it went against the "categorical commands of the Qurʾān and hadith" (64). Indeed, in Alkaf's argument she detected a conspiracy: "By producing some 'intellectuals' among Muslims and with their assistance, it is in fact a strategy of the eternal enemy of human beings that such commands [Allah's about women] are attributed only to the wives of the Prophet, and not to common women, so that the door to the spreading of evil is opened" (57).

While Tabassum saw such voices as opening the door to the spreading of evil, others did not. A former member of the SIO who came from Bihar (he preferred not to be named) viewed the condition of women in a markedly different register. After retiring from the SIO, rather than join Jamaat as some of his SIO friends did, he set up a nongovernmental organization. He was an activist-thinker. He had visited nearly every district of the state. In particular, he frequently visited Bihar's eastern districts—economically and educationally more backward than other districts—where his involvement was intense. Notwithstanding his busy activist schedule, he found ample time to read. His perspective was informed by what he called the "people's experience." He called his own mode of thinking and actions dialectical—viewing and working in society from an Islamic perspective and then relooking and reinterpreting Islam in light of the experiences encountered in the first interaction. He clarified that this didn't mean "fitting" Islam into the prevalent experiences. Instead, these experiences enabled him to discover God's message in the face of "on-the-ground realities," which in turn allowed him to view reality and society in a new light. The challenges and excitement, as he saw them, of such activism was what kept him from pessimism, which some of his friends had in abundance.

About the specific issue of women's rights, he felt that Jamaat's approach was top-down and, in some ways, antipeople. Rather than go down to the bylanes of towns and villages to observe and encounter what problems women faced in their day-to-day lives, from their offices in Delhi and elsewhere Jamaat intellectuals dictated what women should do. "Have you noticed the precise words that Jamaat intellectuals use?" he asked me. "Some of them write, 'Demands of Islam from women.' Should it not also be what women want from such men who speak in the name of Islam by monopolizing knowledge and authority?" In the eyes of this ex-SIO activist, Jamaat intellectuals wrote pamphlets and books about women without bothering to inquire into what women themselves thought about those issues and problems. These "intellectuals" nursed an illusion that they knew Islam because they had read books of theology and certain interpretations of the Qur᾽ān, or they had acquired degrees of some sort from a center of learning. As knowledge is dialectical in Islam, he argued, writing books and pamphlets the ways scholars did in the past was no longer entirely pertinent. To this end, he narrated an experience he had had with a prominent female member of Jamaat.

This woman was active in the women's wing of the Bihar unit. She was highly educated and wrote articles on women. However, there was nothing new in her articles. She more or less repackaged what Maududi had already said on the issue of women. My interlocutor asked her if she had also observed the "on-the-ground realities" of women in villages, especially the conditions of those from the poorest families. Had she ever asked those women what they thought about the Prophet's views on women and the message of the Qur᾽ān? Did their conceptions of Islam differ from those of Jamaat intellectuals? Her response was curious: Such women were neither well-read nor knew Arabic. To which he asked, "Did you educate them? Were not women in Prophet Muhammad's time and after scholars who studied and taught subjects as diverse as hadith, *tafsīr,* logic, philosophy, history, medicine, arts, and so on? Did not men come to such women scholars to learn about Islam and the universe?" In his opinion, the uneducated women might not know the specific injunctions of theology, but based on their lived experiences they probably knew better than many men did how Islam's message of *inṣāf* (justice) and compassion could effectively be instituted to transform their lives. The former SIO activist concluded this part of the conversation by recommending a set of books on Islam for her to read, including Simone de Beauvoir's *The Second Sex.*

It was after I had published an article from this research (see below) that I came to know the works of Mohammad Akram Nadwi. As his name shows, he was a graduate of Nadva, a famous madrasa in Lucknow. On learning about my project about Islam and women, a Deoband scholar based in Delhi advised me to read Nadwi's works. But few in Jamaat mentioned him or his work to me. Even outside of the Jamaat circle, still fewer discussed the role of women scholars in Muslim history and society: the subject of Nadwi's forty-volume project, the introductory volume (*Muqaddimah*) of which alone is over 300 pages. Nadwi (2007, xi) modestly began the project to write a single-volume biographical dictionary of women scholars of hadith, *muḥaddīsāt* (in the plural). For the purpose of this chapter, I will rely on *Muqaddimah.* At the time of its publication in 2007, Nadwi worked as a fellow at the Oxford Centre for Islamic Studies in the United Kingdom. In a story on Nadwi's work, the *New York Times* described it as "a secret history" because it rediscovered "a long-lost tradition of Muslim women" acquiring, teaching, and expanding knowledge (Power 2007).

Nadwi's principal contention was as follows: The Qur'ānic conception of women was neither in terms of their inferiority nor in terms of deficiency or any sort of primordial sin. They were "independent moral beings," autonomous and responsible for their actions as were men for theirs. Prophet Muhammad himself called for equal treatment of sons and daughters. Such a Qur'ānic conception of individuals allowed women to excel in whatever field of knowledge they chose for themselves. Women were not simply transmitters or narrators of hadith; they were also its teachers. To take one example, Umm al-Dardā (d. 700) was a renowned scholar of hadith in what is now Syria. She taught hadith both at home and in the mosques of Damascus and Jerusalem (note that both men and women attended mosques). She taught men as well as women.

As a matter of fact, the caliph of the time, Abdul Malik Ibn Marwan, attended her lectures and learned from her. In delivering lectures and formulating a position on a particular issue (when sought by the public), she did not simply do her job. Thinking about thought interactionally marked Umm al-Dardā's life. Translated into European terms, hers was a "life of the mind" (Arendt 1978; Marsden 2005, 109).[18] When asked if she felt tired, she replied, "I have sought worship in everything. I did not find anything more relieving to me than sitting with scholars and exchanging [knowledge] with them" (qtd. in Nadwi 2007, 43; brackets in original). Hers was not a solitary example. Nadwi (2007, x, 9, 37, 179, 150, 152, 249, 259, 266–67) devoted five of his volumes to women like Umm al-Dardā during the seventh century of Hijra alone.

Women's prominent roles as scholars were not absent from the Indian subcontinent either, though their number was comparatively smaller. Zaibun Nisāʾ, daughter of Awrangzeb (d. 1707), who ruled India, had memorized the Qurʾān, for which she received gifts from her father. She studied religious sciences as much as philosophy, logic, mathematics, and other sciences. In nineteenth-century Delhi, Amat ul Ghafur—whose father was Ishaq Dehlavi and who himself was a noted scholar of hadith—was considered an authority in discussion about hadith. So knowledgeable was she that when her husband (also a scholar of hadith) encountered any difficulty in scholarly matters he consulted her and she would come to his rescue (Nadwi 2007, 119, 263, 272). Among other women scholars in India the names Shamsun Nisāʾ (d. 1890 AD) and Saliha (d. 1900 AD) are also notable.

Though not formulated directly in relation to Maududi's view that it is "impossible that even a single person of the stature of Aristotle, Avicenna, Kant, Hegel . . . would be born in the fair sex," based on archival and literary sources, Nadwi's *Muqaddimah* (and forty additional volumes) did enough to puncture claims such as Maududi's. And what Nadwi did through archival-textual analysis, the former SIO activist did in conversation.

More important, Nadwi's *Muqaddimah* demonstrates that gender was no bar to women's becoming scholars. What mattered was the knowledge itself. But knowledge at that time was not neatly separable from deeds or practice (*ʿamal*). To be knowledgeable was to also practice and exemplify what one knew, for authority and reputation stemmed from the combination of knowledge and practice (Nadwi 2007, 273–90). And in this respect women excelled as much as men did. Women scholars were not unusual. They were ubiquitous to the extent of being "normal"—a fact that not only the female member of Jamaat but also many "secular" intellectuals seem to ignore. Consider the case of Arifa Subh Khan (2009, 11, back cover), a young Pakistani scholar whose 2009 book—*Urdu tanqīd kā aṣlī chehrā* (*The Real Face of Urdu Critique*)—I discussed in chapter 3. While applauding her book, Jameel Jalibi and Gopi Chand Narang wrote that "despite being a woman" she wrote an important book on critique. Neither Jalibi nor Narang is considered in public to be "religious"; they are well-known "secular" literary critics from Pakistan and India, respectively. While the former has a Muslim name, the latter has a Hindu one. Curiously, the author (or publisher?) didn't find it problematic to publish such patriarchal endorsements of her book. Patriarchal prejudice was instead decorated in full color and presented as a trophy of academic excellence.

So far, I have discussed many shades of critique leveled against Maududi's ideology by intellectuals and activists related to Jamaat and the ways they gesture toward a new discourse. I showed how Zurti, a former Jamaat member, critiqued Maududi's views on women's issues and offered a substantially different reading of the Qurʾān. I then shifted my focus to lay out the theological reasoning of Islahi, then an active Jamaat member. Subsequently I discussed the critical views of Jamal, an SIO activist, as well as a heated debate over the practice of veiling that was published in *Zindegī-e-nav*. I concluded with a critique by a former SIO member (then active in a nongovernmental organization) of Jamaat's position vis-à-vis women. Important to that critique was the relationship among gender, knowledge, and religious authority, and how, unlike from the nineteenth century onward, women in earlier times were visible in their roles as teachers and scholars. In the remainder of this chapter, I will discuss the context and factors that went into critiquing Maududi's neopatriarchate and what such a critique means analytically.

◆ Context of Transformation

Writing about the Haitian revolution, in *Silencing the Past*, anthropologist Michel-Rolph Trouillot (1995, 89) argues that it "thought itself out politically and philosophically as it was taking place," in a context where "discourse always lagged behind practice." A largely similar process seems at work in Jamaat's changing discourse on women. The dissenting, critical voices I discussed above found a place in discourse because in part they were already being played out in practice. The levels at which these practices got staged were multiple. And the factors that contributed to this transformation were many.

To start with, in the Islamist arena itself, Maududi's ideas over time were less strictly followed. In the mid-1970s, Nazar was an Islamist student activist at AMU. Then newly married, he did not let even his friends meet his wife. Under Maududi's influence, he believed in the complete veiling of women.

In 1975, when Indira Gandhi banned Jamaat, several of its leaders in Aligarh were put in prison. One key leader of Jamaat, a professor at AMU, was jailed. When Nazar went to visit the professor in jail, he also saw the latter's wife. She was not wearing a niqab. Even her scarf (*dupaṭṭā*) was not properly placed. To Nazar's surprise, she even wore lipstick. Later, Nazar learned that she did not consider wearing a niqab to be a religious obligation. If not wearing a niqab is against Islam, she asked, were the unveiled women studying in AMU not Muslim? In Nazar's account, the professor himself didn't consider veiling to be a traditional Islamic obligation. Let me offer another example of practice preceding discourse. To Maududi, coeducation was "destructive." However, most postgraduate SIO activists at AMU had studied alongside women. In Jamal's Communicative English course, comprising twenty-one students, nine were women and only two of them wore the veil. Jamal didn't consider studying with women un-Islamic; indeed, he talked to and spent time with women at the university canteens.

Practices within the Islamist arena have also been intimately linked to a much broader context. This context includes notable changes in Muslim society and Indian social-political formations generally. The process of change began in the 1970s, an important decade for the women's movement in India. Considered to be the decade of "reawakening," the 1970s saw massive mobilizations by women throughout India. The "reawakening" was clearly influenced by international developments, the women's movements of the 1960s in the West being a crucial factor. The relative lull of the 1950s and 1960s gave way to a heightened feminist consciousness in the 1970s (Calman 1989; Mazumdar and Agnihotri 1999; Patel 1988). A similar change was registered on the landscape of AMU. Prior to 1947, veiled women came in palanquins (covered chairs) to attend classes. During the 1950s, classrooms at postgraduate levels were partitioned with a curtain to separate men from women (undergraduate classes were segregated by gender, as they are today). The 1970s saw postgraduate gender separation wither away. Delhi's Jamia Millia Islamia, another important university for many Muslims, did not lag behind. The number of Muslim women attending AMU and Jamia Millia Islamia continued to shoot up.

Women's visibility was not limited to universities. Many women achieved success in politics and even became cabinet ministers. As a primetime national TV newsreader, Selma Sultana became a household name in the 1980s (Shaheen 1990). The visibility of women in the public domain, especially in an increasingly diverse array of professions, was closely connected to urban social formation. Owing to a maze of factors, with the postcolonial developmental state as an important agent, the size of the middle class expanded from the

1970s on. In the 1930s, there were no more than a dozen Muslim women with matriculation degrees in Bihar (Daudi 2001). By the 1970s, their number had significantly risen and a considerable number of women were attending universities. Writing about the position of the Tunisian Islamist party, Mouvement de la Tendance Islamiste (Movement of the Islamic Trend, or MTI), Muhammad Mahmoud (1996) linked the loosening of its gender rigidity to the aspirations of this nascent middle class, MTI's main constituency. A similar link can be observed in Jamaat's case. In *The Veil*, Maududi ruthlessly critiqued the middle class and its "revolt" against Islam as manifest in women's freedom. From the 1970s on, Jamaat began to address itself to a segment of this very middle class, or those aspiring to middle-class status. In *Sex in Islam*, Islahi discussed the practice of going on a honeymoon and concluded that Islam allowed it; in fact, he called it "desirable." As I noted, he also discussed the relative benefits of different contraceptives (e.g., condoms, the pill, and IUDs), and he informed readers about their prices. Clearly, desires like that for a honeymoon are hardly those of the Indian working classes. One telling index of Islahi's (and Alkaf's) assumed middle-class audience was the assumption of a desire for privacy. Islahi considered the joint family harmful, for it failed to facilitate the privacy desired by its members.

The transnational ties of one segment of Jamaat's leadership were another significant factor. Elsewhere, I have dealt with the ways this segment influenced Jamaat's shift in favor of secular democracy (see Ahmad 2009b). Here I will dwell on the views of such leaders on "the woman question." During the 1970s, some influential Jamaat leaders from Aligarh went to work in Saudi Arabia, the Gulf countries, and the United States. They also visited Britain, France, and many countries in the Middle East (or what most Indians call "West Asia"). The views of these leaders carried weight, as most of them were university teachers and members of the Jamaat's *shūra*, an executive committee similar to the politburo of communist parties. One such member, Nejatullah Siddiqi, lamented that Jamaat kept an eerie silence about women's role in public life. Calling for women's involvement in political processes, he pleaded for a rethinking of Jamaat's position on women (Siddiqi 2003, 99; 2000, 416–18; also see 1995). In this rethinking, he urged the participation of women who were equally well-versed in modern and Islamic education. If there were no such women, he proposed, steps should be taken to develop them. Siddiqi was not alone in his call for a rethinking. The editor of *ZN* also believed that Jamaat needed to recast itself in accordance with new challenges, particularly those relating to women. Without naming Maududi, he told me that *ʿulema* were wrong in equating the Indian custom of *pardāh* with Islam. Views such as those of Siddiqi and the *ZN* editor were, to an extent, also a part of a wider change in the discourses of Islamist movements worldwide. In my telephone interviews with him, Siddiqi often favorably mentioned Tunisia's Rashid Ghannoushi and urged me to read his works. As John Esposito and John Voll (2001, 91–117) observe, Ghannoushi was one of the first to argue for women's participation in political processes.

To a certain extent, Maududi's death in 1979 paved the way for a thorough critique of his ideology. Though the Indian Jamaat had stopped obediently heeding him while he was still alive, his death left no room for Jamaat hardliners to consult "the authority," Maududi.[19]

◆ Terms for Use

In an article I published in *Modern Asian Studies* in 2008, the opening paragraph of the conclusion posed a question as follows: "Analytically, what does the critique of Maududi's neopatriarchate by his followers mean? For lack of a better term, I submit that it gestures a move towards an Islamic feminist discourse" (Ahmad 2008, 569). Stanley Tambiah (1990, 85) endorsed Lucien Lévy-Bruhl's usage of "primitive mentality" and "pre-logical mentality" on the ground that what mattered was not the label but the "substantive" issue at stake. I largely agree with Tambiah on this point. In the specific case of this chapter, the label, however, is as important as the substantive issue it aims to signify. The reasons for my reluctance to continue to use the term "Islamic feminism" as an analytical grid are many. Foremost among them is that none of my interlocutors themselves used it. They simply related their thoughts and conducted their critiques of Maududi's position on women through the vocabulary of Islam, with barely any homage to feminism, at least not in the way the term is understood in the dominant Western frames. For all Jamaat activists, including Maududi's critics, Islam remains the frame of reference; none, for example, thought intimate relationships outside marriage were legitimate. Likewise, family—considered to be the prime institution of patriarchy in Marxist analyses—remains important to them. What this chapter demonstrates, then, is an important transformative moment in the Islamist movement on "the woman question." Central to this current is a serious engagement with Islamic traditions—the Qurʾān and hadith in particular—to question Maududi's representation of the neopatriarchate. As compelling works by Leila Ahmed, Riffat Hassan, Asghar Ali Engineer, Fatima Mernissi, and others (see early part of this chapter) show, there exists a strong possibility for an antipatriarchal, egalitarian reading of Islam in its full complexity and diversity. This transformative current marks an important moment that the Iranian writer, Nayereh Tohidi, describes as an "egalitarian ethics of Islam" (qtd. in Moghadam 2002, 1147). This moment is far from finished. Both as a phenomenon and an analytical field, it continues to be in the making.

In this chapter, I have focused on the ways Indian Islamists have called into question an array of tenets at the center of Maududi's neopatriarchate. First, for Maududi, home was the natural place for women. They were, therefore, forbidden to leave the home unless there was dire need. And if a woman stepped out, Maududi obligated her to veil from head to toe. It was also for this reason that he described coeducation as destructive. Second, since he considered man to be the ruler over woman, he did not allow women to assume key political roles. Third, Maududi regarded woman as naturally inferior to men. All these elements at the core of Maududi's ideology derived their legitimacy from a particular reading of the Qur'ān and hadith. For a long time, Maududi's ideology reigned in Jamaat as the sole authentic version of Islam. But from the 1970s on, activists and intellectuals connected to Jamaat began to question it. I showed how in different ways, my interlocutors Zurti, Islahi, Jamal, Alkaf, and the former SIO member critiqued Maududi and arrived at alternative readings. According to their readings, the home ceased to be the natural place for women. And Islam did not prevent women from working outside or participating in the public domain, including even films. Indeed Maududi's critics called for women's participation in every domain. According to them, there was no sound reason that prevented women from becoming prime ministers or other heads of state. The argument that women are intellectually inferior to men has lost validity. Even for those in a minority who continue to hold on to it, it has become embarrassing to voice it, certainly in public. Drawing on important archival works by others, such as Akram Nadwi, I also discussed how alternative readings of Islamic history and society showed women working as scholars, which critics of Maududi mobilized to argue for a greater role for women in the present and in the future.

Alternative readings of the Qur'ān, such as those indicated in the debates on veiling in *Zindegī-e-nav*, or in Zurti's and Islahi's employment of *mā'rūf* to encompass "popular" practices, call into question the assumption—central to both Winter and Moghissi—that Islam or the Qur'ān has a patriarchal "essence" and that no other interpretation favorable to women is possible. Intense debates on veiling, women's right to become a head of state, and their participation in the public domain indeed show that the Qur'ān can be open to multiple and at times competing interpretations. Thus the Qur'ān can also be put to use, against Winter's atheistic proposition, for a discourse empowering women. From this perspective, tradition, religion, and sacred texts are not necessarily "a compromise with patriarchy"; they may instead be a critical medium and instrument for questioning a neopatriarchiate such as Maududi's and for continually enlarging women's rights. In 1999, the Jamaat *shūra* discussed the invisibility of women in the leadership (in 2000, out of 4,776 members, only 303 were women). It proposed that the Jamaat president should be authorized to nominate fifteen women to the body from which *shūra* members (at the all-India level) are democratically elected (*ZN* June 1999, 62–63). Though there is still no woman in the *shūra*, the proposal itself is of momentous salience. After all, it was barely a decade ago that the first woman became a member of the politburo of the Communist Party of India (Marxist).

This chapter and the previous one lay bare, I hope, some of the forms, modalities, nature, and mechanisms of critique in printed texts as well as in conversations among the educated and intellectuals. Critique, however, is not the sole preserve of intellectuals. Nor is it limited to the printed world. It is to the mundane life of ordinary subjects and critique of and in it that we turn in the final chapter.

7

THE MUNDANE

Critique as Social-Cultural Practice

> Without *tanqīd* [critique] life is impossible in the same way as we will die if we stop breathing.... Each and every domain of life feels its power and impact.... There is hardly a moment in life when we don't make critical [*tanqīdī*] judgments.... Everywhere and in everything it is our critical capacity that guides us. Whether a judge or a thief, a commoner or a trader, a scientist or a craftsman, a lawyer or a doctor, a soldier or a philosopher, or even a prostitute, all are steeped in critique [*naqd v intiqād*], and the success of each depends on whether he/she correctly employs his/her critical capacity and integrity.
>
> —KALIMUDDIN AHMAD (2006, 34–35)

In order to fully accomplish the objective of this monograph, this chapter marks a significant shift from earlier chapters in part 2, which described critique among intellectuals (*ʿulema*) in texts as well as in conversation. This chapter focuses instead on critique by ordinary subjects (nonintellectuals), going well beyond the realm of texts. In the introduction I discussed why attending to critique by ordinary subjects is important, underscoring the pervasive equation of criticism with literary critique and arguing that this equation is limiting and unproductive. To this end, I quoted Kalimuddin Ahmad, an Urdu literary critic (see epigraph above), who tore this equation apart to posit critique at the center of life for everyone, including ordinary subjects with no educational degrees. By arguing to accord salience to critique by ordinary subjects and to life itself, it is apt to also articulate my dissatisfaction with anthropology's orientation to the domain demarcated as literary.

During my master of philosophy training in sociology at Delhi's Jawaharlal Nehru University in the mid-1990s, in an interaction with Imtiaz Ahmed, considered to be the "expert" anthropologist on Muslims, I asked him to suggest references on doing fieldwork to prepare for my own. The pat response came: "Read *Notes and Queries on Anthropology*." Subsequently, I asked him if I could use poetry and literary pieces such as novels in anthropological analysis. Unenthusiastically, he advised me to avoid them, for they either accentuated or disfigured "reality" and did not constitute "proper data." As an underground poet and literary reader, I found his responses strange; and they stayed with me. Later I discovered that his advice to avoid poetry and literature also stemmed from *Notes and Queries on Anthropology*, according to which "literature deals with ideal behavior, not with actual customs. . . . Literary records also tend to stress the unusual rather than everyday occurrence," and, therefore, they "can't be used to give a picture of everyday custom" (CRAI 1954 [1874], 34). Neither Ahmed nor *Notes and Queries on Anthropology*, however, noted that this was a repetition of the Enlightenment position. In *Anthropology*, Kant (2006 [1798], 5) wrote that plays, novels, and other literary works "are not actually based on experience and truth but only on invention."

If judged from this premise, to some, portions of the previous two chapters might appear to be "unreflective" of so-called reality. But as readers may have rightly noticed, I have already broken with this specific anthropological conceptualization of reality as my prose is interspersed, inter alia, with poetry. The recounting of the tale above is not meant to suggest that nothing has changed since the time of *Notes and Queries on Anthropology*; only to let readers know of a facet of my own anthropological trajectory.

Many works have critiqued and shown the innocence, if not futility, of an iron fence—maintained by advocates on either side—between anthropology and ethnography, on the one hand, and art, poetry, and fiction, on the other. Didier Fassin's (2014) exposition on the boundary between ethnography and fiction is the most recent one. Much of what Fassin says, however, is well known and previously written about, albeit differently (see Berger 1977; Dannhauser 1995; Lennard 1980; McWilliams 1995; Spencer 1954; and Srinivas 1998). He frames the issue in relation to French scholarship; authors I cite here thus don't figure in his text. Also missing is a discussion of poetry. What is particularly productive in Fassin's analysis, however, is the heuristic differentiation he makes between *reality* and *truth*. Against the likely equivalence between reality and truth, he instead views them as concepts in perpetual tension: "the real being that which exists or has happened and the true being that which has to be regained from deception and convention." Drawing on Martha Nussbaum's works, he takes anthropology as an enterprise to "articulate the real and the true—the horizontal and the vertical—in the exploration of life." The quest for the real and the true at times may mean going past bare and known facts as well as instituting a relation to facts, events, structure, and history unnoticed by the interlocutors. Fiction and anthropology are thus different ways of accessing and investigating truth. Calling into question the popular premise that fiction explores truth and anthropology (and social sciences) reality, he states that anthropological forms of inquiry into truth lead to the articulations of "various levels of reality." Interestingly, he compares his own ethnographic work on policing in French *banlieues* to the American crime drama *The Wire*. To this end, he cites sociologist William Wilson's remark on *The Wire*: "Although [a] fiction ... its depiction of the systemic urban inequality that constrains the lives of the urban poor is more poignant and compelling than that of any published study, including my own." Fassin (2014, 41, 45, 52, 48, 53) nonetheless notes that what bestowed credibility on his published work was that it depicted "reality," not fiction.[1]

In the first part of this chapter, I discuss the Ḳhudāī Ḳhidmatgār (servants of God) movement (begun in the first quarter of the last century) as an illustration of critique in everyday life and beyond the highly educated group studied the previous chapters. I have not observed the Ḳhudāī Ḳhidmatgār, as it had petered out by 1947 or shortly thereafter. I rely on historical sources, including an oral account based on Mukulika Banerjee's (1999, 2001) ethnographic fieldwork in the early 1990s that recounts events, memories, and political struggles of the surviving Ḳhudāī Ḳhidmatgār activists prior to the bloody partition of the subcontinent in 1947. Contra Fassin's "direct" observation and depiction of "reality," the account presented here is based on published sources. The "facts" are therefore not mine, but the analytical account surely is. So is the interpretive frame oriented to depict the reality and truth of critique. In Fassin's terms, I am not merely describing reality that existed or happened anthropologically but also aiming to regain the true from deception and convention; that which existing accounts and narratives elide, ignore, or may even find utterly foreign. In so doing I hope to relationally illuminate the true as much as the real. As far as I know, little to no work on the Ḳhudāī Ḳhidmatgār has viewed that movement and its life as a work of critique. In the second section, I continue the theme of critique in everyday life by focusing on three important proverbs drawn from my own fieldwork and that of others from Pakistan. Here I show how by erecting and circulating "nonshifter" (see below) proverbs, discourses—scholarly and popular alike—institute a particular regime of truth. I, therefore, introduce a "shifter" proverb to show a different portrait: a hawker as critic.

◆ Critique in Movement

Most writings on the Ḳhudāī Ḳhidmatgār movement revolve around its founder, Khan Abdul Ghaffar Khan (1890–1988), often described in Indian accounts and in accounts influenced by Indian writings as the "Frontier Gandhi" (e.g., Muhammad Korejo's 1994 book of the same name).[2] In popular parlance also (e.g., in 2011 a television report by NDTV) he is referred to as the "Frontier Gandhi" or its Hindi equivalent. The documentary on Khan by Teri McLuhan (2008), daughter of the famed media theorist Marshall McLuhan, is likewise titled *Frontier Gandhi: Badshah Khan, a Torch for Peace*. People of the Frontier Province—the area currently in Pakistan where the Taliban predominantly comes from—whom Ghaffar Khan worked with and led, however, never called him the "Frontier Gandhi"; for them, he was Badshah Khan (King Khan), Bacha Khan, Baba, and/or Khan Sahib (Abdussattar 2009 [1969], 4; Marwat 2012; Pal 2011, 99). In his autobiography, narrated to K. N. Narang and published in 1969, Ghaffar Khan himself never used the term "Frontier Gandhi" (Pal 2011, 120, 242n5). It was a title created by outsiders for cultural subordination and assimilation. The prefix "frontier" not only makes "Gandhi" a proper noun but simultaneously renders Ghaffar Khan invisible and subservient to Mohandas Gandhi, who had been mythicized and made larger than life. The postcolonial deployment of "Frontier Gandhi" as a metonym for Ghaffar Khan is indeed a colonial trope at the service of a hegemonic enterprise.

It was the British orientalist William Jones who had described Kalidas (d. fifth century AD), a Sanskrit poet and dramatist born more than a millennium before Shakespeare, as the "Shakespeare of India" (Lal 1991, 171). In strict temporal terms, Shakespeare should have been called the Kalidas of England. Jones's description, however, is not simply anachronistic but an ideological move that recognized Indian literature only as a subordinated appendix to English literature, the supreme yardstick against which everything else should search for its definition. Thus, many Indians like me grew up hearing Kanpur described as the Manchester of India and Allahabad University as the Oxford of India. While commenting on my prefieldwork doctoral proposal, the political sociologist Claus Offe (2015), from the "second generation of Frankfurt School theorists," advised me to read Thomas Pantham, a political scientist. When I did not immediately give a gesture of recognition of his name, Offe remarked: "You don't know him? He is considered to be the Habermas of India." Clearly, behind all such formulaic descriptions of A as B—in education, economy, literature, and politics alike—there is a hierarchical valuation and violent evaluation, the pivot of which is ultimately culture, albeit often expressed through the catalog of nationalized geography. The metonym "Frontier Gandhi" belongs to the same repertoire of violent descriptions.

Ghaffar Khan stood for peace, led one of the most spectacular movements against colonial oppression and in favor of freedom, derived inspiration from Islam, and included people of other faiths in his movement. But he could accomplish all this, so tells the dominant scholarship as well as demotic common sense, only under the influence of Gandhi, perceived as *the* symbol of nonviolence, tolerance, and ethical politics, the mainspring of which is construed as Hinduism. So entrenched is this belief that in McLuhan's documentary, when an Indian schoolgirl is asked who Badshah Khan (Ghaffar Khan) was, she says: "He was almost very same to Gandhi *jī*. *But* he was a Muslim." Another girl observed: "His method was *also* non-violence *just like* Gandhi *jī*" (YouTube 2010; italics for English words mine). The words "but," "also," and "just like" speak volumes about the hierarchical valuation of religion/culture at play.[3] Whether or not Gandhi advocated nonviolence and if it was a mere contingent tactic or principle (see Ahmad 2014b; and Sifton 2015) should not detain us here. What is important is the certitude of derivativeness, in the hands of analysts and writers, of Ghaffar Khan's struggle and philosophy from Gandhi. This derivativeness is instilled even in those few accounts that apparently claim to interrogate the convention. Thus Amitabh Pal notes that "in India Ghaffar Khan has been handled with unfairness," for he is "portrayed as adjunct of Gandhi (hence the term 'Frontier Gandhi')." Yet, Pal finds it soothing to conclude: "The 'Frontier Gandhi' is a person whose achievements can truly be compared with the *original* [Gandhi]" (Pal 2011, 122–23; italics mine). The much-discussed biography of Ghaffar Khan by D. G. Tendulkar, as Banerjee aptly notes, is also no more than an "appendage to Gandhi." Banerjee's (2001, 3, 209) work is almost an exception (in English) to the industry that writings on Gandhi have become.

It is unclear what Pal has in mind as the relational opposite of "the original"—is it a photocopy, fake, or something else? My aim here, as alluded to earlier, is to regain the true life of Ghaffar Khan and his movement as an autonomous entity. The task I undertake may be described as belonging to retrieval of subjugated or stigmatized knowledge (Ahmad 2012, 901n4). A writer who came close to a facet of what I argue here was J. S. Bright, a contemporary of Ghaffar Khan. Below I quote him at length for he does not figure in most writings on either the Ḳhudāī Ḳhidmatgār or Ghaffar Khan, including work by Rajmohan Gandhi (2004)—a politician and Gandhi's grandson—and Banerjee (2001).

> Ghaffar Khan is in complete accord with the principle of nonviolence. . . . He has reached it. And reached it independently. Independently like a struggler after truth. No doubt, his deep study of Koran [*sic*] has influenced his doctrine of love. . . . Of the two, Ghaffar Khan and Mahatma Gandhi, my personal view is that the former has achieved a higher level of spirituality. . . . Ghaffar Khan, like Shelley, has come from heaven to the earth, while Mahatma Gandhi, like Keats, is going from earth to the heaven. Hence, I do not understand why Ghaffar Khan should be called the Frontier Gandhi. There is no other reason except that the Mahatma was earlier in the field, more ambitious than spiritual, and has been able to capture, somehow or the other, a greater publicity. If we judge a person by spiritual qualities, Mahatma Gandhi should rather be called the Indian Khan than Ghaffar Khan the Frontier Gandhi: true, there the matter ends. (Bright 1944, 103–4)

Hierarchical subordination and cultural assimilation is not the only aspect of works on Ghaffar Khan. From the Pakistani side, scholars and nonscholars alike have maintained silence on the Ḳhudāī Ḳhidmatgār. Scholarship on Pakistan either ignores the movement (Akbar Ahmed 2003; Allana 1988; Jalal 2008; Khan 2012) or mentions it inconsequentially (e.g., see Marsden 2005, 196; Shaikh 2009, 186; and Zaman 2012, 232). A recurrent theme has been the depiction of the Ḳhudāī Ḳhidmatgār and Ghaffar Khan as traitors to the so-called Pakistani nation-state (Banerjee 2001, 1; *Humshehri.org* 2014; Makki 2003; Pal 2011, 121; Quraish 2010). Geopolitics has been at the core of Indian and Pakistani attitudes to the Ḳhudāī Ḳhidmatgār and the frontier area they inhabited—the history of which goes back to the Great Game between imperial Britain and tsarist Russia to implant their respective dominations (Ahmad 2011a, 32). To the Simon Commission, it was "an international frontier of the first importance from the military point of view for the whole [British] Empire" (qtd. in Bright 1944, 11). If the Pakistani state dismantled the Ḳhudāī Ḳhidmatgār for their "anti-national" activities and "sedition," on the Indian side, there has been support—sometimes explicit, sometimes implicit—for an independent state of Pashtuns. Gandhi himself backed such an idea (Pal 2011, 115).[4] How the colonial dovetails into the "postcolonial" is demonstrated, for example, by the fact that the Pakistani state imprisoned Ghaffar Khan for the same duration as the British had done—fifteen years (Abdussattar 2009 [1969], 5).

To the extent it is possible, in what follows I aim to evacuate the Ḳhudāī Ḳhidmatgār movement from the bloody debris of nation-(un)thinking and state-(un)making to read it as a movement of critique. A suitable place to begin is with the life of Ghaffar Khan.

Born in 1890 in the village of Utmanzai, Hashtnagar, Peshawar, Ghaffar Khan's father, Bahram Khan, was an influential khan (chief/leader). But unlike the major khans of the landed aristocracy that formed the support base of colonial rule (Banerjee 2001, 30–31; Shah 2013, 111), he was a small khan who never entered a relationship of sycophancy with the then rulers. Nor was he authoritarian in his approach. As Ghaffar Khan (2009) recounted in his autobiography, which this section heavily draws on, his father was uneducated, pious, God-oriented, and big-hearted; he responded to the bad with the good. His mother, a virtuous and gentle woman, would often cook extra food for neighbors and travelers. Though he had servants, his father would carry the basket of bread and vegetables over his head to feed the travelers. Unlike the major khans who sided with the British, Ghaffar Khan's grandfather had fought against the British.

In 1901, the British created North West Frontier Province (NWFP)—with Peshawar as its capital—out of the Punjab, but built only a few schools, where the medium of instruction was not Pashto, the local language. In the countryside there were hardly any schools. In 1901, the literacy rate in the NWFP stood at 5.5 percent, only to fall in 1911 to 5.1 percent (Marwat 2012, 128; Shah 2007, 87). In Ghaffar Khan's narrative, at the behest of and in league with the British, local mullahs forbade children from going to schools on the pretext that gaining a worldly education was *kufr* and would prevent the students from reaching paradise. The education given at mosques was largely religious, but even that was not meant for all because "the so-called mullahs" thought as Brahmans did. To Ghaffar Khan, this was because of the influence of Hinduism, which Pashtuns had left to embrace Islam.[5] By the time Islam reached the frontier, he maintained, it had lost the spiritual light, Godly impulse, and piety brought by Prophet Muhammad. Arabs had by then become intoxicated with monarchy and bereft of the spirit to spread virtues. At five, he enrolled in school and was taught the Qur'ān. Subsequently, he joined the boardinghouse of Mission High School of Peshawar (run by Christian missionaries), where his elder brother was also enrolled (later this brother would go to the United Kingdom to become a medical doctor). A well-built man, six feet three inches tall, he aspired to join the British army and was accepted; but seeing the humiliation heaped on a fellow Pashtun at the hands of the British, he chose not to. While Ghaffar Khan was studying at the Mission school, pastor-teacher M. E. Wigram impressed him. Wigram's service to the poor and the subalternated influenced

Ghaffar Khan, making him ask why Pashtuns didn't help each other. For his higher education, he moved to Mayo College, Aligarh, and stayed there for a year as a day scholar. His elder brother wanted him to join him in Britain. Ghaffar Khan was all set to go, but he submitted to his mother, whom he loved and who didn't desire his departure. He didn't pursue any further education (2009, 6–20).

Instead Ghaffar Khan turned to social reform, especially for the spread of education. To this end, he was guided by the Haji of Turangzai, a graduate of Darul Uloom Deoband, a fiercely anticolonial activist, and a respected figure. In 1910, Ghaffar Khan (2009 [1969], 30) and his associates founded an independent Islamic school, the Azad school. The initiative for schools gathered momentum in the 1920s with their number rising to seventy; some of them secured affiliation with Delhi's Jamia Millia Islamia (Shah 2007, 92). Many such schools were attached to village mosques, where Ghaffar Khan made persuasive speeches. Money to run schools was drawn from the pool of *zakāt*, which in the recollection of one Ḳhudāī Ḳhidmatgār activist in the early 1990s was 10 percent of one's property. The subjects taught at these schools were history, the Pashto language, math, the Qur'ān, and hadith, as well as vocational skills like carpentry, tailoring, and weaving. There was a particular emphasis on the teaching of the Qur'ān and hadith to crush the fatalism spread by the mullahs and major khans (Banerjee 2001, 51–52). Ghaffar Khan synthesized his educational activism with reading newspapers and magazines, like *Al-Hilāl* and *Al-Balāgh* of Abul Kalam Azad and *Zamīndār*[6] of Zafar Ali Khan (1873–1956). He also met *ʿulema* of Deoband. There was a resonance between the *ʿulema* of Deoband and Ghaffar Khan as they all aspired to gain freedom from colonial rule. Two *ʿulema* he met and was impressed by were Mahmudul Hasan (1851–1920), known as Shaikhul Hind, and his disciple Ubaidullah Sindhi (d. 1944).[7] In 1914, Ghaffar Khan received a letter from Hasan to meet him in Deoband. With Fazal Mahmud and Fazal Rabbi, he traveled to Deoband. Hasan and his associates aimed to drive the British out through jihad. They saw the NWFP and Afghanistan as a base to meet this objective and called upon people to migrate (*hijrat*) there. Anticipating arrest, however, Hasan went for the hajj, after which he aimed to mobilize Turkey's support for India's freedom. In 1917, Sheriff Husain of Mecca arrested and handed Hasan over to the British to whom Husain was loyal. They jailed Hasan and his colleagues in Malta for three years (Kidwai 1985, 406). Ghaffar Khan (2009, 38, 54) had taken part in that failed *hijrat* movement. He also met the poet-philosopher Muhammad Iqbal (d. 1938) and Zafar Ali Khan (Khan 2009, 105).

Following the end of World War I, India experienced a heightened phase of anti-British mobilization due to the combination of the Ḳhilafat movement with opposition to the 1919 Rowlatt Act, which aimed to crush all dissent as sedition. With his associates, Ghaffar Khan organized an anti-imperialism meeting that attracted over 100,000 participants. Quick to action, the British jailed Ghaffar Khan in Peshawar for six months. Having terrorized his native village with the raw display of guns and canons, they imposed a collective fine of ₹30,000 on the village of Utmanzai and arrested 150 of its residents. A few villagers worked as agents of the British. Terrible though the event was for the entire village, it also inaugurated political life in the province (Khan 2009 [1969], 46–47).

Before 9/11, it was standard in anthropology—from Fredrik Barth in the 1950s through Akbar Ahmed in the 1970s and Charles Lindholm in the 1980s, to Mukulika Banerjee in the early 2000s—to write about Pashtuns not as Muslims but primarily as Pathans/Pakhtuns, as the titles of these scholars' respective books testify. After 9/11, Lindholm (2002, 113–16) acknowledged how little he knew or how uncurious he was about Islam during his fieldwork in the 1960s. The anthropological focus was cast on social structure or culture; in some cases they overlapped. Thus Banerjee (2001, 28–33) titled a subsection of her book "Fundamentals of Pathan Culture," in which she described its segmentary lineage system. From there she proceeded to devote a paragraph to the "caste-like social stratification" among Pathans followed by shame and honor (*nāmūs*—things with which a man surrounds himself: guns, land, and women). Honor, she informed readers, is encoded in the larger idea of *pakhtunwali*. Central to this is *badal* (revenge, feud, or vendetta). Pathans' customs had it that, when sought, sanctuary could not be refused to even an enemy. In Pashto, it was called *nanawati*, which literally means "coming in" but more properly translates as "sanctuary." *Melmastia* is the offering of sanctuary and hospitality and thus an extension of *nanawati*. Two related notions are *pardah* and *jirga*. Whereas the former means the seclusion of women and arrangement of domestic life, the latter means the honorable organization of public life through an assembly of male elders. Banerjee complemented her description of the "fundamentals of Pashtun culture" with the mention of major and minor khans, *ʿulema*, and *lambardars* (quasi-hereditary revenue tax collectors). Factions, feuds, violence, and alliances marked relationships among such actors. Elsewhere, Banerjee (1999, 184) described Pathans' "classic segmentary structure, . . . overlain by a highly developed . . . code, *pakhtunwali*, which was founded on several inter-related institutions and concepts."

Though Banerjee noted the neglect of colonial history in Barth, promised to deliver a "more dynamic ethnographic model of Pathan society" rather than a "static" one, and cursorily and indecisively discussed orientalism, she seldom presented an alternative account, even as her book title, *The Pathan Unarmed*, sought to contest the colonial hubris of the "notoriously violent" Pathans (Banerjee 2001, 3, 14, 9, 15). A key reason, as she herself noted, was that her aim was "not to challenge the veracity of earlier anthropological accounts." Wedded to a British style of political anthropology (Ahmad 2009a, 2015c, 2015d), her account was largely in a realist mode and nearly blind to the representational nature of anthropological works and its power (Asad 1986b; Van Maanen 1988). Like other scholars, she did not mention, let alone address, Asad's (1972, 75, 80) critique of Barth's Weberian analysis premised on a Hobbesian view of human nature. A segmentary lineage system, *badal*, and the like, or what Banerjee called the "Fundamentals of Pathan Culture" might be real in monographs to some, but to many they may not necessarily be true to the tradition and vision of a moral world that Pathans discursively and conflictually hold. It was by recalling, retrieving, and renewing the religious tradition and its moral vision that Ghaffar Khan critiqued what anthropologists such as Banerjee called the "Fundamentals of Pathan Culture." For him, the "Fundamentals of Pathan Culture" was simply an unjust constellation of power relations dating to precolonial times but consolidated and transformed under colonialism.

Ghaffar Khan's autobiography contains ample insights and facts to read what anthropologists usually take as culture (cf. Crehan 2002, chaps. 1 and 3) are in fact power relations. Describing the Frontier Crime Regulation Act (FCRA, implemented after the creation of the NWFP in 1901) as "terrifying," Ghaffar Khan discussed how, in the wake of its pervasive use, "factionalism, division, and mutual enmities [*dushmanīyāñ*] began to be born." This law allowed the filing of a fictitious case, with no evidence needed, against anyone unfriendly to the British. The alleged criminal was then brought to a *jirga* under the control of local men working as agents of the British to pronounce a sentence of fourteen years of imprisonment (Khan 2009 [1969], 22, 7, 46, 8, 32, 12, 23). The recruitment of local people to work as proregime witnesses or as spies was the cause as much as consequence of division or enmity among people. Implementation of laws like the FCRA through a *jirga* was simply unthinkable without the khans, whom he termed "*ḥākim parast* [ruler-worshippers]." This is not to say that all khans were ruler-worshippers—he claimed his father was not—but they formed the base supporting colonial rule. Likewise, the presence of "caste-like social stratification," as Ghaffar Khan saw it, was a remnant of Brahmanism endorsed by some "so-called" *ʿulema* steeped in "ignorance and degeneration." For Ghaffar Khan, the fact that local *ʿulema* discouraged children from going to school was neither a reflection of Islam nor of Pashtun culture;

he held that Islam made it mandatory for boys and girls to study. For Ghaffar Khan it was instead a result of an "alliance between the British and the so-called mullah," the latter obscuring Islam to further the interests of his own group and those of the colonial regime.

We saw above that Ghaffar Khan's description of his parents as God-fearing and virtuous was already a critique of the machismo attributed to Pathan culture. In his account, his father was not authoritarian and submitted to his mother's wishes rather than let his brother's and his own wish to go to Britain for education prevail. We also saw that he bemoaned the lessening of godly impulse and piety brought by Prophet Muhammad, and the Arabs' subsequent intoxication with monarchical rule. That distancing from the piety of Prophet Muhammad notwithstanding, some people with knowledge of and depth in piety wandered around the world in a quest for Islam and they brightened the fields of philosophy, intellect, knowledge, and Sufism. Such souls were *k̲hudā parast* (God-worshippers) rather than *zar parast* (wealth-worshippers) (Khan 2009 [1969], 15, 32). Ghaffar Khan himself wandered around the world. With his sister and wife, he travelled to Hijaz to perform the hajj and also visited what are now Lebanon, Syria, and Iraq (including Baghdad, Basra, and Karbala). During the journey to Baytul-Maqdis, his wife died. He resolved not to remarry and devoted himself to the service of community and country (*mulk v millat*). After the hajj, he spent some days in Ṭāʾif. While he was walking through the town a bearded stranger called to him (in Arabic). When the stranger approached him, the man said, "Here lies a hair of the Prophet's beard as well as a stone with his footprint." Ghaffar Khan responded, "I have not come here for this; I have come instead to see the fortitude/steadfastness [*ṣabr*][8] and courage [*himmat*] of the Prophet who, for the good of the people, comes from Mecca to Ṭāʾif. Inhabitants of Ṭāʾif throw stones at, beat, and humiliate him. Yet he is not disappointed with his community. Instead his hands go up in *duʿā*: God, guide my community so that they tread the path of virtue" (100).

It was this journey of Prophet Muhammad and his message that became the fountainhead of Ghaffar Khan's movement: the K̲hudāī K̲hidmatgār. Recalling the challenges in leading the anticolonial movement and the constant imprisonment he faced, he observed, "Religion is also like a movement."[9] For it to succeed, it required virtuous and selfless people dedicated to serving community and country for the sake of God. Such people would benefit God's creation and also make their community prosperous (Khan 2009 [1969], 51, 32). Cultivating piety in the path of God, however, entailed knowing His words in the language revealed. Earlier he had lamented that he was taught the Qurʾān without truly understanding it. One principal reason for his appreciation of

Ubaidullah Sindhi was that he taught the Qurʾān to modern educated youth to generate an "ethos for love, devotion, and service." In jail, he observed, "The language of worship for Hindus is Sanskrit and ours is Arabic. This is why we don't understand the meanings of words and sentences during prayer. Nor do Hindus understand theirs. Now ponder over it: will he who is neither familiar with his religion nor understands its religious text ever achieve progress [*taraqqī*]?" (83).

As this quotation demonstrates, for Ghaffar Khan Islam was a source of inspiration for the anticolonial movement to secure freedom and correct the wrongs of the society he lived in. Asking which came first was irrelevant. Both were simultaneous. However, neither would be possible without reform (*iṣlāḥ*), a concept emanating from Islamic tradition (on which, see Ahmad 2015d). The task of *iṣlāḥ* occupied him throughout his political life—in prisons, rallies, streets, and households alike. In jail, he did the *iṣlāḥ* of a Hindu friend who had subscribed to the British propaganda that Pathans drank human blood by asking him if he had ever met and interacted with Pathans or visited them (Khan 2009 [1969], 83). Likewise, within his household he broke the prevalent custom of the husband eating first; he and his wife dined together (Gandhi 2004, 53). In this task, Ghaffar Khan was inspired, inter alia, by the *iṣlāḥ* mission of the Haji of Turangzai, who had established an Islamic school in the province and conducted jihad against "useless customs and mores" (29). In 1924, Ghaffar Khan founded Anjuman Iṣlāḥul Afghānā (Society for the Reform of Afghans, hereafter AIA). The AIA's motto was expressed in a verse from the Qurʾān: "You are the best of peoples, evolved from mankind, enjoining what is good, forbidding what is wrong, and believing in God" (qtd. in Marwat 2012, 132). The AIA exhorted people to pursue education, especially for their children, and abandon harmful, useless practices. It also worked as a vehicle to articulate people's positions and grievances vis-à-vis the government on a number of issues, including the coercive payment of land revenue even when the harvest had gone bad. In May 1928, he launched a newspaper in Pashto: *Pashtūn* (Khan 2009 [1969], 102).

◆ Homo Ḳhidmatiqus

Ghaffar Khan's most prominent initiative was forming the Ḳhudāī Ḳhidmatgār in 1929 to "ignite passion to serve community and country for the sake of God." Instead of passion for *ḳhidmat* (service), people sought revenge against each other, including their kith and kin. Ghaffar Khan noted that in the midst of conservative and useless customs dwelled an unusual sense of violent revenge, with an utter absence of good morals (*akhlāq*). To join the Ḳhudāī Ḳhidmatgār, one was required to take an oath: "I am Ḳhudāī Ḳhidmatgār. Since God needs no *ḳhidmat*, therefore, to serve God's creation is to serve the oneness of God. I will thus serve God's creation selflessly and for the sake of God alone." Given the centrality of *ḳhidmat* in the movement's discourse, historian Abdul Karim Khan (1999, 22) described Ḳhudāī Ḳhidmatgār activists as "Homo Ḳhidmatiqus."[10] Integral to the membership oath was also the promise "to lead a life of simplicity, abstention from mutual enmities, factionalism, and enactment of virtuous deeds [*nēk kām*] through morals and good conduct." There was no monetary remuneration. It was mandatory for members—poor or rich—to do two hours of physical training and drills every day (Khan 2009, 112–13).

Structurally, the organization resembled an army, and its members had titles similar to army officers. But they carried no weapons, only the weapon of service and peace (for more, see Banerjee 2001, chap. 3; and Gandhi 2004, 84). Women also joined. Their participation mattered to Ghaffar Khan. In August 1928, before the formation of the Ḳhudāī Ḳhidmatgār, 2,000 women had already participated in a public meeting. Flouting local customs, Ghaffar Khan sent his daughter to study at Allahabad University, the "Oxford of India." In one account, she was the first woman from the Frontier to receive a university education. Ghaffar Khan also did not favor the prevalent practice of veiling (*pardāh*). Women in his own household broke away from many traditional customs; his sister actively participated in the movement. During the 1930s, women began to take up leadership roles to address public meetings (Marwat 2012, 134). Women's inequality, he held, stemmed from a customs-centered structure of patriarchy that Islam opposed: "In the holy Qur'ān, you have an equal share with men. You are today oppressed because we men have ignored the commands of God and the Prophet. Today we are followers of custom" (qtd. in Easwaran 1999, 133).

Another element of oath was the vow that "I will serve all God's creatures alike; and my object shall be attainment of the freedom of my country and religion" (qtd. in Johansen 1997, 59). "God's creatures" included nonhumans and people of all faiths. Though predominantly Muslim, the Frontier had Hindu and Sikh "minorities" who also joined the Ḳhudāī Ḳhidmatgār. Interreligious brotherhood and the promotion of "Hindu-Muslim unity" were indeed crucial, and Ghaffar Khan stressed them in nearly all his speeches. Interreligious solidarity was not limited to the Frontier. On many occasions, Ḳhudāī Ḳhidmatgār activists went to help their Hindu brethren in the adjacent province of Punjab. A Hindu candidate had solicited from Ghaffar Khan the assistance of some Ḳhudāī Ḳhidmatgār "soldiers" during an election. As promised, Khan extended the help. Following World War II, when violence against Hindus and Sikhs broke out, thousands of Ḳhudāī Ḳhidmatgār activists swung into action to ensure the safety of their lives and property. In subsequent years, as violence erupted in Bihar and elsewhere, Ghaffar Khan toured those areas to appeal for peace (Banerjee 2001, 50, 95; Marwat 2012, 137; Pal 2011, 103).

Probably the most salient element of the membership oath was unwavering commitment to nonviolence, which became the "puzzle" informing Banerjee's research.[11] It read, "I will not resort to violence, nor will I take revenge against anyone. No matter who inflicts oppression and excesses [*z̤ulm v zeyādtī*] on me, I will forgive him" (Khan 2009 [1969], 112–13). In other accounts, this idea was expressed as follows: "I will live in accordance with the principles of nonviolence [*ʿadm tashaddud*]" (qtd. in Johansen 1997, 59). To those possibly aghast at the proclamation of peace and nonviolence, Ghaffar Khan said, "There is nothing surprising in a Muslim or a Pathan like me subscribing to the creed of nonviolence. It is not a new creed. It was followed fourteen hundred years ago by Prophet Muhammad all the time he was in Mecca, and it has since been followed by all those who wanted to throw off an oppressor's yoke" (qtd. in Johansen 1997, 60).

Elsewhere, he stated that nonviolence (*ʿadm tashaddud*) was required by the Qurʾān itself. Much like *ṣabr, ʿadm tashaddud* should not be narrowly construed, as it is often done, as mere absence of violence. *ʿAdm tashaddud* is closely connected to the notion of *ḳhidmat,* which, an Indian Foreign Service expert recalled after meeting Ghaffar Khan in 1987, to him meant, "Service to our fellow-humans is the greatest form of worship" (qtd. in Sohoni 1995, 39, 42; see also Hameed 1995). Neither *ḳhidmat* nor *ʿadm tashaddud,* however, would cohere if not anchored by a firm faith in God and the building of a world with His attributes: justice, peace, and harmony.

In 1930, the year after the group's founding, the Ḳhudāī Ḳhidmatgār had barely 1,000 members (Banerjee 2001, 60).[12] By 1931, however, 25,000 new members had joined, and the movement had more sympathizers. In 1938, the membership had shot up to over 100,000. At their peak, the Ḳhudāī Ḳhidmatgār had over 1 million members (Banerjee 2001, 61; Pal 2011, 100; Hameed 1995, 114). A major turning point occurred on 23 April 1930 with the Qissa Khani Bazar Massacre in Peshawar, an event comparable to the well-known Jalianwala Bagh massacre of 1919 in Amritsar, but obscured in Indian historiography and public knowledge. Locally, it was known simply as *san tīs shahīdān* (year thirty of martyrs). From the perspective of this book, the Qissa Khani Bazar massacre was an embodied critique by the colonized: an extraordinary street critique of the colonial order and its reign of terror by ordinary subjects as they fearlessly kissed death with fortitude (*ṣabr*) as their only weapon and the Qurʾān clutched to their chests.

During the 1930s, noncooperation and civil resistance against the British government had gathered momentum throughout India. The NWFP was no exception. It is important to note that the Qissa Khani Bazar Massacre and the exemplification of nonviolence by the Ḳhudāī Ḳhidmatgār occurred before they had aligned themselves with the Gandhi-led Congress (which happened in August 1931; see Banerjee 2001, 69; and Johansen 1997, 62). On 19 and 20 April, over 1,000 Ḳhudāī Ḳhidmatgār activists and the Frontier Provincial Congress Committee met at Utmanzai (Ghaffar Khan's native village) to mark the anniversary of the Azad school. Ghaffar Khan called for civil resistance against the occupying power. On his way to Peshawar, on 23 April 1930, police arrested him and his associates (Ahmad Shah, Abdul Akbar, Sarfaraz, and Shahnawaz) at the village of Naqi and imprisoned him for three years under the FCRA. Thousands gathered to protest the arrests. Several rounds of arrests were made in Peshawar as well. There too protests followed, leading to a throng of people to a public square. They marched to Kabuli Thana (the police station) where the arrested activists were being held. About 800 people gathered to chant slogans like "Long Live Revolution [*inqilāb zindābād*]" (Khan 2009 [1969], 119–23; Marwat 2012, 144–45; Shah 2013, 99). The people mobilized were certainly indignant, but not violent at all. Three armored cars appeared on the scene and with frightening speed drove into the crowd, instantly killing many. The British troops opened fire on the unarmed, peaceful people. Protesters agreed to disperse, provided they were allowed to attend to the injured and collect the dead bodies, and provided the armored cars left the scene. However, officials refused to leave; so then did the protesters. The troops repeatedly opened fire on the protesters, to which they responded with "God is great." Many held the Qurʾān to their chests as they embraced death (Johansen 1997, 62). In one account: "When those in front fell down wounded by the shots, those behind came forward with their breasts bared and exposed themselves to the fire, so much so that, some people got as many as 21 bullet wounds in their bodies, and all the people stood their ground without getting into a panic" (Sharp 1960, 110).

The shooting continued from eleven in the morning until three in the afternoon. A recent study (Shah 2013, 100) estimated the death toll at between 200 and 300, with several hundred injured. Those killed—many Hindus and Sikhs among them—"were mostly Mohammedans"; the British burned their bodies in unknown places (Sharp 1960, 111). Zafar Ali Khan, journalist-poet, versified the massacre as follows (qtd. in Shah 2013, 105):

Mulkul maūt kō ḵhāṯir mēñ na lānē vālē [Those who didn't fear the angel of death]
Gōliān tānē huē sīnē pē kẖānē vālē [Those who faced bullets with their bare chests]
Qabr tak ṣabr kō sāthi huē jānē vālē [Those who went to the grave with no rage]
Ṣabr kā moʿjezaʾ dunyā kō dikẖānē vālē [Those who showed the miracle of fortitude to the age]

The colonial horror was not restricted to Peshawar, nor did it stop on 23 April 1930; it continued afterward and spread to the countryside to crush the Ḵhudāī Ḵhidmatgār. On 16 May, Ghaffar Khan's village was besieged by troops. They burned down the offices of the Ḵhudāī Ḵhidmatgār and ransacked the entire village. The troops continued their reign of terror in the villages of Prang and Charsadda. When the Ḵhudāī Ḵhidmatgār organized a protest meeting on 28 May, twenty of their activists were killed by machine-gun fire. This terror included the destruction of grain and the humiliation of people through strip searches. At Bannu on 24 August, troops opened fire at a protest meeting, killing seventy people (Khan 2009 [1969], 124–26; Marwat 2012, 145; Pal 2011, 109; Shah 2013, 99). In 1932, over 10,000 Ḵhudāī Ḵhidmatgār members were jailed in Haripur Prison alone. In spite of British provocation and notwithstanding their huge membership, Ḵhudāī Ḵhidmatgār activists never responded with violence (Johansen 1997, 62–63). Committed to their Islamic ideals and oath to peace, they displayed *ṣabr* (that is, by not responding to police bullets with violence of their own, Ḵhudāī Ḵhidmatgār volunteers indeed displayed honor). A remarkable aspect of the Qissa Khani Bazar Massacre was the refusal by the Royal Garhwal Rifles soldiers, largely comprised of Hindus, to shoot at protesters. The following conversation between the French journalist Charles Petrasch (1932) and Gandhi speaks volumes about who genuinely stood for nonviolence: Ghaffar Khan or Gandhi.

CHARLES PETRASCH: Why did you not see that . . . soldiers, who had refused to fire on an unarmed crowd, were included in the truce? How do you reconcile that with your doctrine of non-violence, since these men were punished for having refused to be party to an act of violence?

GANDHI: I cannot ask officials and soldiers to disobey, for when I am in power I shall in all likelihood make use of those same officials and those same soldiers. If I taught them to disobey I should be afraid that they might do the same when I am in power [*sic*]. (Petrasch 1932; *sic* in brackets in original).

To be sure, more can be said about the Ḳhudāī Ḳhidmatgār's subsequent intense activism. However, it will scarcely advance the goal of this chapter, which is to show the Ḳhudāī Ḳhidmatgār to be a movement of critique. I hope to have demonstrated that critique is a preserve not simply of the educated elite but also and equally of ordinary men and women. Unlike Maududi and many others I discussed in previous chapters, Ghaffar Khan was by no means a typical scholar (*ʿālim*). Nor were hundreds of thousands of his followers, most of whom were unlettered and peasants. In the remainder of this chapter, I will shed light on critique in everyday life, outside of social movements like the Ḳhudāī Ḳhidmatgār.

◆ Critique in Everyday Life: The Power of Proverbs

In Hindu and Islamicate cultures of the subcontinent it is quite a common practice to use proverbs in everyday life. Called *ẓarbul maṡl, qaōl,* and/or *moḥāvarā* in Urdu and *kahāvat* and *bachan* in both Urdu and Hindi (*Fīrozullog̣hāt* 2014), in anthropological literature, proverbs are also known as "speaking folklore." So ubiquitous and important are proverbs that in Africa they are deployed in judicial processes to contest and make arguments (Arewa and Dundes 1964; Siran 1993). Proverbs, as well as antiproverbs, abound in popular culture, advertising, and mass media. To boost its sales, in the 1970s, the German car company Volkswagen played with the proverb "Different strokes for different folks" to create "Different Volks for different folks." It is also the case that many proverbs contain stereotypes and prejudices. Invariably impersonal in nature, proverbs are taken as expressions of truth and wisdom passed down from one generation to another. They function as tools to "summarize experiences and observations into nuggets of wisdom" to reflect, constitute, and transform the social world. Proverbs are, however, not taken to be a "logical philosophical system" because the wisdom expressed in them is rarely agreed upon or true for all times, peoples, and societies. As a matter of fact, for every proverb there is often a counterproverb canceling the wisdom of the former. For instance, the proverb "Absence makes the heart grow fonder" coexists with "Out of sight, out of mind," and "Look before you leap" with "He who hesitates is lost." Interestingly, there are proverbs about proverbs (Mieder 2004, 1, 151, 3).

Proverbs have been studied from a variety of perspectives and disciplines. In fact, there is a distinct science called *paremiology,* the study of proverbs, whose history, like that of all modern knowledges, is traced back to the Greeks and Aristotle. In some accounts, the German scholar Karl Wilhelm Wander (1803–79) is regarded as the first modern paremiologist. There is a yearbook

Proverbium: Yearbook of International Proverb Scholarship. In linguistics, there is a well-established field of study, phraseology, which inquires, among other topics, into the units and expressions of proverbs. Likewise, proverbs have attracted the attention of sociologists, historians, psychologists, cultural and performance studies scholars, folklorists, and practitioners in many other disciplines (Mieder 2004, xii–xiii, 125). Theologians also have written about proverbs extensively (e.g., see Martin 1995; McKane 1970). As is well known, proverbs and religion have been intimately intertwined; the Bible's Book of Proverbs, "a compendium of Israelite wisdom texts" (Whybray 1994, 7; Sandoval 2006), being perhaps the most obvious example. There are many writings about proverbs, known as "wisdom literature," in other religions as well (Mieder 2004, 144–45).

My concern here is with the role of the proverb as critique. A proverb often has a set of unsaid assumptions that are required knowledge to make it discernible (of course, not transcontextually). A proverb often prefigures and condenses a story. This requires knowing proverbs not merely as linguistic statements but as expressions of and in culture. Anthropologically, therefore, what is more fruitful is to examine the situational settings that proverbs express and in which they are used. As E. Ojo Arewa and Alan Dundes (1964, 70) noted, knowing proverbs and applying them in appropriate situations are not the same. The epigraph of their article has a quote from a Western-educated Nigerian scholar at the University of California, Berkeley: "I know the proverbs but I don't know how to apply them." However, as I have noted, since one proverb is often contested, even contradicted, by another, focusing merely on its usage is far from sufficient; indeed it is unproductive. One ought to also ask: Why is a particular proverb and not others used in a given context, and by whom and for what purposes? Is the use of a specific proverb (to the exclusion of others) meant to make a universal claim about truth(s)? Christopher Crocker (1977) and David Sapir (1977) described, rather awkwardly, the first instance as "shifter" and the second as "non-shifter" (see also Parkin 1984, 359). Nonshifters are claims to "global truths," disregarding and transcending the specificity in which proverbs are uttered, invoked, and bestowed with significations (Parkin 1984, 359).

◆ The Greed of the Mullah, the Creed of the Ungodly

The three proverbs I discuss relate squarely to religion. The first two I take from recent ethnographic works on Pakistan. The third is from my own fieldwork. These proverbs, however, don't figure in R. C. Temple's list of north

Indian proverbs published in 1885. Editing and commenting on Fallon's *A Dictionary of Hindustani Proverbs*, Temple listed with their English translations 37 Persian, 81 Urdu, 190 Hindi, and 79 Punjabi proverbs[13] (in the order Temple enumerated).

Used in different situations and locations, the first and second proverbs refer to a similar theme: the status of *mavlvī* (theologian/scholar, see below) in the eyes of non-*mavlvī*, implied to be the educated, nonreligious (if not antireligious), and rich. Here the object of the proverbs is the figure of *mavlvī* and the agent the non-*mavlvī*. The message conveyed by both proverbs is that poor *mavlvīs* are greedy, overzealous, bigoted, and ignorant. From the perspective of this book, however, these proverbs are more forms of criticism and less critique insofar as neither the proverbs themselves nor the ethnographers writing about them examine the condition of their provenance or currency to suggest how things could also be other than what they are or how they are portrayed. That is, I interrogate the very assumptions behind the deployment of these proverbs and their failure to see the world differently. To this end, from my own ethnography I introduce a shifter proverb in which the agent and the object are markedly different. While the object of the third proverb is rich and nonpious, its agent is poor and pious. It is by introducing the shifter proverb that the limits of and assumptions behind the "global truths" of the first two proverbs can be unveiled to show how the poor-pious as agents of the proverb, rather than mere objects thereof (as in the first two proverbs), view the world dominated by the rich as lacking in piety.

In an ethnographic study of an urban neighborhood in Rawalpindi concerned with the interplay of Islam and everyday life, Muhammad Bilal (2014) examined the social status that imams of mosques enjoyed in the community. He learned that their economic status was rather abysmal. The monthly salary of one imam (an imam being one who leads prayer), though possessing a proper educational degree, was as low as 7,000 rupees (US$81). The imams thus also earned money from other sources. These included remunerations received for performing a *nikāḥ* (wedding) or money they received as *ṣadaqāh* (voluntary charity). "The financial susceptibility of *ʿulema*," writes Bilal, "gave birth to a popular rhetoric of insult and sarcasm: mavlvī ḥalvā ḳhōr (*mavlvī* sweet-eater)." The same attitude is conveyed in a "popular expression" through a semipoetic line: "Jahan ḥalvā vahāñ maulvī kā jalvā (where there is sweet, there is a theologian [*mavlvī*])." Interestingly, the ethnographer begins his account about imams but later uses imams and *ʿulema* interchangeably. Explaining the proverb, Bilal observed that the term *mavlvī* "does not apply to an *ʿālim* or an imam"; rather "it is in general use[d] to refer to someone who is religious, or embraces a religious outlook." As for halvah (*ḥalvā*), it is a dessert, made from semolina, served to invitees to mark a joyful event, like a wedding, which an *ʿālim* is called to officiate. The deployment of halvah in the proverb is to depict *ʿulema* as "greedy for money and food."[14] While offering details, Bilal never tells readers who are the agents of and subscribers to what he calls "popular expression" or "popular rhetoric." Clearly, *ʿulema* themselves don't hold such a view. As a matter of fact, they don't even think in terms of what anthropologist calls "salary," otherwise an etic term. They think it as an "affront to the very spirit of Islam" to call what an imam does an "occupation." Thus when Bilal asked if he considered his role to be an occupation or profession, an imam observed, "My father warned me never to commit the mistake of considering *imāmat* a professional thing but always to take it as *khidmat*. . . . [It] is an Islamic ideal" (41–42, 45).

Rather than take the self-perception of his interlocutor seriously and reexamine the provenance and salience of the proverb beyond the obvious, Bilal just leaves it there, depriving his readers of a potentially productive insight. In my view, the proverb is not simply a critique of *ʿulema* as representatives of religious knowledge; it is equally a critique of the very society in which *ʿulema* are at the mercy of mammon. It is common knowledge that at the time of Prophet Muhammad and long thereafter imams were not salaried. To call to prayer or lead it was open to anyone. If the Prophet and his companions led prayer, they did so as a duty, and the idea of salary was foreign to them. In some accounts, taking money for attending to godly calls or duties is at least unappreciable, if not outright forbidden. There is nothing in Islam that prevents, for example, a highly salaried bureaucrat from leading prayer. Rather than situate it in a wider frame and view it as a societal problem of the priestification of Islam, the proverb "Jahān ḥalvā vahāñ mavlvī kā jalvā" particularizes it to target *ʿulema*. The imam's invocation of *khidmat* was similar to Ghaffar Khan's notion of *khidmat*: for and by all.

My point is not that the description Bilal offers is incorrect; instead I ask, Are not non-*ʿulema*, the "enlightened seculars," also "greedy for money and food"? If so, is there a proverb about them? If yes, Bilal mentions no "shifter," which I will come to in a moment. First, a word about divergent naming of the same act expressed in folklore I have often used in my teaching. In a feast, the village chief and an extremely poor man both eat copiously. To the chief, another poor villager said, "Sir, you have such a good diet." To the fellow poor man, he said, "You are such a *pētū* [glutton or gourmand]."[15]

Returning to *ʿulema* in Pakistan and proverbial sarcasm against them, in *Muslim Becoming*, Naveeda Khan (2012, 4) largely follows a similar path. She discusses at length the proverbial idea of *jāhil mavlvī*, which has the oxymoronic meaning "ignorant scholar-theologian." Though she doesn't say so explicitly, early on in her book it is apparent from her ethnography that this proverb originates from the secular—"two clean-shaven [as opposed to her bearded interlocutors] men" interjected to say that "these people [the bearded, religious ones] are *jāhil* [ignorant]." In a later chapter devoted entirely to this subject, she defines the term *ʿulema* as a "community of religious scholars who serve as the guardians, transmitters, and interpreters of the *sharīʿā*." Though *mullah* means "learned master," she says how, together with *mavlvī*, it has become derogatory, now meaning one who is "overzealous," "a bigot," and "a censor." Given the concern of her book, she relates the proverb *jāhil mavlvī* not to the malevolent *mavlvī* alone but to a condition or attitude residing within "every Pakistani." It is only at the end of her analysis that we briefly read responses of two *mavlvīs* to the secularist proverb of *jāhil mavlvī*. While one response was "defensive," another clamored for "incorporation" in the mainstream (2012, 148–50, 169–70).

To begin with, limiting the word *ʿulema* to mean "clerics" or "theologians" is incorrect and of relatively recent origin. Not only in the distant past, but also in the twentieth century, *ʿulema* themselves used the term to mean scholars in a general sense without necessarily limiting it to theology, religion, or sharia. As I noted in chapter 3, Maududi called Aristotle and Plato "*ʿulemā-e-yūnān* [*ʿulema* of Greece]" and elsewhere described natural scientists as "*ʿulemā-e-sāins*." Also absent in Khan's discussion are different categories of *ʿulema*: *ʿulemāʾ-e-sū*, false scholars, and *ʿulemāʾ-e-ḥaq*, scholars of truth (see Ahmad 2015d). As I noted in chapter 3, many *ʿulema* stood for freedom of thought and critique vis-à-vis the power that flogged scholars such as Imam Mālik, and uprooted his arms from his shoulders. Imprisoned by the uncritical embrace of the notions of *mavlvī ḥalvā ḳhōr* and *jāhil mavlvī*, neither the conceptual apparatus of Bilal or Khan nor the capacity of their narrative can enunciate the truth of Imam Mālik.

Seen from this perspective, figures like Ghulam Ahmad Pervez (1903–85) clearly belonged to the category of *ʿulema*. But seldom is the proverb *jāhil mavlvī* applied to *ʿulema* like Pervez, who offered theological justification for the dictatorship of Pakistan's General Ayub Khan. Curiously, Pervez does not figure in Naveeda Khan's book, certainly not in its index. Pervez rationalized Ayub's dictatorship by arguing that the general's disenfranchising notion of "basic democracy" was akin to the Islamic idea of *shūra* and that "the type of democracy introduced by Western civilization has no place in Islam" (qtd. in Sayeed 1961, 255; also see chap. 6). Similarly, an "enlightened secular" like Bilal Zuberi (1999, 5), who cheered the coup by General Pervez Musharraf in

1999, is not called *jāhil mavlvī*. The same can be said about the mufti and *ʿulema* like Egypt's Ali Gomaa and Shawki Ibrahim Abdel-Karim Allam, who justified the killings of peaceful democracy protesters (Egypt's Ḵhudāī Ḵhidmatgār), the overthrow of the first democratically elected government led by Mohammad Morsi, and the installation of Fattah al-Sisi's dictatorship (Ahmad 2015b). Contra Naveeda Khan, are not *ʿulema* who theologically justify dictatorships also "overzealous" and "bigoted"?

That such questions are not dealt with in the ethnography of either Muhammad Bilal or Naveeda Khan is due mainly to the fact that both focus on the nonshifter proverbs to depict a specific truth to the exclusion of others. Had they also focused on anti- or counterproverbs about the ungodly, the picture emerging from their respective ethnographies would have been significantly different. So, what could the shifter proverb be? Possibly this one:

Jō dēgā sō mavla dēgā (Whatever I get God gives)
Āṣif davlā kēyā dēgā (What can Asaf-ud-Daula give?)

[The translation doesn't capture the lyricism of the Urdu with its rhyme]

Once I passed through an elite neighborhood of Aligarh in late afternoon. From a distance I heard a skinny old man, standing at the gigantic iron gate of an imposing house, say, "In the name of Allah, please help this poor and disabled person." As I approached him, he continued repeating that line. But there was no response. When I got closer to him, I saw him walk away from that house. By the time I reached him, I heard a hawker, with a flowing beard and white skullcap, say to the old man, "Jō dēgā sō mavla dēgā, āṣif davlā kēyā dēgā." I instantly stopped. I remembered my unlettered paternal uncle, the late Mohammad Faheem, from whom I had heard these very same words for the first time. As a teenager, I remember asking him, Who is Asaf-ud-Daula? I was told that he was a king (*bādshāh*). My uncle explained to me, "Nephew, never ask for anything from a human, even if he is a king. Do hard work [*jam kē meḥnat kar*] and rely [*bh̲arōsā*] on Allah alone."

As if he was my uncle, I asked the hawker the same question. Looking at my appearance and taking me as one not knowledgeable, he elaborated that Asaf-ud-Daula (d. 1797) was a king of Lucknow who, removed from God, led a life of excessive indulgence and opulence. He did not care about his people and succumbed to British deceit. He considered himself to be a king but actually he was not. The British wielded the real power. I saw the hawker give the old man some money. As the old man left, the hawker continued talking to me. Familiar with the neighborhood, he informed me that its people were rich but with little or no genuine concern for God. He had seen many people like the old man return empty-handed from houses resembling palaces. The rich, intoxicated with their wealth and power, did not know that it is Allah who made them so and, therefore, He could also take it all away. King Sikandar (Alexander) went to the grave, he observed, empty-handed. If people had firm faith in God and followed His message of *inṣāf* (justice) as conveyed to Prophet Muhammad, the hawker continued, the old man would not ask for money and he himself would not be a petty hawker shouting just to survive.

The hawker was a critic.

EPILOGUE

If to critique is to judge and assess (Koselleck 1988 [1959]; Maududi 1956a), then how do we judge what we judge? Is a judgment reached at a certain time and in a specific setting eternal as some judges claim, presumably because the source (*dīn*) they base their judgment on is believed to be eternal? Put differently, is judgment derived from the framework of religion deemed eternal itself eternal, or is it also an upshot of an understanding of religion in a given age, society, culture, or polity that judges inhabit, often not out of their own sovereign will alone? It is this epistemological, anthropological, and political condition, which enables or restricts the enterprise of critique, that this epilogue preliminarily reflects on. To unravel that condition is to arrive at an anthropologically and sociologically grounded theory of critique. That is, given that the enterprise of immanent critique is identified as "fragile" by Qasim Zaman (2012, 311), my endeavor is to make it a little agile.

Abdolkarim Soroush, the Iranian philosopher, offers what he calls a "theory of contraction and expansion [*qabz v bast*]." Anchored in the tradition of thought that includes Maulana Rum/Rumi, Shah Valiullah, Muhammad Iqbal, Ali Shariati, and many others, Soroush's theory aims at explaining change in Islamic social formations. Soroush takes up Iqbal's proposition to distinguish between eternity and temporality and render them compatible at the same time. The epigraph of his book chapter detailing the theory of contraction and expansion of religious interpretation has the following passage from Iqbal: "[Islam] demands loyalty to God, not to thrones. . . . The ultimate spiritual basis of all life, as conceived by Islam, is eternal and reveals itself in variety and change. A society based on such a conception of Reality must reconcile, in its life, the categories of permanence and change" (qtd. in Soroush 2000, 26).

Soroush's theory is an elaboration of Iqbal's insight about the importance of differentiating the constant from the variable in religion as well as reconciling the eternal and the temporal. Central to this "epistemological theory" is the distinction between religion and knowledge of religion.[1] Concomitantly, Soroush suggests, "religion is sacred and heavenly, but the understanding of religion is human and earthly." And since knowledge about religion is "a branch of human knowledge," "a transformation in the mode of knowledge and life of humanity is the remote cause of a transformation of religious knowledge." In short, understanding of religion is in flux because other branches of human knowledge are likewise in flux. "Religious knowledge," Soroush (2000, 31–34) thus concludes, "changes, evolves, contracts, expands, waxes, and wanes." What may seem implicit to some readers of Soroush is made explicit by his commentator, who sees expansion as positive and contraction as negative. He reads expansion as broadening one's horizon and contraction as narrowing it. He especially dwells on "extrareligious" knowledge produced in modernity: the contributions made in the form of the Copernican revolution and the theories of Darwin, Freud, Marx, and so on (Kamali 1995).

I find Soroush's analytical distinction between religion and understandings of religion insightful. It is an important tool to grasp the dynamic of change, reform, and renewal in order to judge what is essential to retain and what requires change and how. However, in my view, the remaining components of his theory are problematic on four counts. First, he strictly separates the religious and the secular. Second, he accords a necessarily positive valuation to modern sciences. At the risk of sounding relativist, one might be prompted to ask, On what basis can we say with certitude that knowledge the "primitive" had was narrow whereas the knowledge we moderns have is expanded (Tambiah 1990)? Relatedly, knowledge deemed narrow now was expanded in its own time, in the same way as expanded knowledge of today might well become narrow in the future. Third, by grounding his theory solely in the realm of pure epistemology, Soroush evades the ontology of asymmetrical world politics that impacts, though not always directly, the exercise of understanding. Fourth, and flowing from the third point, the notion of "understanding" that permeates his text is flawed and in need of reformulation. If to understand is to stand "under," as Edward Tiryakian (2005, 305) fittingly posits, what is that "under" under which one stands to attain an understanding? My contention is that "under" is not simply epistemological but also, perhaps equally, political. Whether or not, or the extent to which, a specific epistemology is considered "theirs" or "our own," and how one adapts to or adopts it is very much predicated on and informed by the "extraepistemological"—a point variously made by, inter alia, Hilary Putnam (1981) and Martin Rudwick (1986). It is high time we reminded readers of philosophers' innocence about epistemology as a sovereign field, to the utter neglect of the political, broadly conceptualized. Let me illustrate my argument.

There has been/was almost a consensus among modern *ʿulema* of the Indian subcontinent that taking, keeping, and displaying (in bedrooms or living rooms) the photographs of living beings, including those of God's creations in the animal world, is *ḥarām* (Qasmi 2012, 336–57).[2] When photographs became necessary for the purpose of governmentality—as in identity cards, for completing administrative forms, and so on—the *ʿulema* allowed it with a heavy heart, qualifying that these photos' use must not extend to other domains. This was the position of Maududi as well as of most *ʿulema*, including Deoband's Mufti Muhammad Kifayatullah, whom we met in chapter 4 (Maududi 1943, 124–27). A person walking onto the campuses of Islamic colleges with a camera was viewed with considerable suspicion and scorn. Islamic newspapers and magazines long filled their pages only with text—no photos, drawings, or cartoons. In the 1950s, when a reader asked Maududi (1962, 97) why he allowed publication of his photo in a newspaper when he considered photos to be *ḥarām*, Maududi defensively responded that he didn't know that he was being photographed and that no one sought his permission to publish the photo. In the 1990s, when *Al-Balāgh*, an Urdu magazine published from Bombay and belonging to the Ahl-e-ḥadīs̱ school, began to publish photos, it blurred faces in them. The prohibition against the making and installation of statues of living beings was even stronger. One of the few statues of Muslim personalities in India is that of the poet Ghalib on the campus of my alma mater, Jamia Millia Islamia, in Delhi. To my knowledge there exists no statue of any *ʿulema* on the subcontinent.

The reason for declaring photographs *ḥarām* originally derived from the general consensus that making a statue was *ḥarām*—more than one hadith condemns the making of statues. Obviously, photography as a technology belongs to the nineteenth century: 1839 to be precise (Berger 2002; Dadi 2016). The key reason for this prohibition was that since power and the attribute (*ṣifat*) of creation belong to God alone, for a human being to make a statue or taking a photograph was akin to "mimicking and approximating [*naqqālī avr hamsarī*]" (Qasmi 2012, 355) God to appropriate, claim, or resemble His attribute (*ṣifat*) of creation. Furthermore, the presence of a statue might prompt the veneration, glorification, and eventually even worship, of beings other than God. An oft-heard reason was that on seeing the photograph of a living being in a house the angel of compassion (*raḥmat*) left.

Fatwas (opinions) declaring photographs *ḥarām* are published even today. Archives belonging to nearly all schools of Islamic thought bear witness to this. But their credibility is in fast decline. Not only do commoners possess photos on their mobile phones, on the walls or tables of their homes, in family albums, or in Facebook posts, many *ʿulema* also desire to see their photos splashed across newspapers. Today, the written fatwas declaring photos *ḥarām* exist in dissonance with the practice of their being halal—among commoners as well as among many *ʿulema*. That they are today largely halal, or at least acceptable to most, is not only a result of pure epistemology and its expansion, as Soroush wants us to believe. It is due also to the mundane practices of commoners and their own understanding, not necessarily linked to the adoption of formal and conscious epistemology, that makes them halal. A theory like Soroush's that is oblivious to the salience of practice among the nonscholarly and commoners as knowledge in its own right (obviously not identical to disciplinary knowledge produced, among other places, in academia) is grossly defective. It is the notion of *mʿārūf*, as explicated, among others, by Zurti in chapter 6, that becomes the basis of judgment and change. My emphasis on mundane practice among the nonscholarly and commoners is an invitation to rehabilitate the salience of practice in the Islamic tradition.

No less significant is the confidence in and of a culture and tradition at work in the formulation and enactment of a given judgement. A visitor to the Alhambra in Spain would certainly notice statues of tigers at the base of the fountain installed at the very center of the royal palace. It is likely that certain scholars objected to those statues. However, the statues' presence also has and had a rationale.

Between my PhD defense and finishing my scholarship stipend there was a gap of almost a year. With very little money left, in Amsterdam I lived in a shared flat with a taxi driver from the subcontinent and an Egyptian "illegal immigrant,"[3] Anwar. Anwar had an underpaid job where he worked longer hours than the officially approved duration chopping potatoes for French fries. He once showed me some photographs of his family and friends. As Anwar was considerably religious, I asked him if he did not find it odd to be religious and keep or show photographs to his friends. His response was a confident "no." For him, the prohibition against statues and paintings of living beings pertained to the people living in the time of Prophet Muhammad. Since at that time polytheism was widespread and monotheism still nascent, said prohibition was a necessity. Today no Muslim with a firm faith in monotheism would even think of glorifying a statue as on a par with God, let alone worshipping it. The prohibition against the making of statues in subsequent times was, therefore, less than necessary.[4] To buttress his argument, Anwar cited the presence of statues of tigers at Al-Hambra. He further held that, rather than making new discoveries and expanding the existing knowledge beneficial to people of

Statues of tigers at Al-Hambra, 2004. Photograph by the author.

all faiths, contemporary Muslims—politically defeated as they are—rushed merely to ask if this or that technology or knowledge was halal or *ḥarām*.

If understanding is predicated on confidence and confidence on the grasp of tradition and culture, then the latter are, contrary to the anthropological consensus, in part also individual. In *Al-hilāl*, which Abdul Kalam Azad launched as editor at the age of twenty-four (he had created *Lisānuṣṣidq* when he was barely sixteen; Ram 1989, 51–59), he published photographs of Jamaluddin Afghani, Muhammad Abduh, and Rashid Rida in its inaugural issue (13 July 1912). He continued publishing photos of many other people, including Mohandas Gandhi (in the 3 December 1913 issue). For him the question was not if the photo was halal but of if its quality was adequate. On the front page of the 1 August 1912 issue, he promised his readers that if things went as planned, soon they would see color photographs in *Al-hilāl*. Ten or so years later, Sulaiman Nadvi, a scholar of the Nadvatul Ulema, wrote a series of articles in *Al-jamᶜīat* justifying why photos and statues were not *ḥarām*. Of his many rationales, the principal one was this: if the making of statues was *ḥarām*, then why in the palace of the Prophet Sulaiman (Solomon), as mentioned in the Qurʾān, were there many statues of living beings (see also Isa 1955, 267)?[5] As an individual,

Sulaiman Nadvi, like Azad, contested the prevailing tradition by critically engaging with that very tradition.

What enables or disables the enterprise of critique and change is not related purely and solely to epistemology; political and social-cultural coordinates are equally significant to that constellation we ought to call critique.

An effective, enduring, meaningful, and immanent critique inspired by a quest for justice-oriented freedom and beauty is usually what dialectically (re)institutes the relationship between the critic and the theme of critique—indeed the wider community of shared concerns—in such a way that it becomes like an unhazy mirror in which all, if they sufficiently summon their courageous sincerity with vision and insight, can see their faces—faces that may appear starkly familiar or intimately strange, or both at once. At times the labor and fruit of critique may lead to the making of a new mirror, meticulously assembled from things that in themselves, when properly analyzed and historically situated, are neither entirely novel nor wholly unfamiliar.

Over to you, my dear readers, to judge *Religion as Critique*!

Notes

Prologue

1. That to many it might not have been rational then, or may not be rational *now,* is a different matter.

2. I have relied on the Urdu translation of *Ḥujjat Allāh al Bāligha*. English speakers who do not read Urdu may consult Marcia Hermansen's (1996) translation, which includes a crisp, learned introduction. Hermansen notes a similarity between Valiullah's theory of civilizational/societal development (*irtefāqāt*) and Ibn Khaldun's—a point not explored here. Nor do I dwell on her insight that Valiullah's *Ḥujjat Allāh al Bāligha* anticipated "some major twentieth-century Western social theories" (Hermansen 2008, 394).

3. Associated with Ibn Arabi (1165–1240), ontological monism posits that "the ultimate reality is identical to what is found [*al-wajūd*]" (Rizvi 2005, 234). It follows that God alone is existent and everything else nonexistent. Proponents of this position, in a state of ecstasy, considered God's appearances and flashes as "One-in-all and All-in-one"—that is, everything is Him (Aziz Ahmad 1964, 187; Abdurrahman 1970, 168–93). This position, its opponents held, had an immanent, as opposed to a transcendent, view of God, leading to pantheism. Many *ʿulema* viewed proponents of *vaḥdat al-vajūd* as unbelievers and *zindīq* flouting elementary *sharīʿā* (Abdurrahman 1970, 176). Phenomenological monism, *vaḥdat al-shahūd*, associated with Shaykh Ahmad Sirhindi (1564–1624), himself a Sufi, held that what the mystic thought was the unity of being, erasing any difference between immanent and transcendent, was not the reality of being per se but its appearance to a specific mystic. Sirhindi replaced "everything is Him" with "everything is from Him," reasserting God's transcendence and observance of *sharīʿā*, the violation of which was visible among many Sufis who didn't pray or fast, and even remained naked (Abdurrahman 1970, 169–71). To Sirhindi, *vaḥdat al-vajūd* was a negation of the oneness of God (Dallal 1993, 346). For more, see Ahmad 2015d.

Chapter 1

1. A colonial officer in India remarked that Muslims' heads were unfit for mathematics (Nazeer Ahmad 1918, 79). Describing the European as a "close reasoner" and "natural logician," the British consul-general of Egypt, Baring Cromer (d. 1917), held that "the mind of the oriental . . . is eminently wanting in symmetry . . . [and] singularly deficient in the logical faculty" (qtd. in Nasr 1999, 564). Such views about Islam were not limited to a given region; they were transregional (see Ahmad 2011c).

2. I thank José Casanova for signaling a link to the axial age and suggesting references.

3. I use social imaginary as employed by Charles Taylor (2004).

4. On this point, there seems to be some commonality with Hindu tradition, according to which the "soul [*ātman*] is the seat of reason" (Ganeri 2003, 425).

5. My formulation departs from Michael Walzer's (1987, 1988), who, like George Marcus

and Michael Fischer (1999), is reluctant to consider a commoner as a critic. His *The Company of Critics* includes a list of eleven well-known critics like George Orwell, Albert Camus, and Michel Foucault. I also disagree with his anchoring of an effective critic within the precincts of the nation-state (Walzer 1988, 234–38).

6. Given his disciplinary training, such an anthropological expectation of Sen is perhaps unfair. However, I expected some discussion of the derailment or suppression of argumentative tradition as I discuss it vis-à-vis Muslim tradition in chapter 3. How can we construe the cutting of Ekalavya's thumb at the demand of Drona (Shankar 1994) from the perspective of argumentative tradition? It is significant that Sen's text opens with the *Mahābẖārata*. Furthermore, Sen's idea of public debate as central to democracy doesn't address how the media effaces, distorts, and brackets things out, thereby inhibiting and silencing public discussions; see Ahmad 2014a.

7. Wolfe's (2002, 377–78) key point is that Hindu reformist principles, traced to European influence, were already present in Ram Mohan Roy's 1804 *Tuhfat-ul-Muwahhiddin*, a rationalist tract that discussed, among other topics, Islamic thoughts. Roy wrote it well before he learned English.

8. I grew up in rural Bihar and moved to its capital, Patna, for higher study. Biharis often praised (with envy) Bengalis' skill in argument. I have heard "ḥujjat-e-bengāl" (argument of Bengal) and "ḥikmat-e-chīn" (wisdom/philosophy of China) uttered in a single phrase. I have also heard Bangla-speaking friends use *ḥujjat*. In the Bangla dictionary the first meaning of *ḥujjat* is *tarkatarki* (argument) (Biswas 1984 [1957], 723). *Ḥujjat* in Arabic, as in the title of Shah Valiullah's book *Ḥujjat Allāh al Bāligha*, means "argument." Is Sen's argumentative Indian connected to *ḥujjat* as alluded to here? This is a conjecture other scholars may explore. I thank Nabanipa Bhattacharjee (University of Delhi) for looking up this word in Bangla and clarifying its meaning (e-mail communication, 15 December 2014).

Chapter 2

1. In addition to promoting conferences and books, the CCF launched journals like *Encounter, China Quarterly,* and *Quadrant*. In *Encounter,* Shils attacked *Sociological Imagination,* calling C. Wright Mills a "horseman," a "rough-tongued brawler"—anything but an intellectual (qtd. in Brewer 2004, 329).

2. Since Kant is the "greatest Western philosopher of the last three hundred years," philosophy itself is divided into pre-Kantian and post-Kantian eras and schools (Priest 2016).

3. Bruce Kapferer's (2007, 85) observation that anthropology may be viewed "as Reason's Doubt" is brilliant. So is his attention to "other forms" of reason. However, he remains wedded to the Enlightenment, asserting it contains its own critique. My aim, in contrast, is to show critique that can't be subsumed within the Enlightenment narrative. Sahlins's (1999, xxi) take is different, suggesting that the Enlightenment in Africa finally arrived only when it broke from the Western idea of development. If Sahlins's concern is development and the "death" of indigenous cultures (and hence of anthropology), Kapferer's is to defend anthropology as a threatened discipline.

4. As in *Lectures on Logic* (Kant 1992, 537, 25).

5. Will and Ariel Durant's (1963) seventh volume of *Story of Civilization* is subtitled, *The Age of Reason Begins: A History of Western Civilization in the Period of Shakespeare, Bacon, Montaigne, Galileo, and Descartes, 1558–1648.*

6. In anthropology, the term "ethnicity" came in vogue to replace "tribe" (as in Malinowski 1922, 11, 1945, 30). Examples of ethnicity in Thomas Eriksen's (2001, 261–74) textbook are

from the non-West; the lone exception of Norway's Sami only proves my point. Likewise, in Conrad Kottak's (2008, 299–325) textbook, reference to ethnicity—textual and pictorial—is in relation to nonwhites; inhabitants of the former Yugoslavia being an exception. For an overview of anthropology and ethnicity, see Jenkis 2008, 3–27.

7. In Australia, when Indians meet, they often ask each other, "You got PR [permanent residence]?"

8. Peter Fenves (1993) translates it as "On a Newly Arisen Superior Tone of Philosophy."

9. Kant described the character of Hindus as "*pusillanimity*." Judaism "drew upon itself the charge of *misanthropy*," and "strictly speaking, Judaism is not a religion at all. . . . [It] stands in absolutely no essential connection to . . . ecclesiastical faith [Christianity]" (1998 [1793], 130, 6:125; italics Kant's).

10. Three of its pages deal with Islam (Almond 2009, 49). Stuart Elden and Eduardo Mendieta's *Reading Kant's Geography* (2011) and David Harvey's (2011) article on Kant, however, say little about religion.

11. The couplet reads (Saadi 1949, 632):

بسیار سفر باید تا پخته شود خامی　　صوفی نشود صافی تا درنکشد جامی

12. John Miller, in 1844, translated it into English as *Mahomet the Impostor*; its performance took "the London stage by storm" (Perchard 2015, 470).

13. Bernhard Giesen (1998, 229) notes Voltaire's hypocrisy, "which seems not to have caused any problem in the French Enlightenment": "A critic of the king and of censorship, he was at the same time a spy in the pay of the French government." Champion of *la raison*, Voltaire extolled "the lie as a virtue."

14. A comment on my article—"As Mohamed Morsi Faces the Gallows, Where Are the Defenders of Democracy?"—on the Australian Broadcasting Corporation website said, "Mr Morse [*sic*] does not come from that level of society, or *a religion that allows democracy*" (qtd. in Ahmad 2015a; italics mine).

15. For Dietrich Bonhoeffer (d. 1945), secularism "represents a realization of crucial motifs of Christianity itself" (Keane 2000, 14).

16. Define so as to rule, as Mahmood Mamdani (2012) thoughtfully put it in his book *Define and Rule*.

17. Though connected and interchangeably used, in Kant's writings *critique* differs from *criticism*. Criticism is an exchange of claim and counterclaim. This approximates one of the meanings of criticism that Raymond Williams (1983, 84–86) identified as "fault-finding." For Kant, the to-and-fro of claim and counterclaim between skeptics and dogmatists was criticism. If dogmatists placed their own assumptions above questioning, skeptics questioned every assumption to derail endeavors by the former to impose rules. The ground beneath the feet of dogmatists and skeptics was the same, for the disagreement between them concerned only "*facta*." In *Critique of Pure Reason*, Kant went beyond *facta* to investigate the very nature, scope, and grounds of reason. For Kant, reason was not there to merely think about *facta* but about itself. Doubt prepares the ground for criticism which, when exhausted and pushed to its limits, inaugurates critique. Critique comes about when it critiques criticism (Kant 1998 [1781], A761/B789, A7641/B792, 653–66; MacKenzie 2004, xxv, 1–10; Thorpe 2015, 57). Iain MacKenzie (2004, 11, 89), however, contends that Kant himself "transformed it [critique] back into an idea of criticism" because he failed to question "his own dogmatic assumption about the unity and purpose of reason." The difference between criticism and critique obtains beyond Kant as well, though less rigorously and epistemologically. Critique is a "sustained criticism" of a position, or argument. Marx (1976)

thus gave *Capital* the subtitle *Critique of Political Economy* to better illuminate the workings of capitalism while also showing its limitations (Macey 2000, 76).

18. On criticism and debates in "Indic" religions in general—Hinduism, Buddhism, and Jainism—see Ganeri 2003; Sen 2005; Jaiswal 2000; Matilal 1989; Sangari 1990; and Heesterman 1985.

19. On the axial age, Brahmanism, and Buddhism, see Pollock 2005; and Thapar 1975. More generally, see "Wisdom, Revelation, and Doubt" 1975 (special issue of *Daedalus*).

20. It is only recently that anthropologists got interested in the axial age; see Thomassen 2010.

21. In Shah Valiullah's (n.d., 19) theology, God sent prophets to lead humanity from "darkness to light" and from "restraint to openness." The word he used is "prophets [*ambeāy'*]," not "prophet." Going by Valiullah's account, the Enlightenment took place long, long ago, in a time we can't even date.

22. Muslims' modernity, to cite Robert Bellah (1991, 151–52), was "manifest in the high degree of commitment, involvement, and participation expected from the rank-and-file members of the community" and the "openness of its leadership position to ability judged on universalistic grounds."

23. On the use of reason in the explanation of the Islamic notion of prophecy, see Griffel 2010, which describes how Muslim philosophers—such as Al-Farabi, Ibn Sina, and Al-Ghazali—offered a rational explanation of prophecy using the Greek philosophical postulates.

24. The Indian sociologist J. P. S. Uberoi made this point in a different context during an informal lecture at JNU in November 2000.

25. Thus, in the 1999 preface to *Gender Trouble*, Judith Butler (2007, vii) writes: "I understood myself to be in an embattled . . . relation to certain forms of feminism, even as I understood the text to be part of feminism. I was writing in the tradition of immanent critique that seeks to provoke critical examinations of the basic vocabulary of the movement of thought to which it belongs." Soon a disclaimer differentiating "self-criticism" from "criticism" is issued: the former "promises a more democratic and inclusive life," whereas the latter "seeks to undermine it [feminism]."

26. As crisply put by John Caputo (2013, 127): "For Kant, a law is a law is a law. It does not matter who pronounces it, or where or when, or whether that person is wearing a hat that day."

27. For a nonanthropological work on this theme, see Qasim Zaman's (2012) outstanding book (especially chapters v and ix); see also the epilogue of this book.

28. The domain of *nafs* (soul) can be controlled by the fourth potentiality and transformed into a better state, which scholars identify as *al-nafs al-ammāra* (the soul that controls the self); *al-nafs al-lawwāmā* (the soul that faults itself for its own frailties); and *al-nafs al-muṭmainnā* (the soul in tranquility and bliss) (Chittick 2011, 15; Hallaq 2013, 130).

29. For an unorthodox view, see Griffel 2016, x; and Hallaq 2013, chap. 5.

30. Noted Indian Marxist historian Irfan Habib (2013, 7, 11n1) recently reproduced this view of Islam's opposition to reason in general and Ghazali's "rejection of rationality" in particular. Clearly, he didn't read Shibli Nomani (who is absent from his text). Habib called his own judgment of Ghazali "tentative"; it should be perhaps called "imitative" instead, for many of his sources and much of his frame are orientalist, as is his judgment derived, inter alia, from a shallow invoking of Marx's view of religion as "the opium of the people."

Chapter 3

1. I use *tanqīd/intiqād/naqd*, as does Jeffrey Sacks (2007) vis-à-vis Arabic, to mean both "criticism" and "critique." The distinction between the two in English (see chap. 2, n. 17) does not securely obtain in Urdu.

2. I quote Khan's article from *Aligarh Magazine* (*Inteḳhāb number*) of 1971 where it was republished from *Aligarh Monthly* (February 1904).

3. Ahmad's writings first appeared as articles in 1940s and were later published as books (Mazhari 2013, 50).

4. Faruqi reckons that Qudama Ibn Jafar's *Naqd al- sheʿr* (tenth century) is an important work of poetic criticism in Arabic. However, in one account Mohammad Ibn Sallam al-Jumahi's (d. 846) *Tabaqat al-shuʿraʾ* "sowed the first seed of the principle of criticism" (Nadvi 1990, 86). In Arabic, it was in the early twentieth century that *naqd* replaced *intiqād* (Hallaq 2014). In Farsi, *intiqād* and *naqd* are both used for criticism (Mehdi 1999, 18; Zaheer Siddiqi 2000, 1).

5. Based on personal communication with Rizwan Ahmad of University of Michigan, Ann Arbor, who did his doctoral fieldwork (in 2006) on Urdu in Old Delhi and interviewed Gulzar Dehlvi.

6. To fully rule out the biographical is perhaps incorrect. Faruqi began his career declaring "belief in God is a pleasant sentiment which we litterateurs ought to embrace" (qtd. in Usmani 1999, 33–34).

7. This assumption equally informs historical writings. The second volume of compiler-historian Mushirul Hasan's anthology—*Islam in South Asia*—is titled *The Realm of the Traditional* (2008) and the fourth, *The Realm of the Secular* (2009). To Hasan, as to Faruqi, this division (and separation) into "traditional [religious]" and "secular" is too "natural" to require an explanation.

8. Masihuzzaman's (2003 [1954]: 39) history of critique in Urdu is one such example. Contra Vazir Agha, Nurul Hasan Naqvi, and many others (see below), he makes no reference to critique in Greece or to its Western pedigree. He begins his account with critique in Arabic poetry then shifts to Persian poetry, both of which he takes as the "source [*sarchashmā*]" of critique in Urdu, mainly in poetry.

9. This disregards declarations like that of the poet Kalim Ajiz, who asserted that the cause (*sabab*) of his poetry was the 1946 political riots in which many members of his family were killed. For Ajiz (2005, 368), "my poetry is related to my life" and "each of my *ghazals* and couplets is a chapter in history."

10. For Bernal's argument I draw mainly on his interview with Walter Cohen (1993). For a balanced review of his works, see Levine 1998. Many responses to Bernal were hostile; Josine Blok (1996, 708) accused him of conveying "political views" that can't be "acceptable history" (for his response to such charges, see Bernal 2007, 5). Blok saw no politics in her own accusation, however.

11. Only in 1986 was the first department of anthropology founded in Greece (Herzfeld 2002, 911).

12. In his book on India's Hasrat Mohani (1875–1951)—poet, journalist, anticolonialist, Sufi—Abdus Shakur (1954, 4–5) says of Mohān, Mohani's place of birth in Uttar Pradesh, "Yūnān kō muddat sē t̲h̲ī mohān sē nisbat [for ages Greece had relations with Mohān]." For those baffled, Shakur adds a note: "Mohān was and is famous for its philosophers [*ḥokmāʾ*] and doctors; therefore, Mohan is called part [*ḳhiṭṭā*] of Greece." Note that it is not Mohān which has relations with Greece but the other way around. *Yūnān* and *mohān* rhyme to en-

hance the poetic beauty. Importantly, the subcontinent still has a medical system known as *yūnānī* (Greek); see Narain 2002; and Quaiser 2012.

13. Also known as moral (*akhlāqī*), purposive (*maqṣadī*), or Islamic literature, it deems itself as the trustee of "certain universal, positive values [*qadrōṅ*]" (Sajjad 1994, 52). Its key text is *Islāmī adab* by Maududi (1979), who defined *adab* as a synthesis between the "beauty of *kalām* and its effect [*tā sīr*]."

14. Among social scientists, the historian Irfan Habib (2013, 6) is a prime example of such a pedestrian, reductionist, if not vulgar, view.

15. Thus said Kant (2006 [1798], 215; italics in original): "Flattery *corrupts* while criticism *improves*."

16. Maududi (1927, 11) described the Buddha as a determined human who reformed (*iṣlāḥ*) Brahmanism. At age twenty-four, in *Al-Jihad fil Islam*, he discussed theories of war in Hinduism. In 1945, he replied to a reader that "your objection that I have relied on European translations rather than citing directly from Sanskrit and Hindu scriptures is correct." He also admitted that he didn't have the caution necessary for research when he wrote it. Promising he would investigate anew everything he didn't know from direct sources if he rewrote it, he asked his reader if he would help him in his research. He scarcely engaged with Hinduism after Partition, when he settled in Pakistan.

17. Maududi (1954, 298) cites examples relating to the prophets Yūsuf (Joseph), Nūḥ (Noah), Mūsā (Moses), and so on.

18. On the figure of Khiẓr in Iqbal's poetry, see Omar 2004.

19. Usually rendered as "Islamic law," *sharīʿā* means things exclusively Muslim. However, in another tradition, crystalized in Imam Shatibi (d. 1388) and continued by scholars like Muhammad Ashur (2007), it concerns humanity at large (Siddiqi 2004). See also Ahmad 2015d; and Moad 2007.

20. The word *ʿulema* is widely, though erroneously, taken to mean "clerics" or "theologians"; the correct meaning is "scholar." Maududi (1990a, 162) called Aristotle and Plato "*ʿulemā-e-yūnān* [scholars of Greece]" and elsewhere described natural scientists as "*ʿulemā-e-sāins*" (Maududi 1939, 43). Writing about Babylonian civilization, Malik Ram (1992, 213), an Urdu litterateur, described European scholars like Engelbert Kaempfer (interested in history and archeology) as "Europe's *ʿulema*."

Chapter 4

1. The term *qalādāh* refers to a ring put around the necks of slaves and animals. In one reading, the root of *taqlīd* (imitation) is *qalādāh*. See Farhad n.d., 77; and *Haqulmubeen.com* 2012.

2. On the tradition of Athenian funeral oration, see Pritchard 1996.

3. Nasr 1996 is perhaps the most comprehensive academic biography of Maududi in English (in Urdu there are many). For a brief account of Maududi's life, see Ahmad 2013a; and Ahmad 2009b, chap. 2. English readers may read a short autobiographical account of Maududi (1971, 21) written in Urdu in 1932 and translated into English by Nasr (1995).

4. There is no minority before the rise of nationalism, the nation-state, and democracy; see Bilgrami 2014, 100–101; Liebich 2008; Killian 1996; and Wirth 1945.

5. Contra the deification of Gandhi as a symbol of so-called Indian secularism, he indeed worked for Hindu domination. Anthropologist Nirmal Kumar Bose (1961 [1929]: 82), who also served as Gandhi's secretary, wrote: "In this new form of organized action, Gandhi tacitly formed an alliance with those who believed in a restoration of Hindu domination."

6. I have made this argument earlier; see Ahmad 2013c, 2011b, and 2009b.

7. Maududi cited articles 119, 121, 122, and 124 of the Constitution of Czechoslovakia and R. W. Seton-Watson's *The New Slovakia* (1924).

8. On Yugoslavia, he cited C. D. Hazen's *Europe since 1815* (1910), A. M. Morley's *The New Democratic Constitution of Europe* (1928), and the entry "Yugoslavia" in the *Encyclopedia Britannica*.

9. Maududi (1980 [1979], 290) reiterated this position as late as 1975, four years before his death.

10. Maududi used "we" to refer to himself—a practice common in Urdu and Hindi as well as Arabic.

11. Wael Hallaq (2009, 113) is one of the few scholars to highlight this important point.

12. Maududi had two main criticisms of Western-modern education, particularly of the kind established by Sayyid Ahmad Khan (1817–98), founder of Aligarh's Mohammedan Anglo-Oriental College. First, it made students "black Englishmen" or "comrades." Second, it did not foster an Islamic ideal among the students (Maududi 1991). For details, see Ahmad 2008.

13. It first appeared in *Al-furqān* (published from Bareli) in its special issue on Shah Valiullah; see below.

14. Integral to Islamic tradition, the task of renewing Islam has been invoked throughout history. For instance, the eleventh-century scholar al-Khatib al-Baghdadi invoked it (Anjum 2012, 23n74). Also see Ahmad 2015c.

15. Generally, there are/have been two types of *ʿulema*: *ʿulema-e-sū* (false scholars) and *ʿulema-e-ḥaq*, scholars of truth (Faruqi 1986, 13).

16. For recent works on Ghazali, see Moosa 2005; and Hallaq 2013. Wael Hallaq calls Foucault a Ghazalian.

17. "Secular" scholars like David Smith (2003, 55) also wrote about such practices introduced by Akbar.

18. For more on this, see Ikram 1964; Malik 1980; and Metcalf 1982.

19. On this theme Maududi (1991, 39) had also written three articles in *Tarjumānul Qurʾān* between April 1933 and November 1934, as he mentioned in his 1936 write-up published in *Tarjumānul Qurʾān* in September 1936. The 1936 article is included as chapter 2 in Maududi's *Tāʿlīmāt* (1991).

20. Compare this with Marshal Hodgson's formulation of Islamic/Islamicate civilization; especially see the "General Prologue" (1974a, 71–99) and "Epilogue" (1974b, 411–41). See also the learned commentary on Hodgson and others, including Ibn Khaldun, by Bruce Lawrence (2009).

21. Translated into English as *Towards Understanding Islam* (Maududi 1981).

22. I use *fiṭrat*, not *fiṭra*, which is common to Arabic speakers, who don't pronounce the *t* if it occurs at the end of a word. Some Urdu speakers now follow the Arabic style.

23. Anjum (2012, 215–27) and Ashur (2007, 78–86) offer learned summaries of the notion of *fiṭrat* in the writings of, among others, Ibn Sina, Avicenna (d. 1037), al-Mawardi (d.1058), Zahir Ibn Hazm (d. 1064), Umar al-Zamakhshari (d. 1144), and Ibn Taymiyya (d. 1328).

24. On scholarly treatment of this issue, see Nesbitt 1997; Singh 2014; and Uberoi 1990.

25. Such a premise about "nature" is not entirely dissimilar from liberalism's claim about human nature—at best a first principle or original position that is ultimately hard to substantiate. Alfred Deakin (1986 [1895]: 2), founder of the first Australian Liberal Party and thrice prime minister of Australia, traced liberalism back to "ancient Greece." His fellow liberals George Brandis, Tom Harley, and Don Markwell (1986, 216) noted that "liberalism commences with a theory of the nature of human society." In this context John Rawls

is no exception (Matsuda 1986), as is the entire liberal tradition, beginning with John Locke (Pabst 2013). Partisans of Europe's Enlightenment held that its principles were "rooted in nature" (Owen and Owen 2011, 8).

26. For a similar description, see Gulen 2004, 17–19.

27. For this distinction in Maududi's *tafsīr*, see *sura an-nūr*, 7 (Maududi n.d.).

28. This distinction between *takvīnī* and *tashrīʿī* is further delineated to explicate the goal of Jamaat in its constitution (Maududi 1942, 174).

29. The copy of volume 3 I have is undated. Since one of its chapters was earlier published in *Tarjumānul Qurʾān* in Muḥarram 1360 (January–February 1941) and also contains the constitution of Jamaat-e-Islami, formed in August 1941, it is safe to say that it was published in 1941 or 1942. Nasr (1994, 278; 1996, 199) loosely and oddly dates all volumes as published between 1938 and 1940.

Chapter 5

1. His grandson, Yahya Nomani, communicated his life span in an e-mail to me, 19 June 2010.

2. Though different in tenor, Nomani had published a critique even earlier, in 1951. Abullais published a response to Nomani in the November–December 1951 issue of *Zindegī*.

3. The absence of precise temporality is abundant, as are "probably" and "perhaps," in Nomani's text.

4. On Jewish and Christian injunctions on hair, see Derrett 1973. Saint Paul held that it was a dishonor for a man to wear his hair long.

5. This quote is from a long footnote in the 1998 edition of Nomani's book. Admitting that earlier he did not give details of the impiety for which "Maududi's supporters" critiqued him, he wrote, "Now with pain in my heart, I record them." Importantly, not all Urdu books mention the original year of publication when they are reprinted. The preface of Nomani's 1998 book (which I cite) states that it was first published as a series of articles in 1958 and then as a book in 1980.

6. To Nasr (1994, 25), Nomani's critique aimed to "unseat" Maududi from leadership. In *The Tale*, however, Nomani states more than once that he didn't consider himself suitable to lead Jamaat.

7. Fatima Jinnah lost to Ayub Khan. While 79,700 valid votes went in favor of Khan, 28,691 went to Jinnah. "Basic Democrats" numbered 80,000 (Tai 1974, 357).

8. This is known as the Machchi Ghot Affair, which took place from 1955 to 1957 and led to the defection, expulsion, and resignation of some fifty-six members; see Nasr 1994, 31–40; and Moten 2003, 395–96. Israr Ahmad (1932–2010), a prominent member, also resigned and published a critique; see Israr Ahmad 1966.

9. The Indian state viewed Jamaat with ample suspicion. After 1947, some of its publications were confiscated and its members jailed (*RIR* 1951, 117). Questions about Jamaat's loyalty to the state were raised in 1953 in the Parliament. The then president, Rajendra Prasad, and Home Minister K. N. Katju, took part in that debate (Hasan 1997, 202). In the early 1960s, several Jamaat members were imprisoned under the Defense of India Rules Act. Jamaat was banned in 1975 during the Emergency and in 1992 after the demolition of the Babri *masjid* (*MMS* 1997, 163–69).

10. On *ḥikmat*, see Yaman 2008 and Farahi 1996. Hamiduddin Farahi was a scholar who influenced Maududi. Farahi had studied philosophy with Thomas Arnold, who taught at Aligarh Muslim University (Masud 1996, 10). Both Farahi and Arnold died in 1930.

11. Nomani (1998, 83–92) also touched on Maududi's exposition of these four terms.

12. In Urdu literary culture, a special issue of a journal is called "number" (transliterated in Urdu), occurring as it often does after the theme of the issue: for example, "critique number" or "poetry number."

13. The *ʿulema* of Deoband and Jamiatul Ulema-e-Hind were perhaps the first to critique Jamaat. In 1951 Deoband published many fatwas (opinions): "Wipe Out Maududi Mischief (*fitna*)," "Followers of Maududi Are Deviant," and so on (*Zindegī*, June–August 1951, 51–53). In 1951 Mazāhirul Ulum, Saharanpur, expelled a teacher influenced by Maududi (*Zindegī* October 1951, 38). On Deoband's critique of Jamaat and the latter's response, see the exchange between Hussain Ahmad Madani (1879–1957) and Abullais (Markazi Maktaba Islami 1984). Key to the critique was Maududi's position that Prophet Muhammad's companions were not beyond critique, which Deoband found disrespectful; see Zakarya 1976. Madani sarcastically described Maududi as "only with a degree from Cambridge, Oxford, or a college," "lacking sufficient competence in religion and Arabic," yet decreeing that earlier scholars did not know Islam well (in *Markazī maktabā islāmī* 1984, 12). So vast is the Deoband literature on Maududi and Jamaat that it could be a subject of study in its own right.

14. For a biographical and a partial account of Sadruddin's over twenty books, see Islam 1999.

15. I could not locate *Niẕām*, a monthly published from Kanpur, where it first appeared in December 1965.

16. Niazi left Jamaat and became a minister under Zulfikar Bhutto's premiership; see Niazi 1973.

17. Such views were also expressed in print; see Ayyub 1996, 4; and Husain 1991.

18. This couplet is in *Maśnavī* 2; see Rumi 1974, 173.

19. For a learned exposition of this *sura* and details on divorce, see El-Sheikh 2003, 20–30.

20. These included works by, among others, Yusuf al-Juwayni, Ghazali, Raghib Isfahani, Abd al-Wahhab Khallaf, Shah Valiullah, Ishaq al-Shatibi, and Ibn Taimiyah.

21. Notably, Kahlid Masud's work on al-Shatibi and Mazen Hashem's on *tajdīd* (renewal).

22. When Nomani published his critique of Maududi (in 1951), Ahsan defended the latter in a book titled *Tanqīdāt* (*Critiques*; 1973 [1955], chap. 4). Ahsan then dismissed Nomani: "I am not fanatical enough to jeopardize the future of Islam over the length of Maududi's beard" (qtd. in Nasr 1994, 26). In the wake of the Machchi Ghot Affair (see chap. 5, n. 8), Ahsan, arguably the most prominent member and considered second in stature and scholarship to Maududi (Saleem 2009, 105–8), left Jamaat. Later he critiqued Maududi on many counts, one of which was his diehard opposition to Jamaat's support of Fatima Jinnah's candidacy. Ahsan took this as a betrayal of Islam, likening Maududi to Fazlur Rahman (of the University of Chicago) and Ghulam Pervez, considered to be a denier of *ḥadīś*. Given the choice between Islam and democracy, Ahsan (2000, 222–24) sarcastically noted, Maududi chose the latter. For Javded Ghamdi (b. 1951), a noted Pakistani "liberal" scholar, and many of his associates, Ahsan became a source of inspiration (Saleem 2009, 102–11; also see Amin 2010).

23. Notwithstanding Maududi's clarification that he favored the "real Sufism of Islam," the description of the prevalent Sufism as opium in his later writings in a specific context (see chap. 3) was taken by his critics as opposition to Sufism generally. Some Jamaat members like Amin Ahsan (1973 [1955]: 190–201) read it along similar lines.

Chapter 6

1. I equally disagree with Fred Halliday's characterization of the post-Revolution Iranian regime as "Islam with a fascist face" (qtd. in Harman 2002 [1999], 9). Bronwyn Winter's (2001a, 2001b) comparison of Islamist parties with the racist parties in Europe is, to say the least, misplaced. Their respective contexts and genealogies, I submit, are markedly different.

2. In the name of universal principles and constitution, the philosopher Jürgen Habermas justified the war against Iraq in 1991 while ignoring what Mike Hill and Warren Montag (2000, 7) call the "rationalization of the violence and barbarism of the constitutional orders themselves."

3. The scholarship on Indian Muslim women has largely focused on reform movements (e.g., Ali 2000; Devji 1994; Metcalf 2001, 1992; Minault 1998, 1990, 1983; Robinson 2000, 2008) and the controversy over the right of a particular divorced woman, Shah Bano, to seek maintenance costs from her husband, "the Shah Bano case" (see, e.g., Chhachhi 1991; Engineer 1987; Hasan 1994, 1999; Kishwar 1998; Lawrence 1998; McDonough 2002; Mody 1987; and Pathak and Rajan 1989). Other works deal with veiling, education, marriage, divorce, mobility, and so on (see Imtiaz Ahmed 2003; Lateef 1990; Menon 1981; Ruhela 1990; and Hasan and Menon 2004). The Shah Bano case has come to epitomize the "Muslim woman question" in India. Radha Kumar's (1993) history of Indian women's movements deals with the dynamics of Hindu society; the sole chapter on Muslim women is on the Shah Bano case (see also Forbes 1996). Study of Islamic movements and the "woman question" remains considerably neglected. Exceptions are Metcalf 1999 on women in the Tablighi Jamaat and Willmer 1996 on women in the Muslim League. To my knowledge, there is hardly any scholarly work on the Indian Jamaat and women. On Pakistan's Jamaat-e-Islami and women, the recent work of Amina Jamal (2013) combines textual sources and ethnographic work done in Lahore and Karachi.

4. In this specific context, nation (*qaum*), not individual, was the analytical unit for Maududi.

5. Maududi (1953) positioned himself between extremes of excessiveness (*afrāṭ*) and curtailment (*tafrīṭ*). While the Greeks exemplified the former, Hindus did the latter. He noted that a Hindu woman was considered successively a property of her parents, husband, and children and was forced to commit *sati*. She had no right to property or divorce. Similarly, medieval Christianity regarded women as the "gateway to hell" (1953, 16). A nation may hold both attitudes at different times. Maududi presented Islam as a system of balance.

6. Ashraf Ali Thanawi (d. 1943), a renowned reformer who wrote *Bihishtī zēvar* (Metcalf 1992), considered Western education so poisonous that he advised Muslims to send their daughters to brothels rather than marry them to Western-educated men (Thanawi n.d., 530).

7. On women's depiction in the pulp Urdu fiction of Pakistan, see the elegant article by Kamran Asdar Ali (2004).

8. Before it may be construed as exceptionalism, a comparative note is in order. Saint Augustine believed that women should not enter the public domain as "they cause erections even in holy men" (qtd. in Hassan 2001, 68n3). Thus, in the wake of the 1995 United Nations Women's Conference, conservative Christians from "the West" and Muslims from "the East" formed a coalition, led by Pope John Paul II, against women's rights; see Bayes and Tohidi 2001, 1–5.

9. Maududi's reference to Kant is particularly interesting. Kant himself held views

closer to Maududi's. To Kant (2006 [1798], 207), in "establishing womankind . . . *nature's end*" was the preservation of the human species and "the cultivation of society and its refinement by womankind." "*Physical* injury and *timidity*" were in woman's nature and, therefore, she "rightfully demands male protection" (italics in original).

10. To validate such claims, Maududi quoted many Western sources, often without their complete names or other details. Some of them are Weinberg, Dr. Reprev, Dr. Voice Chevsky, and Professor Lapinsky's book *The Development of Personality in Women*.

11. In an earlier publication (Ahmad 2008), I stated that Maududi didn't allow women to even vote. I regret the error.

12. Many Muslim women were active in the Communist movement. Since Islam was not their master frame, I do not focus on them. For a biographical account of a female Communist, see Daudi 2001.

13. It is hard to gauge the extent to which the granting of membership impacted women. In early 1947 their number was only four, all being wives (Maududi's included) of male members. The women held a separate meeting at Jamaat's headquarters in Pathankot (Ali 1988, 231).

14. Since its inception in 1948, *Zindegī* was published from Rampur, Jamaat's second headquarters after Malihabad. When the headquarters shifted to Delhi, its name was changed to *Zindegī-e-nav*.

15. Unlike Abul Kalam Azad's (n.d.b) book, Michael Cook's (2000) work is probably the best example of the conventional interpretation of *mā*ʿ*rūf* and *munkar*.

16. Years after my fieldwork, I learned that Islahi left Jamaat.

17. The defense of Maududi's neopatriarchate by a female Islamist may be seen as a paradox. Gita Sahgal and Nira Yuval-Davis (1992) theorize women's participation in fundamentalist movements as a paradox. How then do we explain the participation of Dalits (formerly called "Untouchables") in Brahmanized Hindu nationalism, *Hindutva* (Guru 1991)?

18. In Abul Kalam Azad's (1967, 78) Urdu it reads, *dimāgh kī zindegī*, literally "life of the mind."

19. In January 1974, Maududi asked Jamaat not to take part in the elections, but they nonetheless participated in the Assembly elections of 1977; see Ahmad 2005, 288–89.

Chapter 7

1. A related issue is the anthropologist as protagonist in novels. In her analysis of over fifteen novels, the depiction of anthropology therein "saddened," not surprisingly, anthropologist Rosemary Firth (1984, 9).

2. The textbook written by Bipan Chandra, Amles Tripathi, and Barun De (1972, 170) and published by National Book Trust, a Government of India agency, states that Ghaffar Khan "came to be known as 'Frontier Gandhi.'" The passive sentence leaves the question "by whom" unaddressed.

3. Citing no source, Vivek Kumar's (2011) report about Ghaffar Khan posted on a German website says he is "called Muslim Gandhi." One may also mention that the colonialist Jan Smuts first called Gandhi "Mahatma" (Aijaz Ahmad 2005, 22).

4. Hari Bhau Joshi's (n.d., xiii; see also Gandhi 2004, 302) book on Ghaffar Khan's life, published in Hyderabad in the late 1960s and translated from the Marathi into Urdu, has a map with international borders showing the demand for an independent Pakthunistan.

5. It is well known that the region where Ghaffar Khan's activism had widest appeal was historically an important site for Buddhist culture and scholarship—a point Khan (2009 [1969], 12–13) himself noted.

6. He also read them aloud to others, the nonliterate. Subscribers to such newspapers were listed as "suspects" by the police (Khan 2009 [1969], 30).

7. For more on Mahmudul Hasan, see Adravi 2002; Kidwai 1985, 402–14; and Ali Usman Qasmi 2011, 44. On Sindhi, see Allana 1988, 173–83; Kidwai 1985, 427–42; Tareen 2017; and Zaman 2012, 11.

8. *Ṣabr* is inadequately translated as "patience" (e.g., by Banerjee 1999, 192; 2001, 80; cf. Easwaran 1999, 243n118). Correct translations are "steadfastness," "fortitude," or "endurance" in times of trial and hardship. As Ishtiaq Danish (2003, 257) puts it, "In Qur'ānic parlance it means to bear all sorts of pangs and difficulties in the way of Allah; to uphold and propagate truth resolutely and face the consequences whatever they might be." For ethnographic explications of this term, see Asad 2003, 90; Hamdy 2009, 180; Jouili 2015, 185; and Mahmood 2005, 170–74.

9. On this point, Ghaffar Khan's view converged with Maududi's and others (Ahmad 2009b, chap. 2).

10. The notion of *hizmet* in Turkish is similar.

11. "The main problematic of my research on . . . the KK [Ḳhudāī Ḳhidmatgār] movement is," writes Banerjee (1999, 198), "how were notoriously violent Pakhtuns converted to an ethic of non-violence." Mark "conversion"! Violence by Pathans is taken as normal; thus, deployment of nonviolence by them is an issue of "conversion"; not, for instance, of its use, adoption, or invocation.

12. Chandra, Tripathi, and De (1972, 171), however, give the figure of 80,000 in 1930.

13. Temple's classification of what is Urdu and what is Hindi is problematic, however.

14. In the Indian proverb, *ḥalvā* is replaced with chicken leg, especially served on such occasions.

15. I owe this to Faiyaz Ahmad Beg and Murari Dwivedi, my batchmates in sociology honors degree studies at Jamia Millia Islamia, New Delhi (1991–94).

Epilogue

1. Soroush calls it "religious knowledge." Going by his own theory, it is more appropriate to call it knowledge about religion, because that knowledge is religious as much as what a commentator on him calls "extra-religious" (Kamali 1995). The premise of a distinction between the religious and the secular is why Soroush calls the knowledge "religious" (see below).

2. Zainul Islam Qasmi (2012, 37, 45) is the mufti of Darul Uloom Deoband, India. I take his position as representing the views of other schools of thought as well. This fatwa (opinion) is recent; made only some years before its publication. The grounds of this fatwa are hadiths, the deeds of Prophet Muhammad's companions, and excerpts of texts by renowned past scholars (*akābir-e-ummat*). Acknowledging that *ʿulema* of Egypt and the Arab world hold a different opinion, Qasmi sticks to the old position, saying that there "is no difference among the *ʿulema* of the subcontinent" (cf. Zaman 2006 on *ijmāʿ*).

3. Though a term backed by international relations, morally I regard "illegal immigrant" as obscene. A world order that considers one's very being, rather than one's actions, as illegal simply because of the movement from one territory to another, reflects the sickness it is built on. See Ahmad 2010.

4. Unlike their counterparts in India, *ʿulema* of Egypt didn't consider taking or publishing photos *ḥarām*. They argued that since machines made photos, there was no question of challenging God's power as creator. Muhammad Abduh, for instance, made an argument similar to Anwar's I cited above. Abduh contended that the likelihood of polytheism was no

longer a possibility because "the representation of persons assumes the same status as the representation of plants and trees" (qtd. in Isa 1955, 264). Muhammad Iqbal had no problem with *moṣṣavarī* (sculpture). He encouraged his son, Javed Iqbal, to pursue it. On his return from Europe, he brought many books of art for Javed to learn from (as noted in Javed Iqbal's 2002 autobiography [36]). Let me quickly add that Plymouth Brethren in England considered reading fiction to be a "sin" because fiction, they held, created a world parallel to God's; see Gosse 1925 [1907].

5. I thank Waris Mazhari, a Delhi-based scholar and a Deoband graduate, for drawing my attention to this and mentioning Sulaiman Nadvi's position in *Al-jamʿīat*.

Bibliography

Abaza, Mona. 2007. *The Dialectics of Enlightenment, Barbarism and Islam*. Ortelius Lecture. Wassenaar: Netherlands Institute for Advanced Study.

Abdullah, Zain. 2014. "A Muslim's Search for Meaning." *Harvard Divinity Bulletin*. Winter/Spring, 23–32.

Abdurrahman, Sabahuddin. 1970. *Hindustan ke salāṯīn, ʿulema avr mashāʾḵh par ek naẕar*, 2nd ed. Azamgarh, India: Dārul muṣannefīn.

Abdussattar. 2009 (1969). "Tʿāruf." In *Āp bītī*, by Khan Abdul Ghaffar Khan, edited and compiled by Jay Prakash Narayan, 3–4. Karachi: Fiction House. http://www.iqbalcyberlibrary.net//en/969-416-227-012.html.

Abousenna, Mona. 2006. "The Absence of Enlightenment in Arabic Culture." *Think: Philosophy for Everyone* 4 (12): 7–12.

Abrahamov, Binyamin. 1998. *Islamic Theology: Traditionalism and Rationalism*. Edinburgh: Edinburgh University Press.

Abullais, Mavlana. 2002. "Ḥiṣṣā dōm." In *Mavlānā Mavdūdī sē mavlānā noʿmān kē iḵhtelāf kā ʿilmī jāʾzā*, edited by Akhtar Hijazi, 109–200. Lahore: ʿIlm-v-ʿirfān.

Abu-Lughod, Lila. 1998. *Remaking Women: Feminism and Modernity in the Middle East*. Princeton, N.J.: Princeton University Press.

———. 2013. *Do Muslim Women Need Saving?* Cambridge, Mass.: Harvard University Press.

Adil, Adnan. 2007. "The Killer Who Got Away." *Newsline*, 14 March. http://www.newslinemagazine.com/2007/03/the-killer-who-got-away/. 29 August 2012.

Adravi, Asir. 2002. *Taḥrīk-e-āzādī avr musalmān*. Deoband, India: Dārul muʿalefīn.

Afary, Janet. 1997. "The War against Feminism in the Name of the Almighty: Making Sense of Gender and Muslim Fundamentalism." *New Left Review* 224: 89–110.

Agha, Vazir. 2011. *Tanqīd avr jadīd urdu tanqīd*. Delhi: Maktabā jāmiʿā.

Ahmad, Aijaz. 2005. "Frontier Gandhi: Reflections on Muslim Nationalism in India." *Social Scientist* 33 (1–2): 22–39.

Ahmad, Aziz. 1964. *Studies in Islamic Culture in the Indian Environment*. Delhi: Oxford University Press.

Ahmad, Irfan. 2002. "Timothy McVeighs of the Orient." *Economic and Political Weekly* 37 (15): 1399–1400.

———. 2005. "From Islamism to Post-Islamism: The Transformation of the Jamaat-e-Islami in North India." PhD diss., University of Amsterdam.

———. 2008. "Cracks in the 'Mightiest Fortress': Jamaat-e Islami's Changing Discourse on Women." *Modern Asian Studies* 42 (2–3): 549–75.

———. 2009a. "Genealogy of the Islamic State: Reflections on Maududi's Political Thought and Islamism." *Journal of Royal Anthropological Institute (NS)* 15: S145–S162.

———. 2009b. *Islamism and Democracy in India: The Transformation of the Jamaat-e-Islami*. Princeton, N.J.: Princeton University Press.

———. 2009c. *An Outline of Abul Kalam Azad's Cosmopolitan Theology*. Paper presented at the 108th Annual Conference of American Anthropological Association, Philadelphia, 2–6 December.
———. 2010. "Is There an Ethics of Terrorism? Islam, Globalization, Militancy—Review Essay." *South Asia: Journal of South Asian Studies* 33 (3): 487–98.
———. 2011a. "The Categorical Revolution: Democratic Uprising in the Middle East." *Economic and Political Weekly* 46 (45): 30–35.
———. 2011b. "Democracy and Islam." *Philosophy and Social Criticism* 37 (4): 459–70.
———. 2011c. "Immanent Critique and Islam: Anthropological Reflections." *Anthropological Theory* 11 (1): 107–32.
———. 2012. "Theorizing Islamism and Democracy: Jamaat-e-Islami in India." *Citizenship Studies* 16 (7): 887–903.
———. 2013a. "Abul Ala Mawdudi." In *The Princeton Encyclopedia of Islamic Political Thought*, edited by Gerhard Böwering, Patricia Crone, Wadad Kadi, Devin J. Stewart, Muhammad Qasim Zaman, and Mahan Mirza, 332–34. Princeton, N.J.: Princeton University Press.
———. 2013b. "In Defense of Ho(s)tel: Islamophobia, Domophilia and the West." *Politics, Religion & Ideology* 14 (2): 234–52. Special issue, "Islamophobia, European Modernity and Contemporary Illiberalism." Guest edited by Natalie Doyle and Irfan Ahmad.
———. 2013c. "Islam and Politics in South Asia." In *The Oxford Handbook of Islam and Politics*, edited by John Esposito and Emad El-Din Shahin, 324–39. New York: Oxford University Press.
———. 2014a. "Kafka in India: Terrorism, Media, Muslims." In *Being Muslims in South Asia*, edited by Robin Jeffrey and Ronojoy Sen, 289–329. New Delhi: Oxford University Press.
———. 2014b. "Gandhi, Palestine and Israel." Kafila.online, 2 August. https://kafila.online/2014/08/02/gandhi-palestine-and-israel-irfan-ahmad/. 10 January 2015.
———. 2014c. "Welcome to Pseudo-democracy: Unpacking the BJP Victory." Kafila.online, 25 May. https://kafila.online/2014/05/25/welcome-to-pseudo-democracy-unpacking-the-bjp-victory-irfan-ahmad/. 26 July 2015.
———. 2015a. "As Morsi Faces the Gallows, Where Are the Defenders of Democracy?" *ABC*, 14 August. http://www.abc.net.au/religion/articles/2015/08/14/4293890.htm. 15 September 2015.
———. 2015b. "As Morsi Faces the Gallows, Where Are the Defenders of Democracy?" *The Conversation*, 14 August. https://theconversation.com/as-morsi-faces-the-gallows-where-are-the-defenders-of-democracy-46068. 15 September 2015.
———. 2015c. "The Importance of C. Wright Mills: Anthropology/Sociology and International Relations." Paper presented at the Australian Anthropological Society Conference, held at University of Melbourne, 3 December.
———. 2015d. "Islamic Reform in Asia." In *Routledge Handbook of Religions in Asia*, edited by Bryan Turner and Oscar Salemink, 144–57. London: Routledge.
———. 2015e. "On the State of the (Im)possible: Notes on Wael Hallaq's Thesis." *Journal of Religious and Political Practice* 1 (1): 97–106.
———. 2015 f. "Talal Asad Interviewed by Irfan Ahmad." *Public Culture* 27 (2): 259–79.
———. 2017. "Nationalism and Disciplinary Knowledge: Othering and the Disciplin(e)ing of Sociology/Anthropology in India." Journal manuscript in search of publication.
Ahmad, Irfan, and Bryan Turner. 2015. "Editorial: Inaugural Statement." *Journal of Religious and Political Practice* 1 (1): 1–6.

Ahmad, Israr. 1966. *Taḥrīk-e- jamāʿt islāmī islāmī: aēk tahqīqī mutāʿla*. Lahore: Dārul ishāʿt islāmīa.
Ahmad, Kalimuddin. 2006. "Tanqīd avr adabī tanqīd." In *Naẕaryātī tanqīd: masāʾl v mabāḥiś*, edited by Abulkalam Qasmi, 34–45. Aligarh, India: Educational Book House.
Ahmad, Khursheed. 1991. "Muqaddima." In *Islāmī reyāsat, Abul Ala Maududi*, edited by Khursheed Ahmad, 17–32. New Delhi: Islamic Book Foundation.
Ahmad, Nazeer. 1918. *Lekchrōñ kā majmūʿa*. Agra, India: Mufīd-e-ʿām.
Ahmad, Sadaf. 2009. *Transforming Faith: The Story of Al-Huda and Islamic Revivalism among Urban Pakistani Women*. Syracuse, N.Y.: Syracuse University Press.
Ahmed, Akbar S. 2003. *Islam under Siege*. Cambridge, U.K.: Polity.
Ahmed, Imtiaz. 1983. "Introduction." In *Modernization and Social Change among Muslims in India*, edited by Imtiaz Ahmed, xvii–xlix. Delhi: Manohar.
———, ed. 2003. *Divorce and Remarriage among Muslims in India*. Delhi: Manohar.
Ahmed, Ishtiaq. 2011. "Women under Islamic Law in Pakistan." In *Politics of Religion in South and South-East Asia*, edited by Ishtiaq Ahmed, 102–19. London: Routledge.
Ahmed, Leila. 1986. "Women and the Advent of Islam." *Signs* 11 (4): 665–91.
———. 1992. *Women and Gender in Islam: Historical Roots of a Modern Debate*. New Haven, Conn.: Yale University Press.
Ahmed, Tariq. 1982. *Religio-political Ferment in the N.W. Frontier during the Mughal Period: The Raushaniya Movement*. Delhi: Idāra-e-adabiyāt.
Ahsan, Amin. 1973 (1955). *Tanqīdāt*. Lahore: Islamic.
———. 2000. *Maqalāt-e-Islāḥī*. Edited by Khalid Masud. Lahore: Fārān Foundation.
Ajiz, Kalim. 2005. *Mērī ẕubān mērā qalam*. Patna, India: Ḵhuda Bakhsh Oriental Public Library.
Akhtar, Saleem. 2014. "Tanqīd, manṯiq, sāins." *Ijrāʾ* (Karachi) 17 (January–March): 19–29.
Al-Ashmawy, M. S. 1998. *Against Islamic Extremism: The Writings of Muhammad Said Al-Ashmawy*. Edited by C. Fluehr-Lobban. Gainesville: University Press of Florida.
Al-Azm, Sadik. 1991. "The Importance of Being Earnest about Salman Rushdie." *South Asia Bulletin* 11 (1–2): 1–20.
Al-hilāl. 1912. Calcutta, 13 July.
Al-Musleh, M. A. 2007. "Al-Ghazali as an Islamic Reformer: An Evaluative Study of the Attempts of the Imam al-Ghazālī at Islamic Reform (iṣlāḥ)." PhD diss., University of Birmingham.
Alam, Israr. 1990. "Afzal hussain sahab avr nayā niẕām-e-tāʿlīm." *Rafīq-e-manzil*, September, 31-54.
Albayrak, Ismail. 2003. "The Classical Exegetes' Analysis of the Qurʾānic Narrative." *Islamic Studies* 42 (2): 289–315.
Alberuni. (1888) 2002. *Alberuni's India*. Delhi: Rupa.
Ali, Azra Asghar. 2000. *The Emergence of Feminism among Indian Muslim Women, 1920–1947*. Karachi: Oxford University Press.
Ali, Kamran Asdar. 2004. "Pulp Fictions': Reading Pakistani Domesticity." *Social Text* 22 (1): 123–45.
Ali, Syed Naqi. 1988. *Sayyid mavdūdī kā aʿhd: Mērī naẕar mēñ*. Rāmpur, India: Zikrā.
Allana, Ghulam. 1988. *Muslim Political Thought through the Ages, 1562–1947*. 2nd ed. Karachi: Royal Book Company.
Almond, Ian. 2009. *History of Islam in German Thought: From Leibniz to Nietzsche*. London: Routledge.

———. 2015. *The Thought of Nirad C. Chaudhuri: Islam, Empire and Loss.* Cambridge: Cambridge University Press.
Alwishah, Ahmed, and Josh Hayes. 2015. "Introduction." In *Aristotle and the Arabic Tradition,* edited by Ahmed Alwishah and Josh Hayes, 1–10. Cambridge: Cambridge University Press.
Ambedkar, B. R. 2003. "Buddha and Future of His Religion." In *Dr. Babasaheb Ambedkar: Writings and Speeches.* Vol. 2, part 2, 97–108. New Delhi: Ministry of Social Justice & Empowerment, Government of India.
Amin, Husnul. 2010. "From Islamism to Post-Islamism: A Study of a New Intellectual Discourse on Islam and Modernity in Pakistan." PhD diss., Erasmus University Rotterdam.
Anidjar, Gil. 2008. *Semites: Race, Religion, Literature.* Stanford, Calif.: Stanford University Press.
———. 2015a. "Christianity, Christianities, Christian." *Journal of Religious and Political Practice* 1 (1): 39–46.
———. 2015b. "The Forgetting of Christianity." *ReOrient: The Journal of Critical Muslim Studies* 1 (1): 27–36.
Anjum, Ovamir. 2011. "Has Modernity Ruptured Islamic Political Tradition?" In *Sociology of Islam: Secularism, Economics and Politics,* edited by Tugrul Keskin, 45–60. Reading: Ithaca, 2011.
———. 2012. *Politics, Law and Community in Islamic Thought: The Taymiyyan Moment.* Cambridge: Cambridge University Press.
Ansari, Abdulhaq. 2003. "Maududi's Contribution to Theology." *Muslim World* 93: 521–31.
Ansari, Asloob Ahmad. 1968. *Adab avr tanqīd.* Allahabad, India: Sangam.
———. 1994. "Pēsh-e-lafẓ." In Ahmad Sajjad, *Tāʿmīrī adabī taḥrīk,* 10–12. New Delhi: Qāzī.
Appadurai, Arjun. 1996. *Modernity at Large: Cultural Dimension of Globalization.* Minneapolis: University of Minnesota Press.
Ar-Raziq, Ali A. 1982. "The Caliphate and the Bases of Power." In *Islam in Transition: Muslim Perspectives,* edited by John Donohue and John Esposito, 29–37. Oxford: University Press.
Arberry, A. J. 2008 (1957). *Revelation and Reason in Islam.* London: Routledge.
Arendt, Hannah. 1978. *The Life of the Mind.* San Diego: Harvest.
Arewa, E. Ojo, and Alan Dundes. 1964. "Proverbs and the Ethnography of Speaking Folklore." *American Anthropologist* 66: 70–85.
Arkoun, Mohammed. 2003. "Rethinking Islam Today." *The ANNALS of the American Academy of Political and Social Science* 588 (1): 18–39.
Arkush, Allan. 1993. "Voltaire on Judaism and Christianity." *AJS Review* 18 (2): 223–43.
Asad, Talal. 1972. "Market Model, Class Structure and Consent: A Reconsideration of Swat Political Organisation." *Man,* n.s., 7 (1): 74–94.
———. 1986a. "The Concept of Cultural Translation in British Social Anthropology." In *Writing Culture: The Poetics and Politics of Ethnography,* edited by James Clifford and George Marcus, 141–64. Berkeley: University of California Press.
———. 1986b. "The Idea of an Anthropology of Islam." Occasional Papers Series, Center for Contemporary Arab Studies, Georgetown University.
———. 1993. *Genealogies of Religion: Discipline and Reason of Power in Christianity and Islam.* Baltimore: John Hopkins University Press.
———. 1997. "Brief Note on the Idea of 'an Anthropology of Europe.'" *American Anthropologist* 99 (4): 719–21.

———. 2003. *Formations of the Secular: Christianity, Islam, Modernity*. Stanford, Calif.: Stanford University Press.
———. 2009. "Free Speech, Blasphemy, and Secular Criticism." In *Is Critique Secular? Blasphemy, Injury and Free Speech*, edited by Talal Asad, Wendy Brown, Judith Butler and Saba Mahmood, 20–63. Berkley: University of California Press.
———. 2012. "Thinking about Religion, Belief and Politics." In *The Cambridge Companion to Religious Studies*, edited by Robert Orsi, 36–57. Cambridge: Cambridge University Press.
Asad, Talal, Wendy Brown, Judith Butler, and Saba Mahmood. 2009. *Is Critique Secular? Blasphemy, Injury and Free Speech*. Berkeley: University of California Press.
Ashenden, Samantha, and David Owen, eds. 1999. *Foucault Contra Habermas*. London: Sage.
Ashur, Muhammad al-Tahir Ibn. 2007. *Treatise on Maqāsid al-Sharīʿā*. London & Washington: International Institute of Islamic Thought.
Ayoob, Mohammed. 2008. *The Many Faces of Political Islam*. Ann Arbor: University of Michigan Press.
Ayubi, Nazih. 1991. *Political Islam: Religion and Politics in the Arab World*. London, New York: Routledge.
Ayyub, Hakim Muhammad. 1996. *Yē bēchārē mamūlē*. Azamgarh, India: n.p.
Azad, Abul Kalam. 1967. *Ghōbār-e-khāṭṭir*. Edited by Malik Ram. New Delhi: Sāhitya akādmī, 1967.
———. 2004 (1968). *Tarjumānul Qur'ān-jild 1*. New Delhi: Sāhitya akādmī.
———. N.d.a. *Ḥaẓrat yūsuf*. Delhi: Farīd buk depo.
———. N.d.b. *Ṣadā-e-ḥaq*. Delhi: Farīd buk depo.
Azam, K. M. 2010. *Ḥayāt-e-sadīd: bānī dārul islām neyāz ʿalī khāñ*. Lahore: Nashrīāt.
Azmi, Altaf. 1999. *Aḥyā-e-millat avr dīnī-jamʿātēñ*. Aligarh, India: Idāra taḥqīq.
Azmi, Fakhrul Islam. N.d. "Sabras kā tanqīdī jā'za." In *Sabras sē mazāmīn-e-rashīd tak*, edited by Fakhrul Islam Azmi, 1–18. Azamgarh, India.
Badran, Margot. 2002. "Islamic Feminism: What Is in a Name?" *Al-Ahram Weekly Online*, 17–23 January. http://weekly.ahram.org.eg/2002/569/cu1.htm\.
Baghpati, Mateen Tariq. 1979. *Mavlānā mavdūdī aur fikrī inqilāb*. Delhi: Markazī maktabā islamī.
Banerjee, Mukulika. 1999. "Justice and Non-violent Jihad: The Anti-colonial Struggle in the North West Frontier Province of British India." *Etudes Rurales* 149–50: 181–98.
———. 2001. *The Pathan Unarmed: Opposition and Memory in the North West Frontier*. New Delhi: Oxford University Press.
Barelvi, Ibadat, ed. 1970. *Urdu tanqīdnegārī*. Delhi: Chaman buk depo.
Bari, Sayyid Abdul. 1997. *Afkār-e-tāzā*. Delhi: Published by author.
Barker, Philip. 2008. *Religious Nationalism in Modern Europe: If God Be for Us*. London: Routledge.
Barnett, S. J. 2003. *The Enlightenment and Religion: The Myths of Modernity*. Manchester: Manchester University Press.
Barth, Fredrik. 1969. Introduction to *Ethnic Groups and Boundaries: The Social Organization of Culture Difference*, edited by Fredrik Barth, 9–38. London: George Allen & Unwin.
Barton, Greg. 1997. "Indonesia's Nurcholish Madjid and Abdurrahman Wahid as Intellectual Ulama: The Meeting of Islamic Traditionalism and Modernism in Neo-modernist Thought." *Islam and Christian-Muslim Relations* 8 (3): 323–50.
Bausani, Alessandro. 2012. "Ghālib." *Encyclopaedia of Islam*. 2nd ed., edited by P. Bearman,

Th. Bianquis, C. E. Bosworth, E. van Donzel, and W. P. Heinrichs. *Brill Online*. http://referenceworks.brillonline.com/entries/encyclopaedia-of-islam-2/ghalib-SIM_2452.
Bayat, Asef. 1998. "Revolution without Movement, Movement without Revolution: Comparing Islamic Activism in Iran and Egypt." *Comparative Studies in Society and History* 40 (1): 136–69.
Bayes, John H., and Nayereh Tohidi, eds. 2001. *Globalization, Gender and Religion: The Politics of Women's Rights in Catholic and Muslim Societies*. New York: Palgrave.
Baynes, Kenneth. 2004. "The Transcendental Turn: Habermas' 'Kantian Pragmatism.'" In *The Cambridge Companion to Critical Theory*, edited by Fred Rush, 194–218. Cambridge: Cambridge University Press.
Bazmesukhan.com. 2015. "'Āmir uṡmānī." http://www.bazmesukhan.com/author.php?aid=3.
BBC. 2007. "Mohtasib ki khair ho." 24 February. http://www.bbc.com/urdu/miscellaneous/story/2007/02/070224_zille_huma_column.shtml.
———. 2015. "India's Maharashtra State Bans Beef." 3 March. http://www.bbc.com/news/world-asia-india-31712369.
Becker, Carl. 1932. *The Heavenly City of the Eighteenth-Century Philosophers*. New Haven, Conn.: Yale University Press.
Bell, Lucinda. 2004. "The 1858 Trial of Mughal Emperor Bahadur Shah Zafar II for 'Crimes against the State.'" PhD diss., Melbourne University.
Bellah, Robert N. 1991. *Beyond Belief: Essays on Religion in a Post-traditionalist World*. Berkeley: University of California Press.
———. 2005. "What Is Axial about the Axial Age?" *Archives Européennes de Sociologie* 46 (1): 69–87.
Berger, John. 2002. "The Ambiguity of the Photograph." In *The Anthropology of Media: A Reader*, edited by Kelly Askew and Richard Wilk, 47–55. Malden, Mass.: Blackwell.
Berger, Morroe. 1977. *Real and Imagined World: The Novel and the Social Science*. Cambridge, Mass.: Harvard University Press.
Bernal, Martin. 2006. *Black Athena: The Afroasiatic Roots of Classical Civilization*. Vol. 3, *The Linguistic Evidence*. New Brunswick, N.J.: Rutgers University Press.
Bernasconi, Robert, and Tommy Lott, eds. 2000. *The Idea of Race*. Indianapolis: Hackett.
Besson, Samantha. 2005. *The Morality of Conflict: Reasonable Disagreement and the Law*. Oxford, U.K.: Hart.
Bhagavan, Manu. 2008. "The Hindutva Underground." *Economic and Political Weekly* 43 (37): 39–48.
Bhattacharya, Sabyasachi. 2005. "The Acquiescent Indian." *Economic and Political Weekly* 40 (41): 4425–28.
Bilal, Muhammad. 2014. "Allah's Community: The Interplay of Islam and Everyday Life in Pakistan. Ethnography of a Rawalpindi Urban Community." PhD diss., Macquarie University, Sydney.
Bilefsky, Dan, and Ian Fisher. 2006. "Across Europe, Worries on Islam Spread to Center." *New York Times*, 11 October, http://www.nytimes.com/2006/10/11/world/europe/11muslims.html?pagewanted=all.
Bilgrami, Akeel. 2014. "Secularism: Its Content and Context." In *Boundaries of Toleration*, edited by Alfred Stepan and Charles Taylor, 79–129. New York: Columbia University Press.
Biswas, Shailendra. 1984 (1957). *Sansad Bangla Abhidan*. Calcutta: Sahitya Samsad.

Blok, Josine. 1996. "Proof and Persuasion in Black Athena: The Case of K. O. Muller." *Journal of History of Ideas* 57 (4): 507–24.
Blond, Phillip. 1998. "Theology before Philosophy." In *Post-secular Philosophy: Between Philosophy and Theology,* edited by Phillip Bond, 1–66. London: Routledge.
Blond, Philip, and Adrian Pabst. 2005. "The Roots of Islamic Terrorism." *New York Times,* 28 July.
Bohannan, Laura. 1966. "Shakespeare in the Bush." *Natural History* 75: 28–33.
Bose, Nirmal Kumar. 1961 (1929). *Cultural Anthropology.* Rev. ed. London: Asia.
Bosworth, Edmund. 1976. "The Prophet Vindicated: A Restoration Treatise on Islam and Muhammad." *Religion* 6 (1): 1–12.
Bouma, Gary. 2007. "Religious Resurgence, Conflict and the Transformation of Boundaries." In *Religion, Globalization and Culture,* edited by Peter Beyer and Lori Beaman, 187–202. Leiden, the Netherlands: Brill.
Bourdieu, Pierre, and Loïc Wacquant. 1992. *An Invitation to Reflexive Sociology.* Chicago: Chicago University Press.
———. 1999. "On the Cunning of Imperialist Reason." *Theory, Culture and Society* 16 (1): 41–58.
Bowen, John. 1993. *Muslims through Discourse: Religion and Ritual in Gayo Society.* Princeton, N.J.: Princeton University Press.
Bowker, John. 2003. "Fiṭra." *The Concise Oxford Dictionary of World Religions.* http://www.oxfordreference.com/view/10.1093/acref/9780192800947.001.0001/acref-9780192800947-e-2447?rskey=d9Gs7z&result=2447.
Boy, John D., and John Torpey. 2013. "Inventing the Axial Age: The Origins and Use of a Historical Concept." *Theory and Society* 42: 241–56.
Brague, Rémi. 2002. *Eccentric Culture: A Theory of Western Civilization.* Translated by Samuel Lester. South Bend, Ind.: St. Augustine's.
Brandis, George, Tom Harley, and Don Markwell. 1986. "Liberal Values." In *Australian Liberalism: The Continuing Vision,* edited by Yvonne Thompson, George Brandis, and Tom Harley, 216–25. Melbourne: A Liberal Forum Publication.
Brewer, John. 2004. "Imagining *The Sociological Imagination*: The Biographical Context of a Sociological Classic." *British Journal of Sociology* 55 (3): 317–33.
Bright, J. S. 1944. *Frontier and Its Gandhi.* Lahore: Allied Indian.
Browers, Michaelle, and Charles Kurzman. 2004. "Introduction: Comparing Reformations." In *An Islamic Reformation,* edited by Michaelle Browers and Charles Kurzman, 1–17. Lanham, Md.: Lexington.
Brown, Wendy. 2005. "Political Idealization and Its Discontents." In *Dissent in Dangerous Times,* edited by Austin Sarat, 23–45. Ann Arbor: University of Michigan Press.
Bruce, Steve. 2004. "Did Protestantism Create Democracy?" *Democratization* 11 (4): 3–20.
Bukay, David. 2007. "Can There Be an Islamic Democracy?" Review essay. *Middle East Quarterly,* Spring, 71–79.
Butler, Judith. 2003. "What Is Critique? An Essay on Foucault's Virtue." http://eipcp.net/transversal/0806/butler/en.
———. 2007. *Gender Trouble.* New York: Routledge, 2007.
Calhoun, Craig, Eduardo Mendieta, and Jonathan VanAntwerpen, eds. 2013. *Habermas and Religion.* Cambridge, U.K.: Polity.
Calman, Jeslie J. 1989. "Women and Movement Politics in India." *Asian Survey* 29 (10): 940–58.

Caputo, John. 2013. *Truth: Philosophy in Transit*. London: Penguin.
Caputo, John, and Mark Yount. 1993. *Foucault and the Critique of Institutions*. University Park: Pennsylvania State University Press.
Carson, Craig. 2012. "Religion and the French Revolution, or Politics of Incarnation." In *Sacred and Secular in Early Modern France: Fragments of Religion*, edited by Sanja Perovic, 160–72. New York: Bloomsbury.
Casanova, José. 2006. "Secularization Revisited: A Reply to Talal Asad." In *Powers of the Secular Modern: Talal Asad and His Interlocutors*, edited by David Scott and Charles Hirschkind, 12–30. Stanford, Calif.: Stanford University Press.
———. 2009. "The Religious Situation in Europe." In *Secularization and the World Religions*, edited by Hans Joas and Klaus Wiegandt, 206–27. Liverpool: Liverpool University Press.
———. 2012. "Religion, the Axial Age, and Secular Modernity in Bellah's Theory of Religious Evolution." In *The Axial Age and Its Consequences*, edited by Robert Bellah and Hans Joas, 191–221. Cambridge, Mass.: Belknap Press of Harvard University Press.
Chandra, Bipan, Amales Tripathi, and Barun De. 1972. *Freedom Struggle*. New Delhi: National Book Trust.
Chatterjee, Partha. 1993. *The Nation and Its Fragments*. Princeton, N.J.: Princeton University Press.
Chhachhi, Amrita. 1991. "Forced Identities: The State, Communalism, Fundamentalism and Women in India." In *Women, Islam and the State*, edited by Deniz Kandiyoti, 144–75. London: Macmillan.
Chicago Chronicle. 1995. "Obituary: Edward Shils, Committee on Social Thought, Sociology." 2 February. http://chronicle.uchicago.edu/950202/shils.shtml.
Chigateri, Shraddha. 2008. "'Glory to the Cow': Cultural Difference and Social Justice in the Food Hierarchy in India." *South Asia* 31 (1): 10–35.
Chishti, Unvan. 2012. *Urdu mēṅ klāsīkī tanqīd*. Delhi: Maktabā jāmiʿā.
Chittick, William. 2011. "Reason, Intellect and Consciousness in Islamic Thought." In *Reason, Spirit and the Sacred in the New Enlightenment*, edited by Anna-Teresa Tymieniecka, 11–35. New York: Springer.
Cohen, Walter. 1993. "An Interview with Martin Bernal." *Social Text* 35: 1–24.
Cohn, Bernard. 1996. *Colonialism and Its Forms of Knowledge*. Princeton, N.J.: Princeton University Press.
Collingwood, R. G. 1985 (1946). *The Idea of History*. Madras: Oxford University Press.
Collins, Patricia Hill. 1989. "The Social Construction of Black Feminist Thought." *Signs* 14 (4): 745–73.
Cook, Michael. 2000. *Commanding Right and Forbidding Wrong in Islamic Thought*. Cambridge: Cambridge University Press.
CRAI (Committee of the Royal Anthropological Institution of Great Britain and Ireland). 1954 (1874). *Notes and Queries on Anthropology*. 6th rev. ed. (rewritten). London: Routledge & Kegan Paul.
Crehan, Kate. 2002. *Gramsci, Culture, and Anthropology*. London: Pluto.
Crocker, Christopher. 1977. "The Social Functions of Rhetorical Forms." Edited by David Sapir and Christopher Crocker, 33–66. *Daedalus* 127 (3): 221–50.
Culler, Jonathan. 2012. "Criticism." In *The Princeton Encyclopedia of Poetry and Poetics*, 4th ed., edited by Ronald Greene, Stephen Cushman, Clare Cavanagh, Jahan Ramazani, and Paul Rouzer, 316–19. Princeton, N.J.: Princeton University Press.
Dadi, Iftikhar. 2016. "Enclosure/Erasure: Imran Channa and Partition." *Tanqeed.org*,

March. http://www.tanqeed.org/2016/03/enclosure-erasure-imran-channa/#identifier_0_11520.
Dale, Stephen. 1988. "Religious Suicide in Islamic Asia: Anti-colonial Terrorism in India, Indonesia and the Philippines." *Journal of Conflict Resolution* 32: 37–59.
Dallal, Ahmad. 1993. "The Origins and Objectives of Islamic Revivalist Thought, 1750–1850." *Journal of the American Oriental Society* 113 (3): 341–59.
Danish, Ishtiaq. 2003. "Values and Ethics: The Islamic Perspective." In *World Religions and Islam: A Critical Study*, part 2, edited by Hamid Naseem Rafiabadi, 253–61. Delhi: Sarup & Sons.
Dannhauser, Werner. 1995. "Poetry vs. Philosophy." *PS: Political Science & Politics* 28 (2): 190–92.
Das, Veena, Michael D. Jackson, Arthur Kleinman, and Bhrigupati Singh. 2014. "Experiments between Anthropology and Philosophy: Antagonism and Affinities." In *The Ground Between: Anthropologists Engage Philosophy*, edited by Veena Das, Michael D. Jackson, Arthur Kleinman, and Bhrigupati Singh, 1–26. Durham, N.C.: Duke University Press.
Dasgupta, Priyanka. 2012. "Freedom of Speech Being Gagged: Taslima." *Times of India*, 26 February. http://articles.timesofindia.indiatimes.com/2012-02-26/books/31020759_1_kolkata-book-fair-free-speech-parties.
Dastūr asāsī jamīʿatulʿulemā hind. N.d. Passed in April 1949. Delhi: Jamiatul Ulema-e-Hind.
"Dastūr Jamāʿt-e-Islāmī." 1942. In Abul Ala Maududi, *Musalmān avr maujudah seyāsī kashmakash—ḥissa 3*, 171–84. Pathankot, India: Daftar Risāla Tarjamānul Qurʾān.
Daudi, Zohra. 2001. *Manzil-e-gurēzāñ*. Karachi: Al-banoria.
Davis, Robert Con, and Ronald Schleifer. 1991. *Criticism and Culture: The Role of Critique in Modern Literary Theory*. Essex, U.K.: Longman.
De Castro, Eduardo. 2004. "Perspectival Anthropology and the Method of Controlled Equivocation." *Tipit´i: Journal of the Society for the Anthropology of Lowland South America* 2 (1): 3–22.
de Gruchy, John W. 2004. "Democracy." In *The Blackwell Companion to Political Theology*, edited by Peter Scott and William Cavanugh, 439–54. Malden, Mass.: Blackwell.
De Leeuw, Marc, and Sonja van Wichelen. 2005. "'Please, Go Wake Up!' *Submission*, Hirsi Ali, and the 'War on Terror' in the Netherlands." *Feminist Media Studies* 5 (3): 325–40.
Deakin, Alfred. 1986 (1895). "What Is Liberalism?" In *Australian Liberalism: The Continuing Vision*, edited by Yvonne Thompson, George Brandis, and Tom Harley, 2–5. Melbourne: A Liberal Forum Publication.
Derrett, Duncan. 1973. "Religious Hair." *Man*, n.s., 8 (1): 100–103.
Derrida, Jacques. 2002. *Acts of Religion*. Edited and introduced by Gil Anidjar. London: Routledge.
Devji, Faisal. 1994. "Gender and the Politics of Space: The Movement for Women's Reform, 1857–1900." In *Forging Identities: Gender, Communities and the State*, edited by Zoya Hasan, 22–37. Delhi: Kali for Women.
Dhar, Pulak Narayan. 1987. "Bengal Renaissance: A Study in Social Contradiction." *Social Scientist* 15 (1): 26–45.
Dhume, Sadanand. 2008. "The Paradox of Muslim Weakness." *Yale Global Online*, 27 May. http://yaleglobal.yale.edu/content/paradox-muslim-weakness.
Dillon, Michael. 1996. *Politics of Security: Towards a Political Philosophy of Continental Thought*. London: Routledge.
Dumont, Louis. 1985. "A Modified View of Our Origins: The Christian Beginnings of

Modern Individualism." In *The Category of the Person: Anthropology, Philosophy, History*, edited by Michael Carrithers, Steven Collins, and Steven Lukes, 93–122. Cambridge: Cambridge University Press.

Durant, Will, and Ariel Durant. 1963. *Story of Civilization*. Vol. 7, *The Age of Reason Begins: A History of Western Civilization in the Period of Shakespeare, Bacon, Montaigne, Galileo, and Descartes, 1558–1648*. New York: Simon and Schuster.

Eagleton, Terry. 2005 (1984). *The Function of Criticism*. London: Verso.

———. 2009. "Atheism as Islamophobia." http://www.youtube.com/watch?v=YuAOncRoIpU.

Easwaran, Eknath. 1999. *Nonviolent Soldier of Islam: Badshah Khan, a Man to Match His Mountains*. 2nd ed. Berkeley: Nilgiri Press.

Edel, Abraham. 1953. "Some Relations of Philosophy and Anthropology." *American Anthropologist* 55 (5): 649–60.

Eickelman, Dale. 1985. *Knowledge and Power in Morocco: The Education of a Twentieth-Century Notable*. Princeton, N.J.: Princeton University Press.

Eickelman, Dale, and James Piscatori. 1996. *Muslim Politics*. Princeton, N.J.: Princeton University Press.

Elden, Stuart, and Eduardo Mendieta, eds. 2011. *Reading Kant's Geography*. Albany: SUNY Press.

El-Sheikh, Salah. 2003. "Al-Mujādalah and Al-Mujādilah Then and Now: Kalām, Dialectical Argument, and Practical Reason in the Qur'ān." *Muslim World* 93 (1): 1–50.

Engineer, Asghar Ali. 1998. *Rethinking Issues in Islam*. Hyderabad, India: Orient Longman.

———, ed. 1987. *The Shah Bano Controversy*. Bombay: Sangam.

EPW (Economic and Political Weekly). 2007. "Editorial: SOS from Nandigram." *EPW* 42 (12): 991–92.

Eriksen, Thomas. 2001. *Small Places, Large Issues: An Introduction to Social and Cultural Anthropology*. 2nd ed. London: Pluto.

Eriksen, Thomas, and Finn Sivert Nielsen. 2015. *A History of Anthropology*. 2nd ed. London: Pluto.

Ernst, Carl. 2004. *Rethinking Islam in the Contemporary World*. Edinburgh: Edinburgh University Press.

———. 2011. "The Limits of Universalism in Islamic Thought: The Case of Indian Religions." *Muslim World* 110: 1–19.

Esposito, John, ed. 2003. *The Oxford Dictionary of Islam*. Oxford: Oxford University Press.

Esposito, John, and John Voll. 2001. *Makers of Contemporary Islam*. Oxford: Oxford University Press.

Euben, Roxana. 2002. "Killing (for) Politics: Jihad, Martyrdom, and Political Action." *Political Theory* 30 (1): 4–35.

Eze, Emmanuel. 2002. "What Remains of Enlightenment?" *Human Studies* 25 (3): 281–88.

Fabian, Johannes. 1983. *Time and the Other: How Anthropology Makes Its Object*. New York: Columbia University Press.

———. 1991. "Dilemmas of Critical Anthropology." In *Constructing Knowledge: Authority and Critique in Social Science*, edited by Lorraine Nencel and Peter Pels, 180–202. London: Sage.

Falkenhayner, Nicole. 2010. "The Other Rupture of 1989: The Rushdie Affair as the Inaugural Event of Representation of Post-secular Conflict." *Global Society* 27 (1): 111–32.

Farahi, Hamiduddin. 1996. *Ḥikmat-e-Qur'ān*. Translated by Khalid Masud. Azamgarh, India: Dāera'Ḥamīdiā.
Farhad, Husain Amir. N.d. *Ḥaqā'q avr afsāanē*. Karachi: Idārah ṣaōtulḥaq.
Farooqi, Mehr Afshan. 2004. "Towards a Prose of Ideas: An Introduction to the Critical Thought of Muhammad Hasan 'Askari.'" *Annual of Urdu Studies* 19: 175–90.
Faruqi, Shahnavaz. 2014. "Mavlānā mavdūdī per tanqīd kī bunyādēñ." *Freelancer.co.in*. URL no longer available. Accessed 28 February 2014.
Faruqi, Shamsur Rahman. 1981. *The Secret Mirror: Essays on Urdu Poetry*. Delhi: Academic Literature.
———. 2004. *Tanqīdī afkār*. 2nd rev. ed. Delhi: Qaumī kāunsil barā-e-faroghē Urdu.
———. 2008. "Keyā naqqād kā vajūd ẓarūrī hay?" *Naī ketāb*, July–September, 7–10.
———. 2010. *Ṣurat v m'ānā sokhan*. New Delhi: MR.
Faruqi, Ziaul Hasan. 1986. "Hindustān meñ islamī rāsikhul aqīdgī kī rivāyat." In *Hindustān meñ Islamī ʿulūm-v-adabiyāt*, edited by I. H. Faruqi, 11–27. Delhi: Maktabā jāmiʿā.
Fassin, Didier. 2014. "True Life, Real Lives: Revisiting the Boundaries between Ethnography and Fiction." *American Ethnologist* 41, no.1): 40–55.
Fenves, Peter, ed. 1993. *Raising the Tone of Philosophy: Late Essays by Immanuel Kant, Transformative Critique by Jacques Derrida*. Baltimore: Johns Hopkins University Press.
Fernea, Elizabeth Warnock. 1998. *In Search of Islamic Feminism*. New York: Doubleday.
Firestone, Chris, and Stephen Palmquist. 2006. "Preface." In *Kant and the New Philosophy of Religion*, edited by Chris Firestone and Stephen Palmquist, xix–xxii. Bloomington: Indiana University Press.
Fīrozullоghāt. 2014. Delhi: Kutubkhāna ḥamīdīa.
Firth, Rosemary. 1984. "Anthropology in Fiction: An Image of Fieldwork." *RAIN* 64: 7–9.
Fischer, Michael, and Mehdi Abedi. 1990. *Debating Muslims: Cultural Dialogue in Postmodernity and Tradition*. Madison: University of Wisconsin Press.
Fitzgerald, Timothy. 1999. "Ambedkar, Buddhism, and the Concept of Religion." In *Untouchables: Dalits in Modern India*, edited by S. M. Michael, 57–71. Boulder, Colo.: Lynne Rienner.
Forbes, Geraldine. 1996. *Women in Modern India*. Cambridge: Cambridge University Press.
Foucault, Michel. 1972. *The Archaeology of Knowledge and the Discourses on Language*. Translated by A. M. Sheridan Smith. New York: Pantheon.
———. 1996. "What Is Critique?" In *What Is Enlightenment*, edited by J. Schmidt, 382–98. Berkeley: University of California Press.
Franklin, Todd. 2002. "The New Enlightenment: Critical Reflections on the Political Significance of Race." In *The Blackwell Guide to Social and Political Philosophy*, edited by Robert Simon, 271–91. Malden, Mass.: Blackwell.
Gandhi, Rajmohan. 2004. *Ghaffar Khan: Nonviolent Badshah of the Pakhtuns*. New Delhi: Penguin.
Ganeri, Jonardon. 2003. "Hinduism and the Proper Work of Reason." In *The Blackwell Companion to Hinduism*, edited by Gavin Flood, 411–46. Malden, Mass.: Blackwell.
Gay, Peter. 1957. "Carl Becker's Heavenly City." *Political Science Quarterly* 72 (2): 182–99.
———. 1996. "The Living Enlightenment." Tanner Lectures on Human Values, University of Toronto. http://tannerlectures.utah.edu/_documents/a-to-z/g/Gay98.pdf.
Geertz, Clifford. 1985. Foreword to *Knowledge and Power in Morocco: The Education of a Twentieth-Century Notable*, edited by Dale Eickelman, xi–xiv. Princeton, N.J.: Princeton University Press.

Gellner, Ernest. 1992. *Postmodernism, Reason and Religion*. London: Routledge.
Geuss, Raymond. 1999. *Morality, Culture & History*. Cambridge: Cambridge University Press.
Ghalib, Asadullah Khan. 1993. *Dīvān-e-Ġhālib*. Deluxe ed. Delhi: Ghalib Academy.
Giddens, Anthony. 1990. *The Consequences of Modernity*. Stanford, Calif.: Stanford University Press.
Giesen, Bernhard. 1998. "Cosmopolitans, Patriots, Jacobins, and Romantics." *Daedalus* 127 3 (Summer): 221–50.
Glassberg, David. 1996. "Public History and the Study of Memory." *Public Historian* 18 (2): 7–23.
Godlove, Terry. 2014. *Kant and the Meaning of Religion: The Critical Philosophy and Modern Religious Thought*. New York: IB Tauris.
Goody, Jack. 2006. *The Theft of History*. Cambridge: Cambridge University Press.
Gorski, Philip, David. K. Kim, John Torpey, and Jonathan VanAntwerpen, eds. 2012. *The Post-secular in Question: Religion in Contemporary Society*. New York: New York University Press.
Gosse, Edmund. 1925 (1907). *Father and Son: A Study of Two Temperaments*. London: Heinemann.
Gourgouris, Stathis. 2008. "De-transcendentalizing the Secular." *Immanent Frame*. http://blogs.ssrc.org/tif/2008/01/31/de-transcendentalizing-the-secular/.
Graham, William. 1993. "Traditionalism in Islam: An Essay in Interpretation." *Journal of Interdisciplinary History* 23 (3): 95–522.
Gramsci, Antonio. 1996. *Selections from the Prison Notebooks*. Hyderabad, India: Orient Longman.
Griffel, Frank. 2010. "Muslim Philosophers' Rationalist Explanation of Muhammad's Prophecy." In *The Cambridge Companion to Muhammad*, edited by Jonathan E. Brockopp, 158–78. Cambridge: Cambridge University Press.
———. 2016. Preface to *Islam and Rationality: The Impact of al-Ghazali Papers Collected on His 900th Anniversary*, edited by Frank Griffel, vii–xv. Leiden, the Netherlands: Brill.
Grimshaw, Jean. 1986. *Philosophy and Feminist Thinking*. Minneapolis: University of Minnesota Press.
Guha, Ramachandra. 2005. "Arguments with Sen." *Economic and Political Weekly* 40 (41): 4420–25.
Gulen, Fatehullah. 2004. *Essays, Perspectives, Opinions*. Rev. ed. Somerset: Light.
———. 2013. "Mufīd tanqīd kā uṣūl." *Gulen.com*, 26 June. http://fgulen.com/ur/books-pk/the-broken-jug/36084-essentials-for-fruitful-criticism.
Guru, Gopal. 1991. "Hinduisation of Ambedkar in Maharashtra." *Economic and Political Weekly* 26 (7): 339–41.
Habermas, Jürgen. 1981. "Modernity versus Postmodernity." *New German Critique* 22: 3–14.
———. 1987. *The Philosophical Discourse of Modernity: Twelve Lectures*. Translated by Frederick Lawrence. Cambridge, U.K.: Polity.
Habib, Irfan. 2013. "Questionings within Religious Thought: The Experience of Islam." *Social Scientist* 41 (5–6): 3–13.
Haj, Samira. 2002. "Reordering Islamic Orthodoxy: Muhammad Ibn ʿAbdul Wahab." *Muslim World* 92: 333–70.
Hali, Altaf Hussain. 1998. *Muqaddamah-e-shēʿr-v-shāʿrī*. New Delhi: Maktabā jāmiʿā.
Hallaq, Boutros. 2014. "Adab: Modern Usage." In *Encyclopaedia of Islam*, vol. 3, edited by Kate Fleet, Gudrun Krämer, Denis Matringe, John Nawas, and Everett Rowson. *Brill*

Online. http://referenceworks.brillonline.com/entries/encyclopaedia-of-islam-3/adab-e-modern-usage-COM_23653.
Hallaq, Wael. 1984. "Was the Gate of Ijtihad Closed?" *International Journal of Middle East Studies* 16 (1): 3–41.
———. 2009. *Sharia: Theory, Practice, Transformation*. Cambridge: Cambridge University Press.
———. 2013. *The Impossible State: Islam, Politics, and Modernity's Moral Predicament*. New York: Columbia University Press.
Hamdy, Sherine. 2009. "Islam, Fatalism, and Medical Intervention: Lessons from Egypt on the Cultivation of Forbearance (*Sabr*) and Reliance on God (*Tawakkul*)." *Anthropological Quarterly* 82 (1): 173–96.
Hameed, Sayeda. 1995. "Non-violence in Islam." In *Khan Abdul Ghaffar Khan: A Centennial Tribute*, edited by Nehru Memorial Museum and Library, 97–115. Delhi: Har-Anand.
Hampson, Norman. 1990. *The Enlightenment: An Evaluation of Its Assumptions, Attitudes and Values*. London: Penguin.
———. 2001. "The Enlightenment." In *Early Modern Europe: An Oxford History*, edited by Euan Cameron, 265–97. Oxford: Oxford University Press.
Hanson, Victor. 2006. "Traitors to the Enlightenment." *National Review*, 2 October. http://www.nationalreview.com/article/218870/traitors-enlightenment-victor-davis-hanson.
Haq, Abdul. 1953. "Muqaddima." In *Sabras*, edited by Mulla Wajhi, 1–51. N.p.: n.p. http://mausc1.blogspot.com.au/.
Haqulmubeen.com. 2012. http://haqulmubeen.com/home/mazameen/haqiqat-ghair-muqallidiyat/298-hazrat-aukarwi-ka-ilhami-malfuzat.
Harman, Chris. 2002 (1999). *Prophet and the Proletariat: Islamic Fundamentalism, Class and Revolution*. Updated ed. London: Socialist Workers Party.
Harris, Olivia. 2004. "Braudel: Historical Times and the Horror of Discontinuity." *History Workshop Journal* 57: 161–74.
Harvard, Jonas. 2013. "Catholicism and the Idea of Public Legitimacy in Sweden." In *European Anti-Catholicism in a Comparative and Transnational Perspective*, edited by Yvonne Maria Werner and Jonas Harvard, 223–36. Amsterdam: Rodopi.
Harvey, David. 2000. "Cosmopolitanism and the Banality of Geographical Evils." *Public Culture* 12 (2): 529–64.
———. 2011. "Cosmopolitanism in *Anthropology* and *Geography*." In *Reading Kant's Geography*, edited by Stuart Elden and Eduardo Mendieta, 267–84. Albany: SUNY Press.
Hasan, Aziz Ibnul. N.d. *Urdu tanqīd: Chand manzilēñ*. Lahore: Purab Academy.
Hasan, Mushirul. 1997. *The Legacy of a Divided Nation: Indian Muslims since Independence*. London: Hurst.
———. 1998. "Aligarh's 'Notre Eminent Contemporain': Assessing Sayyid Ahmad Khan's Reformist Agenda." *Economic and Political Weekly* 33 (19): 1077–81.
———. 2008. *Islam in South Asia*. Vol. 3, *The Realm of the Traditional*. Delhi: Manohar.
———. 2009. *Islam in South Asia*. Vol. 4, *The Realm of the Secular*. Delhi: Manohar.
Hasan, Zoya, ed. 1994. *Forging Identities: Gender, Communities and the State*. Delhi: Kali for Women.
———. 1999. "Muslim Women and the Debate on Legal Reforms." In *From Independence towards Freedom: Indian Women since 1947*, edited by Bharati Ray and Aparna Basu, 120–34. Delhi: Oxford University Press.

Hasan, Zoya, and Ritu Menon. 2004. *Unequal Citizens: A Study of Muslim Women in India*. New Delhi: Oxford University Press.
Hassan, Riffat. 1991a. "The Issue of Woman-Man Equality in the Islamic Traditions." In *Women's and Men's Liberation: Testimony of Spirits*, edited by Leonard Grob, Riffat Hassan, and Haim Gordon, 65–82. Westport, Conn.: Greenwood.
———. 1991b. "Muslim Women and Post-patriarchal Islam." In *After Patriarchy: Feminist Transformations of the World Religions* (Faith Meets Faith Series), edited by Paula M. Cooey, William R. Eakin, and Jay B. McDaniel, 39–64. New York: Orbis.
———. 2001. "Challenging Stereotypes of Fundamentalism: An Islamic Feminist Perspective." *Muslim World* 91 (1–2): 55–70.
Hastrup, Kristen. 2005. "Social Anthropology: Towards a Pragmatic Enlightenment?" *Social Anthropology* 13 (2): 133–49.
Heesterman, J. C. 1985. *The Inner Conflict of Tradition: Essays in Indian Ritual, Kinship, and Society*. Chicago: University of Chicago Press.
Hermansen, Marcia. 1996. "Translator's Introduction." In Shah Waliullah, *The Conclusive Argument from God: Shāh Walī Allāh of Delhi's "Ḥujjat Allāh al Bāligha,"* xv–xxxviii. Leiden, the Netherlands: Brill.
———. 2008. "Shāh Walī Allāh." In *The Islamic World*, edited by A. Rippin, 390–95. New York: Routledge.
Herzfeld, Michael. 1987. *Anthropology through the Looking-Glass: Critical Ethnography through the Margins of Europe*. Cambridge: Cambridge University Press.
———. 1997. "Theorizing Europe: Persuasive Paradoxes." *American Anthropologist* 99 (4): 713–15.
———. 2002. "The Absent Presence: Discourses of Crypto Colonialism." *South Atlantic Quarterly* 101 (4): 899–926.
Hill, Mike, and Warren Montag, eds. 2000. *Masses, Classes, and the Public Sphere*. London: Verso.
The Hindu. 2015. "Muslim Population Growth Slows." 27 August. http://www.thehindu.com/news/national/census-2011-data-on-population-by-religious-communities/article7579161.ece.
Hodges, Matt. 2010. "The Time of the Interval: Historicity, Modernity, and Epoch in Rural France." *American Ethnologist* 37 (1): 115–31.
Hodgson, Marshal G. S. 1974a. *The Venture of Islam*, vol. 1. Chicago: University of Chicago Press.
———. 1974b. *The Venture of Islam: Conscience and History in a World Civilization*, vol. 3. Chicago: University of Chicago Press.
Hogan, Desmond. 2010. "Kant's Copernican Turn and the Rationalist Tradition." In *The Cambridge Companion to Kant's "Critique of Pure Reason,"* edited by Paul Guyer, 21–40. Cambridge: Cambridge University Press.
Honneth, Alex. 2009. *Pathology of Reason: On the Legacy of Critical Theory*. New York: Columbia University Press.
Horkheimer, Max, and Theodore Ador(2002. *Dialectic of Enlightenment: Philosophical Fragments*. Edited by G. S. Noerr and translated by E. Jephcott. Stanford, Calif.: Stanford University Press.
Hudson, Wayne. 2005. "The Enlightenment Critique of 'Religion.'" *Australian E-Journal of Theology* 5: 1–12.
Humshehri.org. 2014. "Bacha Khan." http://humshehri.org/history/bacha-khan/?lang=ur.

Husain, Ashfaq Muhammad. 1991. *Vaḥiduddīn ḳhān sāḥab kī fikrī qalābāziyāñ*. Hyderabad, India: Majlis aḥyāē sunnat.
Husain, Ehtesham. 1965. *'Atebār-e-naẕar*. Lucknow, India: Kitāb.
———. 1983. *Urdu adab kī tanqīdī tārīḳh*. Delhi: Taraqqī Urdu Bureau.
Hyder, David. 2003. "Foucault, Cavaillès, and Husserl on the Historical Epistemology of the Sciences." *Perspectives on Science* 11 (1): 107–29.
Ikram, S. M. 1964. *Muslim Civilization in India*. Edited by Ainslie T. Embree. New York: Columbia University Press.
Indian Express. 2010. "Mirwaiz Punched in Face at Chandigarh Seminar." 25 November. http://www.indianexpress.com/news/mirwaiz-punched-in-face-at-chandigarh-seminar/715944/.
Iqbal, Javed. 2002. *Apnā garēbāñ chāk*. Lahore: Sang-e-mīl.
Iqbal, Muhammad. 1934. *The Reconstruction of Religious Thought in Islam*. London: Oxford University Press.
———. 1990. *Kulliyāt-e-Iqbāl*. Lahore: Iqbāl akādmī.
———. 2014. *Stray Reflections: A Notebook of Allama Iqbal*. Edited by Javed Iqbal. Lahore: Sang-e-mīl.
Iqtidar, Humeira. 2011. *Secularizing Islamists? Jama'at-e-Islami and Jama'at-ud-da'wa in Urban Pakistan*. Ranikhet, India: Permanent Black.
Isa, Ahmad Muhammad. 1955. "Muslims and Taswir." *Muslim World* 45 (3): 50–68.
Islahi, Ayaz Ahmad. 1997. "Mavdūdī: Fikrī pasmanzar avr taṣṣavvur-e-tāʿlīm." *Rafīq-e-manzil*, May–June, 97–109.
Islahi, Sultan Ahmad. 1997. "Jadīd zarāʾiblāġh avr islām." *Mujalla ʿul ūm-e- islāmīa* (Aligarh, India) 22 (1): 55–98.
———. 2000 (1994). *Islām kā nazarīya-e-jins*. Aligarh, India: ʿIlm-v-adab.
Islam, Zafrul. 1999. "Mavlāna ṣadruddīn iṣlāḥī marḥūm." *Fikr-v-naẕar* 35 (4): 35–52.
Izutsu, Toshihiko. 1964. *God and Man in the Koran: Semantics of the Koranic Weltanschauung*. Tokyo: Keio Institute of Cultural and Linguistic Studies.
Jackson, Sherman. 2005. *Islam and the Blackamerican: Looking toward the Third Resurrection*. Oxford: Oxford University Press.
Jaiswal, Suvira. 2000. "Change and Continuity in Brahmanical Religion with Particular Reference to Vaisnava Bhakti." *Social Scientist* 28 (5–6): 3–23.
Jalal, Ayesha. 1991. "The Convenience of Subservience: Women and the State in Pakistan." In *Women, Islam and the State*, edited by Deniz Kandiyoti, 77–114. London: Macmillan.
———. 2008. *Partisans of Allah: Jihad in South Asia*. Cambridge, Mass.: Harvard University Press.
Jamal, Amina. 2013. *Jamaat-e-Islami Women in Pakistan: Vanguard of a New Modernity?* Syracuse, N.Y.: Syracuse University Press.
Jamāʿt islāmī hin kī policy avr program. 1964. Delhi: Jamāʿt islāmī hind.
Jaspers, Karl. 1962 (1957). *Kant*. Edited by Hannah Arendt and translated by Ralph Manheim. San Diego: Harvest/HBJ.
Jeffery, Patricia. 1979. *Frogs in a Well: Indian Women in Purdah*. London: Zed.
Jenkis, Richard. 2008. "Anthropology and Ethnicity" and "From Tribes to Ethnic Groups." In *Rethinking Ethnicity: Arguments and Explorations*, 2nd ed., 3–16. London: Sage.
Joas, Hans. 2012. Introduction to *The Axial Age and Its Consequences*, edited by Robert Bellah and Hans Joas, 9–29. Cambridge, Mass.: Belknap Press of Harvard University Press.

Johansen, Robert. 1997. "Radical Islam and Nonviolence: A Case Study of Religious Empowerment and Constraint among Pashtuns." *Journal of Peace Research* 34 (1): 53–71.

Joshi, Hari Bhau. N.d. *Bādshāh khān: Savāneḥ ḥayāt*. Translated from the Marathi into Urdu. Hyderabad, India: Sangam.

Joubin, Rebecca. 2000. "Islam and Arab through the Eyes of the Encyclopédie: The Other as a Case of French Cultural Self-Criticism." *International Journal of Middle East Studies* 32: 197–217.

Jouili, Jeanette. 2015. *Pious Practice and Secular Constraints: Women in the Islamic Revival in Europe*. Stanford, Calif.: Stanford University Press.

Kamali, Hossein. 1995. "The Theory of Expansion and Contraction of Religion." http://www.drsoroush.com/English/On_DrSoroush/E-CMO-19950200-1.html.

Kant, Immanuel. 1992. *Lectures on Logic*. Translated and edited by Michael Young. Cambridge: Cambridge University Press.

———. 1998 (1781). *Critique of Pure Reason*. Translated and edited by Paul Guyer and Allen Wood. Cambridge: Cambridge University Press.

———. 1998 (1793). *Religion within the Boundaries of Mere Reason and Other Writings*. Edited by Allen Wood and G. di Giovanni. Cambridge: Cambridge University Press.

———. 2002. *Critique of Practical Reason*. Introduced by Stephen Engstrom and translated by Werner Pluhar. Indianapolis: Hackett.

———. 2006 (1798). *Anthropology from a Pragmatic Point of View*. Edited by Robert Louden with an introduction by Manfred Kuehn. Cambridge: Cambridge University Press.

———. 2007 (1784). "What Is Aufklärung?" In Michel Foucault, *The Politics of Truth*, edited by S. Lotringer and introduced by J. Rajchaman, 29–37. Los Angeles: Semiotext(e).

Kapferer, Bruce. 2007. "Anthropology and the Dialectic of Enlightenment: A Discourse on the Definition and Ideals of a Threatened Discipline." *Australian Journal of Anthropology* 18 (1): 72–94.

Karmi, Ghada. 1996. "Women, Islam and Patriarchalism." In *Feminism and Islam: Legal and Literary Perspectives*, edited by Maya Yamani, 69–86. Reading, U.K.: Ithaca.

Kavka, Martin. 2012. "Translation." In *The Cambridge Companion to Religious Studies*, edited by Robert Orsi, 186–208. Cambridge: Cambridge University Press.

Kazemi, Farhad. 2000. "Gender, Islam and Politics." *Social Research* 67 (2): 453–74.

Keane, John. 2000. "Secularism?" *Political Quarterly* 71: 5–19.

———. 2009. *The Life and Death of Democracy*. New York: Norton.

Khan, Abdul Karim. 1999. "The Servants of God in the North-West Frontier Province of British India." *ISIM Newsletter* 3: 22.

Khan, Arifa Subh. 2009. *Urdu tanqīd kā aṣlīī chehrā*. Lahore: ʿIlm-v-ʿirfān.

Khan, Haji Mohammad. 1971. "Urdu adab mēñ fan-e-tanqīd kī kamī." *Aligarh Magazine (Intkhāb number)*. Republished from *Aligarh Monthly* 2 (2 (February 1904).

Khan, Khan Abdul Ghaffar. 2009 (1969). *Āp bītī*. Edited and compiled by Jay Prakash Narayan. Karachi: Fiction House. http://www.iqbalcyberlibrary.net//en/969-416-227-012.html.

Khan, Naveeda. 2012. *Muslim Becoming: Aspiration and Scepticism in Pakistan*. Durham, N.C.: Duke University Press.

Khan, Sayyid Ahmad. 1907. *Mukammal majmūʿ lekcharz v ispīchez*, edited by Muhammad Imamuddin Gujarati. Lahore: n.p.

Khan, Sher Banu A. L. 2010. "The Sultanahs of Ache, 1641–99." In *Ache: History, Politics,*

Culture, edited by Arndt Graf, Susanne Schröter and Edwin Wieringa, 3–25. Singapore: Institute of Southeast Asian Studies.
Khan, Vahiduddin. 1995 (1963). *Tʿābīr kī ghalaṭī*. New Delhi: Maktabā Arrisāla.
Kidwai, Muhammad Hashim. 1985. *Jadīd Hindustān kē seyāsī avr samājī afkār*. New Delhi: Taraqqī Urdu Bureau.
Kifayatullah, Mufti. N.d. *Tāʿlīmul islām*. 4 vols.Delhi: Kutubkhāna ʿazīzīa.
Killian, Lewis M. 1996. "What or Who Is a 'Minority?'" *Michigan Sociological Review* (10): 18–31.
Kishwar, Madhu. 1998. *Religion at the Service of Nationalism and Other Essays*. Delhi: Oxford University Press.
Kocabas, S. 1987. *The Qurʾānic Concept of Intellect*. London: Islamic Philosophical Society.
Kontopoulos, Kyriakos. 1995. "The Dark Side of Fire: Postmodern Critique and the Elusiveness of the Ideological." *Argumentation* 9: 5–19.
Korejo, Muhammad Soaleh. 1993. *The Frontier Gandhi: His Place in History*. 1st ed. Karachi: Oxford University Press.
Koselleck, Reinhart. 1988 (1959). *Critique and Crisis: Enlightenment and Pathogenesis of Modern Society*. Cambridge, Mass.: MIT Press.
Kottak, Conrad. 2008. *Anthropology: The Exploration of Human Diversity*. 12th ed. Boston: McGraw-Hill.
Kramer, Gudrun. 1993. "Islamist Notions of Democracy." *Middle East Report* 183: 2–8.
Kraybill, Donald B. 1993a. "Negotiating with Caesar." In *The Amish and the State*, edited by Donald B. Kraybill, 3–20. Baltimore: John Hopkins University Press.
———. 1993b. "Preface and Acknowledgements." In *The Amish and the State*, edited by Donald B. Kraybill, ix–xi. Baltimore: John Hopkins University Press.
Kresse, Kai. 2003. "'Swahili Enlightenment'? East African Reformist Discourse at the Turning Point: The Example of Sheikh Muhammad Kasim Mazrui." *Journal of Religion in Africa* 23 (3): 279–309.
———. 2007. *Philosophising in Mombasa: Knowledge, Islam and Intellectual Practice on the Swahili Coast*. Edinburgh: Edinburgh University Press.
Krystal, Arthur. 2002. *Agitations: Essays on Life and Literature*. New Haven, Conn.: Yale University Press.
Kuehn, Manfred. 2006. Introduction to Immanuel Kant, *Anthropology from a Pragmatic Point of View*, edited by Robert Louden with an introduction by Manfred Kuehn, vii–xiv. Cambridge: Cambridge University Press.
Kuhns, Richard. 1980. "Philosophical Anthropology." *Social Research* 47 (4): 721–33.
Kumar, Radha. 1993. *The History of Doing: An Illustrated Account of Movements for Women's Rights and Feminism in India, 1880–1990*. London: Verso.
Kumar, Vivek. 2011. "Abdul Ghaffar Khan: 'Muslim Gandhi.'" 10 April. http://www.dw.com/ur/.
Kurzman, Charles, ed. 1998. *Liberal Islam: A Sourcebook*. New York: Oxford University Press.
Lal, Malashri. 1991. "Culture and Power." *Indian Literature* 34 (4): 168–74.
Lapidus, Ira. 1984. "Knowledge, Virtue and Action: The Classical Muslim Conception of *Adab* and the Nature of Religious Fulfillment in Islam." In *Moral Conduct and Authority: The Place of Adab in South Asian Islam*, edited by Barbara Metcalf, 38–61. Berkeley: University of California Press.
Larmore, Charles. 1986. *The Morals of Modernity*. Cambridge: Cambridge University Press.
Lateef, Shahida. 1990. *Muslim Women in India*. London: Zed.

Latour, Bru(2004. “Why Has Critique Run Out of Steam? From Matters of Fact to Matters of Concern.” *Critical Inquiry* 30 (2): 225–48.

Lawrence, Bruce. 1998. *Shattering the Myth: Islam beyond Violence*. Karachi: Oxford University Press.

———. 2003. “Islamicate Civilization: The View from Asia.” In *Teaching Islam*, edited by Brannon Wheeler, 61–74. New York: Oxford University Press.

———. 2009. “Islam in Afro-Eurasia: A Bridge Civilization.” In *Civilization in World Politics: Plural and Pluralist Perspectives*, edited by P. J. Katzenstein, 157–75. New York, London: Routledge.

Leaman, Oliver. 2002 (1985). *An Introduction to Classical Islamic Philosophy*. Cambridge: Cambridge University Press.

Lennard, Davis. 1980. “A Social History of Fact and Fiction: Authorial Disavowal in the Early English Novel.” In *Literature and Society*, edited by Edward Said, 120–48. Baltimore: Johns Hopkins University Press.

Lester, Tobby. 1999. “What Is the Koran?” *Atlantic Monthly*, January, 43–53.

Levine, Molly. 1998. “Review Article: The Marginalization of Martin Bernal.” *Classical Philology* 93 (4): 345–63.

Liebich, Andre. 2008. “Minority as Inferiority: Minority Rights in Historical Perspective.” *Review of International Studies* 34 (2): 243–63.

Lindholm, Charles. 2002. “Kissing Cousins: Anthropologists on Islam.” In *Interpreting Islam*, edited by Hastings Donnan, 110–29. New Delhi: Vistaar.

Lisānuṣṣidq. 1904. “Inteqād: Ḥāyāt-e-jāvīd.” 20 April, 12–15.

Lloyd, Genevieve. 1984. *The Man of Reason: “Male” and “Female” in Western Philosophy*. Minneapolis: University of Minnesota Press.

———. 2000. “Rationality.” In *A Companion to Feminist Philosophy*, edited by Alison Jaggar and Iris Young, 165–72. Malden, Mass.: Blackwell.

Loimeier, Roman. 2005. “Is There Something Like a ‘Protestant Islam’?” *Die Welt des Islams* 45 (2): 216–54.

Louden, Robert. 2000. *Kant’s Impure Ethics: From Rational Beings to Human Beings*. Oxford: Oxford University Press.

———. 2006. “Applying Kant’s Ethics: The Role of Anthropology.” In *A Companion to Kant*, edited by Graham Bird, 350–63. Malden, Mass.: Blackwell.

MacDonogh, Steven, ed. 1993. *The Rushdie Letters: Freedom to Speak, Freedom to Write*. Lincoln: Nebraska University Press.

Macey, David. 2000. *Dictionary of Critical Theory*. London: Penguin.

MacIntyre, Alasdair. 1988. *Whose Justice? Which Rationality?* Notre Dame, Ind.: University of Notre Dame Press.

———. 2009. *God, Philosophy, Universities: A Selective History of the Catholic Philosophical Tradition*. Lanham, Md.: Rowman and Littlefield.

MacKenzie, Iain. 2004. *The Idea of Pure Critique*. London: Continuum.

Mackenzie, John. 1929. *A Manual of Ethics*. London: University Tutorial.

Mahdi, Muhsin. 2001. *Alfarabi and the Foundation of Islamic Political Philosophy*. Chicago: University of Chicago Press.

Maherulqadri. 1990. “Chand nqūsh-e-zindegī.” In *Mavlānā mavdūdī: apnōñ avr dūsrōñ kī naẕar mēñ*, edited by Yusuf Bhat, 234–45. Delhi: Markazī maktabā islamī.

Mahmood, Saba. 2005. *The Politics of Piety: The Islamic Revival and the Feminist Subject*. Princeton, N.J.: Princeton University Press.

———. 2008. “Is Critique Secular?” *Public Culture* 20 (3): 447–52.

Mahmoud, Muhammad. 1996. "Women and Islamism: The Case of Rashid al-Ghannushi of Tunisia." In *Islamic Fundamentalism*, edited by Abdel Salam Sidahmad and Anoushiravan Ehteshami, 249–65. Boulder, Colo.: Westview.
Makhdum, Shaykh Ziauddin. 2006. *Tuḥfatul Mujāhidīn: A Historical Epic of the Sixteenth Century*. Translated by S. Muhammad Husayn Nainar. Kuala Lumpur: Islamic Book Trust.
Makki, Mokhtar Ahmad. 2003. *Taḥrīk-e-azādī avr hindustānī musalmān*. New Delhi: Qāzī.
Malik, Hafeez. 1980. *Moslem Nationalism in India and Pakistan*. Lahore: People's Publishing.
Malinowski, Bronislaw. 1922. *Argonauts of the Western Pacific*. London: Kegan Paul.
———. 1945. *The Dynamics of Cultural Change*. New Haven, Conn.: Yale University Press.
Malpas, Jeff, and Karsten Thiel. 2011. "Reading Kant's Geography of Reason." In *Reading Kant's Geography*, edited by Stuart Elden and Eduardo Mendieta, 195–214. Albany: SUNY Press.
Mamdani, Mahmood. 2001. *When Victims Become Killers: Colonialism, Nativism, and the Genocide in Rwanda*. Princeton, N.J.: Princeton University Press.
———. 2012. *Define and Rule: Native as Political Identity*. Cambridge, Mass.: Harvard University Press.
Marcus, George, and Michael Fischer. 1999. *Anthropology as Cultural Critique: An Experimental Moment in the Human Sciences*. 2nd ed. Chicago: University of Chicago Press.
Markazī Maktabā Isāmī. 1984. *Mavlānā abullayṡ nadvī avr mavlānā ḥusayn aḥmad madnī kī morāselat*. Delhi: Markazī maktabā islamī.
Marsden, Magnus. 2005. *Living Islam: Muslim Religious Experience in Pakistan's North-West Frontier Province*. Cambridge: Cambridge University Press.
Martin, James. 1995. *Proverbs*. Sheffield, U.K.: Academic.
Martin, Richard, Mark Woodward, and Dwi Atmaja. 1997. *Defenders of Reason in Islam*. Oxford, U.K.: Oneworld.
Marwat, Fazal-ur-Rahim. 2012. "Origins, Growth and Consolidation of Ḳhudāī Ḳhidmatgār Movement." *Pakistan Perspectives* 17 (1): 123–51.
Marx, Karl. 1976. *Capital: A Critique of Political Economy*. London: Penguin.
Masihuzzaman. 2003 (1954). *Urdu tanqīd ki tārīḳh*. 4th ed. Lucknow, India: Uttar Pradesh Urdu Academy.
Masud, Khalid. 1996. "Pēsh-e-lafẓ." In *Ḥikmat-e-Qur'ān*, by Hamiduddin Farahi,edited and translated by Khalid Masud, 9–25. Azamgarh, India: Dāera'Ḥamīdiā.
Masud, Muhammad Khalid. 2006. *Shatbi's Philosophy of Islamic Law*. Delhi: Adam.
Matilal, Bimal. 1989. "Darma and Rationality." In *Rationality in Question: On Eastern and Western Views of Rationality*, edited by Shlomo Bidermann, Ben Ami Scharfstein, 192–216. Leiden, the Netherlands: Brill.
———. 2015 (1971). *Epistemology, Logic, and Grammar in Indian Philosophical Analysis*. New ed., edited by Jonardon Ganeri. New Delhi: Oxford University Press.
Matin, Abdul. 2001. "Ibtedāī Urdu adabī tanqīd par ʿarabī shēʿrīyāt kā aṡarāt." PhD diss., Jawaharlal Nehru University, New Delhi.
Matsuda, Maria. 1986. "Liberal Jurisprudence and Abstracted Visions of Human Nature: A Feminist Critique of Rawls' Theory of Justice." *New Mexico Law Review* 16: 613–30.
Matthews, David J. 1993. "Eighty Years of Dakani Scholarship." *Annual of Urdu Studies* 8: 82–99.
Maududi, Abul Ala. 1927. "Qur'ān apnē lānē vāloñ ko kis rang mēñ pesh kartā hai." *Tafhīmāt-ḥissa*: 9–38.

———. 1937. *Musalmān avr maujudah seyāsī kashmakash*, vol. 1. Pathankot, India: Daftar Tarjumānul Qurʾān.
———. 1938. *Musalmān avr maujudah seyāsī kashmakash*, vol. 2. Pathankot, India: Maktabā jamāʿt islāmī.
———. 1939. *Risālaʾ-e-dīnīyāt*. Lahore: Daftar Tarjumānul Qurʾān, 1939.
———. 1940–41. "Tajdīd-v-aḥyāē dīn." *Tarjumānul Qurʾān* 17 (4–5) (December–January): 17–98.
———. 1942. *Musalmān avr maujudah seyāsī kashmakash*, vol. 3. Pathankot, India: Daftar Risāla Tarjamānul Qurʾān.
———. 1943. "Foto kā masʾala." In *Rasāʾl v masāʾl—ḥissa-1*, 124–27.
———. 1944. "ʾAsmat-e-amb ēyā." In *Rasāʾl v masāʾl—ḥissa-1*, 21–22.
———. 1945. "Aēk hindū dost kā ḳhaṭ avr us ā javāb." In *Rasāʾl v masāʾl*, 1:119–27.
———. 1951. "Savālat tafhīmul Qurʾān." In *Rasāʾl v masāʾl—ḥissa-2*, 82–85.
———. 1952. "Insān kē fiṭrat par paida honē kā mafhūm." In *Rasāʾl v masāʾl—ḥissa-2*, 97–100.
———. 1953 (1940). *Purdāh*. Delhi: Markazī maktabā islāmī.
———. 1954. "Risālat avr uskē aḥkām." In *Tafhīmāt—ḥissa-1*, 282–317.
———. 1956a. "Iṭmām-e-ḥujjat." In *Kya jamāʿt islāmī ḥaq par hai*, edited by Abdur Rahim Ashraf, 186–91. Laelpur, Pakistan: Maktabā tahzīb-e-millat.
———. 1956b. "Taqlīd avr ittebāʿ." In *Rasāʾel v masāʾel*, 3:266–67. New Delhi: Markazī maktabā islāmī.
———. 1959a. "Lafẓ fiṭrat kā mafhūm." In *Rasāʾl v masāʾl—ḥissa-4*, 50–51.
———. 1959b. *Tanqīḥāt*. Delhi: Markazī maktabā islāmī.
———. 1960. "Shahādat Ḥusayin kā ḥaqīqī maqṣad." In *Tafhīmāt—ḥissa-3*, 323–36.
———. 1962. "Tasvīr sē izhār-e-bar ā ʾt." In *Rasāʾel v masāʾel—ḥissa-4*, 96–97. New Delhi: Markazī maktabā islāmī.
———. 1963. "Sīnema." In *Taḥrīk islāmī*, edited by K. Ahmad, 438. Lahore: Chirāgh-e-rāh.
———. 1965. "Kitāb v sunnat v aqamāte-dīn." *Tajallī*, February–March, 44–49.
———. 1971. "Maiñ Abul ʿAlā Mavdūdī hūñ." *Zindegī*, January, 21–30.
———. 1972. *Islām ka naẓarya-e-seyāsī*. Delhi: Markazī maktabā islāmī.
———. 1976a. *Mavlānā Mavdūdī kī taqārīr*. Edited by Sarvat Saulat. Lahore: Islamic.
———. 1976b. "Saḥābā kē mēʿaar-e-ḥaq honē kī baḥaṡ." In *Rasāʾl v masāʾl—ḥissa-5*, 177–80.
———. 1977a. *Islāmī tahzīb avr uskē usūl v mabādī*. Delhi: Markazī maktabā islāmī.
———. 1977b. *Islām avr zabt-e-valādat*. Delhi: Markazī maktabā islāmī.
———. 1979. *Islāmī adab*. Delhi: Markazī maktabā islāmī.
———. 1980 (1979). *Taṣrīḥāt*. Edited by Salim Mansur Khalid. Rāmpūr, India: Maktabā zikra.
———. 1981. *Towards Understanding Islam*. Rev. ed. Delhi: Markazi Maktaba Islami.
———. 1981 (1940). *Towards Understanding Islam*. Translated by Khurshid Ahmad. Rev. ed. Delhi: Markazī maktabā islāmī.
———. 1982. *Yahūdīat avr naṣrānīat*. Compiled by Naim Siddiqi. Delhi: Markazī maktabā islāmī.
———. 1990a. "Iḳhlāqīāt avr seyāsī āt." In *Mavlānā Mavdūdī: apnōñ avr d dūsrōñ kī naẓar meñ*, edited by Yusuf Bhatta, 161–63. Delhi: Markazī maktabā islāmī.
———. 1990b. "Mazdūrōñ kī jamīʿat ṣirf mazdūrōñ tak hī maḥdūd na rahnī chāhīʾē." In *Mavlānā Mavdūdī: apnōñ avr d dūsrōñ kī naẓar mēñ*, edited by Yusuf Bhatta, 105–9. Delhi: Markazī maktabā islāmī.

———. 1990c. "Sav baras pahlē kā hindustān." In *Mavlānā Mavdūdī: Apnōñ avr d dūsrōñ kī naẓar mēñ*, edited by Yusuf Bhatta, 149–61. Delhi: Markazī maktabā islāmī.
———. 1991. *Tāʿlīmāt*. New Delhi: Markazī maktabā islāmī.
———. 1992 (1919). *Pandit madan mohan mālavīya*. Patna, India: Ḵhudabakhsh Oriental Public Library.
———. 1997 (1943). *Dīn-e-ḥaq*. Lahore: Islamic.
———. 1999a. *Rasāʾel-v-masāel ḥissa 1*. New Delhi: Markazī maktabā islāmī.
———. 1999b. *Rasāʾel-v-masāʾel ḥissa 2*. New Delhi: Markazī maktabā islāmī.
———. 1999c. *Rasāʾel-v-masāʾel ḥissa 3*. New Delhi: Markazī maktabā islāmī.
———. 2001a. *Ḵhilāfat v mulūkiat*. New Delhi: Markazī maktabā islāmī.
———. 2001b. *Tafhīmāt—ḥissa-1*. New Delhi: Markazī maktabā islāmī.
———. N.d. *Tafhīmul Qurʾān*. http://www.urduquran.net/?surah=24&rukuh=7.
Mazhari, Kausar. 2013. *Bāzdīd aur tabṣerey*. Delhi: Arshia.
Mazumdar, Vina, and Indu Agnihotri. 1999. "The Women's Movement in India: Emergence of a New Perspective." In *From Independence towards Freedom: Indian Women since 1947*, edited by Bharati Ray and Aparna Basu, 221–38. Delhi: Oxford University Press.
McDonough, Sheila. 2002. "Muslim Women in India." In *Women in Indian Religions*, edited by Arvind Sharma, 166–88. Delhi: Oxford University Press.
McKane, William. 1970. *Proverbs: A New Approach*. London: SCM.
McLuhan, Teri. 2008. *Frontier Gandhi: Badshah Khan, a Torch for Peace*. http://www.thefrontiergandhi.com/about.html.
McWilliams, Wilson. 1995. "Poetry, Politics and the Comic Spirit." *PS: Political Science & Politics* 28 (2): 197–200.
Mehdi, Tabish. 1999. *Urdu tanqīd kā safar*. Delhi: Published by author.
Mehta, Uday. 1999. *Liberalism and Empire: A Study in Nineteenth-Century British Liberal Thought*. Chicago: University of Chicago Press.
Menon, Indu. 1981. *Status of Muslim Women in India*. Delhi: Uppal.
Mernissi, Fatima. 1985. *Beyond the Veil: Male-Female Dynamics in Muslim Society*. London: Saqi.
———. 1993. *Islam and Democracy: Fear of the Modern World*. London: Virago.
Messick, Brinkley. 1993. *The Calligraphic State: Textual Domination and History in a Muslim Society*. Berkeley: University of California Press.
Metcalf, Barbara. 1982. *Islamic Revival in British India: Deoband, 1860–1900*. Princeton, N.J.: Princeton University Press.
———. 1984. Introduction to *Moral Conduct and Authority: The Place of Adab in South Asian Islam*, edited by Barbara Metcalf, 1–20. Berkeley: University of California Press.
———. 1992. *Perfecting Women: Maulana Ashraf Ali Thanawi's Bihishti Zewar, a Partial Translation with Commentary*. Delhi: Oxford University Press.
———. 1999. "Women and Men in a Contemporary Pietist Movement: The Case of the Tablighi Jamaat." In *Resisting the Sacred and the Secular: Women's Activism and Politicized Religions in South Asia*, edited by Amrita Basu and Patricia Jeffery, 107–21. Delhi: Kali for Women.
———. 2001. "Reading and Writing about Muslim Women in British India." In *Islamic Contestations: Essays on Muslims in India and Pakistan*, 99–119. Delhi: Oxford University Press.
Mieder, Wolfgang. 2004. *Proverbs: A Handbook*. Westport, Conn.: Greenwood.

Miettinen, Timo. 2012. "On the Philosophical Foundations of Universalism: Reason, Task, Critique." *SATS: Northern European Journal of Philosophy* 13 (1): 19–38.
Milbank, John. 2013. "What Lacks Is Feeling: Hume Versus Kant and Habermas." In *Habermas and Religion*, edited by Craig Calhoun, Eduardo Mendieta and Jonathan VanAntwerpen, 322–46. Cambridge, U.K.: Polity.
Miller, Larry. 1984. "Islamic Disputation Theory: A Study of the Development of Dialectic in Islam from the Tenth through Fourteenth Century." PhD diss., Princeton University.
Minault, Gail. 1983. "Hali's Majlis-un-Nisa: Purdah and Women Power in Nineteenth Century." In *Islamic Society and Culture: Essays in Honor of Prof. Aziz Ahmad*, edited by Milton Israel and N. K. Wagle, 39–49. Delhi: Manohar.
———. 1990. "Sayyid Mumtaz Ali and 'Huquq un-Niswan': An Advocate of Women's Rights in Islam in the Late Nineteenth Century." *Modern Asian Studies* 24 (1): 147–72.
———. 1998. *Secluded Scholars: Women's Education and Muslim Social Reform in Colonial India*. Delhi: Oxford University Press.
Mirza, Qudsia. 2005. "Islamic Feminism: Possibilities and Limitations." In *Women and Islam: Critical Concepts in Sociology*, vol. 3, edited by Haideh Moghissi, 300–319. London: Routledge.
Mitchell, Timothy. 2000. "The Stages of Modernity." In *Questions of Modernity*, edited by Timothy Mitchell, 1–34. Minneapolis: University of Minnesota Press.
MMS. 1997. *Markazī majlis-e-shūra jamāʿt islāmī hind kī qarārdādēn̈, July 15, 1961 tā July 7, 1997*. New Delhi: Shoʿba-e-tan ẓīm jamāʿt islāmī hind.
Moad, Edward Omar. 2007. "A Path to Oasis: Sharīʿā and Reason in Islamic Moral Epistemology." *International Journal of Philosophy of Religion* 62: 135–48.
Mody, Nawaz. 1987. "The Press in India: The Shah Bano Judgment and Its Aftermath." *Asian Survey* 27 (8): 935–53.
Moghadam, Valentine. 2002. "Islamic Feminism and Its Discontent: Towards a Resolution of the Debate." *Signs* 24 (4): 1135–71.
Moghissi, Haidah. 1999. *Feminism and Islamic Fundamentalism*. London: Zed.
Mohamed, Sayed. 1968. *The Value of Dakhni Language and Literature* (Special Lectures). Mysore, India: University of Mysore.
Mohanty, J. N. 1992. "On Matilal's Understanding of Indian Philosophy." *Philosophy East and West* 42 (3): 397–406.
Mojab, Shaharzad. 2005. "Islamic Feminism: Alternative or Contradiction?" In *Women and Islam: Critical Concepts in Sociology*, vol. 3, edited by H. Moghissi, 320–25. London: Routledge.
Monier-Williams, Monier. 1963 (1898). *Sanskrit-English Dictionary*. Delhi: Motilal Banarsi Das.
———. 1976. *English-Sanskrit Dictionary*. Delhi: Motilal Banarsi Das.
Monk, Paul. 2015. "The Challenge of an Islamic Reformation." *Quadrant*, July–August. https://quadrant.org.au/magazine/2015/07-08/ayaan-hirsi-alis-reformation-challenge-islam/.
Moors, Annelies. 2005. "Submission." *ISIM Review* 15 (Spring): 8–9.
Moosa, Ebrahim. 2005. *Ghazali and the Poetics of Imagination*. Chapel Hill: University of North Carolina Press.
Moten, Abdul Rashid. 2003. "Mawdudi and the Transformation of Jama'at-E-Islami in Pakistan." *Muslim World* 93 (3): 391–413.
Mughni, Abdul. 1981. *Islāmī adab avr uskē masāʾl*. In *Adab kī tʿāmīrī jehat*, edited by Anjum Naim, 86–95. Aligarh, India: Crescent.

———. 1988. "Ḡhālib ka ikhlāqī noq ṭa-e'-na ẓar." *Sayyārā* 54 (3–4): 33–43.
Murphy, John, and Emil Visnovsky. 2006. "Age of Enlightenment." In *Encyclopedia of Anthropology*, edited by H. Birx, 818–22. Thousand Oaks, Calif.: Sage.
Murtagh, James G. 1946. *Democracy in Australia*. Melbourne: Catholic Social Guild.
Nadvi, Abul Hasan Ali. 1980. *ʿAṣr-e-ḥāẓīr mēñ dīn kī tafhīm v tashrīḥ*. Lucknow, India: Dār-e-ʿarafāt.
———. 2000a. *Karvān-e- zindegī*. Lucknow, India: Maktabā islāmī.
———. 2000b. *Purānē cherāgh*. Lucknow, India: Maktabā firdaus, 2000b.
Nadvi, Muhammad Iqbal Husain. 1990. *ʿArabī tanqīd: Moṭāʿlā v ja'zā*. Hyderabad, India: Central Institute of English and Foreign Languages.
Nadvi, Sulaiman. 1985 (1914). *Islām avr mushtashreqīn*. Azamgarh, India: Dārul muṣannefīn.
Nadwi, Muhammad Akram. 2007. *Al-muḥaddithat: The Women Scholars in Islam*. Oxford, U.K.: Interface.
Nair, Harish. 2015. "Supreme Court Backs CBSE Ban on Head Scarves in Pre-medical Exam." *India Today*, 25 July. http://indiatoday.intoday.in/story/cbse-ban-on-head-scarves-all-india-pre-medical-entrance/1/453963.html.
Naqvi, Nurul Hasan. 2013 (1990). *Fann-e-tanqīd v tanqīd negārī*. 2nd ed. Aligarh, India: Educational Book House.
Narain, Abhilash. 2002. "India World Leader in Unani Medicine." *Azad Academy Journal*, July, 33–34.
Narang, Gopi Chand. 2002. "Ḡhālib: Andāz-e-bāyāñ avr." *Samkālīn bhāratiya sāhitya*, January–February, 5–10.
———. 2009. Endorsement on back cover of *Urdu tanqīd kā aṣlīī chehrā*, edited by Arifa Subh Khan, 464. Lahore: ʿIlm-v-ʿirfān.
Nasr, Seyed Hossein. 2004. *The Heart of Islam: Enduring Values for Humanity*. New York: HarperOne.
Nasr, Syed Vali Reza. 1994. *The Vanguard of Islamic Revolution: The Jamaat-e-Islami of Pakistan*. Berkeley: University of California Press.
———. 1995. "Mawlana Maududi's Autobiography." *Muslim World* 85 (1–2): 49–62.
———. 1996. *Maududi and the Making of Islamic Revivalism*. New York: Oxford University Press.
———. 1999. "European Colonialism and the Emergence of Modern Muslim States." In *The Oxford History of Islam*, edited by John Esposito, 549–600. Oxford: Oxford University Press.
Navaz, Muhammad. 1965. "Taṣṣavvur-e-dīn." *Tajallī*, February–March, 67–87.
NDTV. 2010. "Right-Wing Activists Attack Kashmiri Separatist Leader Mirwaiz in Delhi." http://www.ndtv.com/article/india/right-wing-activists-attack-kashmiri-separatist-leader-mirwaiz-in-delhi-69636.
———. 2011. "Frontier Gandhi: A Forgotten Hero." http://www.ndtv.com/video/player/india-matters/frontier-gandhi-a-forgotten-hero/189293.
———. 2015. "Pak Islamic Body Says Full Face Veil Not Mandatory for Women." http://www.ndtv.com/world-news/pak-islamic-body-says-full-face-veil-not-mandatory-for-women-1234339. Accessed 4 March 2016.
Nesbitt, Eleanor. 1997. "The Body in Sikh Tradition." In *Religion and the Body*, edited by Sarah Coakley, 289–305. Cambridge: Cambridge University Press.
Neumann, Peter. 2009. *Old & New Terrorism: Late Modernity, Globalization and the Transformation of Political Violence*. Cambridge, U.K.: Polity.

Niazi, Kausar. 1973. *Jamāʿt islāmī avāmī ʿadālat mēñ*. Lahore: Qavmī kutubḳhāna.
Nietzsche, Friedrich. 2003. *The Genealogy of Morals*. New York: Dover.
Nomani, Maulana Manzur. 1998. *Mavlānā Mavdūdī kē sātẖ mērī refāqat kī sarguzasht avr ab mērā mavqaf*. Lucknow, India: Al-furqān.
Nomani, Qayyum Hasrat. 1970a. "Mēʿāar-e-naqd." In *Urdu tanqīdnegārī*, edited by Ibadat Barelvi, 65–100. Delhi: Chaman buk depo.
———. 1970b. "Urdu mēñ tanqīd kā irteqāʾ." In *Urdu tanqīdnegārī*, edited by Ibadat Barelvi, 147–243. Delhi: Chaman buk depo.
Nomani, Shibli. 1901. *Al-ghazālī*. Delhi: Farīd buk depo.
———. 1955. *Maqālāt-e-Shiblī -jild*, vol. 3, compiled by Syed Sulaiman Nadwi. Azamgarh, India: Dārul muṣannefīn.
O'Donnell, Patrick. 2011. "Poetry and Islam: An Introduction." *Crosscurrents*, March, 72–87.
O'Keeffe, Brian. 2014. "Jacques Rancière: The Misadventures of Criticism and the Adventures of Hope." In *Criticism after Critique*, edited by Jeffrey Di Leo, 183–208. New York: Palgrave: McMillan.
Offe, Claus. 2015. "Professor Claus Offe." http://baumaninstitute.leeds.ac.uk/people/claus-offe/.
Ohmann, Richard. 1981. "What Is Criticism?" *Radical Teacher* 18: 19–32.
Omar, Irfan. 2004. "Khiẓr-i rāh: The Pre-eminent Guide to Action in Muhammad Iqbal's Thought." *Islamic Studies* 43 (1): 39–50.
Onfray, Michel. 2007 (2005). Preface to *Defence of Atheism: The Case against Christianity, Judaism and Islam*. London: Arcade.
Outram, Dorinda. 2005. *The Enlightenment*. 2nd ed. Cambridge: Cambridge University Press.
Owen, John, IV, and Judd Owen. 2011. "Religion, the Enlightenment, and the New Global Order." In *Religion, the Enlightenment, and the New Global Order*, edited by John Owen IV and Judd Owen, 3–36. New York: Columbia University Press.
Oxford English Dictionary Online. 2009a. "Literary, adj. and n." http://www.oed.com/view/Entry/109067?redirectedFrom=Literary+Criticism. Accessed 18 December 2016.
———. 2009b. "Text, n.1." http://www.oed.com/view/Entry/200002?. Accessed 18 December 2016.
Oxford Islamic Studies Online. 2012. "Women and Islam." http://www.oxfordislamicstudies.com/article/opr/t125/e2510.
Pabst, Adrian. 2013. "Liberalism." In *Handbook on the Economics of Reciprocity and Social Enterprise*, edited by Luigino Bruni and Stefano Zamagni, 217–26. London: Edward Elgar.
Pal, Amitabh. 2011. *"Islam" Means Peace: Understanding the Muslim Principle of Nonviolence Today*. Santa Barbara, Calif.: Praeger.
Palmquist, Stephen. 2016. *Comprehensive Commentary on Kant's Religion within the Bounds of Bare Reason*. Malden, Mass.: Wiley Blackwell.
Parkin, David. 1984. "Political Language." *Annual Review of Anthropology* 13: 345–65.
Patel, Vibhuti. 1988. "Emergence and Proliferation of Autonomous Women's Groups in India: 1974–1984." In *Women in Indian Society*, edited by Rehana Ghadially, 249–56. Delhi: Sage.
Pathak, Zakia, and Rajeswari Sunder Rajan. 1989. "Shahbano." *Signs* 14 (3): 558–82.
Patterson, Thomas. 2009. "The Enlightenment and Anthropology." In *Karl Marx, Anthropologist*, 9–37. New York: Berg.
Pedersen, Esther Oluffa, and Sune Liisberg. 2015. "Introduction: Trust and Hope." In

Anthropology and Philosophy: Dialogues on Trust and Hope, edited by Sune Liisberg, Esther O. Pedersen and Anne L. Dålsgard, 1–19. New York: Berghahn.
Pellat, Ch. 2012. "Ḥamāsa." In *Encyclopaedia of Islam*, 2nd ed., edited by P. Bearman, Th. Bianquis, C. E. Bosworth, E. van Donzel, and W. P. Heinrichs. *Brill Online*. http://referenceworks.brillonline.com/entries/encyclopaedia-of-islam-2/hamasa-COM_0258.
Perchard, Adam. 2015. "The Fatwa and the Philosophe: Rushdie, Voltaire, and Islam." *Journal of Commonwealth Literature* 51 (3): 1–18.
Perovic, Sanja. 2012. "French Revolution as World Religion." In *Sacred and Secular in Early Modern France: Fragments of Religion*, edited by Sanja Perovic, 125–43. New York: Bloomsbury.
Peters, Rudolph. 1990. "Reinhard Schulze's Quest for an Islamic Enlightenment." *Die Welt des Islams*, n.s., 1 (4): 160–62.
Petrasch, Charles. 1932. "An Interview with Gandhi." *Le Monde*, 10 February. https://www.marxists.org/history/international/comintern/sections/britain/periodicals/labour_monthly/1932/04/x02.htm#1b.
Pocock, J. G. A. 1997. "Enthusiasm: The Antiself of Enlightenment." *Huntington Library Quarterly* 60 (1–2): 7–28.
———. 2008. "Historiography and Enlightenment: A View of Their History." *Modern Intellectual History* 5 (1): 83–96.
Poliakov, Leon. 1982. "Racism from the Enlightenment to the Age of Imperialism." In *Racism and Colonialism*, edited by Robert Ross, 55–64. The Hague: Martinus Nijhoff.
Pollock, Sheldon. 2005. "Axialism and Empire." In *Axial Civilizations and World History*, edited by Johann P. Arnason, S. N. Eisenstadt and Björn Wittrock, 397–450. Leiden, the Netherlands: Brill.
Popper, Karl. 1969. *The Open Society and Its Enemies*. London: Routledge and Kegan Paul.
———. 1972. "On Reason and the Open Society." *Encounter* 37 (5): 13–18.
Power, Carla. 2007. "A Secret History." *New York Times Magazine*, 25 February. http://www.nytimes.com/2007/02/25/magazine/25wwlnEssay.t.html.
Preckel, Claudia. 2008. "Philosophers, Freedom Fighters and Phantomimes: South Asian Muslims in Germany." In *Islam and Muslims in Germany*, edited by Ala Al-Hamerneh and Jorn Thielmann, 299–328. Leiden, the Netherlands: Brill.
Pricthard, David. 1996. "Thucydides and the Tradition of the Athenian Funeral Oration." *Ancient History* 26: 137–50.
Priest, John. 2016. "Philosopher of the Month: Immanuel Kant." *Oxford University Press Blog*, 3 April. http://blog.oup.com/2016/04/philosopherotm-immanuel-kant/.
Pritchett, Frances. 1994. *Nets of Awareness: Urdu Poetry and Its Critics*. Berkeley: University of California Press.
Putnam, Hilary. 1981. *Reason, Truth and History*. Cambridge: Cambridge University Press.
Qadir, Abdul. 2009. "Modern India and the West: A Study of Urdu Prose." In *Islam in South Asia*, vol. 4, *The Realm of the Secular*, edited by Mushirul Hasan, 217–30. Delhi: Manohar.
Qasmi, Abul Kalam. 1981. "Jadīd afsāanē mēñ rūḥānīyat avr mʿādīyat kī kashmakas." In *Adab kī tʿāmīrī jehat*, edited by Anjum Naim, 36–45. Aligarh, India: Crescent.
Qasmi, Ali Usman. 2011. *Questioning the Authority of the Past: The Ahl al-Quran Movements in the Punjab*. Karachi: Oxford University Press.
Qasmi, Ikhlaq Husain. 2000. "Āh! Tāʿlīmul islām vālē muftī sāḥib." *Al-jamīʿat* 13 (May): 14–15. Muftī–e–ʿ āẓam nabmar of *Al-jamīʿat* 23 February 1953, with new arrangement and addition. New Delhi.

Qasmi, Mohammad Aslam. 2011. *Urdu tanqīd avr uskā pasmanzar*. Meerut, India: 3 ZR.
Qasmi, Moʿizuddin Ahmad. 2000. "Gulshan-e-q āsmī k ā gul-e-sarsabz." *Al-jamīʿat* 13 (May): 135–40. Muftī–e-ʿ āẓam nabmar of *Al-jamīʿat* 23 February 1953, with new arrangement and addition. New Delhi.
Qasmi, Mufti Zainul Islam. 2012. *Chand aham ʿaṣrī masāʾl*. Deoband, India: Maktabā dārul ʿulūm.
Quadri, Safdar Imam. n.d.. "Kalīmuddīn Aḥmad kī tanqīdāt pe dāktar abdul moghnī kī āra." In *Kalīmuddīn Aḥmad sēmīnār kē maqālē*, edited by Bihar Urdu Academy, 1–6. https://www.academia.edu/12139558/The_Evaluation_of_Dr_Abdul_Moghnis_opinion_about_famous_Urdu_critic_Kalimuddin_Ahmad.
Quaiser, Neshat. 2012. "Unani Medical Culture: Memory, Representation, and the Literate Critical Anticolonial Public Sphere." In *Contesting Colonial Authority: Medicine and Indigenous Responses in Nineteenth- and Twentieth-Century India*, edited by Poonam Bala, 115–35. Lanham, Md.: Lexington.
Quinn, Fredrick. 2008. *The Sum of All Heresies*. New York: Oxford University Press.
Quraish, Qazi Ali Mustafa. 2010. "Manzil unhēñ mīlī jo sharīk-e-safar na thē." *Dosrārukh*. https://dosrarukh.wordpress.com/2010/08/13/61/.
Radin, Paul. 1927. *Primitive Man as Philosopher*. New York: Appleton.
Rahnema, Ali. 2007. "Ali Shariati: Teacher, Preacher, Rebel." In *Pioneers of Islamic Revival*, updated ed., edited by Ali Rahnema, 208–50. London: Zed.
Ram, Malik. 1989. *Kuchch abul kalām āzād kē bārē mēñ*. New Delhi: Maktabā jāmiʿā.
———. 1992. *Ḥambūrābi avr bābulī tahzīb v tamaddun*. New Delhi: Maktabā jāmiʿā.
Ramadan, Tariq. 2004. *Western Muslims and the Future of Islam*. New York: Oxford University Press.
Rancière, Jacques. 2009. *The Emancipated Spectator*. Translated by Gregory Elliott. London: Verso.
Rasch, William. 2009. "Enlightenment as Religion." *New German Critique* 36 (3): 109–31.
Rawls, John. 1993. *Political Liberalism*. New York: Columbia University Press.
Reiss, Hans. 1991 (1970). "Postscript." In *Kant's Political Writings*, 2nd ed. enlarged, edited by Hans Reiss, 250–72. Cambridge: Cambridge University Press.
RIR. 1951. *Rūdāde ijtimāʿ rāmpūr jamāʿt islāmī hind 1951*. Delhi: Jamāʿt islāmī hind.
Rizvi, Sajjad. 2005. "Mysticism and Philosophy: Ibn Arabi and Mulla Sadra." In *The Cambridge Companion to Arabic Philosophy*, edited by Peter Adamson and R. C. Taylor, 224–46. Cambridge: Cambridge University Press.
Robertson, Jennifer. 2002. "Reflexivity Redux: A Pithy Polemic on 'Positionality." *Anthropological Quarterly* 75 (4): 785–92.
Robinson, Francis. 2000. *Islam and Muslim History in South Asia*. Delhi: Oxford University Press.
———. 2008. "Islamic Reform and Modernities in South Asia." *Modern Asian Studies* 42 (2–3): 259–81.
Rooney, Phyllis. 1991. "Gendered Reason: Sex Metaphor and Conceptions of Reason." *Hypatia* 6 (2): 77–103.
Roy, Olivier. 1994. *The Failure of Political Islam*. Translated by Carol Volk. Cambridge, Mass.: Harvard University Press.
Rudwick, Martin J. S. 1986. *The Great Devonian Controversy: The Shaping of Scientific Knowledge*. Chicago: Chicago University Press.
Ruhela, Satya Pal, ed. 1990. *Empowerment of the Indian Muslim Women*. Delhi: MD.
Rumi, Jalaluddin Mauvlana. 1974. *Maśnavī, jild 2*. Lahore: Hamid.

Rushdie, Salman. 2005. "Muslims Unite! A New Reformation Will Bring Your Faith into the Modern Era." *Times* (of London), 11 August. http://www.thetimes.co.uk/tto/law /columnists/article2048308.ece.
———. 2006. "Inside the Mind of Jihadists." *New Perspectives Quarterly* 23 (1): 7–11.
———. 2009. "Salman Rushdie and Irshad Manji at 92nd Street Y." http://www.youtube .com/watch?v=lc6oro81dIw.
Russell, Bertrand. 1920. *Practice and Theory of Bolshevism*. New York: Cosimo.
Russell, Ralph. 2000. *The Famous Ghalib*. Delhi: Rolli.
Saadi, Shaikh. 1949. *Kullīyāt-e-sāʿdī*. Edited by Mohammad Ali Foroughi. Tehran: Amīr kabīr.
Sachedina, Abdulaziz. 2001. *The Islamic Roots of Democratic Pluralism*. New York: Oxford University Press.
Sacks, Jeffrey. 2007. "Futures of Literature: Inhitat, Adab, Naqd." *Diacritics* 37 (4): 32–55.
Sadruddin. 1965. "Ḵhaṭ mavlānā ṣadruddīn banām modīr-e-tajallī." *Tajallī*, February–March, 51–63.
Saeed, Ahmad Abu. 1998. *Bisvīn̄ sadī ka qā'ed-e-ʿālā: Abul ʿAlā Mavdūdī*. Hyderabad, India: Idāra Shān.
Sahgal, Gita, and Nira Yuval-Davis, eds. 1992. *Refusing Holy Orders: Women and Fundamentalism in Britain*. London: Virago.
Sahlins, Marshall. 1999. "What Is Anthropological Enlightenment? Some Lessons of the Twentieth Century." *Annual Review of Anthropology* 28: i–xxiii.
Said, Edward. 1995 (1978). *Orientalism*. 2nd ed. London: Penguin.
Sajjad, Ahmad. 1979. *Tanqīd v taḥrīk*. Ranchi, India: Gahvāra-e-adab.
———. 1981. "Islāmī adab avr uskē masā'l." In *Adab kī tʿāmīrī jehat*, edited by Anjum Naim, 86–95. Aligarh, India: Crescent.
———. 1994. *Tāʿmīrī adabī taḥrīk*. New Delhi: Qāzī.
Saleem, Shehzad. 2009. *Islam and Women: Misconceptions and Misrepresentations*. Lahore: Al-Mawrid.
Salman, Ali. 2007. "Sarvar kā qatl ke jurm sē inkār." *BBC*, 10 March. http://www.bbc.com /urdu/pakistan/story/2007/03/printable/070310_zille_huma_hearing_fz.shtml.
Salvatore, Armando. 2007. *Public Sphere: Liberal Modernity, Catholicism, Islam*. New York: Palgrave.
———. 2013. "Islam and the Quest for a European Secular Identity: From Sovereignty through Solidarity to Immunity." *Politics, Religion & Ideology*, 14 (2): 253–64.
Samiuddin, Abida. 2007. *Encyclopaedic Dictionary of Urdu Literature*, vol. 1. New Delhi: Global Vision.
Sandoval, Timothy. 2006. *The Discourse of Wealth and Poverty in the Book of Proverbs*. Leiden, the Netherlands: Brill.
Sangari, Kumkum. 1990. "Mirabai and the Spiritual Economy of Bhakti." *Economic and Political Weekly* 25 (27): 1464–75.
Sapir, David. 1977. Introduction to *The Social Use of Metaphor: Essays on the Anthropology of Rhetoric*, edited by David Sapir and Christopher Crocker, 69–73. Philadelphia: University of Pennsylvania Press.
Sardar, Ziauddin. 2008. "The Reformist." *News on Sunday* (Karachi), 23 November. http:// ziauddinsardar.com/2011/02/the-reformist/.
Sarvar, Muhammad. 1947. "Arẓ-e-mutarjim v pēsh-e-lafẓ." In *Moshāhidāt v maʿārif*, by Shah Valiullah, translated from the Arabic into Urdu and with an introduction by Muhammad Sarvar, 3–16. Lahore: Sindh Sagar Academy.

Sayeed, Khalid. 1961. "Pakistan's Basic Democracy." *Middle East Journal* 15 (3): 249–63.

Sayyid, Salman. 1998. "Anti-essentialism and Universalism." *Innovation: The European Journal of Social Science Research* 11 (4): 377–89.

SBS-1. 2012. "Meet the Amish." Broadcast, 5 September.

Schimmel, Annemarie. 1992. *Islam: An Introduction*. Albany: State University of New York Press.

Schott, Robin. 2000. "Kant." In *A Companion to Feminist Philosophy*, edited by Alison Jaggar and Iris Young, 39–48. Malden, Mass.: Blackwell.

Schulze, Reinhard. 2000. "Is There an Islamic Modernity?" In *The Islamic World and the West: An Introduction to Political Cultures and International Relations*, edited by Kai Hafez, 21–32. Leiden, the Netherlands: Brill.

Scott-Smith, Giles. 2010. "The Congress for Cultural Freedom: Constructing an Intellectual Atlantic Community." In *Defining the Atlantic Community: Culture, Intellectuals, and Policies in the Mid-Twentieth Century*, edited by M. Mariano, 132–45. London: Routledge.

Sen, Amartya. 2005. *The Argumentative Indian: Writings on Indian History, Culture and Identity*. London: Allen Lane.

Sen, Arup Kumar. 2008. "Nandigram: A Tale of Developmental Violence." *Economic and Political Weekly* 43 (37): 31–32.

Shah, Sayed Wiqar Ali. 2007. "Abdul Ghaffar Khan, the Ḳhudāī Ḳhidmatgārs, Congress and the Partition of India." *Pakistan Vision* 8 (2): 86–115.

———. 2013. "The 1930 Civil Disobedience Movement in Peshawar Valley from the Pashtoon Perspective." *Studies in History* 29 (1): 87–118.

Shaheen, Shabana. 1990. "Family Environment, Education and Vertical Social Mobility: Ten Case Studies of Highly Successful Indian Muslim Women in Different Professional Fields." In *Empowerment of the Indian Muslim Women*, edited by Satya Pal Ruhela, 37–76. Delhi: MD.

Shaikh, Farzana. 2009. *Making Sense of Pakistan*. Delhi: Foundation.

Shaikh, Nermeen. 2004. "The Jew, the Arab: An Interview with Gil Anidjar." *Asia Society*. http://asiasociety.org/jew-arab-interview-gil-anidjar.

Shakur, Abdus. 1954. *Ḥasrat mohānī*. 4th ed. Lucknow, India: Anwar.

Shankar, S. 1994. "The Thumb of Ekalavya: Postcolonial Studies and the 'Third World' Scholar in a Neocolonial World." *World Literature Today* 68 (3): 479–87.

Shaqqa, Abdulhalim Abu. N.d. *Ḳhavātīn ki āzādī ʿahd-e-risālat mēñ*. Translated into Urdu by Hasnain Nadvi. Herndon, Va.: International Institute of Islamic Thought.

Sharar, Abdul Halim. 2009. "The Development of Urdu Prose." In *Islam in South Asia*. Vol. 4, *The Realm of the Secular*, edited by Mushirul Hasan, 201–5. Delhi: Manohar.

Shariati, Ali. 1979. *On the Sociology of Islam*. Translated by Hamid Algar. Berkeley, Calif.: Mizan.

Sharp, Gene. 1960. *Gandhi Wields the Weapon of Moral Power: Three Case Histories*. Ahmedabad, India: Navajivan.

Shaz, Rashid. 2006. *Islam: Negotiating the Future*. Delhi: Milli.

Shils, Edward. 1972. *The Intellectual and the Powers, and Other Essays*. Chicago: University of Chicago Press.

Shumway, David. 2014. "Criticism and Critique: A Genealogy." In *Criticism after Critique*, edited by Jeffrey Leo, 15–25. London: Palgrave Macmillan.

Siddiqi, Naeem. 1999. *Muḥsin-e-insānīyat*. New ed. Delhi: Markazī maktabā islāmī.

Siddiqi, Nejatullah. 1995. *Taḥrīk-e-islāmī ʿaṣr-e-ḥāẓir mēñ*. Delhi: Markazi markazī maktabā islāmī.

———. 2000. *Islām, maʿāshiāt avr adab: Ḳḳhaṭūṭ kē āʾīne mēñ*. Aligarh, India: Educational House.

———. 2003. "Taḥrīk-e-islāmī: Āj kē qāabil-e- ghaur masāʾl." In *Taḥrīk-e-islāmī badalt ē huē ḥ ālāt mēñ*, edited by Mumtaz Ali, 89–102. New Delhi: Markazī maktabā islāmī.

———. 2004. "Maqāṣid al-sharīʿat: ēk ʿaṣrī mut āʿla." *Fikr-v-naẓar* 41 (4): 3–34.

Siddiqi, Zaheer Ahmad. 2000. *Tanqīd v taḥqīq-e-adbīyāt*. Lahore: GC University.

Sieg, Katrine. 2010. "Black Virgins: Sexuality and the Democratic Body in Europe." *New German Critique* 37 (1): 147–85.

Sifton, John. 2015. *Violence all Around*. Cambridge, Mass.: Harvard University Press.

Silverman, Sydel. 2005. "The United States." In Fredrik Barth, Andre Gingrich, Robert Parkin, and Sydel Silverman, *One Discipline, Four Ways: British, German, French and American Anthropology*, 257–347. Chicago: Chicago University Press.

Singh, Bhupinder. 2014. "The Five Symbols of Sikhism." *Sikh Formation: Religion, Culture, Theory* 10 (1): 105–72.

Singh, Yogendra. 1972. *Modernization of Indian Tradition: A Systemic Study of Social Change*. Jaipur, Delhi: Rawat.

Siran, Jean-Louis. 1993. "Rhetoric, Tradition and Communication: The Dialectics of Meaning in Proverb Use." *Man*, n.s., 28 (2): 225–42.

Smith, David. 2003. *Hinduism and Modernity*. Malden, Mass.: Blackwell.

Smith, Wilfred Cantwell. 1946. *Modern Islam in India: A Social Analysis*. London: Victor Gollancz.

Sohoni, Shrinivas Rao S. 1995. "Badshah Khan: Islam and Non-violence." In *Khan Abdul Ghaffar Khan: A Centennial Tribute*, edited by Nehru Memorial Musuem and Library, 35–49. Delhi: Har-Anand.

Soroush, Abdulkarim. 2000. *Reason, Freedom, and Democracy in Islam: Essential Writings of Abdolkarim Soroush*. Translated and introduced by Mahmoud Sadri and Ahmad Sadri. New York: Oxford University Press.

Spencer, Robert. 1954. "The Humanities in Cultural Anthropology." In *Method and Perspective in Anthropology*, edited by Robert Spencer, 126–44. Minneapolis: University of Minnesota Press.

Spivak, Gayatri Chakravorty. 1990. *The Post-colonial Critic: Interviews, Strategies, Dialogues*. Edited by Sarah Harasym. New York: Routledge.

Srinivas, M. N. 1998. "Social Anthropology and Literary Sensibility." *Economic and Political Weekly*, 26 September, 2525–28.

Stahl, Titus. 2013. "Habermas and the Project of Immanent Critique." *Constellations* 20 (4): 533–52.

Stanford University Press website. 2006. "About the Author." Description of Jonathan Culler, *The Literary in Theory*. http://www.sup.org/books/title/?id=9845.

Stark, Rodney. 2006a. "A Civil Religion: How Christianity Created Free and Prosperous Societies." *American Enterprise*, May, 16–19.

———. 2006b. *The Victory of Reason: How Christianity Led to Freedom, Capitalism, and Western Success*. New York: Random House.

Stephens, Mitchell. 2014. *Imagine There's No Heaven: How Atheism Helped Create the Modern World*. New York: St. Martin.

Stowasser, Barbara. 2001. "Old Shaykhs, Young Women, and the Internet: The Rewriting of Women's Political Rights in Islam." *Muslim World* 91 (1–2): 99–120.

Suroor, Al-e Ahmad. 2011. *Tanqīd keyā hai*. New Delhi: Maktabā jāmiʿā.
Tai, Hung-chao. 1974. *Land Reform and Politics: A Comparative Analysis*. Berkeley: University of California Press.
Tambiah, Stanley. 1990. *Magic, Science and Religion and the Scope of Rationality*. Cambridge: Cambridge University Press.
Tarcov, Nathan, and Thomas Pangle. 1987. "Epilogue: Leo Strauss and the History of Political Philosophy." In *History of Political Philosophy*, 3rd ed., edited by Leo Strauss and Joseph Cropsey, 907–38. Chicago: Chicago University Press.
Tareen, SherAli. 2017. "Revolutionary Hermeneutics: Translating the Qur'an as a Manifesto for Revolution." *Journal of Religious and Political Practice* 3 (1–2): 1–24.
Tarrow, Sidney. 1998. *Power in Movement*, 2nd ed. Cambridge: Cambridge University Press.
Taylor, Charles. 2004. *Modern Social Imaginaries*. Durham, N.C.: Duke University Press.
Tayob, Abdulkader. 2010. *Religion in Modern Islamic Discourse*. London: Hurst.
Temple, Capt. R. C. 1885. "North Indian Proverbs." *Folk-Lore Journal* 3 (1): 16–44.
Thanawi, Ashraf Ali. N.d. *Ashraful javāb*. Deoband, India: Kutubḳhāna naʿīmīa.
Thapar, Romila. 1975. "Ethics, Religion, and Social Protest in the First Millennium B.C. in Northern India." *Daedalus* 104 (2): 119–32.
Thomassen, Bjørn. 2010. "Anthropology, Multiple Modernities and the Axial Age Debate." *Anthropological Theory* 10 (4): 321–42.
Thompson, Yvonne, George Brandis, and Tom Harley, eds. 1986. *Australian Liberalism: The Continuing Vision*. Melbourne: A Liberal Forum Publication.
Thorpe, Lucas. 2015. *The Kant Dictionary*. London: Bloomsbury.
Tilly, Charles. 1984. "Social Movement and National Politics." In *State-Making and Social Movements*, edited by Charles Bright and Susan Harding, 294–317. Ann Arbor: University of Michigan Press.
Tiryakian, Edward. 2005. "Durkheim, Solidarity, and September 11." In *The Cambridge Companion to Durkheim*, edited by Jeffrey Alexander and Philip Smith, 305–21. Cambridge: Cambridge University Press.
Tompkins, Jeff. 2013. "Interview: Debut Novelist Weighs In with Towering Portrayal of 19th-Century India." *Asiasociety.org*, 22 August. http://asiasociety.org/blog/asia/interview-debut-novelist-weighs-towering-portrayal-19th-century-india.
Trouillot, Michel-Rolph. 1995. *Silencing the Past: Power and Production of History*. Boston: Beacon.
Trumpbour, John. 2003. "The Clash of Civilizations: Samuel Huntington, Bernard Lewis, and the Remaking of the Post–Cold War World Order." In *The New Crusades: Constructing the Muslim Enemy*, edited by E. Qureshi and Michael A. Sells, 89–130. New York: Columbia University Press.
Turner, Bryan. 2007. "Minorities and Modernity: The Crisis of Liberal Secularism." *Citizenship Studies* 11 (5): 501–8.
———. 2016. "Max Weber and the Sociology of Religion." *Revue Internationale de Philosophie* 70 (276): 140–50.
Uberoi, J. P. Singh. 1990. "The Five Symbols of Sikhism." In *Sikhism*, edited by L. M. Joshi, 131–46. Patiala, India: Punjabi University.
Urdu Point. 2007. "Ḳhātūn ṣūbāī vazīr kā qatl." 1 March. http://daily.urdupoint.com/article/all/khatoon-sobai-wazir-zilly-huma-ka-qatal-1461.html.
Usmani, Amir. 1965. "Vaḥiduddīn ḳhān sāḥab kī tʿābīr kī ghalaṭī." *Tajallī*, February–March, 99–125.
———. 1973. "Tafhīmul Qurʾān per chand ʿetarāẓāt." *Tajallī*, May, 43–65.

———. 2002. "Ḥiṣṣā avval." In *Mavlānā mavdūdī sē mavlānā noʿmān kē iḳhtelāf kā ʿilmī jā'zā*, edited by Akhtar Hijazi, 21–103. Lahore:ʿIlm-v-ʿirfān.
Usmani, Shah Rashad. 1999. *Adab kā islāmī tanāẓur*. Delhi: Applied.
Vadet, J. C. 2012. "Ḳalb." In *Encyclopaedia of Islam*, 2nd ed., edited by P. Bearman, Th. Bianquis, C. E. Bosworth, E. van Donzel, and W. P. Heinrichs. *Brill Online*. http://referenceworks.brillonline.com/entries/encyclopaedia-of-islam-2/kalb-COM_0424.
Valiullah, Shah. 1947. *Moshāhidāt v maʿārif*. Translated from the Arabic into Urdu and introduced by Muhammad Sarvar. Lahore: Sindh Sagar Academy.
———. 1996. *The Conclusive Argument from God: Shāh Valī Allāh of Delhi's "Ḥujjat Allāh al Bāligha."* Translated by M. K. Hermansen. Leiden, the Netherlands: Brill.
———. N.d. *Ḥujjat Allāh al Bāligha*. Translated by Mavlana Khalil Ahmad. Delhi: ʿEtaqād.
Van der Veer, Peter, ed. 1996. *Conversion to Modernities: The Globalization of Christianity*. London: Routledge.
———. 2001. *Imperial Encounters: Religion and Modernity in India and Britain*. Princeton, N.J.: Princeton University Press.
Van Ess, Josef. 2006. "Islam and the Axial Age." In *Islam in Process: Historical and Civilizational Perspectives*. Vol. 7 of *Yearbook of the Sociology of Islam*, edited by Johann Arnason, Armando Salvatore, and Georg Stauth, 220–37. Bielefeld, Germany: Transcript.
van Kley, Dale. 2012. "Robert Palmer's Catholics and Unbelievers in Eighteenth-Century France: An Overdue Tribute." In *Sacred and Secular Agency in Early Modern France: Fragments of Religion*, edited by Sanja Perovic, 13–36. New York: Bloomsbury.
Van Maanen, John. 1988. *Tales of the Field: On Writing Ethnography*. Chicago: University of Chicago Press.
Van Schendel, Willem. 2009. *A History of Bangladesh*. Cambridge: Cambridge University Press.
Vincent, Joan. 2002. "Introduction" and "Introduction to Part I." In *The Anthropology of Politics: A Reader in Ethnography, Theory and Critique*, 1–13, 16–20. Malden, Mass.: Blackwell.
Viswanathan, Gauri. 1989. *Masks of Conquest: Literary Study and British Rule in India*. Delhi: Oxford University Press.
———. 2008. "Secularism in the Framework of Heterodoxy." *PMLA* 123 (2): 466–76.
Voll, John. 2007. "Islam and Democracy: Is Modernization a Barrier?" *Religion Compass* 1 (1): 170–78.
Voltaire. 2000. *Treatise on Tolerance and Other Writings*. Translated and edited by Simon Harvey. Cambridge: Cambridge University Press.
Wajhi, Mulla. 1953. *Sabras*. N.p.: n.p. http://mausc1.blogspot.com.au/.
Walbridge, John. 2010. *God and Logic in Islam: The Caliphate of Reason*. Cambridge: Cambridge University Press.
Walzer, Michael. 1987. *Interpretation and Social Criticism*. Cambridge, Mass.: Harvard University Press.
———. 1988. *The Company of Critics: Social Criticism and Commitment in the Twentieth Century*. New York: Basic Books.
Watt, M. W. 1988. *Islamic Fundamentalism and Modernity*. London: Routledge.
Weber, Cynthia. 2005 (2001). *International Relations Theory: A Critical Introduction*. 2nd ed. London: Routledge.
Weber, Max. 1992. *The Protestant Ethic and the Spirit of Capitalism*. Translated by Talcott Parsons. London: Routledge.

Weiss, Anita. 2014. *Interpreting Islam, Modernity, and Women's Rights in Pakistan*. New York: Palgrave.
Werner, Yvonne Maria, and Jonas Harvard. 2013. "European Anti-Catholicism in Comparative and Transnational Perspective—The Role of a Unifying Other: An Introduction." In *European Anti-Catholicism in a Comparative and Transnational Perspective*, edited by Yvonne Maria Werner and Jonas Harvard, 13–22. Amsterdam: Rodopi.
West, Ed. 2012. "Can Islam Ever Accept Higher Criticism?" *Telegraph*, 29 August.
Whine, Michael. 2001. "Islamism and Totalitarianism: Similarities and Differences." *Totalitarian Movements and Political Religions* 2 (2): 54–72.
Whybray, R. Norman. 1994. *The Composition of the Book of Proverbs*. Sheffield, U.K.: Academic.
Williams, David. 2012. "Voltaire." In *The History of Western Philosophy of Religion*. Vol. 3, *Early Modern Philosophy of Religion*, edited by Graham Oppy and Nic Trakakis, 197–209. Durham, U.K.: Acumen.
Williams, Raymond. 1983. *Keywords: A Vocabulary of Culture and Society*. Rev. ed. New York: Oxford University Press.
Willmer, David. 1996. "Women as Participants in the Pakistan Movement: Modernization and the Promise of a Moral State." *Modern Asian Studies* 30 (3): 573–90.
Winter, Bronwyn. 2001a. "Fundamental Misunderstandings: Issues in Feminist Approaches to Islamism." *Journal of Women's History* 13 (1): 9–41.
———. 2001b. "Naming the Oppressor, Not Punishing the Oppressed: Atheism and Feminist Legitimacy." *Journal of Women's History* 13 (1): 53–57.
Wirth, Louis. 1945. "The Problem of Minority Groups." In *The Science of Man in the World Crisis*, edited by Ralph Linton, 347–72. New York: Columbia University Press.
"Wisdom, Revelation, and Doubt: Perspectives on the First Millennium BC." 1975. Special issue, *Daedalus* 104 (2.
Wittgenstein, Ludwig. 1958. *Preliminary Studies for the "Philosophical Investigations" Generally Known as "The Blue and Brown Books."* New York: Harper and Row.
———. 1980 (1977). *Culture and Value*. Edited by G. V. Von Wright and Heikki Nyman and translated by Peter Winch. Chicago: University of Chicago Press.
Wittrock, Bjorn. 2012. "The Axial Age in Global History: Cultural Crystallizations and Societal Transformations." In *The Axial Age and Its Consequences*, edited by Robert Bellah and Hans Joas, 102–25. Cambridge, Mass.: Belknap Press of Harvard University Press.
Wolfe, Patrick. 2002. "Can the Muslim Speak? An Indebted Critique—Review of Spivak's *A Critique of Postcolonial Reason*." *Theory and History*, 41 (3): 367–80.
Wulf, Christoph. 2013. *Anthropology: A Continental Perspective*. Translated by Deirdre Winter, Elizabeth Hamilton Margitta, and Richard Rouse. Chicago: Chicago University Press.
Yaman, Hikmet. 2008. "The Concept of *Hikmah* in Early Islamic Thought." PhD diss., Harvard University.
YouTube. 2010. "Bacha Khan Documentary 6." https://www.youtube.com/watch?v=jv4nV9eCmL8.
Yusuf, Mufti Mohammad. 1999 (1964). *Mavlānā Mavdūdī par ʿetaraẓāt k ā ʿilmī jāʾezā, ḥiṣṣā 1*. Delhi: Markazī Maktabā Isāmī.
Zakarya, Muhammad Mavlana. 1976. *Fitna-e-mavdūdīat*. Saharanpur, India: Ishāʿtul ʿulūm.

Zaman, Muhammad Qasim. 2006. "Consensus and Religious Authority in Modern Islam: The Discourses of the Ulema." In *Speaking for Islam: Religious Authorities in Muslim Societies*, edited by Gudrun Kramer and Sabina Schmidtke S, 153–80. Leiden, the Netherlands: Brill.

———. 2012. *Modern Islamic Thought in a Radical Age: Religious Authority and Internal Criticism*. Cambridge: Cambridge University Press, 2012.

Zia, Afiya Shehrba(2015. "Faith-Based Challenges to the Women's Movement in Pakistan." In *Contesting Feminisms: Gender and Islam in South Asia*, edited by Huma Ahmed-Ghosh, 181–204. Albany: State University of New York Press.

Zindegī. Jamā't Islāmī Hind's monthly Urdu journal published from Rāmpūr. June–August, October 1951; March 1958; May 1961; August 1964; September 1980.

Zindegī-e-nav (*ZN*). Jamā't Islāmī Hind's new monthly Urdu journal published from New Delhi. June 1999; January–June 2002.

Zuberi, Bilal. 1999. "The Pakistan's Coup: Other Side." *The Tech*, 22 October.

Index

Page numbers in italics refer to illustrations.

Abduh, Muhammad, 207, 220n4
Abdullah of Deccan, Sultan, 74
Abdussattar, 184
Abedi, Mehdi, 13, 50, 93
Abousenna, Mona, 60
Abraham, 15, 55–56, 80, 116–17
Abrahamov, Binyamin, 48, 62
Abu Bakr, 143, 167
Abullais, 217n13. *See also* Nadvi, Abul Hasan Ali
Abu-Lughod, Leila, 156
"Across Europe, Worries on Islam Spread to Center" (*New York Times*), 7–8
Adab, 67–68, 76
Adam, 56, 80, 113
Adil, 151–53
Adil, Adnan, 155
Afary, Janet, 156
Afghani, Jamaluddin, 207
Afghanistan, 91
Agamben, Giorgio, 152
Agha, Vazir, 63, 72, 213n8
Agnihotri, Indu, 174
Ahl-e-ḥadīs school, 141
Ahmad, Aijaz, 158, 164
Ahmad, Irfan, 11, 20, 80, 94, 157, 176, 183, 199–200, 219n11
Ahmad, Kalimuddin, 19, 65, 71–72, 179
Ahmad, Khursheed, 56
Ahmad, Nazir, 161
Ahmad, Sadaf, 156
Ahmad, Sayyid, 107
Ahmed, Akbar, 184, 187
Ahmed, Imtiaz, 156, 179–80, 218n3
Ahmed, Ishtiaq, 155
Ahmed, Leila, 156, 176
Ahmed, Qazi Hussain, 163
Ahmed, Tariq, 57
Ahsan, Amin, 217n22
Ajiz, Kalim, 213n9
Akbar, Ijaz, 145–47
Akhtar, Saleem, 71
Al-Ashmawy, Muhammad Said, 133
Al-Azm, Sadik, 10
Al-Balāgh, 186, 205
al-Banna, Hasan, 92, 99
Albayrak, Ismail, 85
Al-Beruni, 42
al-Bustani, Butrus, 68
al-Dardā, Umm, 172
Al-Furqān (journal), 123–24
Al-Hambra, 207
Al-Hilāl, 186, 207
al-Hudaybi, Hassan Ismail, 134
Ali, Ayaan Hirsi, 10–11
Ali, Azra Asghar, 218n3
Ali, Kamran Asdar, 218n7
Aligarh, 147, 151, 174–75, 186, 200, 215n12
Aligarh Monthly, 64–65
Aligarh Muslim University (AMU), 23, 140–41, 145, 165, 168, 216n10
Al-Jihad fil Islam (Maududi), 214n16
Al-Juwaini, 58
al-Juwayni, Yusuf, 144
Alkaf, Abdurrahman, 169, 175, 177
Allahabad University, 182, 191
Allam, Shawki Ibrahim Abdel-Karim, 200
Allana, Ghulam, 184
al-Mawardi, 215n23
Almond, Ian, 38–39, 41, 77
Al-Musleh, M. A., 80
al-Samarqandi, Shams al-Din Muhammad bin Ashraf al-Husaini, 58
al-Shafi, Imam, 105

al-Sisi, Fattah, 200
al-Sulayhiyya, Malika Arwa Bint Shihab, 159
al-Tabari, Muhammad Ibn, 135
al-Zamakhshari, Umar, 215n23
Ambedkar, B. R., 22, 55
Amish, 16–17
Amritsar, 192
Anderson, J. N. D., 57
Anidjar, Gil, 9, 13, 33
Anjum, Ovamir, 93, 111, 215n23
Anjuman Iṣlāḥul Afg hānā (Society for the Reform of Afghans) (AIA), 190
Ansari, Abdulhaq, 100
Ansari, Asloob Ahmad, 65, 71
Anthropology, Geography (Kant), 39–40
Anthropology as Cultural Critique (Fischer), 50
Anthropology from a Pragmatic Point of View (Kant), 15, 38, 40–41
Anthropology of Politics, The (Vincent), 33
Appadurai, Arjun, 101
ʿAql, 17, 50–53, 60–61, 99–109, 112. *See also* Reason
Arabic language, 17–18, 57, 61, 65, 68, 82–83, 111, 141
Arab Mind, The (Patai), 66
Arberry, A. J., 62
Arendt, Hannah, 172
Arewa, E. Ojo, 196
Argumentative Indian, The (Sen), 19–24
Aristotle, 41, 74–75, 161, 172, 214n20
Arkoun, Mohammed, 12
Arkush, Allan, 44
Arnold, Matthew, 19, 71
Arnold, Thomas, 216n10
Aron, Raymond, 30
Ar-Raziq, Ali, 133
Aryans, 73
Asad, Talal, 13–14, 31, 34, 38, 59–60, 64, 69, 122, 134, 188
Asaf-ud-Daula, 200
Ashenden, Samantha, 45
Ashur, Muhammad, 111, 214n19, 215n23
Askari, Hasan, 70
ʿAṣr-e-ḥāẓīr mēñ dīn kī tafhīm v tashrīḥ (Nadvi), 134
Atheism, 12–13, 177
Atmaja, Dwi, 48
Atwood, Margaret, 10, 12
Avicenna, 75, 161, 172, 215n23
Awrangzeb, 172
Axial age, 16, 34, 54–56
Ayubi, Nazih, 93
Azad, Abul Kalam, 15, 17–18, 23–24, 65, 77, 186, 207, 219n15
Azam, K. M., 126
Azamgarh, 130, 166
Aziz, ʿOmar bin Abdul, 26, 94, 104, 106–7
Azmi, Altaf, 162

Badran, Margot, 155
Baghpati, Mateen Tariq, 126
Bai, Rani Lakshmi, 168
Banerjee, Mukulika, 181, 183, 185–88, 192–93
Bannu, 194
Bano, Shah, 218n3
Barber, Benjamin, 13
Barelvi, Ibadat, 71
Bari, Sayyid Abdul, 65
Barker, Philip, 46
Barnett, S. J., 45
Barth, Fredrik, 36–37, 187–88
Barton, Greg, 50
Bausani, Alessandro, 78
Bayat, Asef, 157
Bayes, John H., 218n8
Bayly, Chris, 20
Baytul-Maqdis, 189
Becker, Carl, 47
Bedar, Rahmat, 143–45
Beg, Faiyaz Ahmad, 220n15
Belgium, 7
Bell, Daniel, 30, 78
Bellah, Robert, 27, 55–56, 118–19, 212n22
Benedict, Ruth, 66
Benedict XVI (pope), 7, 31, 44
Benjamin, Walter, 14
Bentham, Jeremy, 16
Berger, John, 205
Berger, Monroe, 180
Berlusconi, Silvio, 11
Bernal, Martin, 25, 64, 73–74, 76, 213n10
Bernasconi, Robert, 25
Berzelius, Jöns, 107

Besson, Samantha, 2
Bharatiya Janata Party (BJP), 97
Bhattacharya, Sabyasachi, 23–24
Bible, 118, 196
Bijnauri, Sayyid Ahmad, 83–84
Bilal, Muhammad, 197–98
Birth control, 175
Black Athena (Bernal), 73
Blond, Phillip, 45
Blood: A Critique of Christianity (Anidjar), 33
Blunt, William, 11
Bohannan, Laura, 36
Bonhoeffer, Dietrich, 211n15
Bose, Nirmal Kumar, 24, 214n5
Bose, Subhash Chandra, 148
Bosworth, Edmund, 55
Bouma, Gary, 48
Bourdieu, Pierre, 21, 156
Bowen, John, 13, 49–50
Boy, John D., 55
Brague, Rémi, 25, 74–75
Brahmanism, 56
Brandis, George, 215n25
Braudel, Fernand, 91–92
Briffault, Robert, 74
Bright, J. S., 183
Brown, Wendy, 42
Bruce, Steve, 46
Buddha, 55–56, 214n16
Bukay, David, 95
Burhan, Muhammad, 150–51
Bush, George W., 91
Butler, Judith, 54, 212n25

Caliphate, 87, 105–6, 143
Calman, Jeslie J., 174
Capitalism, 95–96
Caputo, John, 30, 33, 37–38, 212n26
Carson, Craig, 46
Casanova, José, 15, 49, 55
Catholicism, 31, 118–19
Chandra, Bipan, 219n2
Charity, 39
Charsadda, 194
Chatterjee, Partha, 23, 159
Chhachhi, Amrita, 218n3
Chicago Chronicle (newspaper), 30
China Quarterly (journal), 210n1
Chitral, 52–53
Chittick, William, 61
Cohen, Walter, 73, 213n10
Cohn, Bernard, 101
Cold War, 9, 32, 48
Collingwood, R. G., 47, 49
Collins, Patricia Hill, 25
Colonialism, 20, 53, 148
Committee of the Royal Anthropological Institution of Great Britain and Ireland (CRAI), 180
Communism, 48, 219n12
Comte, Auguste, 107
Congress for Cultural Freedom (CCF), 30, 32, 210n1
Congress Party (India), 22
Continuity, 91–93, 123–35
Contraception, 175
Cook, Michael, 219n15
Cosmology, 112–13
Creation, 112
Criticism: critique vs., 211n17; literary, 19, 63–64, 68
Critique of Judgment (Kant), 41
Critique of Postcolonial Reason, A (Spivak), 23
Critique of Practical Reason (Kant), 38–39
Critique of Pure Reason (Kant), 37–38, 211n17
Crocker, Christopher, 196
Culler, Jonathan, 18
"Cultural heritage," 75
Czechoslovakia, 97

Dadi, Iftikhar, 205
Dale, Stephen, 88
Danish, Ishtiaq, 220n8
Dannhauser, Werner, 180
Darul Islam, 126–27, 140, 150
Das, Veena, 35
Dāūd, 81–82
Daudi, Zohra, 175
David, 81–82
De, Barun, 219n2
Deakin, Alfred, 215n25
Debating Muslims (Fischer and Abedi), 50
de Beauvoir, Simone, 171
De Castro, Eduardo, 14
Defamiliarization, 51
Dehlavi, Ishaq, 172

Dehli, 95, 123, 170–71, 205
Dehlvi, Gulzar, 66
De Leeuw, Marc, 10
Deleyre, Alexandre, 58
Democracy, 96–99, 117, 128, 149, 152–53, 214n4, 217n22
Deoband, 82–83, 88, 95, 109, 120, 156, 171, 186, 205, 217n13, 220n2
Derrida, Jacques, 43–45
Descartes, René, 36
Devji, Faisal, 159, 218n3
Dhar, Keval, 168
Dhume, Sadanand, 8
Dictionary of Hindustani Proverbs, A (Fallon), 197
Diderot, Denis, 44
Dieu et les Hommes (Voltaire), 44
Dignity, 149–50
Dillon, Michael, 37
Dīn-e-ḥaq (Maududi), 108–9
Divine critique, 80–88
Djavann, Chahdortt, 11
Do Muslim Women Still Need Saving? (Abu-Lughod), 156
Dualism, 17, 48
Dumm, Thomas, 37
Dumont, Louis, 46
Dundes, Alan, 196
Durant, Ariel, 210n5
Dwivedi, Murari, 220n15

Eagleton, Terry, 12
Eccentric Culture: A Theory of Western Civilization (Brague), 25, 74–75
Economy, 143–44
Edel, Abraham, 37
Education, 161, 215n12
Egypt, 60, 72–73, 152, 157, 220n4
Eickelman, Dale, 13, 50–52
Ekalavya, 210n6
Elden, Stuart, 211n10
Elements of Criticism (Lord Kames), 18
Eliot, T. S., 71
el-Sādāt, Anwar, 152
El-Sheikh, Salah, 57–58
Encounter (journal), 210n1
Encyclopedia of Islam (Brill), 61, 77–78
Encyclopédie, 15, 30, 42–44
Engineer, Asghar Ali, 156, 176, 218n3
England. *See* United Kingdom
Enlightenment, the, 14–15, 17, 30–34, 121; colonialism and, 53; critique before, 54–56; ethnicity and, 34–49; in France, 42–45, 211n13; nationalism and, 33; "secular," 45–46
Eriksen, Thomas, 32, 36, 210n6
Ernst, Carl, 55
Esposito, John, 176
"Essay on the Illness of Head, An" (Kant), 38
Ethnicity: the Enlightenment and, 34–49; Other and, 36–37; as term, 210n6
Euben, Roxana, 13
Eze, Emmanuel, 25
Ezra, 80

Fabian, Johannes, 66
Fahlcrantz, Eric, 31
Faith, reason and, 60–61
Falkenhayner, Nicole, 9–10
Fallon, S. W., 197
Family, 160–61
Famous Ghalib, The (Russell), 77
Farahi, Hamiduddin, 216n10
Farooq, Mirwaiz Omar, 11
Farsi language, 65, 68, 78, 88, 213n4
Faruqi, Shahnavaz, 83
Faruqi, Shamsur Rahman, 63–71, 78, 213n4
Fassin, Didier, 29, 180–81
Fasting, 115
Fatalism, 33, 48
Fatehpuri, Neyaz, 65
Fatima, Sultana, 160
Fernea, Elizabeth Warnock, 156
Fichte, Johann Gottlieb, 107
Fiqh, 132, 144
Firdausi, 77
Firth, Rosemary, 219n1
Fischer, Michael, 13, 50–51, 93
Fitzgerald, Timothy, 55
Folly of Interpretation, The (Khan), 130–31
Foucault, Michel, 14, 30, 54–55, 72
Four Basic Terms of the Qur'ān (*Qur'ān kī chār bunyādī iṣṭelāḥēñ*) (Maududi), 132–35, 137
France, 42–45, 211n13

Franklin, Todd, 25
Freedom, 8–12, 79–80, 86–87, 149–50, 154, 158, 186, 208
Free society, 10–11
Frontier Crime Regulation Act (FCRA), 188
Frontier Province, 182
Fundamentalism, 9, 26, 32–33, 60, 76, 219n17. *See also* Islamism
Fuyudul al-ḥaramain (Shah Valiullah), 1, 3

Gadgil, D. R., 24
Galvani, Luigi, 107
Gandhi, Indira, 174
Gandhi, Mohandas, 24, 95, 148, 150, 182, 194, 207, 214n5
Gandhi, Rajmohan, 183
Ganeri, Jonardon, 20
Gay, Peter, 47–49
Gayo highlands, 49–50
Geelani, Ali Shah, 11
Geertz, Clifford, 50
Gehlen, Arnold, 35
Gellner, Ernest, 9–10
Gender Trouble (Butler), 212n25
Genealogy of Religion (Asad), 59
Germany, 8
Geuss, Raymond, 72
Ghaffari, Abu Zar, 57
Ghaffar Khan, Khan Abdul, 28, 182–95, 219n3, 219n5
Ghafur Amat ul, 172
Ghalib, Asadullah Khan, 65, 70, 76–79, 205
Ghamdi, Javded, 217n22
Ghannouchi, Rachid, 143
Ghazal, 65, 69
Ghazali, Imam, 26, 42, 62, 94, 102, 104–5, 212n30
Gibb, H. A. R., 57
Giddens, Anthony, 47, 53–54
Giesen, Bernhard, 211n12
Glassie, Henry, 22
Globalization, 47, 144
Goethe, Johann Wolfgang von, 31
Gomaa, Ali, 200
Gonman, Patrick, 7–8
Goody, Jack, 74–75
Gorski, Philip, 45
Gosse, Edmund, 221n4
Gramsci, Antonio, 18
Grass, Günter, 11
Great Britain. *See* United Kingdom
Greece, 16, 25–26, 41–42, 50, 57, 64, 69, 71–76, 105, 158, 213n8, 213n12, 214n20
Griffel, Frank, 212n23
Grimshaw, Jean, 25
Guha, Ramachandra, 21, 23–24
Gujranwala, 154
Gulen, Fatehullah, 86
Guru, Gopal, 55
Gurvitch, Georges, 91–92

Habermas, Jürgen, 11, 32, 47, 60, 218n2
Habib, Irfan, 212n30, 214n14
Hadith, 1, 51, 87, 116, 126–27, 142, 171–72, 186
Hafiz, 70, 77
Hai, Maulvi Abdul, 106
Haiti, 173
Haj, Samira, 61
Haji of Turangzai, 186, 190
Hajj, 115–16
Hali, Altaf Hussain, 65–68, 87
Hallaq, Wael, 39, 45, 57, 61, 74
Halliday, Fred, 218n1
Hameed, Sayeda, 192
Hampson, Norman, 14
Hanbal, Imam, 105
Hanifa, Imam, 105, 167
Hanson, Victor, 31
Haq, Abdul, 77
Harley, Tom, 215n25
Harman, Chris, 157
Harris, Olivia, 92
Harvard, Jonas, 31
Harvey, David, 40, 211n10
Hasan (grandson of the Prophet), 86
Hasan, Aziz Ibnul, 71
Hasan, Mahmudul, 186
Hasan, Mushirul, 23, 213n7
Hasan, Zoya, 218n3
Hasrat, 77
Hassan, Riffat, 156, 176, 218n7
Hastrup, Kirsten, 32–33
Heart, 61. See also *Qalb*
Heavenly City of the Eighteenth-Century Philosophers, The (Becker), 47

Hedgewar, Keshav Baliram, 148
Hegel, G. W. F., 107, 161, 172
Heidegger, Martin, 35
Herberg, Will, 48
Herder, Johann Gottfried, 107
Hermansen, Marcia, 3, 29
Herzfeld, Michael, 25, 34, 64, 73–74, 76
Hijaz, 62
Hill, Mike, 218n2
Hind, Shaikhul, 186
Hinduism, 22, 66, 77, 112, 160, 183, 185, 191–92
Hitchens, Christopher, 12
Hobbes, Thomas, 2, 46
Hodges, Matt, 92
Hogan, Desmond, 37
Honneth, Alex, 59
Hūd (prophet), 116
Hudson, Wayne, 45
Ḥujjat Allāh al Bāligha (*The Conclusive Argument from God*) (Valiullah), 2–3, 88, 209n2
Huma, Zille, 154–55
Hume, David, 25, 60
Huntington, Samuel, 9
Husain, Imam, 86–87
Husain, Ehtesham, 69, 71
Husain, Sheriff, 186
Hussain, Saddam, 152
Hussain, Zakir, 24
Husserl, Edmund, 34
Hyder, David, 34
Hyderabad, 95

Ibn Abbas, Abdullah, 83
Ibn Arabi, 209n3
Ibn Hazm, Zahir, 215n23
Ibn Khaldun, 209n2
Ibn Sina, 215n23
Ibn Taymiyyah, 26, 94, 104–5, 165
Ibrāhīm, 80, 116–17
Idea of History, The (Collingwood), 47
Ifadi, Mehdi, 64
Ijtihād, 57, 94, 99–109, 145. *See also* Reason
Income disparity, 95–96
Indian National Congress, 95
Individualism, 46
Indonesia, 144
International relations theory, 2
Intiqād, 63, 65–66, 179, 213n1
Iqbal, Muhammad, 1–2, 30, 77, 79, 126, 186, 203–4
Iqtidar, Humeira, 156
Iran, 157, 218n1
Iraq, 91, 152, 189
ʿIsā, 80, 116. *See also* Jesus
Isa, Ahmad Muhammad, 207, 221n4
Islahi, Ayaz, 161, 177
Islahi, Sultan Ahmad, 165–68, 175
"Islam and Arabs through the Eyes of *Encyclopédie*: The 'Other' as a Case of French Cultural Self-Criticism" (Joubin), 42–43
Islami, Markazi Maktaba, 217n13
Islamic Civilization: Its Principles and Sources (Maududi), 109
Islamism, 92–93, 157, 173–74, 177, 218n1. *See also* Fundamentalism; Jamaat-e-Islami
Ismail, Shah, 106
Izutsu, Toshihiko, 111

Jaanam, Burhanuddin, 77
Jackson, Sherman, 50
Jafar, Qudama Ibn Jafar, 213n4
Jalal, Ayesha, 162, 184
Jalianwala Bagh massacre, 192
Jalibi, Jameel, 173
Jamaat-e-Islami, 13, 56, 81–82, 94, 116, 120–21, 123, 126–34, 138–39, 143, 146, 157–78, 216n9, 218n3, 219n13, 219n19. *See also* Student Islamic Organization
Jamal, Amina, 163, 177
Jami, 77
Jamia Millia Islamia, 108, 174, 186, 205
Jamiatul Ulema-e-Hind (JUH), 95, 162, 216n13
Jaspers, Karl, 37, 42, 55, 122
Jauhar, Muhammad Ali, 150
Jawaharlal Nehru University, 179–80
Jeffery, Patricia, 156
Jesus, 27, 55–56, 80, 94, 116–17
Ji, Badruddin Tayab, 24
Jihad vs. McWorld (Barber), 13
Jilani, Abdul Qadir, 102
Jinnah, Fatima, 128–29
Jinnah, Muhammad Ali, 128, 148

Joas, Hans, 31, 56
Johansen, Robert, 191–93
Jones, William, 182
Joseph (prophet), 80
Joshi, Hari Bhau, 219n4
Joubin, Rebecca, 42–44
Juan Manuel, Prince of Villena, 9
Judaism, 211n9
Justice: critique and, 82; democracy and, 149; in Maududi, 100; Muhammad and, 145; Qur'ān and, 164; rape and, 147; religion and, 142; women and, 165, 169; in Zurti, 165

Kabir, 77
Kalidas, 182
Kalimatul haqā'q (Jaanam), 77
Kamali, Hossein, 220n1
Kanpur, 182
Kant, Immanuel, 2, 15, 25, 30, 32, 35–42, 45, 54, 58, 122, 161, 172, 210n2, 211n9, 211n17, 214n15, 218n9
Kapferer, Bruce, 14, 33–34, 210n3
Karmi, Ghada, 155–56
Kavka, Martin, 48
Keane, John, 25, 46, 64, 74, 76
Kelek, Necla, 11
Kenya, 35–36
Keywords (Williams), 18
Khadija, Sultana, 160
Khakheperresenb, 72
Khan, Abdul Karim, 191
Khan, Ali Akbar, 23
Khan, Arifa Subh, 72, 172–73
Khan, Ayub, 199
Khan, Bahram, 185
Khan, Haji Mohammad, 64–65
Khan, Muhammad Ayub, 128
Khan, Naveeda, 198–200
Khan, Sayyid Ahmad, 18, 23, 65, 77
Khan, Sher Banu A. L., 160
Khan, Vahiduddin, 27, 83, 88, 120, 130–34, 137–40, 147, 151
Khan, Zafar Ali, 186, 193–94
Ḳhilāfat, 123
Ḳhilāfat v mulūkīat (Maududi), 147
Ḳhiẓr, 85
Khomeini, Ayatollah Ruhollah, 10
Khoury, Elias, 68
Ḳhudāī Ḳhidmatgār (servants of God), 28–29, 181–86, 189–95, 200, 220n11
"Ḳhuṯba adab al-ʿArab" (al-Bustani), 68
Kidwai, Muhammad Hashim, 186
Kifayatullah, Mufti Muhammad, 109, 205
Kishwar, Madhu, 218n3
Kluckhon, Clyde, 51
Knowledge, 1–2, 102–3, 203–4, 220n1. *See also* Revelation
Kontopoulos, Kyriakos, 54
Korejo, Muhammad, 182
Kosambi, D. D., 24
Koselleck, Reinhart, 2, 20, 54, 203
Kottak, Conrad, 211n6
Kramer, Gudrun, 95
Kresse, Kai, 13, 35–36
Krystal, Arthur, 72
Kuehn, Manfred, 39
Kuhns, Richard, 35, 37
Kumar, Radha, 218n3
Kumar, Vivek, 219n3
Küng, Hans, 55
Kurzman, Charles, 9
Kuyper, Abraham, 27, 118

Lahore, 123, 126
Lajjā (Nasreen), 10
Lal, Malashri, 182
Language, 23–24. *See also* Arabic language; Farsi language; Urdu language
Lapidus, Ira, 67
Larmore, Charles, 46, 74
Lateef, Shahida, 218n3
Lavoisier, Antoine, 107
Law, 152
Lawrence, Bruce, 25, 218n3
Leaman, Oliver, 62
Leavis, F. R., 71
Lebanon, 189
Lectures on Logic (Kant), 41
Le Fanatisme, ou Mahomet le Prophète (Voltaire), 44
Leibniz, Gottfried, 37
Lennard, Davis, 180
Lessing, Gotthold Ephraim, 107
Leviathan (Hobbes), 46
Lewis, Bernard, 9

Liberalism, in India, 20–21
Life and Death of Democracy, The (Keane), 74
Liisberg, Sune, 35
Lindholm, Charles, 187
Lipset, Seymour, 30
Lisānuṣṣidq (journal), 65
Listening, 11–12
Literary criticism, 19, 63–64, 68
Literature, 67, 69–71, 76–80
Living Enlightenment, The (Gay), 48
Lloyd, Genevieve, 25
Locke, John, 25, 32
Loimeier, Roman, 11
Lone, Bilal, 11
Lord Kames, 18
Lott, Tommy, 25
Louden, Robert, 39, 41
Luther, Martin, 8, 31

MacDonogh, Steven, 10
Machchi Ghot Affair, 216n8, 217n22
MacIntyre, Alasdair, 58, 74, 94
MacKenzie, Iain, 211n17
Madani, Hussain Ahmad, 217n13
Madjid, Nurcholish, 50
Madni, Husaan Ahmad, 82
Madrasatul Islah, 166
Maghfur, 147–50
Mahābḫārata, the, 210n6
Mahmood, Saba, 156
Mahmoud, Muhammad, 175
Mahmud, Fazal, 186
Mahmud, Ghaffar, 186
Makhdum, Shaykh Ziauddin, 87–88
Making of Humanity, The (Briffault), 74
Malaviya, Madanmohan, 22, 95
Malaysia, 144
Maldives, 160
Malihabad, 219n14
Mālik, 87
Malik, Imam, 105
Malinowski, Bronislaw, 121, 210n6
Mallet, Abbé Edme, 44
Malpas, Jeff, 38
Malraux, Rhoda, 66
Malta, 186
Malthus, Thomas, 107
Mamdani, Mahmood, 24, 211n16
Manji, Irshad, 10–11
Maqāṣid al-Sharīʿā, 28, 122, 143–45
Marcus, George, 13, 50–51
Markwell, Don, 215n25
Marsden, Magnus, 14, 52–53, 121, 172, 184
Martin, James, 196
Martin, Richard, 48
Marwan, Abdul Malik Ibn, 172
Marwat, Fazal-ur-Rahim, 185, 192–94
Marx, Karl, 211n17, 212n30
Marxism, 69–70
Masihuzzaman, 213n8
Maṣlaḥa, 2–3
Masud, Muhammad Khalid, 48
Matilal, Bimal, 20
Matin, Abdul, 83, 87
Matthews, David, 77
Maududi, Abul Ala, 13, 26–28, 50, 56, 64, 77, 80–83, 86–87, 91–119, 122–50, 156–78, 203, 205, 214n16, 214n20, 215n12, 215n19, 216n6, 217n13, 218n5, 219n19
Mavlānā Mavdūdī kē sāth mērī refāqat kī sar-guzasht avr ab mērā mavqif (*The Tale of My Friendship with Maulana Maududi and My Current Stand*) (Nomani), 123, 124, 127–30
Mavlvī, 197–200
Mayo College, 186
Mazāhirul Ulum, 217n13
Mazhari, Jameel, 70–71
Mazhari, Kausar, 71, 213n3
Mazhari, Waris, 221n5
Mazrui, Sheikh Al-Amin, 36
Mazumdar, Vina, 174
McDonough, Sheila, 162, 218n3
McKane, William, 196
McLuhan, Marshall, 182
McLuhan, Teri, 182
McWilliams, Wilson, 180
Mead, Margaret, 66
Mehdi, Imam, 104
Mehdi, Tabish, 65, 83
Mehta, Uday, 30
Mendieta, Eduardo, 211n10
Menon, Indu, 218n3
Merkel, Angela, 8
Mernissi, Fatima, 156, 176
Messick, Brinkley, 121

Metaphysics, 37–38, 40
Metcalf, Barbara, 67, 159, 218n3, 218n6
Mieder, Wolfgang, 195–96
Miettinen, Timo, 42
Milbank, John, 45, 60–61
Mill, John Stuart, 16, 58, 107
Miller, John, 211n12
Miller, Larr, 57
Minault, Gail, 218n3
Mir, 77
Miriam, Sultana, 160
Mirror of Man (Kluckhon), 51
Mirza, Qudsia, 155
Modern Asian Studies (journal), 176
Modernity, 47, 53, 63, 212n22
Modernization theory, 51–52
"Modern Media and Islam" (Islahi), 166
Mody, Nawaz, 218n3
Moghadam, Valentine, 155–56
Moghissi, Haidah, 155–56, 177
Mohamed, Sayed, 77
Mohani, Hasrat, 213n12
Mohanty, J. N., 20
Moigliano, Arnaldo, 56
Mojab, Shaharzad, 155
Monier-Williams, Monier, 20
Monk, Paul, 32
Montag, Warren, 218n2
Mookherjee, S. P., 22, 148
Moors, Annelies, 10
"Moral Courage Project," 10
Morocco, 51–52
Morsi, Mohammad, 200
Moses, 55–56, 80, 116. *See also* Mūsā
Mouvement de la Tendance Islamiste (Movement of the Islamic Trend) (MTI), 175
Mughni, Abdul, 77–79
Muhammad: as critic, 15, 80–81, 85; in Diderot, 44; disrespectful representations of, 8, 13; Ghaffar Khan and, 189–90; and Islam as new religion, 80–81; Jesus and, 56; in Kant, 38–39; in Maududi, 27, 56, 114, 118; as modern, 56; monotheism and, 114; prophets and, 82; in Rumi, 142; Valiullah and, 1; in Voltaire, 44; women and, 162, 169, 171–72
Muir, William, 9
Mujaddid, 103–7, 165
Mukerji, D. P., 24
Munshi, K. M., 22
Muqaddamah-e-shaʿr-v-shāʿrī (Hali), 66–68, 87
Muqaddimah (Nadwi), 171–72
Mūsā, 80, 85, 116, 142
Musalmān avr maujudah seyasī kashmakash (Maududi), 97, 118
Musharraf, Pervez, 199–200
Muslim Becoming (Khan), 198–99
Muslim League, 95, 148, 154, 159, 218n3

Nadvatul Ulema, 133, 207
Nadvi, Abul Hasan Ali, 27, 63, 83, 87, 120, 133–35. *See also* Abullais
Nadvi, Sulaiman, 7, 207–8, 221n5
Nadwi, Mohammad Akram, 171–73, 177
Naidu, Sarojni, 168
Nair, Harish, 157
Nandigram, 149–50
Naqd, 65, 83, 213n1, 213n4. *See also* Criticism
Naqd al- sheʿr (Jafar), 213n4
Naqvi, Nurul Hasan, 213n8
Narang, Gopi Chand, 63, 78, 173
Narang, K. N., 182
Nasr, Syed Vali Reza, 126, 128, 214n3, 216n6
Nasreen, Taslima, 10–11
Nationalism, 214n4; critique and, 63; democracy and, 96; distrust of, 95; Enlightenment and, 33; in India, 22; literary, 65–66; in Maududi, 96–98, 100, 144; of Maududi, 28, 122; of Roy, 21; of Sen, 20
Nationalist Thought and Colonial World (Chatterjee), 23
Nature, 111–12, 215n25
Navaz, Muhammad, 137–38
Nehru, Jawaharlal, 22, 98, 148
Neorealism, 2
Neumann, Peter, 13
"New atheism," 12
"New Education System" (Maududi), 102
New Testament, 118
New World Order (NWO), 31–32, 48
New York Times, 7–8
New York University, 10

Nielsen, Finn Sivert, 32
Nietzsche, Friedrich, 14, 72
9/11 attacks, 12, 187
Noah, 80, 116
Nomani, Manzur, 9, 27, 42, 65, 71, 88, 120, 123–30, 134, 151, 216nn5–6, 217n22
Nomani, Shibli, 62, 77, 212n30
Nonviolence, 28–29, 183–84, 192–94, 220n11
North West Frontier Province (NWFP), 185–86
Notes and Queries on Anthropology (Committee of the Royal Anthropological Institution of Great Britain and Ireland), 180
Nūḥ, 80, 116
Nussbaum, Martha, 180

O'Donnell, Patrick, 87
Offe, Claus, 182
Ohmann, Richard, 18
Old & New Terrorism (Neumann), 13
ʿOmar, 85, 149
"On a Newly Raised Noble Tone of Philosophy" (Kant), 38
Onfray, Michel, 12–13
Open Society and Its Enemies, The (Popper), 9
Orientalism (Said), 38
Outram, Dorinda, 45
Owen, David, 45
Owen, John, 31
Owen, Judd, 31
ʿOzair, 80

Pakistan, 29, 52–53, 107, 128, 147, 150, 154–55, 163–64, 182–89, 192, 218n3
Pal, Amitabh, 183–84, 192, 194
Palmquist, Stephen, 39
Pangle, Thomas, 61
Pardāh (*The Veil*) (Maududi), 158–59, 175
Paremiology, 195–96
Parkin, David, 196
Patai, Raphael, 66
Patani, 160
Patel, Sardar, 22
Patel, Vibhuti, 174
Pathak, Zakia, 218n3
Pathankot, 126–27
Pathans, 29, 187–89, 220n11
Patna, 210n8
Paul, 216n4
Pedersen, Esther Oluffa, 35
Pellat, Ch, 87
Pericles, 91
Pervez, Ghulam, 199, 217n22
Peshawar, 185, 192–94
Peters, Rudolph, 49
Philosophical Dictionary (Voltaire), 43–44
Philosophising in Mombasa (Kresse), 35
Philosophy: anthropology and, 33–38; in Faruqi, 70; gendering of, 25; Greece and, 73–75; Hindu, 20; reason and, 42
Photographs, 161, 205–6
Piscatori, James, 13
Plato, 74, 214n20
Plessner, Helmuth, 35
Pocock, J. H. A., 14
Poetry, 70
Poliakov, Leon, 25
"Political Perspective of Islam" (Maududi), 116
Popper, Karl, 9
Postmodernism, Reason and Religion (Gellner), 9–10
Prang, 194
Prasad, Rajendra, 216n9
Primitive Man as Philosopher (Radin), 48
Pritchard, David, 91
Pritchett, Frances, 79
Prophet and the Proletariat (Harman), 157
Prophets, 55–56, 80–82, 113–14, 117, 212n21
Protestant—Catholic—Jew: An Essay in American Religious Sociology (Herberg), 48
Protestantism, 12, 38, 46, 49
Proverbs, 195–201
Putnam, Hilary, 204

Qadir, Abdul, 68
Qalādāh, 91, 99, 214n1
Qalb, 17–18, 34, 60–61
Qasmi, Abul Kalam, 80
Qasmi, Moʿizuddin, 109–10
Qasmi, Mufti Zainul Islam, 205
Qasmi, Zainul Islam, 220n2
Qazi, Samia Raheel, 163
Qissa Khani Bazar massacre, 192–94

Quadrant (journal), 32
Quadri, Safdar Imam, 65, 77
Quesnay, François, 107
Qur'ān: in alternative genealogy of critique, 64; antipathy toward, 9, 44; critique and, 83, 88, 99; in Diderot, 44; Islamists and, 92; justice in, 145; in Khan, 132–33; knowledge in, 102–3; in Maududi, 100, 102–3, 108, 131; New Testament and, 118; prophets in, 56, 80–82; reason and, 51, 61, 142, 146; in Rumi, 142; in Usmani, 137; women and, 155–56, 160–62, 168–72, 177–78, 191; in Zurti, 141–43, 164–65

Rabbi, Fazal, 186
Racial inequity, 95–96
Radin, Paul, 48
Rahman, Fazlur, 50, 217n22
Rahnema, Ali, 57
Rai, Lajpat, 22, 95–96
Rajan, Rajeswari Sunder, 218n3
Ram, Malik, 214n20
Ramadan, Tariq, 61, 143
Rāmāyṇa, the, 20
Rampur, 219n14
Rape, 147
Rasch, William, 46
Rashtriya Swayamsewak Sangh (RSS), 140
Rawalpindi, 197
Rawls, John, 58, 215n25
Realism, 2
Reason, 16–18, 51; anthropology and, 210n3; Christianity and, in Stark, 47; critique and, 51, 54–55, 57, 121–22; in Eickelman, 52; Enlightenment and, 14, 25, 32–33, 48–49; faith and, 60–61; gendering of, 25; heart and, 60–61; *ijtihād* and, 57; in Joubin, 43–44; in Kant, 38–39, 41–42, 54, 211n17; in Maududi, 101–3, 110, 112–13; Qur'ān and, 51, 61, 142, 146; revelation and, 62; in Sen, 20; universalism and, 25, 32, 34; in Valiullah, 1. See also *'Aql*; *Ijtihād*
Reform, 56–57
Religion within the Boundaries of Mere Reason (Kant), 39
Renan, Ernest, 8–9, 61
"Renewal and Revival of Religion, The" (Maududi), 108–9
Revelation, 50–51, 82, 111, 113. *See also* Knowledge
Revelation and Reason in Islam (Arberry), 62
Richards. I. A., 71
Rida, Rashid, 207
Risāla'-e-dīnīyāt (Maududi), 109–11, 116
Rituals, 114–15
Robertson, Jennifer, 51
Robinson, Francis, 218n3
Rousseau, Jean-Jacques, 107
Rowlatt Act, 187
Roy, Arundhati, 165
Roy, Jacob de, 160
Roy, Olivier, 92–93, 99
Roy, Ram Mohan, 20–21, 23
Rudwick, Martin, 204
Ruhela, Satya Pal, 218n3
Rum, Maulana. *See* Rumi
Rumi, 1, 70, 77, 141–42, 203
Rupture, 92–93, 123–35
Rushdie, Salman, 10, 12, 17
Russell, Bertrand, 9
Russell, Ralph, 77

Sabit, Hassan Bin, 77
Sabras (Wajhi), 77
Sacks, Jeffrey, 213n1
Sadi Shirazi, 77
Sadruddin Islahi, 138–39, 150
Sahgal, Gita, 155, 219n17
Sahiwal, 128
Sahlins, Marshall, 14, 33
Said, Edward, 38
Saint Paul, 216n4
Sajjad, Ahmad, 65, 76, 79, 87
Saleem, Shehzad, 217n22
Ṣāleḥ (prophet), 116
Saliha, 172
Salman, Ali, 155
Salvatore, Armando, 33, 55
Samiuddin, Abida, 71
Ṡānavī Darsgāh, 169
Sapir, David, 196
Sardar, Ziauddin, 17
Sarvar, Ghulam, 154–55
Sarvar, Muhammad, 1–2

Satanic Verses, The (Rushdie), 10
Saudi Arabia, 60
Sayeed, Khalid, 199
Sayyid, Salman, 30
Schacht, Joseph, 48, 57
Scheler, Max, 35
Schlegel, Friedrich, 75
Schleiermacher, Friedrich, 46
Schmitt, Carl, 152
Schott, Robin, 25
Schulze, Reinhard, 48
Science, 104, 108
Second Sex, The (de Beauvoir), 171
Secret Mirror, The: Essays on Urdu Poetry (Faruqi), 65
Sectarianism, 44
Secularism, 63, 211n15, 214n5; Christianity and, 12, 45; Cold War and, 9, 48; critique and, 68; Enlightenment and, 31–32; in Indian constitution, 22; Jamaat-e-Islami and, 175; Maududi and, 96–97; and religious/secular divide, 45–46; universalism and, 36; Urdu literature and, 69, 76
Sen, Amartya, 14, 19–24
Sex, 168
Sex in Islam (Islahi), 168, 175
Shah, Sayed Wiqar Ali, 185, 193–94
Shaheen, Shabana, 174
Shaikh, Farzana, 184
Shaikh, Nermeen, 13
Shakur, Abdus, 213n12
Shamsun Nisā᾽, 172
Shankar, S., 210n6
Sharabi, Hisham, 162
Sharia, 84–85, 129, 140, 146–49, 214n19. See also *Maqāṣid al-Sharīʿā*
Shariati, Ali, 57, 203
Sharp, Gene, 193
Shatibi, Ishaq al-, 144, 214n19
Shaz, Rashid, 56–57
Shikoh, Dara, 22
Shils, Edward, 30–32, 53, 210n1
Shirazi, Saadi, 42
Shoʿaib, 116
Shuʿayb, 80
Siddiqi, Naeem, 15, 175–76
Sidgwick, Henry, 16
Sieg, Katrine, 12
Sikhism, 111–12, 191
Silencing the Past (Trouillot), 157–58
Silverman, Sydel, 66
Simon Commission, 184
Sindhi, Ubaidullah, 156, 186, 190
Singapore, 144
Singh, Yogendra, 55
Sirhindi, Shaykh Ahmad, 26, 94, 104–6, 209n3
Slovakia, 97
Smith, Adam, 107
Smith, Wilfred Cantwell, 101
Sociological Imagination (C. Wright Mills), 210n6
Sociology, 92
Sohoni, Shrinivas Rao S., 192
Solomon, 207
Soroush, Abdolkarim, 29, 50, 203–4, 220n1
Spain, 40–41
Spencer, Robert, 180
Spivak, Gayatri Chakravorty, 19, 23
Srinivas, M. N., 180
Stahl, Titus, 59
Stark, Rodney, 46–47
Stowasser, Barbara, 85
Strauss, Leo, 62
Straw, Jack, 7
Student Islamic Organization (SIO), 13, 164, 168–70, 173
Submission (film), 10
Sufism, 2, 107, 150–51, 189, 217n23
Sulaiman, 207
Sultana, Razia, 159, 168
Sultana, Selma, 174
Sumatra, 49–50
Sunna, 16, 64, 84, 99, 108, 126
Sura Kahf, 85
Ṣurat v mʿānā soḵhan (Faruqi), 69
Suroor, Al-e Ahmad, 66, 71
Switzerland, 97–98
Syria, 171, 189

Tabassum, Farzana, 169
Tābīr kī ghalaṭī (*The Folly of Interpretation*) (Khan), 130–31, 140
Tablighi Jamaat, 162, 218n3
Tafhīmul Qur᾽ān (Maududi), 109, 135, 165

Tāj (Maududi), 96
Tajallī (journal), 27, 83, 121, 124, *125*, 127, 135, *136*, 137–39
Tajdīd v aḥyā-e-dīn (Maududi), 147
Tājul haqā'q (Wajhi), 77
Takhfīf, 84
Tale of My Friendship with Maulana Maududi and My Current Stand (Nomani), 123, 124, 127–30
Tā'līmul islām (Kifayatullah), 109–10
Talmud, 80
Tambiah, Stanley, 176, 204
Tanqīd, 64–65, 81, 84, 213n1. *See also* Criticism
Tanqīd avr jadīd Urdu tanqīd (Agha), 72
Tarcov, Nathan, 61
Tarjumānul Qur'ān (journal), 15, 81–82, 99, 123, 215n19
Tarrow, Sidney, 163
Taylor, Charles, 74
Temple, R. C., 196–97, 220n13
Tendulkar, D. G., 183
Terrorism, 12–13, 97, 152, 192–93; War on Terror (WOT), 31–32
Thailand, 144, 160
Thanawi, Ashraf Ali, 161, 218n6
Thesis Eleven (journal), 11
Thiel, Karsten, 38
Think: Philosophy for Everyone (journal), 60
Thomassen, Bjørn, 55
Thorpe, Lucas, 211n17
Tilak, Bal Gangadhar, 148
Tilly, Charles, 163
Tiryakian, Edward, 204
Tohidi, Nayereh, 218n8
Tompkins, Jeff, 71
Torpey, John, 55
Trevelyan, Charles, 69
Tripathi, Amles, 219n2
Trouble with Islam, The (Manji), 10
Trouillot, Michel-Rolph, 157–58, 173
Trumpbour, John, 9, 21
Tuḥfatul Mujāhidīn (Makhdum), 88
Tulsi, 77
Tunisia, 175–76
Turgot, Anne Robert Jacques, 107
Turkey, 41, 186
Turner, Bryan, 49, 56
Uberoi, J. P S., 212n24
'Ulema, 50, 52, 57, 59–60, 64, 87, 107, 120, 133, 145–46, 186, 188, 197–200, 206, 214n20, 217n13, 220n4
Ummayad, 105
United Kingdom, 40, 69, 98, 117, 152
United States, 16, 27, 31, 48, 97, 152
Universalism, 14, 25, 28, 32, 34, 36, 55, 59, 122, 140–53, 212n22
Urdu language: critique in, 16, 25–26, 63–72, 213n8; familiarity with, 151; in India, 151; literary criticism in, 63–64; proverbs, 195–201
Urdu literature, 17, 68–69, 76–77
Urdu poetry, 66
Urdu tanqīd kā aṣlī chehrā (*The Real Face of Urdu Critique*) (Khan), 173
Usman, 86
Usmani, Amir, 27, 70, 76, 84, 120, 124–25, 127–30, 135–39. See also *Tajallī*
Utilitarianism, 16–17
Utmanzai, 187, 193
Uttar Pradesh, 120, 123, 151, 213n12

Vadet, J. C., 61
Valiullah, Shah, 1–2, 26, 29, 88, 94, 102, 104, 106, 123, 203, 212n21
Van der Veer, Peter, 45–46
Van Ess, Josef, 55, 61–62
van Gough, Theo, 10
van Kley, Dale, 45
Van Maanen, John, 188
Van Schendel, Willem, 22
van Wichelen, Sonja, 10
Veil, The (Maududi), 158–59, 175
Veiling, 173–74
Vico, Giambattista, 72–73
Victory of Reason, The: How Christianity Led to Freedom, Capitalism, and Western Success (Stark), 47
Vincent, Joan, 14–15, 33
Voll, John, 95, 176
Voltaire, 25, 32, 42–45, 54, 107

Wacquant, Loïc, 21, 156
Wahid, Abdurrahman, 50
Wajhi, Mulla, 74, 77
Walbridge, John, 18, 52

Walzer, Michael, 58
Wander, Karl Wilhelm, 195
War on Terror (WOT), 31–32
Watt, Montgomery, 57
Wealth, 57
Weber, Max, 31, 41, 46
Weiss, Anita, 163
Werner, Yvonne Maria, 31
Westernization, 63
"What Does It Mean to Orient Oneself in Thinking?" (Kant), 38
"What Is Aufklärung?" (Kant), 30, 54
"What Is Criticism?" (Ohmann), 18
"What Is Critique?" (Foucault), 54–55
Whine, Michael, 95
White power, 43
Whybray, R. Norman, 196
Wigram, M. E., 185–86
Williams, David, 44
Williams, Raymond, 18, 211n17
Willmer, David, 162, 218n3
Wilson, William, 181
Winter, Bronwyn, 155, 177, 218n1
Wire, The (television program), 181
Wittgenstein, Ludwig, 121–22
Wittrock, Bjorn, 56
Wolfe, Patrick, 23
Women, 128–29, 148, 154–78, 191, 218n3, 219n12, 219n17
Woodward, Mark, 48
World War I, 186–87
World War II, 30, 192
Worship, 114–15
Wulf, Christoph, 35

Yale Global Online, 8
Yazid, 86–87
Yugoslavia, 97
Yusuf, Mufti, 83–85
Yuval-Davis, Nira, 155, 219n17

Zaibun Nisāʾ, 172
Zaman, Muhammad Qasim, 14, 184, 203, 220n2
Zend-Avesta (Zoroaster), 41
Zia, Afiya Shehrba, 155
Zindegi (journal), 125, 163–64, 169, 175, 177, 219n14
Zoroaster, 41
Zuberi, Bilal, 199
Zurti, Akram, 140–43, 164–65, 173, 177, 206
Zutshi, Anand Mohan, 66. *See also* Dehlvi, Gulzar

ISLAMIC CIVILIZATION AND MUSLIM NETWORKS

Irfan Ahmad, *Religion as Critique: Islamic Critical Thinking from Mecca to the Marketplace* (2017).

Scott Kugle, *When Sun Meets Moon: Gender, Eros, and Ecstasy in Urdu Poetry* (2016).

Kishwar Rizvi, *The Transnational Mosque: Architecture, Historical Memory, and the Contemporary Middle East* (2015).

Ebrahim Moosa, *What Is a Madrasa?* (2015).

Bruce Lawrence, *Who Is Allah?* (2015).

Edward E. Curtis IV, *The Call of Bilal: Islam in the African Diaspora* (2014).

Sahar Amer, *What Is Veiling?* (2014).

Rudolph T. Ware III, *The Walking Qur'an: Islamic Education, Embodied Knowledge, and History in West Africa* (2014).

Saʿdiyya Shaikh, *Sufi Narratives of Intimacy: Ibn ʿArabī, Gender, and Sexuality* (2012).

Karen G. Ruffle, *Gender, Sainthood, and Everyday Practice in South Asian Shi'ism* (2011).

Jonah Steinberg, *Ismaʿili Modern: Globalization and Identity in a Muslim Community* (2011).

Iftikhar Dadi, *Modernism and the Art of Muslim South Asia* (2010).

Gary R. Bunt, *iMuslims: Rewiring the House of Islam* (2009).

Fatemeh Keshavarz, *Jasmine and Stars: Reading More than "Lolita" in Tehran* (2007).

Scott Kugle, *Sufis and Saints' Bodies: Mysticism, Corporeality, and Sacred Power in Islam* (2007).

Roxani Eleni Margariti, *Aden and the Indian Ocean Trade: 150 Years in the Life of a Medieval Arabian Port* (2007).

Sufia M. Uddin, *Constructing Bangladesh: Religion, Ethnicity, and Language in an Islamic Nation* (2006).

Omid Safi, *The Politics of Knowledge in Premodern Islam: Negotiating Ideology and Religious Inquiry* (2006).

Ebrahim Moosa, *Ghazālī and the Poetics of Imagination* (2005).

miriam cooke and Bruce B. Lawrence, eds., *Muslim Networks from Hajj to Hip Hop* (2005).

Carl W. Ernst, *Following Muhammad: Rethinking Islam in the Contemporary World* (2003).